D1241520

SOUTHERN LITERARY STUDIES
Louis D. Rubin, Jr., *Editor*

Selected Essays of John Crowe Ransom

Selected Essays of

JOHN CROWE RANSOM

Edited, with an Introduction, by

THOMAS DANIEL YOUNG *and* JOHN HINDLE

Louisiana State University Press

Baton Rouge and London

Designer: Barbara Werden
Typeface: Linotron Primer
Typesetter: G & S Typesetters, Inc.
Printer and binder: Vail-Ballou Press

Library of Congress Cataloging in Publication Data

Ransom, John Crowe, 1888–1974.
Selected essays of John Crowe Ransom.
(Southern literary studies)
Includes index.
I. Young, Thomas Daniel, 1919–   . II. Hindle,
John J., 1946–   . III. Title. IV. Series.
PS3535.A635A6 1984   808.1   83-12041
ISBN 0-8071-1130-9

For
HELEN RANSOM FORMAN

Contents

Acknowledgments

We want to thank Kieran Quinlan and Thomas D. Young, Jr., for their valuable assistance in assembling and preparing these essays for publication. To Mrs. Helen Ransom Forman we owe a special debt of gratitude for allowing us to use many of her father's essays. Other acknowledgments for permission to reprint essays are given at appropriate places in the text. We owe our thanks to Louise Durham and Ann Musgrove for typing the several drafts of the manuscript.

We are grateful to the College of Arts and Science of Vanderbilt University for leaves of absence which permitted the completion of this manuscript and for much-needed financial assistance.

Selected Essays of John Crowe Ransom

Introduction

o OTHER literary critic of this century has devoted as much time and intellectual energy as John Crowe Ransom in attempting to distinguish between scientific prose and poetic discourse. At Oxford as a Rhodes Scholar he helped to establish a literary club to discuss the works of English and continental authors, but it was not until three years later, when he was teaching Latin at the Hotchkiss School, in Lakeville, Connecticut, that he found the area of literary studies that became the compelling interest of his life. On February 4, 1914, Ransom wrote his father, detailing his analysis of the difference between a good translation of prose and one of poetry.

> I recognize a good translation of Vergil with no difficulty and I like it because even the translation is poetry. Yet it lacks meter. Everybody knows that poetry (in its complete form, at least) employs meter: but what else poetry contains no one has yet formulated. . . . The question then is how does the translation that satisfies good taste differ from correct and formal prose? What is unique in the good translation, as a result of a comparison, will be the x, the unknown quality of poetry.

What the good translator is careful to avoid is attempting to smooth out the obscurities of the original. He preserves the "discontinuities, ellipses, the failing to attain preciseness and perfect connection." He retains the words "which mean the given thing yet involve it in accidental associations that provoke the imagination and enrich the logical process." The good translator of poetry is trying to provoke both modes, that of "thought" and that of "imagination." He knows that words have a double nature: "they stand for things and are associated inseparably with thought." Ransom had found his area of greatest interest and for the next half century, though there were brief interludes when the writing of poetry and polemical prose diverted him, he spent a major portion of his creative energy attempting to describe exactly the nature and function of poetic discourse and how it differs from a scientific treatise.

In 1937 Ransom proclaimed in "Criticism, Inc." that the proper function of literary criticism was not to compile data about literature, but to offer a literary judgment. Although he wrote more than a hundred essays in which he engaged in "the proper business of the literary critic," he was careful to create a mask through which he performed. Rather than projecting the image of a "learned pedagogue" issuing proclamations from Mount Olympus intended for others like him, he endeavored to create an impression of the interested and concerned layman discussing matters of importance to all enlightened citizens. Apparently he succeeded, for Elmer Borklund recently wrote that Ransom's style is so disarming and engaging that even when he's wrong we want to agree with him. At the time of Ransom's death Allen Tate wrote: "I risk the guess that Eliot's essays will be read, by that mythical character posterity, for their opinions; Ransom's, for their style, regardless of what they say. For John Ransom wrote the most perspicuous, the most engaging, and the most elegant prose of all the poet-critics of our time."

The end result of this prose style, according to Arthur Mizener, is that the reader is convinced that "Mr. Ransom knows thoroughly, which is to say, with his imagination as well as his practical mind, what he is talking about." Ransom gains this confidence, in spite of the fact, as Graham Hough points out, that "he seems impelled by some minor necessity to put things in a way that would certainly merit censure in an examination paper or a Ph.D. thesis." Marcia McDonald, who has done the most extensive study of Ransom's prose style, lists four qualities of the "fictive personality that delivers" his critical pronouncement: earthiness, wit, irony, and graciousness. Among the quotations she presents to demonstrate her point are the following: "The ten unrhymed lines in Milton's *Lycidas*," Ransom says, are as conspicuous among the 183 rhymed ones as "so many bachelors at a picnic of fast-mated families." An idea, he says in "Poetry: A Note in Ontology," is "the image with its character beaten out of it." The climax of a serious essay on the unique nature of poetry is presented through a simile in which he says poetry is like a chemical compound: its morality and aestheticism are compounded (MA) to make poetry in the same way as sodium (Na) and chloride (Cl) are combined into NaCl, sodium chloride (salt). It is not a mixture like lemonade:

> Lemonade is only a mechanical mixture, not very interesting to chemists. Aside from the water, a drop of lemonade contains lemon and sugar in no standard proportions. If it tastes too sour, add sugar, and if it tastes too sweet, add lemon. (And do not forget to stir the mixture.) No matter what

the final proportions, you can still detect in the lemonade the sweet and the sour; though this is too abstract a matter to bother about if the lemonade is satisfactory, for in that case you simply drink it.

He has made his point—that the constituent elements of poetry, beauty and truth, are irretrievably joined in the only proportions possible—by creating a simile and turning the humor on himself, lest the reader think he is trying to be too highfalutin. Surely Ransom's wit and enjoyment of intellectual play are apparent in his strategic choice of the salt-lemonade analogy.

Ransom's wit is in fact almost as active in his prose as it is in his poetry. Often, as in the poetry, his irony turns to sarcasm, and is used to demolish an antagonist. He often disposes of the Platonists and the Romanticists, two of his worst enemies, by leaving the impression that they are mere incompetents. He ridicules some of the modern poets by parodying the excesses of what we today would call "confessional" verse:

Today young men and women, as noble as Milton . . . try to become poets on another plane, and with rather less success. They write their autobiographies, following perhaps the example of Wordsworth, which on the whole may have been unfortunate for the prosperity of the art; or they write some of their intenser experiences, their loves, pities, griefs, and religious ecstasies; but too literally, faithfully, piously, ingenuously.

One of the passages most often quoted in Ransom's critical prose is the second of Browning's "Pippa's Songs":

> The year's at the spring
> And day's at the morn;
> Morning's at seven;
> The hill-side's dew-pearled;
> The lark's on the wing;
> The snail's on the thorn:
> God's in his heaven—
> All's right with the world.

This, Ransom says, "is a piece of transparent homiletics; for in it six pretty, co-ordinate images are marched, like six little lambs to the slaughter, to a colon and a powerful text." It is the perfect example of the poet's using images to illustrate an idea. At another time he claims this poem makes "nature purposive with an almost excessive clarity, and indeed carries a tag of identification so pointed as to be embarrassing. . . . Little Pippa sings this song in passing, and a pair of guilty lovers recall their lost innocence and take to quarreling, like Adam and Eve after their Fall." The poet is not content to tell us in three concrete details—the hillside, the lark, the snail—that nature shares Pippa's joy in her holiday from the silk mill. He must insert his theological abstraction: "The world rejoices because Pippa's God is now its God too, and he is in his heaven ordering all."

Similarly, in pointing up the weaknesses of Edna St. Vincent Millay's poetry, he virtually demolishes it while ostensibly paying it a compliment. "The college plays," he writes, "were exactly right for their occasions, but *Aria da Capo* comes long afterward and still suggests the prize-winning skit on the Senior Girls' Stunt Night of an unusually good year." He summarizes one of Millay's most ambitious poems in this way. Among the poems in *Second April*, which demonstrate that the author has not consistently grown up, is the longest one in the volume, "a narrative of the Day of Judgment, telling how the narrator witnessed the burning up of the earth, and had to run back at great risk to rescue a poor blue-flag in a bog, but took God's hand and got his special permission to set the plant out and make a little private garden for it in Heaven." Then, he concludes, "I do not think any obligation can lie upon the male adult requiring him to assist at this sort of thing, or, if he must, to smile other than untenderly though God's smile was tender."

Neither can the obvious irony—the distance between what is said and what is meant—be mistaken in Ransom's suggested "cures" for Platonism:

> There are probably two cures. . . . One is by adversity, by the failure of the ideas to work, on account of treachery or violence, or the contingencies of weather, constitution, love, and economics; leaving the Platonist defeated and bewildered, possibly humbled, but on the other hand possibly turned cynical and worthless. Very much preferable is the cure which comes by education in the fine arts, erasing his Platonism more gently, leading him to feel that that is not a becoming habit of mind which dulls the perceptions.

These suggested "cures" for Platonism are offered after Ransom has indicated what will happen if Platonism is allowed to dominate the poem: "The poetry is likely to destroy the conclusions with a sort of death by drowning."

A less obvious kind of irony that permeates Ransom's prose appears in "Poets Without Laurels":

> So I shall try a preliminary definition of the poet's traditional function on behalf of society: he proposed to make virtue delicious. He compounded a

moral effect with an aesthetic effect. The total effect was not a pure effect, but it was rich, and relished highly.

Any student of English literature knows immediately that Ransom is trying to make Sir Philip Sidney's phrase as concrete as possible by playfully using such casual and sensuous words as "delicious" and "relish" instead of the more intellectually rigorous "instruct and delight." In Ransom's critical prose, then, one will also recognize that the poet is never trying for the "pure" effect—such is the ambition of the scientist or theologian—but that the artist always strives for an "impure" effect, one acquired by compounding a "rational structure" with an "irrelevant and irrational" texture.

II

Born in Pulaski, Tennessee, on April 20, 1888, Ransom grew up in half a dozen villages and small towns near Nashville, Tennessee. He attended the Bowen School in Nashville, and in 1909 was graduated from Vanderbilt University first in his class, having had to leave the university for two years following his sophomore year to teach in secondary school. After his graduation he taught one more year in secondary school before attending Christ Church College, Oxford, as a Rhodes Scholar from 1910 to 1913. After a year in Connecticut at the Hotchkiss School, in the fall of 1914 Ransom returned to Vanderbilt to join the English faculty of his alma mater. With him he brought the strong conviction, as John L. Stewart points out, "that modern man is crippled by a dissociation of the reason and sensibility which results in an imbalance whereby the reason, armed with abstract principles which have been spectacularly successful in supplying the material needs of the body, tyrannizes over the sensibility and restricts its innocence," its ability to provide delight "in the vividness and variety of the world." With this conviction went the desire "to restore the sensibility to its proper eminence in man and his society and to enable it to enjoy . . . its harmless indulgence." The bases of his critical system were beginning to solidify. For the next sixty years he would continue to clarify this basic system and attempt to find the most appropriate language through which to express it.

Two developments at Vanderbilt pleased him very much. First, he discovered that the preparation necessary to teach his classes in English literature encouraged him to read closely and analytically a great deal of English literature, an activity vital to the testing of his evolving aesthetic theories. Better still, a group of young faculty members and students were meeting at the apartment of a young Jewish intellectual, Sidney Mttron Hirsch, to discuss literature and philosophy. These discussions, Ransom believed, came to provide another excellent opportunity for him to test some of his theories.

In the spring of 1917 this group dissolved, most of its members serving in World War I. But by the fall of 1920 all the former members had returned, new ones were invited to join, and the meetings had shifted from general literary, religious, and philosophical discussions to considerations of the *craft* of poetry. In *Southern Writers in the Modern World*, Donald Davidson describes a typical meeting in early 1922, just before the group decided to publish its influential little magazine, *The Fugitive*:

> First we gave strict attention, from the beginning, to the *form* of poetry.
> . . . Every poem was read aloud by the poet himself, while the members
> of the group had before them typed copies of the poem. . . . [When] dis-
> cussion began . . . it was likely to be ruthless in its exposure of any tech-
> nical weakness as to rhyme, meter, imagery, metaphor and was often
> minute in analysis of details.

These discussions undoubtedly influenced Ransom, and he wrote the best poetry of his career from 1922 to 1925, the years during which *The Fugitive* was being published. At the same time his participation in the animated discussions aided in the formulation of his theories of the nature and function of poetic discourse. Indeed there were several occasions on which he committed these theories to the printed page. Whenever Allen Tate was out of town, as he was once for several months for reasons of health, he and Ransom exchanged letters, more often than not devoted to intricate discussions of literary theory.

In one such letter to Tate dated December 7, 1922, Ransom outlines some important facets of his theory of poetry, many of which he would never abandon:

> The art thing sounds like the first immediate transcript of reality, but it
> isn't; it's a long way from the event. It isn't the raw stuff of experience.
> The passion in it has mellowed down—emotion recollected in tranquility,
> etc. etc. Above all things else, the core of experience in the record has
> been taken up into the sum total of things and in its relations there dis-
> covered are given the work of art. That is why the marginal meanings,
> the associations, the interlinear elements of a poem are all important. The
> most delicate piece of work that a poet has to do is to avoid a misleading
> connection in his phrasing. There must not be a trace of the expository

philosophical method, but nevertheless the substance of the philosophical conclusion must be there for the intelligent reader.

The continuities of thought in this letter, the letter he wrote his father
nearly ten years before, and his first book of literary criticism, *The
World's Body* (1938), are striking.

It was during the last two years of publication of *The Fugitive* that
Ransom took his first opportunity to discuss formally some of the critical ideas that had been slowly fermenting for more than ten years. In
the first of these brief essays ("The Future of Poetry," February 1924),
Ransom pays his respects to the Imagists, who "declared for honesty of
theme and accuracy of expression." Some of these poets forget, however, that one of the purposes of poetry is to provide a "sense of miracle
before the union of inner meaning and affective form." Some try to produce "pure poetry," but their meters are too regular, "like a string of
beads, all of a size," and their arguments become puerile and platitudi-
nous. The future of poetry is potentially immense, Ransom concludes,
paraphrasing Arnold's familiar prediction, if the poet will remember
that the nature and function of his discourse is different from that
of prose.

In "Mixed Modes" (March, 1925) he expresses his dissatisfaction
with Romantic poetry. So much juvenile poetry is being written, he begins, it is no wonder that H. L. Mencken declares poetry "nothing but
paregoric of lullaby." In Ransom's view the poetry of the nineteenth
century, the simplest, the most autobiographical, the most didactic in
our history, should not be taken as synonymous with the entire literary
tradition. If poetry is going to remain a significant means of cognition,
which Ransom always insisted is poetry's *raison d'être*, it must not
"simplify and prettify" its themes. It must instead present what Ransom calls in the preface to *The World's Body* a "post-scientific poetry,"
one that will engage all of the faculties of those "who have aged in the
pure intellectual disciplines." In the next issue of *The Fugitive* (June,
1925) he argues for a return to the kind of poetry written by Chaucer,
Spenser, Shakespeare, and Milton, one in which the romantic attitude
has been replaced by "mature irony, the ultimate mode of all great
minds," and in the September 1925 number he returns to a discussion
of the unique nature of poetic discourse. Its two different parts—its fable, logical argument, or paraphrasable content—move in one fairly
predictable direction, but other aspects of the poem—the connotation
of the words, the tropes, the allusions—intrude and seem to impede the
logical argument from accomplishing its objective. The nature of this

unique construction, which, unlike science, employs references "free and personal," not "fixed and ideal," is central in Ransom's ontological theory of poetry and will appear in various guises in his critical essays for the remainder of his career.

During the summer and fall of 1926, while on leave from his teaching position at Vanderbilt, Ransom wrote the critical book he had been pondering for more than twenty years. The working title of the manuscript was "The Third Moment," and, as he wrote his chairman at Vanderbilt, Edwin Mims, he was attempting to treat "formally a great mass of observations I have to make about literature" and to prepare for more specialized studies by presenting "a technical philosophy of aesthetics." From his correspondence with Tate and others we know that he spent a great deal of time and effort during the next two or three years preparing a manuscript approximately three hundred pages long which he immediately sent off to Harper's. After several weeks of deliberation the publishers returned it with suggestions for extensive revisions. For two or three years Ransom attempted sporadically to make the suggested revisions, but he finally decided the book was hopelessly abstract, that such a study could "scarcely afford to be pursued in any way except in the constant company of the actual poems"; therefore, as he wrote in the preface to *The World's Body* (1938), he "had the pleasure of consigning . . . [it] to the flames."

Since no copy of this manuscript is extant, its contents can be reconstructed only by carefully reading the letters he wrote during the period of its composition. Throughout this period he and Tate were exchanging long letters in which they were debating the functions of poetic discourse. These letters, one suspects, were of enormous benefit to both men as they were framing their theories of the validity of poetry as a means of cognition, and were in part responsible for Ransom's statement in *The World's Body* that he had observed that when the discussion between him and Tate reached a "certain temperature" it illustrated the "theory of anonymous or communal authorship."

In a letter to Tate on September 5, 1926, Ransom outlined the plan and intentions of the book in some detail (See Appendix A). There are, Ransom wrote, "Three moments in the historical order of experience": the first is the experience itself, "pure of all intellectual content, unreflective, concrete, and singular; there are no distinctions, and the subject is identical with the whole." In the second moment "cognition takes place" and a record is made, but this record includes only a part of the original experience—that portion that may be expressed through concepts. These concepts are the beginning of science, with its emphasis on practicality, because the concepts are abstract statements of isolated parts, formed by subtracting from the whole experience that which may serve some utilitarian purpose. Only in the third moment are we aware of the deficiency of the record, of the fact that "most of the experience is quite missing from it." Neither science nor history can reconstitute the whole experience, including its concrete particularities. At this point art, fancies (day dreams) or dreams enter and attempt to restore to the original experience that which natural science or the social sciences have deleted. Obviously Ransom is concerned here not with the nature of poetry but with its function. He is explaining, as he states in *The World's Body*, why poetry presents "the kind of knowledge by which we must know that which we have arranged that we shall not know otherwise." What we cannot know constitutionally as scientists is the "world which is made of whole and indivisible objects, and this is the world which poetry recovers for us." The intent of poetry, then, is not to "idealize" the world but to make us "realize" it.

Although Ransom in the late 1920s and early 1930s was very much involved in the Agrarian movement—he wrote the introduction and the lead essay to *I'll Take My Stand* (1930)—he continued to write and publish essays of literary criticism. After a book of Agrarian reform, *Land!*, was turned down by his publisher, Ransom salvaged two essays from it ("The State and the Land" and "Land! An Answer to the Unemployment Problem"). His interest in economic questions began to wane, however, and he returned to literary criticism. By mid-1937 he concluded that he had published a sufficient number of essays for a book; therefore he collected them, wrote an introduction, and sent them off to Charles Scribner's. The book was accepted and appeared in 1938 as *The World's Body*.

Although this is an uneven book, it does contain some of Ransom's best and most influential essays, especially on the function of poetry in a mature society. The most significant of these essays, perhaps, is "Poetry: A Note in Ontology," which brings together much of his thinking on this subject for almost a quarter of a century. He begins the essay by classifying poetry into three types: physical, Platonic, and metaphysical. Then he describes, discusses, and explains the strengths and weaknesses of each type. Physical poetry he calls "genuine poetry" because it attempts to present "things in their thingness." As the best example of this type he points to the twentieth-century Imagists and their attempt to create verse that concentrates almost completely upon the concrete object itself. Although this kind of poetry is concerned with the "basic constituent" of all verse—images—it is really only quasi poetry, since all ideas or concepts are scrupulously excluded, and the verse contains little, if any, emotional or intellectual content. The second classification, Platonic poetry, is "bogus," according to Ransom, because it demonstrates no faith in images. They are used merely as decoration or to illustrate (rather than to embody) ideas. The writers of such verse can never expect to create real poetry because their interest is in an abstract idea and not in the presentation of the concrete particularities of the object itself. The third kind he calls metaphysical—although he is not completely satisfied with the designation. This is true poetry because it presents and develops both ideas and images. It is built upon a central figure, "a metaphor that is meant." It is "meant" because it is "developed so literally that it must be meant, or predicated so baldly that nothing else can be meant." Through a blend of both image and idea a fully developed metaphor emerges, one which presents an identity between two objects which "is partial, though it should be considerable, and proceeds to an identification which is complete." In this way the poet attempts to reconstitute the experience itself by presenting a mixed world of images "adulterated with concepts."

The World's Body also contains Ransom's essay "Forms and Citizens," which is occupied with the necessity of literary form (using *Lycidas* to prove the point). Incidentally, however, it presents the philosophical bases for his support of Agrarianism. The society which Ransom wanted to recover was what he called a mature society, that of the old South, one unique in America because it was formed on European principles. Every society, he argues, passes through two phases—the "Pioneering" and the "Mature." In the first stage man's primary obligation is to find the means of assuring his livelihood. In this developmental stage he must examine his natural surroundings and make "whatever concessions he might reasonably be expected" to make in order to secure the material necessities of life. Once the means of providing these economic necessities have been secured, man moves into a second phase because pioneering is no longer necessary. (The antebellum southern civilization, Ransom believes, moved into the second phase but that of the North never did.) The Europeans, for example, do "not make too much of the more intense practical enterprises, but are at pains to define rather narrowly the practical effort which is prerequisite to the reflective or aesthetic life." The mature society knows the value of traditions, manners, rituals, ceremonies, myths, rites, and poetry. The nontraditional society of America, Ransom believes, follows a "gospel of progress," a doctrine counter to the notion that man should adapt himself to his environment and demonstrate that he is intelligent enough to secure with a minimum of effort his material necessities. The traditional man believes he should live with nature "on terms of mutual respect and amity," and not wage an unrelenting war against her.

In the last essay in the volume, "Criticism, Inc.," Ransom says that literary criticism must be placed in the hands of professional critics, men who are able to analyze a poem and render a literary judgment, for the kind of unique knowledge contained in the poem will become available only after an intensive study of the work of art itself. The poem must be read as a poem and not as history, biography, or homiletics. Obviously Ransom is discussing the kind of criticism essential for literature to retain a significant role in the life of civilized man. It is an approach to literature that he had been developing and refining in his own classes for more than twenty years.

Many readers have seen this essay as an urgent appeal for the New Criticism. If so, Ransom did not have to wait long for his plea to be answered, for in that same year two of his former students—Cleanth Brooks and Robert Penn Warren—published *Understanding Poetry* (1938), a widely influential textbook that has undergone numerous editions in the forty years since its publication. Its aim is quite simple and very much in accord with the challenge issued in Ransom's essay: it attempts to demonstrate how a poem should be read. First it suggests three substitutes currently in use for reading the actual poem, three practices to be avoided at all costs: (1) paraphrase of the logical or narrative content; (2) study of biographical or historical materials; (3) inspirational and didactic interpretation. Although the paraphrase of a poem might be useful, it is a means and not an end. A knowledge of an author's life or the times in which he lived may be helpful, but it is preliminary to reading the poem itself, not a substitute for that act. Brooks and Warren followed Ransom's lead and sought to focus attention on the poem as a work of conscious artistry that yields its full meaning only upon careful and intelligent analysis by an informed and intelligent reader.

III

Soon after *The World's Body* was published, Ransom began a new book in which he intended to survey modern criticism. "I am sweating gore," he wrote Tate not too long after he became settled at Kenyon, "finishing off my book for New Directions." The book, *The New Criticism* (1941), is divided into four chapters: one on Richards and Empson, one each on Eliot and Winters, and a final one, added at the suggestion of Delmore Schwartz, who asked for some consideration of Ransom, Tate, Blackmur, and Brooks. Ransom responded by writing one of his most significant essays: "Wanted: An Ontological Critic." A careful examination of this piece indicates that while Ransom's earlier concern had been chiefly with the *function* of poetic discourse, he is now interested in examining its *nature*. But this is not a new interest for Ransom, for it develops some of the ideas offered tentatively in the letter to his father twenty-five or more years before.

A poem, he begins, differentiates itself from prose discourse not by moralism, emotionalism, or sensibility, because any of these can be expressed in prose. It differs because of its unique structure, and the difference is an ontological one. He has searched, he says, for an ontological critic, but he cannot find one. The most helpful critic he has been able to find is Charles W. Morris, a semanticist at the University of Chicago. Eliot and Richards seem to agree that the basic function of a poem is to release emotion; thus they deny the value of poetry as a means of cognition. Empson neglects entirely the logical structure of the poem, Ransom believes, and Winters is oblivious to its rich texture. Although he has read closely those seventeenth-century poets in which "the modern dualism of thought and feeling" is said to have been fused, he has never been able to find any persuasive evidence to convince him that a thought can be felt. Neither can he find an acceptable definition of poetry "which regards it as a single unified experience, and exempts it from the dilemma of logic." He has been unsuccessful, he believes, because he has attempted to fuse "two experiences that always repel one another." Although we cannot "feel a thought," neither can we "conduct a thought [and deny] all innocent or irrelevant feelings in the process." He suggests how this apparent dichotomy may be solved. "We can realize the *structure*, which is the logical thought," he says, "without sacrificing the *texture*, which is the free detail." In Eliot's terms, we can think of the big emotion as being "attached to the main thought"— that is, the logical structure—and the little feeling being attached to the play on words—that is, the local texture.

The odd structure of a poem, which is the principal means by which it is differentiated from prose, is difficult to describe. It is a structure which "is not so tight and precise as a scientific or prose structure usually is," but one that "carries along a great deal of irrelevant or foreign matter which is clearly obstructive." The closest he can come, then, to offering an acceptable definition of poetry is that it is a "loose logical structure with an irrelevant local texture."

Ransom is not only arguing that poetic and prose discourse are different in kind; he is also declaring his conviction that they have different functions. There are many worlds, he says, and the one treated in scientific discourse is "reduced, emasculated, and docile." Poetry attempts, on the other hand, to recover the "denser and more refractory original world which we know loosely through our perceptions and memories." Charles Morris, he repeats, comes closer than any other critic to defining the "radical and ontologically distinct" nature of poetry. Human discourse, Morris contends, is conducted through signs: syntactical (logic), semantical (reference of sign to object), and pragmatical (references in the sign itself). There are, Morris continues, three kinds of discourse: science, art, and technology. Science is objective and knowledge-giving, but in providing knowledge it uses only symbol. Aesthetic signs, on the other hand, are icons or images. They not only refer to objects but they resemble those objects. Whereas scientific symbols are abstract and refer to abstract concepts, aesthetic icons recall whole concrete objects. They do not refer to abstractions, to words, for example, that substitute for mankind in general, but instead are concrete images of human beings, of particular men.

The value of scientific discourse depends upon the purity of its symbols—the reference of a single symbol always to a specific and uniform concept. The icon, which pictures a whole and indivisible object, however, exceeds definition. Since it refers to a specific person, it may change with each reference. The aesthetic discourse, furthermore, will digress from logic through the use of icons. Only the argument, fable, or theme of a poem deals with a single value system. Poetry attempts, furthermore, to make rhythm and sense at the same time. But while this process is occurring, another action is taking place: the argument or structure of the poem is trying to replace the meters, and the meters are attempting to replace the argument. Each poem, therefore, has a determinate meaning (DM) and a determinate sound (DS), but at the same time it has an indeterminate meaning (IM) and an indeterminate sound (IS). The determinate meaning is working against the indeterminate meaning to produce a meaning different from the intended one. The same process is occurring with the meter.

In a later essay Ransom argues that the intent of the critic should be to study the relationship between the structure and texture of the poem. Many critics erroneously believe that anything in a poem that is not directly functional is extraneous, but such an attitude reveals certain limitations in understanding the true nature of a poem. Like Hegel, those critics believe—and Ransom will have much to say on this attitude later—that all the elements of a poem should be assembled under a ruling idea, a Concrete Universal. Although scientific discourse is "one-valued," as he has argued in "Wanted: An Ontological Critic," the poem is not. Poetry "improves on discursive prose" because it makes "five or six pleasures to appear and prose only one." Moreover, and here Ransom thinks he is pursuing an often mistaken view of art, the effect that a poem has on its reader may be astonishingly disproportionate to his interest in the subject it treats. The good critic must have a realistic world view. He must realize that he does not occupy the tidy universe of the scientist; therefore, the reality that the poet is trying to present will be much different—more diffuse—than that of the scientist. Neither should the critic set the value of a poem at the level of the utility it produces, a view that has dominated the whole occidental world. Although in its "argument" or "design" art shows its positivistic nature, the contribution of art to revolutionary causes of any kind is not great.

Ransom's formal declaration of independence from Agrarianism is included, it is commonly believed, in "Art and the Human Economy" (1945). Actually, however, Ransom's interest in the Agrarian cause had been declining for ten years or longer; he explained in a letter to Tate on April 6, 1937: "I enclose a last act of patriotism. I'm signing off a little by degrees. . . . It's been on my conscience for a long time. I can imagine it is a line you yourself might not care to take, feeling that our Agrarian position is stronger if we just urge it simple and pure without reference to politics." The essay Ransom refers to in this letter was never published. A little later that spring he wrote his department chairman, Edwin Mims—after he had received an offer from Kenyon College—that leaving Vanderbilt would be detrimental to his literary career if he intended to do any more writing on regionalism or agrarianism. "But I have about contributed all I have to those movements," he wrote, "and I have of late gone almost entirely into literary work." He is referring, of course, to the fact that all but one of the essays published in *The World's Body* were written in a three-year period during the mid-thirties.

In "Art and the Human Economy," Ransom is ostensibly commenting on W. P. Southard's essay on Robert Penn Warren's poetry, a task which he dutifully and sincerely performs, writing that Warren has found a sympathetic and able critic earlier than most poets. After a

time, though, the tone of the essay suddenly changes. Mr. Southard
wishes for an agrarian economy, Ransom points out, in which "innocence may be recovered." Ransom admits that he, too, once had a similar desire. In such a society, however, Ransom points out, there would
be no "effective science, inventions, and scholarship," no "art, e.g., *Reviews* and contributions to *Reviews*, fine poems and their exegeses."
Once he would have thought, he admits, that the Declaration of Potsdam, compelling the Germans to go back to an agrarian economy, would
produce a much desired state. But now he considers it "an inhuman
punishment." He can now see that the primary contribution of Agrarianism was to make its participants see "the forward-and-backward
movement of the human economy." He is, furthermore, grateful that its
advocates are "defending the freedom of the arts," which is more than
the exponents of "economic progress" are doing. However, even Ransom's conciliatory conclusion did not satisfy Donald Davidson, who, as
Ransom suspected he would, thought the essay "treason and unfriend-
ship." Soon after the essay appeared Davidson wrote Tate: "It's all right
for John to change his mind, of course. . . . Already by his silence on
anything but purely aesthetic issues he had in effect severed his connection with his old friends."

In 1952 Ransom returned to this topic. It has been said that his primary interest in Agrarianism, perhaps, was in attempting to retain a
social order in which art would be regarded as a significant means of
cognition. His thinking during the intervening fifteen years, however,
had changed drastically. Now, he writes, "the heavy hand of politics is
upon us in these times. . . . Like Milton's meager Shadow, Death, we
can sniff where we sit, where we live, 'the smell of mortal change on
Earth.'" Art remains the fullest image of the human experience, and
our civilization would be much the poorer without it. There is no question but that it must be produced and consumed. Ransom notes that
the past few decades had spawned a large group of writers of a quality
seldom equaled in our history, writers who had not merely reflected the
views and attitudes of their generation, but who had produced "a product which was ahead of the immediate acceptance of their readers."
And such, in Ransom's view, is the proper function of the artist. Although he is not a teacher, he should bring "the contemporary mind to
a new elevation of ideas and spirits."

The artist cannot perform his function, however, if he writes only for
himself and others like him. He must have a wider audience. The nature of society has become so complex and specialized that the artist

cannot expect to be received by even a small segment that cuts across all social interests. For this reason Ransom entitled his 1952 essay "The Communities of Letters," and that is exactly the point he is trying to make:

> The public of any important writer forms one [community], and for a long time it may have intense consciousness of its separateness; it is not identical with any other. . . . If in some rude sense, however, we add all the communities up, we will have, in theory at least, a total community having a peculiar role. It may be thought of as a secondary society branching off from the formal or primary society, and easing its requirements, compelling its members to approach to the sense of a common humanity. . . . How could a gentle civilization do without this community?

Less than ten years after he had called for a group of professional critics to make the modern complex poetry available to the common reader, he found a revolt developing against the New Criticism. The reason, he thought, was that the new approach to literary studies did not satisfy the expectations it aroused. He attempted to assess the value of this new means of experiencing poetry in an essay entitled "Poetry: The Formal Analysis." In its emphasis on the total connotation of words, he asserts, the close analysis of verse has achieved a virtual revolution in the "way poetry is read." Now, however, many critics approach a poem as a bee gathers nectar: "he goes from one image to the next," as the bee goes from blossom to blossom without "noticing the tree that holds the blossoms." In their movement from image to image, these critics concentrate on the texture of the poem and disregard its structure, its logical argument. By doing so they have left an impression that a poem is a very disorderly construction.

The fear that Ransom's structure-texture formulation could lead too easily to the false division of a poem into form and content had led Cleanth Brooks to deny that the paraphrase (Ransom's "Structure") is a part of a poem. As a consequence Brooks's defense of poetry, Ransom argues, is not based on "the defense of its human substance." Although the so-called New Critics have power because they have found profound and moving new meaning in the texts of poems, Ransom asserts, they have been as "weak in its psychology as . . . [they have] been brilliant in its semantical effects." The formal analysis of a poem is a linguistical exercise, but the determination of its use is a psychological one. A poem has two kinds of meaning: its "ostensible argument" which can be rendered by paraphrase and a "tissue of meaning" which resists restatement in prose. Too many modern critics give their attention only to the latter. More notice should be given the former because a poem is public and should make formal sense.

Although a paraphrase is not the poem, Ransom admits it is often useful to a critic: (1) if the text of a poem is long and needs explanation, or (2) if a long poem needs paraphrase to provide perspective and proportion. As an example of the first, Ransom offers "Sailing to Byzantium," which, though relatively short, is esoteric, involved, and complicated. A paraphrase is necessary to get the drift of the argument. Of course, Ransom adds, no critic feels his function has been effected when a paraphrase has been executed; he has merely done a part of the preparation necessary to read the poem. Since many modern poems are difficult, "establishing the canonical paraphrase" is a "dignified critical responsibility." The critic should never forget, however, that poetry is in the "pathetic" rather than the "logical" mode, the language of feeling, not of thought. Poetry is a logical discourse, but necessarily an impure one.

The companion essay to this piece, called "Poetry: The Final Cause," is one of Ransom's most familiar critical essays because it contains his definition of "precious object," a category in which he included poetry. He defines a precious object as "one beyond price" or "one valued at more than the market value of such objects." Such an object is important to us because it occupies "so much of our affective life." Besides poetry, the term may include "father and mother, husband and wife, child, friend, home, view, terrain, town; natural objects . . . which familiarly invest our lives, such as sun and moon, sky and sea, mountain and forest, river, plain; and even objects that are far less tangible when we try to comprehend them as wholes . . . such as one's nation, church, God, business, 'causes,' and institutions."

Although a precious object is a familiar one, it is always capable of "exhibiting fresh aspects which are contingent and unpredictable." Because these objects are "loved," they are different from ones that are merely used. In the view of a technician an object has no value beyond that attached to its use. As a result, little value is given to precious objects in contemporary life because they cannot properly be included in scientific prose. A scientific discourse is interested only in useful objects, ones which have been abstracted from substance. And Ransom makes his point: if a poem is a precious object, its paraphrase is its abstraction.

Some critics, Ransom says, argue that the logical argument of a poem (its structure or paraphrasable content) is so powerful that it absorbs and assimilates the discursive elements (texture). But to admit this assumption, he believes, is to argue that a poetic and a prose discourse are the same. To attempt to differentiate between the poem and its prose paraphrase, Ransom resorts to a Freudian analogy. The structure of a poem may be likened to the ego, the texture to the id. The id, rooted in the instincts, is so deeply seated that it scarcely knows what it wants from the outside world and has to depend upon the ego to conduct its business. The ego (structure) is the feeling and reasoning organ and therefore able to conduct the use of the world for the id's (texture's) benefit. But at times a compulsion comes through from the id that the ego cannot handle. So it is with the logical argument of the poem. Sometimes the attraction of the texture exerts such a strong pull on the reader that the even flow of the logical structure is temporarily diverted into interesting, informative, and poetic—though completely illogical—channels.

The psyche sometimes develops certain sentimental attachments to objects, and this attraction is so strong that the ego (structure) is no deterrent. All the reason wants of the precious object is that it perform its utilitarian function, but other considerations of the precious object are so strong that the course of a poetic discourse is often impeded as fact and advanced in other directions.

Some of the most severe criticism Ransom received on *The World's Body* was for his apparently irreverent attitude toward Aristotle. (In "The Cathartic Principle" he had written: "Aristotle's opinion . . . was that of a man with medical training; it amounted to saying that people had better make the best of a delicate situation, and it was precisely like the point of view of a modern military authority legalizing prostitution in the neighborhood of the camp.") Ten years later, he wrote "The Literary Criticism of Aristotle" in which he discusses in more detail the strengths and weaknesses of the Greek's theory of aesthetics. Aristotle's theory is incomplete, Ransom says, because his treatment of epic and comedy are incomplete, and his assessment of tragedy is suspect because it was motivated for utilitarian reasons. The Greeks were addicted to pity and fear, Aristotle was convinced, so they should go to the drama where these unhealthy and undesirable emotions could be purged: "They would be better citizens after such a debauch, or between debauches." Aristotle's greatest contribution to aesthetics, in Ransom's view, was his theory of mimesis. Imitation meant to Aristotle that language should denote natural objects as "given, contingent . . .

to be distinguished from those abstract or working objects." In the literary arts, furthermore, words are mimetic indirectly; they evoke images of the natural object in its fullness, which go beyond the needs of the appetitive or acquisitive life. This fact is important, Ransom says, because it gives us pleasure when the artist's imitation is a particularly high-grade technical achievement. It is not a pleasure that appeals to our economic appetites but to our aesthetic needs.

For Ransom, the weakness of Aristotle's theory of *katharsis* is best demonstrated by Kant. Before Kant it was possible to say a very specialized thing about reason or intellect; that is, it was the instrument of our appetitive life. But Kant, like Schopenhauer, Freud, and Bergson, did not surrender everything to reason. Unlike Hegel, who argued that the Concrete Universal assimilates all the qualities that the sensibility discovers, these philosophers reverted to the abstract or common universal, which does not include all the individual concretions of nature. They still argue that nature is "infinite," "boundless," "inviolable in its contingency and plentitude." (Such an argument, of course, is more compatible with Ransom's "structure-texture" formulation as the unique nature of poetry.)

Although man has used reason as an economic force, as a means of getting what he needs from nature more effectively (and we are an animal species to whom the appetitive life is important), for poetry, for "precious objects" and our other aesthetic needs, it has been of little value, in Ransom's view. To gratify his aesthetic wants man must be transformed from an appetitive animal to one of human sensibility. He must rely, not only on reason, but on poetry, the concrete particularity of nature, the sensibilities, emotions, and feelings for effects which are not fundamentally useful but which "are always brilliant, vivid and aesthetically pleasing."

Late in life Ransom seems to have gained a greater respect for the Romantic poets, especially for Wordsworth and Keats. He wrote an appreciative essay on Wordsworth, and one of the courses he often offered at the Kenyon School of English and at many of the universities he visited after his retirement from Kenyon was on Keats. Wordsworth, he wrote in 1950, "reversed the course of English poetry, revitalized it." Coming as he did at the end of a century known for its restrictive forms and highly artificial diction, Wordsworth's insistence that the diction of poetry is not different from that of good prose was little short of revolutionary, Ransom points out. In his poetry Wordsworth's diction registers factually a human passion for the concrete particularities of a natural object. He endeavored to reconstitute human experience, not to offer some comment about it. But Ransom could not accept, finally, Wordsworth's theory that the diction of poetry and prose are the same. He points out four differences: the poet uses (1) "spreaders," that is, the "words and phrases which explore the vivid concreteness in the objects and events"; (2) "dystatical terms" or "rufflers," that is, the use of inversions, alterations in idiom, ambiguities, and obscurities, faulty series, ellipses, and the omission of rational connectors; (3) metaphorical terms—"foreign terms brought in by way of analogy or association of ideas"; (4) meters—measures imposed on poetry with a regularity not found in prose. In his poetry Wordsworth used items one and four of the above. Although many critics think Wordsworth's verse is too plain, Ransom considers it genuine poetry because Wordsworth always endeavors "to display" the affections in their purest and most elemental form.

IV

Throughout his career, Ransom continued to be less than satisfied with his definition of poetry as a kind of discourse having a *structure*, though not one as tight as a prose structure generally is, and a *texture*, which does not further the central argument of a poem but often impedes it. It was not that he was constantly changing his mind about the nature of poetic discourse but that he had never been able to say exactly what he meant. Between 1954 and 1970 he took up this subject again in a series of three essays, all of which he called "The Concrete Universal."

In the first of these he takes issue with W. K. Wimsatt, who argues that the concrete detail of a poem may be completely consumed in an abstract universal. Ransom recognizes this as the theory of Hegel, but, he writes, he finds Croce's argument, following Kant's, more convincing. Croce was persuaded that it was impossible "to render in purely logical terms the full import of any poem." The paraphrase, in other words, could never include the whole poem. Ransom contends that Eliot is making a similar point when he suggests that though Shakespeare knew which emotion he wanted to arouse in Hamlet—"perhaps an affective version of the Concrete Universal"—he made a mistake when he thought the plot of an old play would be a suitable "objective correlative."

What Hegel failed to consider, Ransom continues, was that although all of one's sensibilities may be employed in a scientific discourse, such is not the case in poetry. Nevertheless, Ransom admits that he thinks he has found the reason why his definition of "texture" has never completely satisfied him:

> Suppose we say that the poem is an organism. Then it has a physiology. We will figure its organs, and to me it seems satisfactory if we say they are three: the head, the heart, the feet. In this organism the organs work all at the same time, but the peculiarity of the joint production is that it still consists of the several products of the organs working individually. Of course a good deal of co-operation among the organs was necessary, on the understanding that each would have to push its product at the expense of the others, requiring some compromises all round.

We may assume, too, that the organs are all intelligent; therefore they are able to speak, and they speak different languages: the head in an intelligent, the heart in an affective, and the feet in a rhythmical language. The product they produce in concert is a poem, and since all three are speaking their three languages simultaneously—often each at the expense of one of the others—we cannot expect the poem always to proceed along predictable lines. Although there are three different languages, the affective and the rhythmical do not distort the intelligent; therefore there will always be a logically organized "argument" (or structure) with a beginning, middle, and end.

In modern poetry, Ransom admits, this argument may not always be easy to detect. To discover it one often has to do an *"explication de texte"* and "then a translation of the composite language into an exclusive language of the intellect." The reason for this paraphrase is obvious; it is important because it "exhibits one working of a principle that is moral or religious or political." There is no reason to believe this paraphrase does violence to the poem, because it comes from the poem and after it is taken the poem is still there for the critic to make whatever use of it he wishes.

Although the language of the head (the paraphrase) may be expressing a concept that is well known or even trite, this is not, of course, always the case. Certainly it is not the entire poem. Wallace Stevens, for example, may be expressing "Notes Toward the Definition of a Secular Culture," and Eliot "Notes Toward the Definition of a Religious Culture." Since all intelligent men are concerned with the nature of present and future cultures, the intelligent language (the structure) can be very significant.

The second half of the essay, which appeared in the *Kenyon Review* nearly a year later (Summer, 1955), announces that the literary world is under the influence of an "aesthetic humanism" which we must call Kantian or post-Kantian. The general definition of poetry under which the Romantics operated was Kantian, but the Victorians' work was much more simplistic than their technique would suggest. Unlike Kant, Hegel argued that "any idea in the mind proposes a little universe or organized working combination of parts, and the heterogenous parts must perform their several duties faithfully to bring it about." One searching for an example to demonstrate the process that Hegel is describing could propose a blueprint, a chemical reaction, a recipe, or even Newman's concept of a university. Any of these will become a concrete universal, Ransom says, when it materializes and is really working. The universal is the design as it exists in the understanding, and the concrete refers to the parts, all of which must work together to make the design materialize. One can find such a universal in science, each part performing perfectly, nothing missing, nothing unnecessary.

But some critics, following Aristotle and Hegel, insist that the same perfect organization exists in a poem, "that the concrete is completely used up in the universal." Ransom, the dualist, however, cannot accept such a theory, for it does not take into consideration that the universal operating in a poem is moral without being didactic. It is different from that working in science because it uses nature as a means not as an end. It goes into nature to explore it, not to use it.

Although the practical world would seem to want us to abandon poetry, Ransom says, Kant is one of its strongest defenders. His argument, simply stated, is that the world taken as a whole cannot be fully comprehended by the understanding. Natural beauty can be known through poetry, whose agent is the imagination. (We are back here to the basic argument of "The Third Moment.") Even such an imperfect poem as the Pippa's song previously referred to gives evidences of nature's beauty: the hillside, the lark, and the snail. The poet is not disciplined, however, to let the concrete particularities be his spokesman; he attempts to provide credibility by adding a theological universal, "a powerful text": "God's in His Heaven— / All's right with the World."

Kant assures us, Ransom says, that metaphor can be used to render a *sense* of nature, an image of the natural world. It can perform this function, though, "only if we proceed by accepting the universal readily into an informal system." And Ransom identifies nature as the system to which the universal may be referred and to which poetry has to look. Poetry cannot abandon nature, because to do so is to abandon metaphor and metaphor is the stuff poetry is made of. Ransom reiterates that the universal of poetry is unlike that of science, in which the particulars are always assimilated into the concrete. In a poem the concrete particulars and the abstract universal are always working against each other: the universal is always trying to consume the concrete particulars and the particulars are always struggling to keep the abstract statement (the universal) from making faultless logical sense. Thus, Ransom concludes, a poem is a genuine dualism with a structure and a texture.

In his final word on this subject, in 1970 Ransom writes:

> It may be said that the notion of the poem as a concretion, but not a universal, must generate more excitement than Episteme. The author of the poem is Spirit residing though partially and intermittently in the poet and, hopefully at least, identical with that Spirit of the universe which is God, or that Spirit of history which continually creates in order to objectify itself. This Spirit is of an order which only concreteness can express. It cannot have its being within the servile restrictions of the technical sciences. The scientific universals are hopelessly abstract; they are mere concepts; and though these mean to hold their ground, it is only to keep what each of them characteristically wants of the world, and to reject more than they take. Quite different are the occasions when the world somewhere seems possessed and sustained through and through by the concretions of the Spirit; for example, when a natural landscape is utterly beautiful . . . still better in the more responsive world of human affairs, when there is realized beside some hearth a scene of perfect familial accord.

Ransom's views of the nature and function of poetry changed little over a long lifetime. For him poetry was always a "loose logical structure with an irrelevant local texture," and its function was always to help us "realize" the world, to provide "the kind of knowledge by which we must know that which we have arranged that we shall not know otherwise, . . . to recover the world of whole and indefeasible objects" which science and social science has taken from us. Poetry can assist us in knowing the world, for in poetry the imagination, through the agency of metaphor, constructs a moral universal, makes that which is abstract and conceptual concrete and perceptual. Without poetry, man's knowledge of the world is fragmentary and incomplete. Fundamentally, Ransom's views of poetry changed little, but he was always trying to clarify and refine his position by supplying additional details or by shifting his metaphor. For that reason, as well as for the style in which they are composed, his essays remain as intellectually cogent and vital today as when they first appeared.

V

The editors have brought what they believe to be Ransom's most important essays into one volume, arranged chronologically, so that the reader
can conveniently trace the development of his theories on the nature
and function of poetry. Such a study demonstrates, as indicated above,
the consistency of Ransom's fundamental views of poetry, a literary
form he believed provided man with knowledge he could gain from no
other source. A far more significant reason for this collection is that
Ransom's essays for the most part are sprinkled through dozens of journals, many of which are no longer printed today. Only a mere handful of
the essays of one of America's few theoretical critics are available in
books today in print. All editorial apparatus, including textual notes,
has been supplied by the editors unless otherwise indicated.

FOUR SHORT PIECES FROM
THE FUGITIVE

THE FUTURE OF POETRY

 HE ARTS generally have had to recognize Modernism—how should poetry escape? And yet what is Modernism? It is undefined. Henry James stopped before a certain piece of sculpture to apostrophize "the beautiful modern spirit"; but he did not attempt a definition where a more incompetent man would surely have done it.

In poetry the Imagists, in our time and place, made a valiant effort to formulate their program. Their modernist manifestoes were exciting; their practice was crude, as was becoming to pioneers, and instructive in more ways than they had intended. They announced at least two notable principles.

In the first place, they declared for honesty of theme and accuracy of expression. Though a poem were but a single minor image, tactile, visual, auditory, or even gustatory, provided it was honest and accurate, they preferred it to the grand performance of the Cosmos-throned-by-Love order, where the whole nature of things was presented in orderly and elegant exposition, if here the conception or the diction came second-handed out of the schools. They spurned as their art-material the stilted platitudes, the sentimental *clichés*, the taught relics of the other generations. They conceived the first duty of the Moderns as being to disembarrass poetry of its terrible incubus of piety, in the full classical sense of that term, and they rendered the service.

Their second principle followed. Emphasizing the newness of the matter, and the spontaneity of the Word, which was sacrosanct with all its edge and pungence just as it came forth, they were obliged to make their meters more elastic to accommodate their novelties. As a matter of fact, they practically gave up meters altogether, pretending that it was

This essay and the three that follow were all first published in *The Fugitive*. "The Future of Poetry" appeared in the February 1924 issue; "Mixed Modes" in March, 1925; "Thoughts on the Poetic Discontent" in June, 1925; and "Prose: A Doctrine of Relativity" in September, 1925. Reprinted by permission of Helen Ransom Forman.

their intention to realize a subtler music for ears that experienced revulsion against the stupid monotone of the school meters; but apparently [they were] unable to adapt their new meanings and phrases to
any formal requirements whatever. Their free verse was no form at all,
yet it made history.

Against the second of these principles there has come a sweeping
reaction. And it does not seem too hazardous to claim that poetry, as one
of the formal arts, has for its specific problem to play a dual role with
words: to conduct a logical sequence with their meanings on the one
hand, and to realize an objective pattern with their sounds on the other.
Now between the meanings of words and their sounds there is ordinarily no discoverable relation except one of accident: and it is therefore
miraculous, to the mystic, when words which make sense can also
make a uniform objective structure of accents and rhymes. It is a miracle of harmony, of the adaptation of the free inner life to the outward
necessity of things.

But we moderns are impatient and destructive. We forget entirely
the enormous technical difficulty of the poetic art, and we examine the
meanings of poems with a more and more microscopic analysis; we examine them in fact just as strictly as we examine the meanings of a
prose which was composed without any handicap of metrical distrac-
tions; and we do not obtain so readily as our fathers the ecstasy which is
the total effect of poetry, the sense of miracle before the union of inner
meaning and objective form. Our souls are not, in fact, in the enjoyment of full good health. For no art and no religion is possible until we
make allowances, until we manage to keep quiet the *enfant terrible* of
logic that plays havoc with the other faculties.

For, take the fact of poetic license as an illustration. Till now poets
were privileged to insert a certain proportion of nonsense—very far in
excess of one-half of one per cent—into their otherwise sober documents. Thence their archaisms, their inversions, their illegal accents.
For their audience appreciated the difficulties under which they labored; or else wanted the main experience of poetry, and were willing to
disregard the invidious details. But now that attitude and that privilege
are gone.

And how can poetry stand up against its new conditions? Its position
is perfectly precarious. When critics are waiting to pounce upon poetic
style on exactly the same grounds as if it were prose, the poets tremble.
They know they cannot at once, waiving all immunities, realize the
standards of style and at the same time meet the requirements of their

meter. They prepare to turn themselves, in grievous numbers, to the composition of pure prose, if they would escape rebuke. And sometimes they are their own severest critics; their own documents, on second reading, have been known to induce in poets a fatal paralysis of the writing digit. For their consecutive verses, wherein they laboriously round off the stanza, are as a string of beads, all of a size, a monstrosity of construction; and the individual lines, as they come to their inevitable climactic rhyme, fall into foolish platitudes, and are puerile.

The future of poetry is immense? One is not so sure in these days, since it has felt the fatal irritant of Modernism. Too much is demanded by the critic, attempted by the poet. For just as long as poetry means accommodation between the inner thought and the objective pattern to which the poet has committed himself, it will be impossible to conduct that thought as freely as though there were no other end in view; and on the basis of thought alone, between poetry and prose as two rival exhibitions of free cerebration, the palm must invariably go to prose. And if the critics will insist on drawing the comparison, they will have to follow Mr. Mencken and seek profit for their souls from the real excitement of prose, while they reduce poetry to the role of a harmless inducer of sleep; and the poets will have to content themselves with an office that is useful but, as measured by their expectations, ignominious.

The intelligent poet of today is very painfully perched in a position which he cannot indefinitely occupy: vulgarly, he is straddling the fence, and cannot with safety land on either side. He can at will perfect a poetry in either of two directions. He can develop sense and style, in the manner of distinguished modern prose, in which event he may be sure that the result will not fall into any objective form. Or he can work it out as a metrical and formal exercise, but he will be disappointed in its content. The New Year's prospect fairly chills his dauntless breast.

MIXED MODES

Plato, a rich and adult mind if there ever was one, decided in his Republic to establish a censorship of music and accordingly he prohibited all but the pure and simple modes. His example is still being followed by the Doctors of the Ars Poetica.

Poetry is a communication between two minds of the same order, and what shall that order be? Not only are separate minds very various, but even the same mind is various. The same man is gentle and horribly wise. One moment he suffers a painful palatal constriction of tenderness, but the next moment he is dissolved in an explosion of brutal irony. For an hour at a time he may be in the possession of the dark half-conscious memories of his lost pre-natal happiness, according to Words-worth, and according to Freud. But then the other modes of his being assert themselves, and there follows an hour in which he has the full command of all his faculties, which interact with each other and pro-duce the richest synthesis of mind. Is he deaf to poetry at that hour?

Speaking roughly, a mind is an integer. But it has the ridiculous ca-pacity of becoming at any time not its whole self, but one of its previous selves, or one of the mere fractions of itself.

Witness the vogue of juvenile poetry in our day. Poetesses of ten summers, and no suspicion of winter, address themselves to readers who at the time of reading subscribe to the same mental age. They are not alone: they are joined by poetesses, and (Forgive us O Lord) poets, whose publishers guarantee that they have become men and women but who have not therefore put away the things of a child. For many poets and for whole multitudes of readers poetry is an exercise in the juvenile modes on mind. H. L. Mencken, with damnable iteration, de-clares that poetry is nothing but paregoric of lullaby, good for making him go to sleep, two teaspoonsful of the drug doing the work if it is sufficiently pure. Maxwell Bodenheim complains bitterly that this is the attitude of the whole modern public, and that poets can't succeed if they don't consider the obvious requirements of their market.[1]

The respectable attainments of much recent poetry exist to contro-vert the view that poets are essentially juveniles. It was a view that could with some reason have been entertained in 1900, following the century of the simplest poetry in English literary history: a century which, being the most recent and also the easiest of comprehension, is generally taken by lazy readers as standing for the English tradition. As for Tennyson and Browning, the former's mind was much simpler than his glittering technique would indicate, and the latter's was simpler than readers are apt to conclude from the state of his grammar. The century outdid itself in the nonsense melodies of Swinburne, and sinis-ter naïveté of the pre-Raphaelites. But going back earlier into that cen-tury, when the stream of the English tradition had not yet been di-verted, it is evident that not Byron nor Keats nor Shelley ever became quite sophisticated, or grown-up, though Byron showed an indefatigable

---

1. Maxwell Bodenheim (1892–1954); poet, novelist, and playwright associated with Bohemian circles in Chicago and New York.

and alarming tendency to devote a complete act of cerebration to each of his poetical themes; and Keats missed writing a second English epic because he was too young when he tried it,—he did not know how to bring his whole mind to bear on his subject as Milton had done, and his Hyperion was an exercise in one mode only and intolerable when executed on an epic scale. Nobody in the whole century knew how to put his whole mind and experience to work in poetry, as had Chaucer, Spenser, Shakespeare, and Milton.

And still the Doctors would have it that youth is the only age for poetry. And the poets generally agree; and if they are not young, they cultivate such an ingenuous and callow simplicity that they appear so, and the full-blooded reader puts them down in disgust and picks up the book of prose, which bears no license-tag permitting it to be silly. But generally and now certainly some poets are not so tractable. These are pre-eminently concerned with the problem of stating their own minds, and not the mind of the hypothetical Wonder-Child; and from a trifling generation they will have to bear the charge of being wilful and obscure. So they are; but may it not be a sin on the nobler side?

For on the face of it, there seems nothing stranger than the notion that wisdom comes out of the mouth of a child. Where did he get it? The apocryphal authorities tell many legends about the miracles that the Holy Child performed to the discomfiture of his elders; but not one of them goes as far as that miracle of sober Scripture, which occurred when Jesus removed himself from the company of his parents, went into the temple, and confounded the elders with his wisdom, both asking and answering questions. Literature never suffered a greater loss than when the chronicler refused to report circumstantially these discussions. What was his understanding of the imagery of the Songs of Solomon? Or of Aristotle's conception of the function of God? But it is the character of miracles that they stagger the comprehension.

Profanely speaking, mind is an entity of slow growth only, and its deliverances are profitable only when it is mature, wise, and sincere. If poetry is worth the candle, poets must report their own mixed modes; but to simplify and prettify the theme is the office of the composers of the Third, Fourth, and Fifth Readers.

THOUGHTS ON THE POETIC DISCONTENT

Not many poets are satisfied with dualism. Mr. Gorham B. Munson, in a remarkable and brilliant analysis, has apparently succeeded in mak-

ing a dualist out of Mr. Robert Frost, but only by a considerable sim-
plification of Mr. Frost's mind, which may or may not be relished by the
owner.[1]

A dualist is a practical man whose mind has no philosophical quality.
It may be that we begin our intellectual lives as dualists, but under the
logic of experience (if our minds entertain the logical categories) we
soon find that the largest problem in our lives is to effect an escape from
dualism. The dualist sees himself as one, and the objective world as
another; this world is not sympathetic, not even sentient, but still fairly
plastic to his will, and capable of being made by hard work to minister
to his happiness: a wilderness which may be transformed into a garden,
a habitat which has the makings of a home. His problem is purely the
physical one: the application of force at the point where it will do the
most good.

Philosophy and metaphysics take their rise most naturally when one
perceives that the object, which is the world, is too formidable to be
controlled altogether by the subject, which is oneself. Defeat humbles
the proud spirit of a mortal. He cannot impose his will upon Nature,
and self-respect will not permit him to deceive himself through the illusion of work, the debauchery of the "practical" life. Insisting upon his
own independence, he is forced to conclude that his personal identity is
a tiny thing fighting a precarious and inevitably a losing fight against
annihilation by superior forces. Then he consents to surrender the idea
of his own dominating personality in exchange for the more tenable
ideas that he is in some manner related by ties of creation to the world,
and entitled to some share in the general patrimony. The second step in
his intellectual career is to discover somehow this community. It is a
mystical community, capable of a great variety of definitions. So he
finds God appointing to Nature and to himself appropriate places in a
system where not a sparrow falls without effect and the hairs of his own
head are numbered. So he is quick to note every sign of understanding
on Nature's part, and his songs are filled with "pathetic fallacies." He is
persistently trying to escape from an isolation which he cannot endure.

These efforts may or may not bring contentment. The romantic constructions of his mysticism are generally obnoxious to the sober observations of his science, and frequently they fall. The romantic poet comes
to the point of puncturing his own illusions, objecting to his own ro-

1. Gorham B. Munson, "Robert Frost," *Saturday Review of Literature,* I (March 28,
1925), 625–26.

mantic treatment of Nature, and cancelling the line which his own creative fancy has projected. He has advanced at this point to a third position which is later and further—though not all would say higher—than the position he has just vacated. Certainly it is not merely a return to his first position, though it is an affirmation of dualism. For too much history has intervened, he is a dualist with a difference—reluctant, speculative, sophisticated rather than ingenuous, and richer by all the pathetic fallacies he has ever entertained. There is a naïve, unqualified, strictly-business sort of dualism, and there is a matured and informed dualism which though critical is also romantic and poetical;—and his is now the latter. It may be that most poetry is composed wholly from the point of view of the second, the purely romantic position. Nearly all the poetry of the Nineteenth Century, for example; Byron returned in great bitterness to dualism, but Wordsworth, Shelley, Tennyson, and Browning continued indefinitely (with few lapses) to find sufficiency in their romantic escapes. But the earlier and greater poets (Chaucer, Spenser, Shakespeare, Donne, Milton) along with or following their own share of lovely romantic adventures, turned back to the stubborn fact of dualism with a mellow wisdom which we may call irony.

Irony may be regarded as the ultimate mode of the great minds—it presupposes the others. It implies first of all an honorable and strenuous period of romantic creation; it implies then a rejection of the romantic forms and formulas; but this rejection is so unwilling, and in its statements there lingers so much of the music and color and romantic mystery which is perhaps the absolute poetry, and this statement is attended by such a disarming rueful comic sense of the poet's own betrayal, that the fruit of it is wisdom and not bitterness, poetry and not prose, health and not suicide. Irony is the rarest of the states of mind, because it is the most inclusive; the whole mind has been active in arriving at it, both creation and criticism, both poetry and science. But this brief description is ridiculously inadequate for what is both exquisite and intricate.

Mr. Frost's poetry is anything but pretentious, it is trim and easy and sometimes apparently trifling, yet it contains plenty of this irony. It is modern in one of the common senses of modern: its spirit transcends the Nineteenth Century mind and goes back to further places in the English tradition for its adult affiliations. It is immensely metaphysical, as Mr. Munson does not seem to admit. When this poet sees the bent birches in the wood, he "likes to think a boy's been swinging them," a hypothesis which would immediately put man and nature into a sodality of merry play. But he is too sceptical to believe that; he is forced to consider that ice storms have bent the birches, and thereupon his romantic impulse, baffled but not yet defeated, takes a new tack and begins to personalize the trees, imagined under their ice-coating. This is not dualism. Whenever he dwells on Nature, he is the same; as when he finds the rotting timbers attempting to warm the forest with the "slow smokeless burning of decay." It would indeed seem that Nature never otherwise puts in an appearance in human art—whether poetry or painting. Always the natural processes are personalized, and art consoles us with its implication of far-flung analogies between our order and the natural order. Mr. Frost is more than ordinarily delicate in making this implication. And sometimes he is at pains to deny the truth of the more obvious implication which he would like to make. We would like to believe that the phoebes were sorrowful when the master's house burned, but he assures us they were not;—

> One had to be versed in country things
> Not to believe the phoebes wept.[2]

This is irony, and rather brutal if salutary. But like all inveterate poets, he commits this irony in a context sprinkled with sly romanticisms.

PROSE: A DOCTRINE OF RELATIVITY

There is both substance and finesse in the philosophy which inspires Robert Graves' new book, *Poetic Unreason*, published in England by Cecil Palmer. It is doubtless the most penetrating book yet written about English poetry. In an earlier book, *On English Poetry*, Graves confines his attention to a statement of the genetics of poetry, basing his theory of the poet's mind upon the new psychology, and almost ignoring the question of the poetic audience, and of poetry as an art of social communication. But here by a sort of corollary to his original doctrine he extends his study to the point of examining into the validity of poetry as an objective and universal record; or in other words, he now discusses what we may call Poetry: An Objective Art.

Graves contends that poetic values are relative and not absolute. This Einsteinian doctrine, elaborated by means of a direct acquaintance with the poetic processes and a formidable learning in English literature, seems to make his book appropriate as the occasion of a brief

2. "The Need of Being Versed in Country Things."

Fugitive editorial—it appears to state the case for a kind of poetry that has been observed to be somewhat this side of universal in its public appeal.

For a poem means many things. There is more to it than its obvious fable, which in itself may not be so innocent as it looks; for there may be a dozen terms in one little poem, as the fable proceeds, which take the mind away into passionate excursions. The terms which poetry uses are not the narrowest possible, in the sense that the terms of science are the narrowest, but the widest possible; it is their function precisely to evoke in our memories the deepest previous experience. They had this meaning with the poet; it is a commonplace that his processes are not rational, and that he does much more than he knows. But it is important to see that they have this meaning also for the reader; though with this qualification, that his evocations are necessarily different from those of the poet, and the evocations of two readers are necessarily different from each other. Poetry is Art rather than Science in respect of the fact that its reference is always free and personal, and never fixed and ideal.

The consequence follows. A poem records, for all its shining look of innocence, an intricate historical experience; but it can only hope to be intelligible to those minds whose history is tangled in just the same way as the poet's. Its communicability varies inversely with its intricacy or completeness. If a poet could bring himself to write with an eye upon the widest possible audience, he would find himself generalizing and simplifying his experience to the point of triteness and stultification. Actually, his composition is spontaneous, and not basely calculated, and he sends out his poem into the world with only some measure of ex post facto alarm as to the fate the poor thing may encounter in its peregrinations.

What then is good poetry? We fall back upon a pragmatic answer: Good poetry is that which fits our own passionate history, and expresses that which needs expression from our private deeps. What is bad poetry? It is the poetry which we do not like because it does not illuminate our private darkness, and which therefore we call unintelligible, or vain and trifling. On this catholic platform honest poets should unite; but to dogmatize our own poetic likings into a standard for others is to subtract fatally from the conception of poetry as a spontaneous and expressive art.

And is there then no universal standard by which to judge poetry? Poetry is saved from being utterly licentious and chaotic by having a form and content based closely (as a general thing) upon the Tradition. It is a familiar art, and we all know what to look for and how to read it when we see a fresh specimen. Its privacy consists perfectly with its conventionality, its formality. But at this point we are getting away from the book that is under discussion; and this brief note is already inadequate as a description of that book.

CLASSICAL AND ROMANTIC

 GOOD MANY authorities have now assured us that science is simply the strict intellectual technique by which we pursue any of our practical objectives. The scientific consideration is always the technical consideration, which fixes narrowly on the road to some special goal. The perfect tribute to science is to say that, where it has elected to apply itself, it is efficient.

But there are one or two observations to be made about that. The first is that the reach of efficient science, is, after all, very limited, and it seems useless to pretend that it is otherwise. It is perhaps in fashion now to assume that our sciences, because they have secured for us so many wonderful things that we may or may not have wanted, are able to furnish us with anything they please, including all the things that we do not want. It is not a fashion which does us much credit. The wants which science is able to gratify for us are rather the minority of our wants; evidently they are only the simplest and most material wants; and elsewhere science cannot really do very much for us.

We must observe also that, however admirable we may consider efficiency when it is the property of a steam engine, or of a course of medical treatment, or of a servant, it does not necessarily impress us as an excellence when it is a property of our own psychic experiences. The experience we have when we appreciate a work of art, or when we worship God, is quite different from the scientific experience, and often it seems preferable for that very reason. Such an experience is far from exercising our minds towards any productive accomplishment, yet we would defend it to the last as an indulgence to which we have a right; and very few of us would consent to abandon our minds wholly to the scientific regimen.

Ardor and rigor, a fever and a coldness, attend the professional scientist on his sublime pursuit of limited and possibly ridiculous objectives. He burns as he contemplates the goal of his desire. But with the coldest

This essay appeared in the *Saturday Review of Literature*, VI (September 14, 1929), 125–27. Reprinted by permission of Helen Ransom Forman.

self-denial he turns from every innocent phenomenon that rises out of the fertility of the world to draw his attention towards the roadside.

The works of art are psychic exercises which are just so many rebellions against science. Together they constitute the formidable reproach which a disillusioned humanity has had to cast at the scientific way of life. At any rate, that is the thesis which frequently occurs to me, as one that is eminently reasonable, and easy to maintain.

Here I wish to refer particularly to two kinds of literary art, the classical and the romantic. They seem to represent the two inevitable forms of the revulsion against science. I am not deterred by the fact that these terms look tolerably unprofitable at first sight, being large and loose, pulled and stretched in too many ways already. Classical and romantic mean a great many things, all of them backed by good authority; there may have been distinguished as many as fifty-seven varieties of either. Under the circumstances there is some temerity implied in the offer of a new pair of definitions; but at the worse it will only increase the fifty-seven by a fifty-eighth, and at the best our new pair may include some meaning now separate, and actually reduce the total number.

Science is the mind devoting itself exclusively to the attainment of a practical purpose. Now there are two events in the history of any practical purpose which equally are critical, and equally dispose us to revise downwards the hopeful valuation which we have placed upon our program. The first is failure; the second is success. Let us consider some one purpose, and trace its career briefly through both events in turn; and let us take the sexual purpose, for the sake of a most distinguished example.

Let us imagine a hero in love; and for the first case, a lady who does not return the compliment. It must not be required that he should love her quite unselfishly, of course, for lovers never do; it is enough that he desires her powerfully, and in the sense which is biologically important, among whatever other senses. He does not desire that she should continue to exist on earth in order that he may regard her beauty, but that she should marry herself, most circumstantially, to him. But she refuses to gratify this desire. For the sake of the example, he is a lover of heroic constancy, and no other lady will do. He therefore tries in every way possible to win her, applying all his wits to the task, and resorting to persuasion, force, and guile; but after a certain number of years of failure he accepts his defeat as definitive.

Now in the degree that he is a hero, with a grand passion in which the other interests of his life are "sublimated," this defeat is crushing. It means to him that the objective world is simply not tractable to his desires. It is a painful lesson. It touches him so deeply that—if we follow the most approved legends—he suffers a complete metamorphosis. Taught by failure, he renounces the practical life so far as possible, and turns into the embittered cynic, or the stoical philosopher, or the grim tragic artist, or the ascetic religionist. He consents under his grievous compulsion to the radical doctrine that the world is not operated on humane principles, is not in sympathy with human needs. He spends his time now in contemplating the vanity of human aspirations, and in confessing to an invincible universe and its inscrutable God.

But in the second case, we are to suppose that the lady accepts him, and he accomplishes his purpose. This case is much the more remarkable for theory. He will now have the opportunity of learning what there is to lose by success. For oddly enough, he does not lose only by the failure of his practical projects; he is cheated also in their success, and he is in fact a creature whose strange constitution will not permit him to find his happiness in either event.

Let us go back a little upon his history. Sex awakened late, when the organs of his general sensibility were well developed and capable of forming the most compound images of objects. Furthermore, sex as a purpose defined itself with an immense leisure, taking, in fact, the whole protracted period known as adolescence. It was therefore specially privileged among his natural purposes. No other one served so gay and irresponsible an apprenticeship as it played among those infinites of qualities which composed the objective world. In the beginning the love-interest had the widest application, seizing on all sorts of objects compounded brilliantly of their colors, forms, odors, sounds, sense-qualities,—dwelling almost aimlessly, like an interest that was not at all pointed, on the pure particulars of experience. But its inevitable destiny was in the direction of an increasing condensation. Presently it had limited itself to that smaller world—which was still an infinite world—that clustered about the beloved one: her history, family, possessions, dress, gestures, words, person. And eventually it arrived at an astonishing degree of exclusion. Love at last defined its specific objective, and its technical or scientific procedure; the lady consented; and desire is consummated.

The fact which probably presents itself now is this, that the lover will remark how disproportionate is the actual consummation to the vast set of interests which it climaxes. The world of love and loveliness, which took the years of his courtship in the building, has unbuilt itself. In the course of its progress it has ascended by a series of diminishing planes like a pyramid and whittled itself down, so to speak, into an effectual point. But this point, in the poverty of its dimensions, is absurd as the ultimate outcome of his program. Love has put away its youthful indeterminism and turned decisively into lust; and the beloved with her manifold of charms has vanished, shrunken into the excessively finite object of an extremely special desire.

It is doubtless for some such consideration as this that the act of love has often seemed shameful to lovers of delicate sensibility. They may take some comfort in the thought that this act is not at all unique in that character, for every other program of action is blind and exclusive and involves itself in a similar anti-climax. Every science, for example, is a technique of heroic indifferences and proceeds to its point by a set of unscrupulous exclusions and the abuse of sensibility; and the knowledge which is scientifically the most effectual is for metaphysics an absurdity, and for religion an impiety.

My illustration is completed at this point, and I cannot undertake the task of redeeming this cheated lover. I do not suppose that his present embarrassment is fatal. His situation is perilous, however. He will have to see if he cannot recover love in its lovely or romantic sense, and stay in love even after marriage has taken place.

Classical art, as I venture to take it, deals with the first of these two situations: the defeat of human purposes. It conducts a sort of experiment in which a purpose is tested to determine whether it is really a practical purpose. It is like the scientific verification of a practical formula. Through previous unfavorable experience we are aware of the hazard attaching to the formulas by which we would realize our desires. Of course we expect that now the formula will be tested impartially and dispassionately to see if it will work. Hence the representation of what is supposed to be the actual course of nature in order to compose a classical work of art.

And it is not to be denied that the formula is sometimes shown in this representation to prosper. The work of art ends happily, and we are permitted to include the formula all the more confidently in our repertory, and to come away greatly uplifted as we contemplate our evident ability to enforce our private purposes upon nature. Such art as this is classical comedy. We content ourselves with the flattering demonstration that we are on the right track, and can go ahead. In a comedy we have a hero acting on moral principles very like our own and turning out quite successful. We also have generally a villain, who acts on principles precisely opposite to our own; it is as important that the wrong principles should fail as that the right ones should triumph. We may also have a few clowns and fools, naturals and originals, who expect to prosper in this world without any principles at all; but these suffer all sorts of buffets and indignities, if not actual adversities, and testify to the need of having some strenuous principles. And so is established, so far as the evidence of a comedy goes, one proposition with two corollaries. Proposition: Our formula is the sufficient cause of prosperity. Corollaries: The opposite formula is not the cause of prosperity but of its opposite; and, The absence of formula is not the cause of prosperity but of its absence. The total effect is sweeping.

But this is the least intelligent and the most dubious of all the forms of art, notwithstanding the favor with which it will always be held by the softer side of the population. It is more characteristic of the classical artist to exhibit the formula as unsuccessful. Classical art becomes tragic art in the hands of the serious artist. He is the artist who submits the formula to such a searching and sustained experimentation that finally he comes to the place where it breaks down. In tragic art the distinction between the hero and the villain tends to disappear, for their formulas issue equally in failure. As for the ridicule which had been intended for the clown, it tends to symbolize the ridicule which lies in wait for all our fumbling human behavior whatsoever, so unable it is to cope with actual events. But the consequence of the tragic outcome is still quite practical: we are convinced that defeat is in store for us and that we had better be prepared to accept it as a regular feature of life. To abridge a famous classical passage:

> Therefore, since the world has still
> Much good, but much less good than ill,
> I'd face it as a wise man should
> And train for ill, and not for good.

Practical science has constructed, let us imagine, a bridge, and classical art tries the bridge. (Mr. Thornton Wilder tried a bridge, and was to that extent a classical artist.) This bridge is observed at length to collapse under its precious human freight. Evidently scientific bridges are not to be relied on. But a code of morals is also a scientific construct, of much more importance than a bridge; so the tragic playwright embodies this code in a hero, who practises for us vicariously the ideals by which we would pursue our happiness. The hero is defeated and, lest there be any question of the finality of this outcome, is killed. Death is the grimmest possible symbol of defeat. It may be superfluity for those who are quick at inference, and Œdipus Tyrannos goes off stage for the time being merely stripped of his kingdom and honor, but Shakespeare takes his tragic heroes more speedily to their mortal end. The lesson of these representations is that a code of morals is not an instrument by which we can guarantee our prosperity in this life.

Technically speaking, the purpose which we would accomplish, through our careful scientific formulation, is defeated always by interferences which could not be predicted, and which may therefore be called contingent. The bridge for some surprising reason did not bear the strain which the best of calculation said it would bear; its hard stone disintegrated, or its steel suffered a crystallization, or an enemy undermined it, or a geological cataclysm loosened its foundations. As for the moral ideal of the hero, it was not good enough after all, whether for inner reasons (the unsuspected tragic "flaw") or because of an outward circumstance that hit him when and where he could not anticipate. Science is a calculation which leads from one step to another by a theoretical necessity, and there are people who cannot see why a perfect efficiency is not its goal; but the bridge it raises or the character it forms is enveloped in a contingency that may at any time choke it up. The practical processes are like a thin stream of history whose materials seem perfectly under control. But the materials after all are not fully understood, and in any case the stream flows through an indifferent universe whose irruption at any point may shatter its continuity.

Probably this is not a highly contemporary doctrine. In these longitudes and in these times the public does not conspicuously ask to receive the lesson of tragedy. We perform wonderful feats in the laboratory and we live in cities made marvelously with hands; we are able to gloze certain facts very obvious to more primitive societies which have never lost contact with earth and the elements or to older societies who have tasted many defeats.

The Genius Loci under the circumstances refuses rather flatly to make the spirit of tragedy into its adoption. On the contrary, it is our public policy to advertise all the positive achievements and to prattle very innocently about man's imminent and even actual control over nature. But there have not yet been eliminated those contingencies that lurk in natural catastrophe, disease, death, envy, and competition.

The friends of science are very busily celebrating its recent triumphs. Physical science has done much to talk about, and biological science and social science are not far behind, at least in the talking. But nature, the total environment which we have to manage, is still the Djinn of the fairy tale, and science is only the golden-haired boy who pursues him.[1] This young prince is armed with a bottle and a stopper; it is his intention to get the Djinn into the bottle and then put in the stopper. Perhaps he will set the bottle on his laboratory shelf and, letting out the Djinn's power through a control valve, perform wonders of safe magic. The sympathy of the public goes out wholeheartedly to the brave prince. But there must be some hard-headed realists to whom his undertaking seems slightly absurd.

The moral of tragedy is not the failure of the specific program, perhaps, so much as it is the failure of programs generally, on the realistic principle that calculation can never allow for the infinite contingency with which the objective world is invested. Sooner or later we shall have to make an adaptation to the world which is submissive and religious, as well as an adaptation which is egotistical and scientific.

The principle that the world is invested with contingency is a principle that we admit ruefully, when we are compelled by a tragic experience. Even so, classical art leads us into metaphysics at last; for it is metaphysical to confess that things are in themselves, when seen fully and objectively, rather more than the simple-featured and manageable entities which our formulas would represent them as being.

On the other hand, romantic art is metaphysical by preference, and from the beginning. Indeed its favorite origin is probably in that hour of disillusionment which follows upon the absolutely successful accomplishment of some purpose. We have pursued this purpose too hard, and now we have eaten greedily of the fruit. But while the organ of appetite is sated and full, we are wretchedly conscious that our minds are empty; we have snatched our morsel from the delicate banquet of nature like a slave rather than a guest, and devoured without taste and without enjoyment. Desperately we seek to repair our ill breeding, and we go again to nature in order that we may prove ourselves more humble, temperate, and attentive. We solicit the pure esthetic experience such as is expressed in romantic art. We are like Lord Byron, who expiated his grievous personal sins in pictures of true romantic love.

In more exact language, I would denote by the term romantic, as a

---

1. Djinn/Jinn/Genie, a supernatural figure who does one's bidding, appears in several of the tales in *Arabian Nights*.

quality in art, just that rare and simple attitude which we call the love of nature. And that means the love of anything for itself. Science is pragmatic, and bent only on using nature. Scientific knowledge is no more than the knowledge of the uses of nature; it does not credit nature with having any life of its own, and it cannot afford to see in nature any content further than what the scientific terms permit. As a way of knowledge it is possible to us only on condition that we anesthetize ourselves and become comparatively insensible. But it is immediately exposed to scorn when we consent again to free our senses and contemplate those infinites of particularity which are the objects in our world; the landscapes, the people, the flora, the merest things. This is the purest esthetic experience.

Hence the images, the representations by imitation, or romantic art. They aim at being representatives which, short of the actual objects themselves, are the fullest possible, and are indeed of infinite fulness. To make them is no matter of practical interest but a labor of love.

Classical art is the criticism of science by science's own standards, witnessing to its failure or success in attaining the purposes at which it aims. But romantic art goes rather deeper, and suspends the whole purpose-and-attainment process.

This general distinction produces some of the famous differences between classical and romantic art. Classical art pursues a thread of history with classical severity, like a scientific experiment with a hypothesis and a demonstration, but romantic art is essentially diffuse. Classical art gives us emotionally either the shallow self-confidence of comedy, or the bitter resignation of tragedy; but the romantic equivalent for the latter is that nostalgic melancholy with which we survey the estrangement wrought by our practice between ourselves and nature, and for the former the pure joy of knowing the world in its fulness, and without desire. Classical art induces religion in a masculine, stoical, and compulsory phase, but romantic art is religious in a feminine, spontaneous, and loving phase. On the whole, classical is perhaps to a large degree the art of antiquity, crystallized in literature in such forms as the heroic epic, the grim ballad, and the tragic drama; romantic art gives us the performance which is characteristically modern, with heroes who are particular rather than typical, lyrics that are scientifically without point, informal essays, and formless novels.

Romantic features often hide, of course, in works that are classical by intention. The modes come generally mixed. I will mention two romantic features that are almost universal in literature.

Any lyrical passage, even from the most classical context, reveals the romantic spirit if we care to construe it as follows:—it escapes the bounds of the argument. It invites excursions of the mind into many directions. It indicates vast territories, not for conquest and use, but for exploration and delight. More technically, the lyric passage forgets the essential logic of the artist's thesis and releases his sensibility to write its diffuse record of the moment while the scientific record must wait, or at least be obscured under the other.

A second such feature, found commonly in classical art, is a simile, or metaphor. A simile looks like a logical feature meant to illustrate the logic of the account. Scientific texts themselves abound in similes. For instance, in stereo-chemistry a molecule might conceivably be described as cruciform in the arrangement of its component atoms; but no reference would be intended to the massive legendary mysteries of the cross. Literary similes, on the other hand, have precisely such excursions in view; for instance, the wine-dark sea of Homer, and the ox-eyed Hera, and the silver-footed Thetis. These epithets have no necessary relevance to Homer's narrative logic where they occur, and so far as we attend to them we plunge into a pure unmotivated image. Some other poet will elect to know the beloved's lips as cherry-red, not to secure definition of their hue, but to provide a second field of observation for us to enter, and to make definition actually impossible. From the same motive her eyes are like stars, and her throat is a swan's. Nothing is more ridiculous than to take these figures literally as scientific or descriptive terms. On principle they are not clarifying but obfuscatory, they bring a nimbus and not a light.

Perhaps no works of art are pure romances. Even a brief, non-philosophical lyric, or a novel without topical unity, offers necessarily a minimum of logical sequence; the pedagogical mind may be trusted to find it there. Most works of art are doubtless compromises whereby we indulge science and sensibility, or pursue thesis and romance, in alternating moments. That element in them is romantic which is diffuse and particularistic and dwelt upon in love, and they are on the whole romantic if that element is the more favored.

It is idle to speculate on whether Shakespeare is more romantic or classical; it is enough to see that he is both. He surrenders the excellence of a cold, classical precision whenever, for instance, his quick imagination leads him to *enter* the puppets that might have been the perfect carriers of his tragic thesis. For then they become alive, and live; that is, they depart from the finitude that classical theory intended for them and become particulars, persons, intractables, and infinites.

The insubordination of the chief character in Hamlet does not improve the work as a classical tragedy, while it furnishes an excellence that a pure classic could not possess. Furthermore, Shakespeare devotes a vast attention to the presentation of a fairly unclassical thing: romantic love. He conceives romantic love at least as grandly as did the neo-Platonists, and is one of the chief of those who have made the literary term romantic almost impossible to dissociate from the popular term by which we denote true love; even comedy is saved at his hands by being bathed in romantic love. But romantic love in this special sense is only one aspect of the romantic love of nature which we find everywhere indulged in his plays. All these romantic features constitute in Shakespeare a deformity upon the body of the classical Aristotelian drama.

We entertain by reason of our constitution very ardent practical desires, and it is well that classical art should try them and speculate upon their practicality. But romantic art is not at all concerned with this issue. In romantic art we revel in the particularity of things, and feel the joy of restoration after an estrangement from nature. The experience is vain and aimless for practical purposes. But it answers to a deep need within us. It exercises that impulse of natural piety which requires of us that our life should be in loving *rapport* with environment.

THE AESTHETIC OF REGIONALISM

URING a summer in New Mexico the philosophical regionalist, as he secretly described himself, made two acquisitions: a scene which he witnessed with his own eyes, and a story which he received on good enough authority.

The scene first. The eastbound train out of Albuquerque, climbing into the mountains, winds through dry and scrubby country which has a certain fascination for green visitors from the green regions and looks incapable of supporting human life. This visitor was going to pull down his window shade and try simply to keep cool, when he was surprised by the sight of human habitation after all, and on a rather large scale: a populous Indian pueblo. A second appeared presently, and then another. One displayed a very good church, but all were worth passing that particular day for this reason: it was threshing time. On the outskirts of each town were the threshing-floors, evidently of home-made concrete and belonging each to a family or unit of the tribal economy. On the floors Indians were beating out the grain; on some the work was nearly done, the grain had been separated from the chaff and lay in a golden pile. The threshers were old and young, of both sexes, and beautifully arrayed. They laughed, and must have felt pleased with their deities, because the harvest was a success, and bread was assured them for the winter.

So this was regionalism; flourishing on the meanest capital, surviving stubbornly, and brilliant. In the face of the efforts of the insidious white missions and the aggressive government schools to "enlighten" these Indian people, their culture persists, though for the most part it goes back to the Stone Age, and they live as they always have lived. It may be supposed that they find their way of living satisfactory, and are so far from minding it that they prefer it above others, receiving from it the two benefits which a culture can afford. First, the economic benefit; for they live where white men could scarcely live, they have sufficient means, and they are without that special insecurity which white men continually talk about, and which has to do with such mysterious

This essay appeared in the *American Review*, II (January, 1934), 290–310. Reprinted by permission of Helen Ransom Forman.

things as the price of wheat; they thresh, bake, and eat their own grain and do not have to suffer if they cannot sell it. And second, a subtler but scarcely less important benefit in that their way of living is pleasant; it "feels" right, it has aesthetic quality. As a matter of fact the Indian life in that one animated scene appeared to the philosophical regionalist one to be envied by the pale-faces who rode with him in painful dignity on the steel train, reflecting upon private histories and futures, but neither remembering nor expecting anything so bright and charming as this.

And now the story. For several consecutive years an Indian tribe suffered from even drier seasons than usual and made insufficient crops. Their distress was such that a voice was raised for them in Congress and a sum of something like $20,000 appropriated for their relief. An agent of the Government came out to make the presentation, and sought the chief. To his surprise the chief did not jump for it; he was rather indifferent, but he agreed to call his counsellors together and deliberate. He reported later to the agent that the tribe would not accept the white man's money *because it would be bad for the young men.*

The interpretation which a philosophical regionalist might place upon this incident is not the one which would probably occur to the mere moralist or Puritan. It was not because the chief was too proud that he refused the white brother's favours, for he was too courteous not to accept them if they were well meant and if there was no harm in them. But the question was whether it was safe to entrust the young men with spending money, when they had never had much of it, if any, and did not live by money. What would they do with it? The chief knew that, while Indians compose in the mass a strong race, there are always weak-headed Indians, and these would want to take the money and buy white men's goods with it to import into the tribal life and corrupt it. The chief knew at least as much about this as did the philosophical regionalist, and the latter knew, having been instructed by his friends when he was going about making some small purchases of Indian things, that Indians are apt to set an inordinate value upon highly-coloured articles sold in the white ten-cent stores, which are less than trash when compared with the beautiful ornaments which Indian weavers, potters, and jewelers make; that Indian bucks fancy white men's shirts, which are unworthy of them; and that they are apt to part with anything in order to secure alarm-clocks. The chief must have looked with apprehension upon importations in general, knowing that a culture will decline and fall when the people grow out of liking for their own native products, and he drew the line at alarm-clocks.

He surrendered an economic advantage which entailed an aesthetic disadvantage; probably possessing firmly the principle that the aesthetic values are as serious as the economic ones, and as governing. Thereupon the philosophical regionalist, seeking to justify the title, regaled himself with certain reflections.

"The Indian of the Southwest is a noble specimen." That is a persistent saying, and every white traveler comes away repeating it—but on what ground? Noble in his hard-headed pride perhaps; and surely every traveler has seen some Indian brave in his gorgeous costume standing on the busy corner of the white city, aloof and disdainful, his arms folded, as if determined to give a public demonstration of his toleration of the whites before they tolerate him. Noble with a more positive merit too, for Indians lead a life which has an ancient pattern, and has been perfected a long time, and is conscious of the weight of tradition behind it; compared with which the pattern of life of the white men in that region, parvenus as they are, seems improvised and lacking in dignity. And noble because the Indians make their life precisely what it is, in every particular, whereas life for the white men depends on what they can buy with their money, and they buy from everybody, including the Indian. The superiority of Indians, by which term the philosophical spectator refers to their obviously fuller enjoyment of life, lies in their regionalism.

Regionalism is as reasonable as non-regionalism, whatever the latter may be called: cosmopolitanism, progressivism, industrialism, free trade, interregionalism, internationalism, eclecticism, liberal education, the federation of the world, or simple rootlessness; so far as the anti-regional philosophy is crystallized in such doctrines. Regionalism is really more reasonable, for it is more natural, and whatever is natural is persistent and must be rationalized.

The reasonableness of regionalism refers first to its economic, and second to its aesthetic.

A regional economy is good in the sense that it has always worked and never broken down. That is more than can be said for the modern, or the interregional and industrial economy. Regionalism is not exactly the prevalent economy today; it has no particular status in Adam Smith's approach to economic theory, which contemplates free trade, and which has proved very congenial to the vast expansions of the nineteenth and twentieth centuries; therefore regionalism suffers a disability. Yet just now, by reason of the crash of our non-regional economy, it tends to have its revival. Of the two economies, the regional is the realistic one. The industry is in sight of the natural resources of the region and of its population. The farmers support themselves and support their cities; and the city merchants and manufacturers have their eyes on a local market and are not ambitious to build up trade with the distant regions; perhaps it occurs to them that an interregional or world trade cannot be controlled. The quantity and quality of world trade which a given community carried on even as late as 1900 are probably changed beyond recognition now, for a great variety of reasons, of which some were predictable and others were not; but at any rate a community can be badly hurt by the storm, if it chooses to fish in the ocean. Regionalism offers an economy as safe as it is modest.

Now it must be great fun to produce on a grand scale, so long as there is consumption for what you produce. The philosophical regionalist is quite disposed to grant that, and to concede the importance of the producer's having fun. But too much fun runs to mischief. It is agreed now that producers' fun must be curtailed, and producers regulated, as if they were irresponsible boys, unable to be trusted with their freedom, and with their grandiose concept of trade as something which will always love them and take care of their production. The interregional business men of the future will not look like joyous producers so much as communistic ants and wasps; and as between the economy of big business and interregionalism, with its privations, and the old regional economy in which producers had every reason to be realistic, and could be left to their own discretion, there is indeed some show of reason for the latter.

The aesthetic of regionalism is less abstract, and harder to argue. Preferably it is a thing to try, and to feel, and that is what it is actually for some Europeans, and for the Indians of our Southwest. They do not have to formulate the philosophy of regionalism. But unfortunately regionalism for white America is so little an experience that it is often obliged to be a theory.

Coming to the theory, the first thing to observe is that nature itself is intensely localized, or regional; and it is not difficult to imagine that the life people lead in one of the highly differentiated areas of the earth's surface is going to have its differences also. Some persons, with a sociological bias, suppose that the local peculiarities of life and custom, for example in the Southern highlands, are due to the fact that the population is old and deeply inbred, and has developed a kind of set because it has been out of communication with the world. Other persons, who are economists, think at once of the natural resources of the region, and the sort of subsistence it affords to its population, and find there the key to the cultural pattern. Both must be right; regionalism is a compound effect with two causes. But the primary cause is the physical nature of the region. A region which is physically distinct supports an economic unit of society; but its population will have much more of "domestic" trade than of foreign, and it will develop special ways and be confirmed in them.

As the community slowly adapts its life to the geography of the region, a thing happens which is almost miraculous; being no necessity of the economic system, but a work of grace perhaps, a tribute to the goodness of the human heart, and an event of momentous consequence to what we call the genius of human "culture." As the economic patterns become perfected and easy, they cease to be merely economic and become gradually aesthetic. They were meant for efficiency, but they survive for enjoyment, and men who were only prosperous become also happy.

The first settlers in a region are occupied with its conquest, and driven by a pure economic motive. Human nature at this stage is chiefly biological, and raw; physical nature, being harried and torn up by violence, looks raw too. But physical nature is perfectly willing to yield to man's solicitations if they are intelligent. Eventually the economic pattern becomes realistic, or nicely adapted to the bounty which nature is prepared in this region to bestow. It is as if man and nature had declared a truce and written a peace; and now nature not only yields up her routine concessions, but luxuriates and displays her charm; and men, secured in their economic tenure, delight in this charm and begin to represent it lovingly in their arts. More accurately, their economic actions become also their arts. It is the birth of natural piety: a transformation which may be ascribed to man's intuitive philosophy; by religious persons, such as Mary Austin, to the operation of transcendental spirit in nature, which is God.[1] It is certainly the best gift that is bestowed upon the human species. The arts make their appearance in some ascending order, perhaps indicated like this: labour, craft, and business insist upon being transacted under patterns which permit the enjoyment of natural background; houses, tools, manufactured things do not seem good enough if they are only effective but must also be ornamental, which in a subtle sense means natural; and the fine arts arise, superficially pure or non-useful, yet faithful to the

1. Mary Hunter Austin (1868–1934), novelist and essayist who championed the culture of Southwest Indians.

regional nature and to the economic and moral patterns to which the community is committed. It is in this stage that we delight to find a tribe of Navajos, or some provincial population hidden away in Europe.

For now the expert travelers come through, saying, Here is a region with a regionalism, and this is a characteristic bona fide manifestation of human genius. The region is now "made" in the vulgar sense (useless to a philosophical regionalist) that the curious and eclectic populations of far-away capitals will mark it on their maps, collect its exhibits for their museums, and discuss it in their literary essays. But for the regionalists who live in the region it is made already, because they have taken it into themselves by assimilation.

The regionalists receive the benefit of regionalism, not the distant eclectics; it is they who have the piety, and for whom the objects and activities have their real or pious meaning. This piety is directed first towards the physical region, the nature who had always given them sustenance and now gives them the manifold of her sensibilia. It is also directed towards the historic community which has dwelt in this region all these generations and developed these patterns. It is their region and their community, and their double attachment might well seem too powerful, and too natural, and also too harmless, to excite the wrath of any reputed philosophers; or it may be the envy, if the philosophers are so abstract and intellectual that they have never sufficiently felt such attachments; yet, whatever the motive be, some philosophers do actually represent themselves as aggrieved by it.

Cookery is one of the activities which go by regions. A cookery owes its form partly to the climate and to the natural foods of the region, and partly to the cumulative experimentation of the generations of native cooks; perhaps in equal measure. So with architecture, furniture, the decorative motif of interiors; so with clothing; so with the social pastimes and pageants; so with speech and idiom; and so with literature and other fine arts. Sometimes the tradition seems more the consequence of the region than of the community, or vice versa; but both have played their part; the region first, naturally, because it isolated the community. Critics of the arts, and of *objets d'art*, if they wish to be up to date, must now require themselves both to trace in them an adaptation to a special variety of physical nature, and also to find the patient historical development of local "schools" which produced them.

In contrast to the regional view that critics have learned to take of the arts, the broad or eclectic view now seems too fatuous. Eclectic minds are doubtless good for something, but they are very dangerous for the health of the arts. If their interest is in the arts they would be well advised not to carry their missionary zeal into the regions, for presently they will extinguish regionalism and have nothing to average up; then they will be without careers. And capital cities, which are the fortresses of eclecticism, should hardly be built and pushed on the assumption that they are to overrun and standardize all their regions. The city is a dangerous necessity in regional society. It is useful, and it is even creative in the way of aesthetic forms; for example, the architecture of capitols and landscaping of parks, the drama, and the other fine arts; in all of which it had better condescend to try to catch the genius of the hinterland. If it invites the patterns from too many regions, in an excess of hospitality, and tries to compose its arts out of perfectly average materials, its aesthetic life will become a mere formality and perish of cold, and then it will be left with a function which is strictly economic and gross. A capital of the world would be an intolerable city. And lesser cities, with more ambition than piety, which build grandly but upon indifferent and eclectic foundations, are nearly as bad. Cities lately are being zoned and planned; but in the planning, if it is not too late, they should aim at the centre of the aesthetic effect, which is regionalism; at the most, nationalism.

But it takes a long time for regionalism to arrive. It is the work of many generations, of which the earliest ones must live and die in war with the region, exploiting it, trying to impose their own economic wishes upon it, not yet knowing the sort of peace that would be lasting. What chance have frontiersmen, backwoodsmen, "colonials," of attaining to the completeness of life? What they may look forward to principally, if they are lucky, is livelihood. They bring ways and means which suit their old region but not the new region. Or they take pains to bring nothing, and to be open-minded, in order to learn as rapidly as possible; which is not very rapidly. Wherever the settlement of the New World has been undertaken by Europeans, it might have been promised at once that the new region would hardly become the seat of a culture comparable to that of the parent European region within any period which was not commensurate with some centuries of European history.

This latter proposition seems to the philosophical regionalist binding; on second thought perhaps too binding. It is true that the immemorial Europeans, those with acute perceptions and even those with the best will in the world, have looked repeatedly with honest deprecation upon their brethren the new settlers in America, Australia, or Argentina, knowing without having to reason about it that a Europe could

not be improvised in these remarkable regions even if it could be realized in time. By their look and their tone, if nothing else, they have ex-
hibited "a certain condescension in foreigners" and caused us much
concern; we could not help resenting it, nor could they help feeling it.
However rich they might believe American life to be materially, they
could not yet believe it to be rich spiritually. Very largely they must have
been right, and must still be right. Nor is it a great consolation to retort
that what we lack in aesthetic attitude we make up in economic power,
whereas the Europeans in more regions than one seem likely, for one
reason or another, to be caught clinging to their attitudes when the economic structure tumbles down and pulls them with it, attitudes and all.
If it is not becoming in Europeans to dislike us for our power, it is not
becoming in us to wish economic evil upon them in order that their
aesthetic superiority may be blotted out of our consciousness. Nevertheless, however that may be, it is just possible that we may have made
or may be making a better and quicker job of regionalism than the Europeans allow for; than a dogmatic philosophical regionalist allows for.
There may be a short cut.

What we have in this country, of course, is not so much a regionalism *de novo* as a transplanted regionalism, if that is possible. The Fathers of the Republic were not savages; or rather, since savages are
likely to have a quite flourishing regionalism, they were not strictly
business men. They were European regionalists, and they set about to
apply to their new regions as much of their European regionalism as
was applicable. New England they meant to be a Puritan England, Virginia an Elizabethan and royalist England. If they could not quite
transfer their economic techniques, in such matters as building, tilling
the soil, travel, and politics, they were more successful in transferring a
language and some of the technique of the fine arts; which is as if to
say that they had to erect a new house but were able to crown it for the
time being with an imported capital. The matter of classical education,
for instance, is a foreign matter for modern Europe as well as for ourselves; yet to some extent it has proved negotiable. We can use Greek, if
we know it, in forming our poetry and politics, and we certainly have
used it in forming our public buildings and our statues. We can also use
English, French, Italian, and German models; but not so easily since
the rise in us of that proper state of mind attested by our declarations of
independence, because we must regard these cultures as competing
and correlative ones, not as our archetypes. Now it must be remembered that what is Greek to us was native and nameless to the Greeks

themselves, and not the same thing at all; and it enters into our regionalism only as some undigested Egyptian influence may have entered
early into theirs. It should be a comfort to us, however, that we scarcely
know for certain of any regional culture anywhere that can be called, in
strictness, "indigenous." A regional culture ordinarily represents an importation, or series of importations, that has been lived with and adapted
for so long that finally it fits, and looks "native." It may be ages before
we can assimilate all the foreign modes that now conglomerate in what
we call our American culture, and only then will they be really ours. In
the meantime they will serve. Some of the regionalism which we have
not had time to acquire we can borrow.

By the year 1850 our continental acquisitions were completed, and
the settlement of North America, by a stock whose language and inher-
itance were largely British, was proceeding irregularly westward, region by region, and perhaps working faster with each advance. The mo-
mentum behind the advance was great, and the formula of settlement,
or at least the formula of open-mindedness, was familiar; these being
the conditions, if any, under which such work may be speeded up. The
destiny of this enormous area must have seemed to the philosophical
regionalists of the period to be roughly definable: to be comfortably occupied by a population which was now distinct, and was distinguished
as "American"; but to fall culturally, as it fell physically, into a great
number of regions, to which the general pattern of Americanism was to
make its adaptations; that is, to develop culturally according to the implications of the political scheme, which was that of sovereign States
within a federal Union. Naturally the States east, which were older as
compared with the States west, and particularly with those empty areas
west whose States were not yet born, were more highly developed; their
economies more stable, and their mode of life more aesthetic. New England had achieved a rather strong regionalism. The South had done
about as well, or if anything better. The peculiar institution of slavery
set this general area apart from the rest of the world, gave a spiritual
continuity to its many regions, and strengthened them under the reinforcement of "sectionalism," which is regionalism on a somewhat extended scale. But what New England and the South had done the other
sections would do; and they might do it more quickly, though no philosophical sectionalist could be sure about that. The future was promising, though the futurist must look a long way ahead. The federal set-up
for the development was admirable.

At about this time, however, the American varieties of regionalism, developing healthily, and at their uneven stages of development, came under a powerful destructive influence, and the philosophical historian of their subsequent course must bear witness that they have nearly been destroyed by it. This influence was not the dissension which resulted in the Civil War; that was destructive, but may now be regarded as one of the incidents in its march. It was nothing less than a whole new economy; it was industrialism, or the machine economy. It was European, and mainly English, in origin, and it was to have a baleful effect upon the charming regionalisms of Europe. But it was to be seized upon with almost mortal infatuation by the Americans; as if they were thinking that if they could not soon equal the Europeans at regionalism, they could distance them quickly at industrialism, and therefore they had better make a switch in their objectives. Only the South consistently opposed it, and may even now be said temperamentally to dislike it; yet the South was eventually to finger it too.

The machine economy, carried to the limit with the object of "maximum efficiency," is the enemy of regionalism. It always has been; not only at the present stage of affairs has the issue between them become really acute, and been raised specifically and publicly in many places; for example, in Southern communities, now agitated as to their proper alignment between the Southern "tradition" and the "new" industrialism. The industrialism is not new, but the awakening of the Southern communities to its menace is new.

The machine economy was bad enough in coming to America, where the regionalisms were at many different periods of growth, but it came to the perfected cultures of Europe with the disruptive force of a barbarian conquest, turning the clock back, cancelling the gains of many mellowing centuries. (Such strong terms will apply of course to those regions which sooner or later allowed the machine economy to take charge of things.) It is no wonder that a good many pious European thinkers have been appalled by a sort of havoc which was much less visible on this side, and which the pious American thinkers, if any, have therefore been at much less pains to think about.

The new economy restored to the act of labour the tension from which it had delivered itself so hardly and so slowly. It returned the labouring population, and in some degree the whole business population, to a strictly economic status; a status with which the Europeans were fairly unfamiliar, and which their history recorded only putatively as the possible status of serfs, or the possible status of the original savages fighting for subsistence; and a status in all respects more ignominious than that of pioneers and frontiersmen in America. For under this economy the labourer is simply preoccupied with tending his abstract machine, and there is no opportunity for aesthetic attitudes. And not much material for them, either, since it is now more and more the machine which makes the contact with nature and not the man. But most of the machines are concerned with processing the materials taken out of the land, and they are housed in factories, while the factories are housed in cities. Therefore the landed population tends to lose its virtue, and the population as a whole becomes more and more urbanized. Now a city of any sort removes men from direct contact with nature, and cannot quite constitute the staple or normal form of life for the citizens, so that city life is always something less than regional. But the cities of a machine age are peculiarly debased. They spring up almost overnight, a Detroit, an Akron, a Los Angeles. They are without a history, and they are without a region, since the population is imported from any sources whatever; and therefore they are without a character.

So painful a reversion must bear the promise of wonderful compensations, and it does. They define themselves in the new volume and multiplicity of the goods for consumption. But since the necessities of consumption were secured already in sufficient volume and multiplicity (sufficient in Europe, abundant in America) the additional volume and multiplicity must have reference to the luxuries; that is, to the hours of leisure and the pure aesthetic enjoyments. Here it must be said that, on the whole, the expectations of the moderns have been cheated. The products of machines may be used, but scarcely enjoyed, since they do not have much aesthetic character. Aesthetic character does not reside in an object's abstract design but in the sense of its natural and contingent materials, and the aesthetic attitude is piety.

The symbol of the aesthetic torpor and helplessness of the moderns lies in their money. There was never so much money in the world, never a time when goods and labours were so universally for sale; and never so little affection lavished on the products of region, which is natural enough when they do not have their real or private value for us but only the value which is determined by the universal market. It is the intention of the machine economy to furnish everybody with money, and then with a free market in which all the goods of the world will be purchasable. The consequence is that persons with much money, who set the standards of taste, go out and buy in with it the houses, furnitures, vases, educations, lectures and doctrines, foods and drinks, clothes and millineries, of all regions impartially; and people with less money do the same in their degree. To say that is simply to say that the age thinks it has discovered an aesthetic principle which is not regionalism.

The philosophical regionalist in conclusion is inclined to exhibit his good faith by professing his concrete or particular regionalism: an Upper South variety, less rich in many respects than the regionalism of Louisiana, which by virtue of its physical nature and its history is most distinct among the Deep South varieties. Traversing by car the east-and-west dimension of Tennessee, and the north-and-south or Delta dimension of Mississippi, he makes his way to Baton Rouge, startled equally by the distinctness and by the unassimilatedness of the regions entered and crossed, finally marvelling at the power of that interregional but sympathetic symbol, the South. There is too much economic settlement yet to be done in this section to permit him to point with too much pride, and in fact it would appear that during some large part of the period from 1865 to the present day the settlers have taken a holiday. In the Mississippi Delta he is forced to believe that the progress has been backward, as it has been in those unsouthern regions which have felt the extreme impact of the machine economy: what could be more like the homelessness of men in those regions than the life of this black population on this black land, resembling the life of a camp, forcing from nature an annual tribute of cotton and otherwise scarcely obtaining a single token of her usual favours? But in Louisiana it seems different.

The darkey is one of the bonds that make a South out of all the Southern regions. Another is the climate. The South is a place in which it is generally pleasant to be in the open air, and nature blooms and waxes prodigiously; one of the earth's areas most easily habitable by man, and perhaps, for the morale of the inhabitants, too easily. The large Negro population, the all-the-year farming—was it not inevitable that the South should develop a distinctly agrarian culture, whose farmers would dominate their cities, which could not be expected to be large? If the Southern cities are growing rapidly now it does not in the least reflect the intelligent consent of their hinterlands, which are the real South, but the coming of industrialism, which destroys the native tradition, and calls the traditionalists "reactionary." The South has had a noble tradition, as traditions go in these longitudes. But at the moment it is just coming out of being intimidated by the get-rich-quick element that has concentrated in its cities, and is only beginning to think about reviewing seriously its old tradition with the thought of a proper future.

The regionalism of Louisiana is most important for the South, in its still divided mind. The region is more charming than others naturally, with its live-oaks hung with moss, its sub-tropical flora, its waters, its soft air; and culturally, in the respect of the finish of its old French features, and its domestic architecture, which is not surpassed in the world.

But regionalism has to fight for its life in Baton Rouge, all the same, just as elsewhere. This fact is written where the least philosophical of regionalists may read it: in the stones. First of all, in the new buildings of the State University.[2] The old buildings still stand, or at least the "Barracks" do, in the heart of the city; the others had to go, since the city needed their room, and the University, with four thousand students, needed still more room and larger buildings. The old buildings are simple, genuine, and moving; precisely the sort of thing that would make a European town famous among the tourists. When the much larger plant of the new University was constructed it seems probable that buildings on the order of the Barracks but on the new scale would not have been economical, nor successful; therefore the builders conceived a harmonious plan for the campus in a modified Spanish, and it suits the regional landscape, and is not altogether foreign to the regional history.

But the visiting regionalist in Baton Rouge cannot escape its most famous feature: the State Capitol. It is nearly 500 feet high, bold in design, sumptuous in detail and finish, perfect in appointments, costing doubtless more money than a State Capitol ever did before—and extremely disconcerting to the sense of regional proprieties. It denotes power and opulence, and this is fitting for the architectural symbol of the State of Louisiana. But the manner of the expenditure of the millions of dollars that went into it was peculiarly unimaginative, like the manner in which money is inevitably spent by new men who have made their pile. The State of Louisiana took its bag and went shopping in the biggest market; it came back with New York artists, French and Italian marbles, African mahogany, Vesuvian lava for the paving. The local region appears inconspicuously in some bas-reliefs and statues, and in the alligators, pelicans, magnolias, sugar canes, and cat-tails worked in bronze in the gates and the door-panels. They are so ineffectual against the shameless eclecticism of the whole that the Louisiana

2. This paper, in substance, was presented as a speech to The Graduate Club of Louisiana State University at Baton Rouge. (Ransom's note)

State Capitol could almost as easily stand in Topeka or Harrisburg or Sacramento as in Baton Rouge.

The State Capitol is a magnificent indiscretion. But the philosophical regionalist does not therefore despair. For many reasons; and because it occurs to him that the ironic perpetuation of the old Barracks, which stand in strange juxtaposition at the base of the Capitol, may bring to many half-hearted regionalists the understanding that what is called progress is often destruction.

FORMS AND CITIZENS

FIRST-RATE poet performs in *Lycidas*, it is plain. And this is plain too: he performs because the decencies of an occasion require it of him, but the occasion catches him at a moment when his faith in the tradition of his art is not too strong, and in the performance rebellion is mixed up with loyalty. The study of the poem leads into a very broad field of discussion, and the topic is the general relation of the poet to his formal tradition.

By formal we are not to mean the metre only; but also, and it is probably even more important, the literary type, with its fictitious point of view from which the poet approaches his object, and its prescription of style and tone. And by tradition we should mean simply the source from which the form most easily comes. Tradition is the handing down of a thing by society, and the thing handed down is just a formula, a form.

Society hands down many forms which the individual is well advised to appropriate, but we are concerned here with those which may be called the aesthetic ones. They contrast themselves with the other and more common forms in the remarkable fact that they do not serve the principle of utility. This point has not been sufficiently remarked, so far as my reading indicates. There are economic forms; there are also aesthetic forms, which are not the same thing. Or, there are work-forms and there are play-forms.

First, the economic forms. We inherit the traditional forms of such objects as plough, table, book, biscuit, machine, and of such processes as shepherding the flock, building, baking, making war. These forms are of intense practicality, and it is a good thing that they exist for the instruction of the successive generations, whose makeshifts, if they had to tutor themselves, would be blundering and ineffectual. Such forms write their own valuations, and very clearly. They are the recipes of maximum efficiency, short routes to "success," to welfare, to the at-

This essay first appeared as "A Poem Nearly Anonymous: The Poet and His Formal Tradition," in *American Review*, I (September, 1933), 444–67; later reprinted as "Forms and Citizens" in *The World's Body*, copyright © 1938 by Charles Scribner's Sons; copyright renewed 1966 by John Crowe Ransom. Reprinted with the permission of Charles Scribner's Sons.

tainments of natural satisfactions and comforts. They are the stock services which society confers upon its members, and the celebrated ones; doubtless in themselves alone a sufficient justification for constituted societies; sometimes, and especially where it is the modern temper which passes on it, the one usefulness which we can imagine attaching to societies, and the whole purpose of the social contract. But that is almost demonstrably an error, proceeding from a blind spot on the organ of insight which we are scarcely in a position to detect. Men absorbed in business and affairs may be excused for making that error, but it would be an egregious one for those who spend of their time and love upon aesthetic effects. It is in the aesthetic effects, if secured in those experiences that record themselves publicly as "art," or for that matter as manners and religion, that the given forms are both more and less than they seem, and not, on the whole, of any conceivable economic advantage.

Chiefly the error is an eidolon of period, a matter of the age and generation. Societies of the old order seemed better aware of the extent of their responsibilities. Along with the work-forms went the play-forms, which were elaborate in detail, and great in number, fastening upon so many of the common and otherwise practical occasions of life and making them occasions of joy and reflection, even festivals and celebrations; yet at the same time by no means a help but if anything a hindrance to direct action. The aesthetic forms are a technique of restraint, not of efficiency. They do not butter our bread, and they delay the eating of it. They stand between the individual and his natural object and impose a check upon his action; the reason must have been known well to the governors of old societies, for they honored the forms with unanimity; it must even yet be recoverable, for the argument shapes itself readily. To the concept of direct action the old society—the directed and hierarchical one—opposed the concept of aesthetic experience, as a true opposite, and checked the one in order to induce the other. Perhaps, since a social psychology is subtle, they fancied that the indissolubility of societies might depend as much on the definition they gave to play as on the definition they gave to labor. If so, our modern societies, with their horror of "empty" forms and ceremonies, and their invitation to men to be themselves, and to handle their objects as quickly and rudely as they please, are not only destroying old arts and customs, which they might not mind doing, but exposing incidentally their own solidarity to the anarchy of too much greed. But that is an incident. The formal tradition in art has a validity more than political, and the latter I am content to waive. What I have in mind is an argument from aesthetics which will justify any formal art, even a formal literature.

II

When a consensus of taste lays down the ordinance that the artist shall express himself formally, the purpose is evidently to deter him from expressing himself immediately. Or, the formal tradition intends to preserve the artist from the direct approach to his object. Behind the tradition is probably the sense that the direct approach is perilous to the artist, and may be fatal. It is feared that the artist who disregards the instruction may discover at length that he has only been artless; or, what is worse, that he will not make this important discovery, which will have to be made for him by the horrid way of autopsy. I suggest, therefore, that an art is usually, and probably of necessity, a kind of obliquity; that its fixed form proposes to guarantee the round-about of the artistic process, and the "æsthetic distance."

A code of manners also is capable of being taken in this fashion; it confers the same benefit, or the same handicap if we prefer, upon its adherent. Let us represent graphically, as in the figure I have entered below, the conduct of a man toward the woman he desires.

CODE

MAN   WOMAN

The event consists in his approach to the object. He may approach directly, and then his behavior is to seize her as quickly as possible. No inhibitions are supposed to have kept the cave-man or pirate, or any other of the admired figures of a great age when life was "in the raw," from taking this severely logical course. If our hero, however, does not propose for himself the character of the savage, or of animal, but the quaint one of "gentleman," then he has the fixed code of his *gens* to remember, and then he is estopped from seizing her, he must approach her with ceremony, and pay her a fastidious courtship. We conclude not that the desire is abandoned, but that it will take a circuitous road and become a romance. The form actually denies him the privilege of going the straight line between two points, even though this line has an axiomatic logic in its favor and is the shortest possible line. But the woman, contemplated in this manner under restraint, becomes a person and an æsthetic object; therefore a richer object.

In fact the woman becomes nothing less than an individual object; for we stumble here upon a fruitful paradox. The natural man, who today sometimes seems to be becoming always a greater man in our midst, asserting his rights so insistently, causing us to hear so much about "individualism," is a predatory creature to whom every object is an object of prey and the real or individual object cannot occur; while the social man, who submits to the restraint of convention, comes to respect the object and to see it unfold at last its individuality; which, if we must define it, is its capacity to furnish us with an infinite variety of innocent experience; that is, it is a source, from which so many charming experiences have already flowed, and a promise, a possibility of future experiences beyond all prediction. There must then, really, be two kinds of individualism: one is greedy and bogus, amounting only to egoism; the other is contemplative, genuine, and philosophical. The function of a code of manners is to make us capable of something better than the stupidity of an appetitive or economic life. High comedy, for example, is technically art, but substantially it is manners and it has the agreeable function of displaying our familiar life relieved of its fundamental animality, filled, and dignified, through a technique which has in it nothing more esoteric than ceremonious intercourse.

To return to the figure, and to change the denotation slightly. Let us have a parallel now from the field of religion. The man is bereaved, and this time the object of his attention is the dead body of his friend. Instead of having a code of manners for this case, let him owe allegiance to a religious society, one which is possessed preferably of an ancient standing, and at all events of a ritual. The new terms for our graph become: Man and Corpse at the base, and Rite at the top and back. The religious society exists in order to serve the man in this crisis. Freed from his desolation by its virtue, he is not obliged now to run and throw himself upon the body in an ecstasy of grief, nor to go apart and brood upon the riddle of mortality, which may be the way of madness. His action is through the form of a pageant of grief, which is lovingly staged and attended by the religious community. His own grief expands, is lightened, no longer has to be explosive or obsessive. A sort of by-product of this formal occasion, we need not deny, is his grateful sense that his community supports him in a dreadful hour. But what interests us rather is the fact that his preoccupation with the deadness of the body is broken by his participation in the pageantry, and his bleak situation elaborated with such rich detail that it becomes massive, substantial, and sufficient.

We may of course eliminate the pageantry of death from our public life, but only if we expect the widow and orphan not really to feel their loss; and to this end we may inform them that they will not find it an economic loss, since they shall be maintained in their usual standards of living by the State. It is unfortunate for the economic calculus that they are likely to feel it anyway, since probably their relation to the one dead was not more economic than it was sentimental. Sentiments, those irrational psychic formations, do not consist very well with the indifference, machine-like, with which some modern social workers would have men fitting into the perfect economic organization. It is not as good animals that we are complicated with sentimental weakness. The fierce drives of the animals, whether human or otherwise, are only towards a *kind* of thing, the indifferent instance of a universal, and not some private and irreplaceable thing. All the nouns at this stage are common nouns. But we, for our curse or our pride, have sentiments; they are directed towards persons and things; and a sentiment is the totality of love and knowledge which we have of an object that is private and unique. This object might have been a simple economic object, yet we have elected to graft upon the economic relation a vast increment of diffuse and irrelevant sensibilia, and to keep it there forever, obstructing science and action. Sometimes we attach the major weight of our being, unreasonably, and to the point of absurdity, to a precious object. The adventitious interest, the sensibility that complicates and sometimes submerges the economic interest, does not seem to ask any odds of it, nor to think it necessary to theorize on behalf of its own existence. We may resent it, but eventually we have to accept it, as, simply, an "aesthetic" requirement, a piece of foolishness, which human nature will not forego. Wise societies legalize it and make much of it; for its sake they define the forms of manners, religions, arts; conferring a public right upon the sensibilia, especially when they organize themselves, or pile up notably, as they do, into the great fixed sentiments.

In Russia[1] we gather that there is a society bent seriously on "per-

---

1. I am not sure at this time of second publication just how true of Russia this representation may be. (Ransom's note in 1968, at the time *The World's Body* was reprinted.)

fecting" the human constitution, that is, rationalizing or economizing it completely. The code of manners and the religious ritual are suspended, while the arts lead a half-privileged, censored, and furtive existence. Already a recent observer notes one result of the disappearance of the sex taboos: there is less sex-consciousness in Russia than anywhere in the Western world. That is to say, I suppose, that the loyal Russians approach the perfect state of animals, with sex reduced to its pure biological business. The above observer wonders painfully whether "love," of the sort that has been celebrated by so much history and so much literature, will vanish from Russia. It will vanish, if this society succeeds in assessing it by the standard of economic efficiency. The Russian leaders are repeating, at this late stage of history, with a people whose spirit is scored by all the traditional complications of human nature, the experiment of the Garden of Eden; when the original experiment should be conclusive, and was recorded, we may imagine, with that purpose in view. The original human family was instructed not to take the life of the beast-couples as its model; and did not, exactly, mean to do so; occupied itself with a certain pretty project having to do with a Tree of Rationalization; and made the mortal discovery that it came to the very same thing. The question is whether the ideal of efficient animality is good enough for human beings; and whether the economic law, by taking precedence at every point over the imperative of manners, of religion, and of the arts, will not lead to perfect misery.

III

And now, specifically, as to art, and its form. The analogy of the above occasions to the occasion called art is strict. Our terms now are Artist, Object, and Form. Confronting his object, the artist is tempted to react at once by registering just that aspect of the object in which he is practically "interested." For he is originally, and at any moment may revert to, a natural man, having a predatory and acquisitive interest in the object, or at best looking at it with a "scientific" curiosity to see if he cannot discover one somewhere in it. Art has a canon to restrain this natural man. It puts the object out of his reach; or more accurately, removes him to where he cannot hurt the object, nor disrespect it by taking his practical attitude towards it, exchanging his actual station, where he is too determined by proximity to the object, and contemporaneity with it, for the more ideal station furnished by the literary form. For example: there is the position, seemingly the silly and ineffectual one, of the man who is required by some quixotic rule of art to think of his object in pentameter couplets, therefore with a good deal of lost motion; and there is the far-fetched "point of view," which will require him to adapt all his thought to the rule of drama. The motion is well lost, if that is what it costs to frustrate the natural man and induce the aesthetic one. Society may not after all be too mistaken in asking the artist to deal with his object somewhat artificially. There will be plenty of others glad to deal with it immediately. It is perfectly true that art, *a priori*, looks dubious; a project in which the artist has a splendid chance for being a fool. The bad artists in the world are cruelly judged, they are the good journeymen gone wrong; and the good artists may be humorously regarded, as persons strangely possessed. But the intention of art is one that is peculiarly hard to pursue steadily, because it goes against the grain of our dominant and carefully instructed instincts; it wants us to enjoy life, to taste and reflect as we drink; when we are always tending as abstract appetites to gulp it down; or as abstract intelligences to proceed, by a milder analogue, to the cold fury of "disinterested" science. A technique of art must, then, be unprepossessing, and look vain and affected, and in fact look just like the technique of fine manners, or of ritual. Heroic intentions call for heroic measures.

We should not be taken in for a moment when we hear critics talking as if the form were in no sense a discipline but a direct help to the "expressiveness"—meaning the forthrightness—of the poem. This view reflects upon the holder's credit for a reach of piety which is prepared to claim everything for the true works of art, and also a suspicion of ingenuousness for their peculiar understanding of the art-process. Given an object, and a poet burning to utter himself upon it, he must take into account a third item, the form into which he must cast his utterance. (If we like, we may call it the *body* which he must give to his passion.) It delays and hinders him. In the process of "composition" the burning passion is submitted to cool and scarcely relevant considerations. When it appears finally it may be said to have been treated with an application of sensibility. The thing expressed there is not the hundred-percent passion at all.

If the passion burns too hot in the poet to endure the damping of the form, he might be advised that poetry can exercise no undue compulsion upon his spirit since, after all, there is prose. Milton may not always have let the form have its full effect upon the passion; some modern poets whom I admire do not; neither of which facts, however, disposes one to conclude that poetry is worse for the formal tradition.

The formal tradition, as I have said, lays upon the poet evidently a double requirement. One is metrical or mechanical; but the measured
speech is part of the logical identity of the poem; it goes into that "character" which it possesses as an ideal creation, out of the order of the
actual. The other requirement is the basic one of the make-believe, the
drama, the specific anonymity or pseudonymity, which defines the poem
as poem; when that goes we may also say that the poem goes; so that
there would seem to be taking place in the act of poetry a rather unprofitable labor if this anonymity is not clearly conceived when a poet is
starting upon his poem, and a labor lost if the poet, who has once conceived it and established it, forgets to maintain it.

IV

We accept or refuse the arts, with their complex intention, according as
we like or dislike the fruits, or it may be the flowers, they bring to us;
but these arts, and their techniques, may be always reinforced by the
example of manners, and the example of religion; the three institutions
do not rest on three foundations but on one foundation. A natural affil-
iation binds together the gentleman, the religious man, and the artist—
punctilious characters, all of them, in their formalism. We have seen
one distinguished figure in our times pronouncing on behalf of all three
in one breath. In politics, royalism; in religion, Anglo-Catholic; in literature, classical.[2] I am astonished upon discovering how comprehen-
sively this formula covers the kingdom of the aesthetic life as it is organized by the social tradition. I am so grateful that it is with hesitation I
pick a little quarrel with the terms. I would covet a program going
something like this: In manners, aristocratic; in religion, ritualistic; in
art, traditional. But I imagine the intent of Mr. Eliot's formula is about
what I am representing; and on the other hand might be only the more
effective to fight with for being so concrete. (Unfortunately its terms
are not suited to Americans; but possibly this is so of mine too.) The
word for our generation in these matters is "formal," and it might even
bear the pointed qualification, "and reactionary." The phrase would
carry the sense of our need to make a return to amenities which the
European communities labored to evolve, and defined as their "civilization." For the intention of none of those societies can have been simply to

2. T. S. Eliot, *For Lancelot Andrewes: Essays on Style and Order* (Garden City, N.Y.,
1929), 1–2.

confirm the natural man as a natural man, or to improve him in cunning and effectiveness by furnishing him with its tried economic forms. It wanted to humanize him; which means, so far as his natural economy permitted, to complicate his natural functions with sensibility, and make them æsthetic. The object of a proper society is to instruct its members how to transform instinctive experience into æsthetic experience.

Manners, rites, and arts are so close to each other that often their occasions must be confused, and it does not matter much if they are. The rule of manners is directed to those occasions when natural appetites and urges are concerned; when we hunger, or lust, or go into a rage, or encounter strange or possibly dangerous persons. The rites take place upon religious occasions; but I suppose this is tautology. It is my idea that religion is an institution existing for the sake of its ritual, rather than, as I have heard, for the sake of its doctrines, to which there attaches no cogency of magic, and for that matter a very precarious cogency of logic. The issues upon which the doctrines pronounce are really insoluble for human logic, and the higher religionists are aware of it. The only solution that is possible, since the economic solution is not possible, is the æsthetic one. When these issues press upon us, there is little that one man, with whatever benefit of doctrines, can do toward the understanding of the event which another man cannot do; and he had better not try too hard to understand the precise event, but enlarge its terms, and assimilate it into the form of an ornate public ritual through which the whole mind can discharge itself. This is a subtle technique, it has been a successful technique; in insisting upon it as the one thing I do not mean to subtract dignity from the world's great religions—which I revere. And what are the specific occasions for ritual? Those which are startling in our biological and economic history, and provoke reflection, and also, for fear we may forget to be startled when we are living for a long interval upon a dead level of routine, some arbitrary occasions, frequent and intercalated; therefore birth, marriage, death; war, peace, the undertaking of great enterprises, famine, storm; the seasons of the year, the Sabbath, the holidays. But as for the artistic process, what are its occasions? What prompts the artist? For we remark at once that many works of art embody ritual, and art is often apparently content to be the handmaiden to religion, as Hegel desired, and as she conceivably is in a painting by Michelangelo, or a poem on the order of *Lycidas*. We know also that works of art have been dedicated to the ceremonious life of society, commemorating chivalry, or some much easier code; art serving manners.

The occasions of art are innumerable; very probably its "future is im-mense." Its field is wider than that of manners, or than that of religion; the field of literary art alone is that. In fact it is about as wide as the field of science itself; and there I think lies the hint for a definition. What is the occasion which will do for the artist and the scientist indifferently? It is the occasion when we propose to "study" our object; that is, when we are more than usually undesirous and free, and find the time to be-come curious about the object as, actually, something "objective" and independent. Out of the surplus of our energy—thanks to the effi-ciency of our modern economic forms we have that increasingly—we contemplate object as object, and are not forced by an instinctive ne-cessity to take it and devour it immediately. This contemplation may take one of two routes; and first, that of science. I study the object to see how I may wring out of it my physical satisfaction the next time; or even how I may discover for the sake of a next time the physical satis-faction which it contains, but not too transparently; analyzing and clas-sifying, "experimenting," bringing it under the system of control which I intend as a scientist to have over the world of objects. It is superfluous to observe that I, the modern scientist, am in this case spiritually just as poor as was my ancestor the cave-man. My intention is simply to have bigger and quicker satisfactions than he had, my head still runs on sat-isfactions. But I may contemplate also, under another form entirely, the form of art. And that is when I am impelled neither to lay hands on the object immediately, nor to ticket it for tomorrow's outrage, but am in such a marvellous state of innocence that I would know it for its own sake, and conceive it as having its own existence; this is the knowl-edge, or it ought to be, which Schopenhauer praised as "knowledge without desire."[3] The features which the object discloses then are not those which have their meaning for a science, for a set of practical val-ues. They are those which render the body of the object, and constitute a knowledge so radical that the scientist as a scientist can scarcely un-derstand it, and puzzles to see it rendered, richly and wastefully, in the poem, or the painting. The knowledge attained there, and recorded, is a new kind of knowledge, the world in which it is set is a new world.

V

Poetry is more complicated than an animal act, which is ordinarily a scientific sort of act; it is even more complicated than the play of an

3. Arthur Schopenhauer (1788–1860), German philosopher who believed in the disin-terested aesthetic contemplation of art works.

animal, though the complication of that act is one difficult for the psychologists to handle. The poetic act involves the general sensibility, with its diffusive ranging, hardly familiar to science. But it certainly involves at the same time a discipline, very like that of science. Perhaps the best way to construe a poetic labor briefly is to take it as the analogue to a scientific one (though this latter is the paragon of labors which are serious and important) and then to fill in the differences.

The poetic labors of John Milton will do for an example. He is never discovered except meditating an object which is formidable, with a scrutiny which is steady, like that of a scientist; infinitely more sensitive. Milton's poetry exceeds most poetry in its logical closeness and symmetry; the difference between his epics and Virgil's is that his are powerfully and visibly motivated at every moment, and he will not if he can recover the purity of narrative, the innocence, that marks the ancient epic. Milton is a strong man, and has intense economic persuasions, if we may bring under that term his personal, moral, and political principles. These are his precious objects; or the situations in which he finds them exercising are. But the situations in the poetry are not his actual ones; they are fancied ones which do not touch him so nearly, distant enough to inhibit the economic impulse, which would have inhibited the sensibility. The result is that Milton's poetry, broadly speaking, may be said always to deal with "important" or highly economic subjects. But the importance of the subject is not the importance of the poetry; that depends more on the sensitiveness and completeness of the experience. The subject will generally be found to have been treated more precisely or practically somewhere in his economic prose; that is, in the ethical, theological, political tracts. It pleases us to imagine, on the strength of Milton's example, that there is no prose which is incapable of becoming a poetry, no subject in his mind so urgent that he is intimidated by it, and cannot feel it, enjoy it, and spread it out; live it, in the way we might call upon some superior man to live it.

So we look briefly and definitely as we may, at the whole net accomplishment of John Milton; starting from a convenient point, which will be *Lycidas*. This poem looks backward upon a long period of minor or practice poetry, and forward to the career of the major poet; while, as I pointed out in my previous essay,[4] it does not fail to betray the man behind the poet.

We do not find in *Lycidas* quite the proper occasion for a modern tract on communism, nor even for a contemporaneous tract on divorce;

4. "A Poem Nearly Anonymous," *American Review*, I (May, 1933), 179–203; reprinted in *The World's Body*, 1–28.

which makes it unnecessary either to regret or to be glad that Milton
has not attempted a demonstration that literature is sociology, or literature is science. We do find in the death of the young clergyman the
occasion for a contemporaneous tract on the degeneration of the clergy;
and Milton, with some difficulty, perhaps, dismisses that temptation.
For his difficulty, if we detect it, he is probably the less an artist. Yet
Milton entertained strict views upon the function of the artist, and only
upon strong compulsion was apostate.

Milton felt the impact of modernity which is perennial in every generation; or, if it is not, of the rather handsome degree of modernity
which was current in his day. He was exposed to specific temptation
because he was a man of his times and held strong views upon the contemporary ecclesiastical and political situations, in a period when the
church and the political order were undergoing revolution; he was of
the party of revolution. He had a natural inclination to preach, and display his zeal; to preach upon such themes as the reform of the clergy,
and the reform of the government; and he tended to preach intemper-
ately when he preached. He knew of this tendency in himself and opposed it. He went so far as to abandon that career in the church which
his father had intended for him and to which he seems at first to have
consented. The career which he chose instead was one which we are
wrong to consider vague and indefinite, for he hardly considered it so—
the career of an artist. He has a good deal to say about this choice. If in
the course of a public controversy much later he argued that he had
given up the church because he could not endure its tyrannical over-
lords, he made no such plea in the affectionate Latin letter written to
his father when the issue was hot. Here he is content to assert the superiority of the poet to other men. He is impressed with the elevation of
the poet's mind, which gives him a sort of aristocracy, an attitude habitually aesthetic; and Milton has studied it, and had it, enough to know.
(We must not suppose, as Milton did not, that a man has to be born
in some statistical manner to this elevation. He may bring himself up
to it.)

This is not quite the same as saying that Milton renounced his position as a man in order to take a position as a poet; he expected to occupy
both positions, but at different times. But he did not consent to define
himself as the man; that is, as the man with a profession, the economic
man. As a man he was too much like any of us; if not too appetitive in
the flesh, at least too zealous in intellectual action, which comes æsthetically to the same thing. He might have elected to become not an

artist but a man of science; a character that is just barely not a man of action, or a professional. Science belongs to the economic impulse and does not free the spirit; its celebrated virtue is due to its position on the economic scale, well distanced from the maw and the mouth of actual red appetite, while its technique is precisely the same.

Like many other people, he had a blind spot. He could scarcely receive from ritual the æsthetic benefit which was intended for him in that dispensation. Ritual turned him suspicious and truculent; a great modernism. Yet the inhibitions lay upon the act of public participation, not so much upon his intuitive understanding of the matter, and we may easily overstate it. It is probably a common variety of Protestantism. When he came under the milder influences of poetry, he composed the kind of effects which he valued, which he constantly received in the traditional poetry of Greeks, Romans, Italians, and Englishmen—poetry nearly as ornate, mythological, religious, as a ritual itself could be. But when he was faced by the ritual, the effective thing itself, administered by priests whom he had determined to hold as hypocritical, he was roused invariably to resistance. So inveterate and passionate did this resistance become that it took him into the extremist Protestant camp to write hard doctrine, and actually to set up his own religion as a project in dialectic. All the time he "knew" better; probably no European poet exceeds him much, either for consistency or for depths of insight, in mythological sense. The same Milton appealed in a Latin exercise to Plato not to banish the myth-makers from the Republic, and some years later would have liked publicly to chase out of England the Anglican ritualists, the adherents of the then myth, as idolators. That is the Milton paradox.

He was obstinate in his idea of what the church must have been for him as a calling. His Anglo-Catholic contemporaries could have told him—probably they told him—that the priest who is charged with the performance of the ritual, and on some occasions with creating ritual on his own responsibility, is eminently in the service of the cult of æsthetic experience. His noble Italian friends certainly told him, during that triumphal tour on which he received honors incredible for a professing Puritan in Rome, except that he may have been regarded as a man not yet too openly committed, and still reclaimable. Among these friends was Manso,[5] to whom it must have seemed a pity that a poet so prodigious, and so true to the ancient traditions of his calling, was capa-

---

5. Giambattista Manso (ca. 1560–1645), Italian nobleman and art patron.

ble of not perceiving that these had anything to do with the majestic ceremonial of a high church. We may imagine that Manso had this anomaly in mind—and not merely the havoc which the young collegiate Milton had wrought with the Catholics, or tried to wreak, in his exuberant exercise on the Gunpowder Plot—when he presented Milton with a fine Latin compliment, to which there was attached all the same an impressive qualification: "If your piety were such as your mind, your form, charm, face, and manners, then you would not be an Angle, but in sober truth an Angel." Manso was cribbing of course from the Sixth-Century Gregory,[6] who had observed the fair-haired Anglian slaves in Rome, and hoped they might one day take their own part in the ritual of a world-wide catholic church. Gregory's hope had been realized, but now in Milton's time it seemed on the point of being deceived; and here was one of the race in question, brilliantly endowed in his mind and person, but stubborn in his barbarism; for Manso could not fail to appreciate just what it meant for a society to cast off its religious forms.

But, as I have said, Milton did know better than he acted; he made his choice and became the artist; and exercised his *métier* with an aristocratic taste that almost never failed him; though he was no more able as layman than he had been as prospective priest to apply this taste to the forms of his worship. We do not regret his decision when we have to follow him during the ten or fifteen years after 1640, the period in which he felt obliged as a citizen to drop the poet and become the preacher, the tractarian, and the economic man. During that period we remember gratefully that he shares our own view of his intractable nature, in which so much of the sin of Adam resides; that he understands his predicament. The formality of poetry sustained him, induced in him his highest nobility, and his most delicate feeling. The ding-dong of contemporary controversy brought out of him something ugly and plebeian that was there all the time, waiting. He took care that the preacher should be the Miltonic rôle for but a period; the artist came back, and may have been the better artist for the ignominy which he had suffered; though I shall not try to argue that.

Art was his deliberate career. It is a career, precisely as science is a career. It is as serious, it has an attitude as official, it is as studied and consecutive, it is by all means as difficult, it is no less important. It may be less remunerative, it is further from offering the sort of values which are materially rewarded; today it may be so unrewarded that, if we

6. St. Gregory the Great (ca. 540–604), Pope and reformer.

agree to regard it like science as a career, we are not inclined to regard it like science as a profession; but so far from being at a disadvantage on that account, it may be better off, as having the more innocence because of it, and finding innocence a good condition for its peculiar process.

It would follow that Milton has been widely if not generally misunderstood, by people who define him primarily as a Puritan moralist, or a theologian, or a political thinker, or an early modern, or a scholar. Some ultra-modern critics, as was inevitable, now have turned upon him "as a man," and in that capacity as one of the damned, having an inherited disease, or a libido, or a crack in his mind—which seems at this distance unimportant if true. He was chiefly and preferably, and on a life-long scale, an artist. Those who will not undertake to gather what this involved for him will be finding themselves constantly rebuffed by the mountains of irrelevance raised against them in the body of his poetry. Milton is the poetry, and is lost to them if they do not know how to make acquaintance there. What on earth will they do with the cool flora that bloom so uselessly in the formal if somewhat tangled garden which is *Lycidas*?

POETRY: A NOTE IN ONTOLOGY

POETRY may be distinguished from a poetry by virtue of subject-matter, and subject-matter may be differentiated with respect to its ontology, or the reality of its being. An excellent variety of critical doctrine arises recently out of this differentiation, and thus perhaps criticism leans again upon ontological analysis as it was meant to do by Kant. The recent critics remark in effect that some poetry deals with things, while some other poetry deals with ideas. The two poetries will differ from each other as radically as a thing differs from an idea.

The distinction in the hands of critics is a fruitful one. There is apt to go along with it a principle of valuation, which is the consequence of a temperament, and therefore basic. The critic likes things and intends that his poet shall offer them; or likes ideas and intends that he shall offer them; and approves him as he does the one or the other. Criticism cannot well go much deeper than this. The critic has carried to the last terms his analysis of the stuff of which poetry is made, and valued it frankly as his temperament or his need requires him to value it.

So philosophical a critic seems to be highly modern. He is; but this critic as a matter of fact is peculiarly on one side of the question. (The implication is unfavorable to the other side of the question.) He is in revolt against the tyranny of ideas, and against the poetry which celebrates ideas, and which may be identified—so far as his usual generalization may be trusted—with the hateful poetry of the Victorians. His bias is in favor of the things. On the other hand the critic who likes Victorian verse, or the poetry of ideas, has probably not thought of anything of so grand a simplicity as electing between the things and the ideas, being apparently not quite capable of the ontological distinction. Therefore he does not know the real or constitutional ground of his liking, and may somewhat ingenuously claim that his predilection is for those poets who give him inspiration, or comfort, or truth, or honest

This essay first appeared in the *American Review*, III (May, 1934), 172–200; later reprinted in *The World's Body*, copyright © 1938 by Charles Scribner's Sons; copyright renewed 1966 by John Crowe Ransom. Reprinted with the permission of Charles Scribner's Sons.

metres, or something else equally "worth while." But Plato, who was not a modern, was just as clear as we are about the basic distinction between the ideas and the things, and yet stands far apart from the aforesaid conscious modern in passionately preferring the ideas over the things. The weight of Plato's testimony would certainly fall on the side of the Victorians, though they may scarcely have thought of calling him as their witness. But this consideration need not conclude the hearing.

I. PHYSICAL POETRY

The poetry which deals with things was much in favor a few years ago with the resolute body of critics. And the critics affected the poets. If necessary, they became the poets, and triumphantly illustrated the new mode. The Imagists were important figures in the history of our poetry, and they were both theorists and creators. It was their intention to present things in their thinginess, or *Dinge* in their *Dinglichkeit*; and to such an extent had the public lost its sense of *Dinglichkeit* that their redirection was wholesome. What the public was inclined to seek in poetry was ideas, whether large ones or small ones, grand ones or pretty ones, certainly ideas to live by and die by, but what the Imagists identified with the stuff of poetry was, simply, things.

Their application of their own principle was sufficiently heroic, though they scarcely consented to be as extreme in the practice as in the theory. They had artistic talent, every one of the original group, and it was impossible that they should make of poetry so simple an exercise as in doctrine they seemed to think it was. Yet Miss Lowell wrote a poem on "Thompson's Lunch Room, Grand Central Station"; it is admirable if its intention is to show the whole reach of her courage. Its detail goes like this:

> Jagged greenwhite bowls of pressed glass
> Rearing snow-peaks of chipped sugar
> Above the lighthouse-shaped castors
> Of gray pepper and gray-white salt.

For most of us as for the public idealist, with his "values," this is inconsequential. Unhappily it seems that the things as things do not necessarily interest us, and that in fact we are not quite constructed with the capacity for a disinterested interest. But it must be noted even here that the things are on their good behavior, looking rather well, and arranged by lines into something approaching a military formation. More technically, there is cross-imagery in the snow-peaks of sugar, and in the lighthouse-shaped castors, and cross-imagery involves association, and will presently involve dissociation and thinking. The metre is but a vestige, but even so it means something, for metre is a powerful intellectual determinant marshalling the words and, inevitably, the things. The *Dinglichkeit* of this Imagist specimen, or the realism, was therefore not pure. But it was nearer pure than the world was used to in poetry, and the exhibit was astonishing.

For the purpose of this note I shall give to such poetry, dwelling as exclusively as it dares upon physical things, the name Physical Poetry. It is to stand opposite to that poetry which dwells as firmly as it dares upon ideas.

But perhaps thing *versus* idea does not seem to name an opposition precisely. Then we might phrase it a little differently: image *versus* idea. The idealistic philosophies are not sure that things exist, but they mean the equivalent when they refer to images. (Or they may consent to perceptions; or to impressions, following Hume, and following Croce, who remarks that they are pre-intellectual and independent of concepts. It is all the same, unless we are extremely technical.) It is sufficient if they concede that image is the raw material of idea. Though it may be an unwieldy and useless affair for the idealist as it stands, much needing to be licked into shape, nevertheless its relation to idea is that of a material cause, and it cannot be dispossessed of its priority.

It cannot be dispossessed of a primordial freshness, which idea can never claim. An idea is derivative and tamed. The image is in the natural or wild state, and it has to be discovered there, not put there, obeying its own law and none of ours. We think we can lay hold of image and take it captive, but the docile captive is not the real image but only the idea, which is the image with its character beaten out of it.

But we must be very careful: idealists are nothing if not dialectical. They object that an image in an original state of innocence is a delusion and cannot exist, that no image ever comes to us which does not imply the world of ideas, that there is "no percept without a concept." There is something in it. Every property discovered in the image is a universal property, and nothing discovered in the image is marvelous in kind though it may be pinned down historically or statistically as a single instance. But there is this to be understood too: the image which is not remarkable in any particular property is marvellous in its assemblage of many properties, a manifold of properties, like a mine or a field, something to be explored for the properties; yet science can manage the image, which is infinite in properties, only by equating it to the one property with which the science is concerned; for science at work is always *a science*, and committed to a special interest. It is not by refutation but by abstraction that science destroys the image. It means to get its "value" out of the image, and we may be sure that it has no use for the image in its original state of freedom. People who are engrossed with their pet "values" become habitual killers. Their game is the images, or the things, and they acquire the ability to shoot them as far off as they can be seen, and do. It is thus that we lose the power of imagination, or whatever faculty it is by which we are able to contemplate things as they are in their rich and contingent materiality. But our dreams reproach us, for in dreams they come alive again. Likewise our memory; which makes light of our science by recalling the images in their panoply of circumstance and with their morning freshness upon them.

It is the dream, the recollection, which compels us to poetry, and to deliberate æsthetic experience. It can hardly be argued, I think, that the arts are constituted automatically out of original images, and arise in some early age of innocence. (Though Croce seems to support this view, and to make art a pre-adult stage of experience.) Art is based on second love, not first love. In it we make a return to something which we had wilfully alienated. The child is occupied mostly with things, but it is because he is still unfurnished with systematic ideas, not because he is a ripe citizen by nature and comes along already trailing clouds of glory. Images are clouds of glory for the man who has discovered that ideas are a sort of darkness. Imagism, that is, the recent historical movement, may resemble a naïve poetry of mere things, but we can read the theoretical pronouncements of Imagists, and we can learn that Imagism is motivated by a distaste for the systematic abstractedness of thought. It presupposes acquaintance with science; that famous activity which is "constructive" with respect to the tools of our economic role in this world, and destructive with respect to nature. Imagists wish to escape from science by immersing themselves in images.

Not far off the simplicity of Imagism was, a little later, the subtler simplicity of Mr. George Moore's project shared with several others, in behalf of "pure poetry."[1] In Moore's house on Ebury Street they talked

1. The expression "pure poetry" was introduced into England with Moore's *An Anthology of Pure Poetry* (1924). For him, it is that poetry which achieves the greatest possible degree of concreteness and objectivity.

about poetry, with an after-dinner warmth if not an early-morning discretion, and their tastes agreed almost perfectly and reinforced one another. The fruit of these conversations was the volume *Pure Poetry*. It
must have been the most exclusive anthology of English poetry that
had yet appeared, since its room was closed to all the poems that dallied
visibly with ideas, so that many poems that had been coveted by all
other anthologists do not appear there. Nevertheless the book is delicious, and something more deserves to be said for it.

First, that "pure poetry" is a kind of Physical Poetry. Its visible content is a thing-content. Technically, I suppose, it is effective in this
character if it can exhibit its material in such a way that an image or set
of images and not an idea must occupy the foreground of the reader's
attention. Thus:

> Full fathom five thy father lies
> Of his bones are coral made.

Here it is difficult for anybody (except the perfect idealist who is always
theoretically possible and who would expect to take a return from anything whatever) to receive any experience except that of a very distinct
image, or set of images. It has the configuration of image, which consists in being sharp of edges, and the modality of image, which consists
in being given and non-negotiable, and the density, which consists in
being full, a plenum of qualities. What is to be done with it? It is pure
exhibit; it is to be contemplated; perhaps it is to be enjoyed. The art of
poetry depends more frequently on this faculty than on any other in its
repertory; the faculty of presenting images so whole and clean that
they resist the catalysis of thought.

And something else must be said, going in the opposite direction.
"Pure poetry," all the same, is not as pure as it is claimed to be, though
on the whole it is Physical Poetry. (All true poetry is a phase of Physical
Poetry.) It is not as pure as Imagism is, or at least it is not as pure as
Imagism would be if it lived up to its principles; and in fact it is significant that the volume does not contain any Imagist poems, which argues a difference in taste somewhere. Imagism may take trifling things
for its material, presumably it will take the first things the poet encounters, since "importance" and "interest" are not primary qualities which
a thing possesses but secondary or tertiary ones which the idealist attributes to it by virtue of his own requirements. "Pure poetry" as Moore
conceives it, and as the lyrics of Poe and Shakespeare offer it, deals with
the more dramatic materials, and here dramatic means human, or at
least capable of being referred to the critical set of human interests.

Employing this sort of material the poet cannot exactly intend to set the human economists in us actually into motion, but perhaps he does intend to comfort us with the fleeting sense that it is potentially our kind of material.

In the same way "pure poetry" is nicely metred, whereas Imagism was free. Technique is written on it. And by the way the anthology contains no rugged anonymous Scottish ballad either, and probably for a like reason; because it would not be technically finished. Now both Moore and De La Mare are accomplished conservative artists, and what they do or what they approve may be of limited range but it is sure to be technically admirable, and it is certain that they understand what technique in poetry is though they do not define it. Technique takes the thing-content and meters and orders it. Metre is not an original property of things. It is artificial, and conveys the sense of human control, even if it does not wish to impair the thinginess of the things. Metrics is a science, and so far as we attend to it we are within the scientific atmosphere. Order is the logical arrangement of things. It involves the dramatic "form" which selects the things, and brings out their appropriate qualities, and carries them through a systematic course of predication until the total impression is a unit of logic and not merely a solid lump of thing-content. The "pure poems" which Moore admires are studied, though it would be fatal if they looked studious. A sustained effort of ideation effected these compositions. It is covered up, and communicates itself only on a subliminal plane of consciousness. But experienced readers are quite aware of it; they know at once what is the matter when they encounter a realism shamelessly passing for poetry, or a well-planned but blundering poetry.

As critics we should have every good will toward Physical Poetry: it is the basic constituent of any poetry. But the product is always something short of a pure or absolute existence, and it cannot quite be said that it consists of nothing but physical objects. The fact is that when we are more than usually satisfied with a Physical Poetry our analysis will probably disclose that it is more than usually impure.

2. PLATONIC POETRY

The poetry of ideas I shall denominate: Platonic Poetry. This also has grades of purity. A discourse which employed only abstract ideas with no images would be a scientific document and not a poem at all, not even a Platonic poem. Platonic Poetry dips heavily into the physical. If Physical Poetry tends to employ some ideation surreptitiously while still looking innocent of idea, Platonic Poetry more than returns the compliment, for it tries as hard as it can to look like Physical Poetry, as if it proposed to conceal its medicine, which is the idea to be propagated, within the sugar candy of objectivity and *Dinglichkeit*. As an instance, it is almost inevitable that I quote a famous Victorian utterance:

> The year's at the spring
> And day's at the morn;
> Morning's at seven;
> The hill-side's dew-pearled;
> The lark's on the wing;
> The snail's on the thorn:
> God's in his heaven—
> All's right with the world![2]

which is a piece of transparent homiletics; for in it six pretty, co-ordinate images are marched, like six little lambs to the slaughter, to a colon and a powerful text. Now the exhibits of this poetry in the physical kind are always large, and may take more of the attention of the reader than is desired, but they are meant mostly to be illustrative of the ideas. It is on this ground that idealists like Hegel detect something unworthy, like a pedagogical trick, in poetry after all, and consider that the race will abandon it when it has outgrown its childishness and is enlightened.

The ablest arraignment of Platonic Poetry that I have seen, as an exercise which is really science but masquerades as poetry by affecting a concern for physical objects, is that of Mr. Allen Tate in a series of studies recently in *The New Republic*.[3] I will summarize. Platonic Poetry is allegory, a discourse in things, but on the understanding that they are translatable at every point into ideas. (The usual ideas are those which constitute the popular causes, patriotic, religious, moral, or social.) Or Platonic Poetry is the elaboration of ideas as such, but in proceeding introduces for ornament some physical properties after the style of Physical Poetry; which is rhetoric. It is positive when the poet believes in the efficacy of the ideas. It is negative when he despairs of their efficacy, because they have conspicuously failed to take care of him, and utters his personal wail:

> I fall upon the thorns of life! I bleed![4]

2. Robert Browning, "Pippa Passes."
3. "Three Types of Poetry," *New Republic*, LXXVIII (March 14, 1934), 126–28; LXXVIII (March 28, 1934), 180–82; LXXVIII (April 11, 1934), 237–40.
4. Percy Bysshe Shelley, "Ode to the West Wind."

This is "Romantic Irony," which comes at occasional periods to interrupt the march of scientific optimism. But it still falls under the category of Platonism; it generally proposes some other ideas to take the place of those which are in vogue.

But why Platonism? To define Platonism we must remember that it is not the property of the historical person who reports dialogues about it in an Academy, any more than "pure poetry" is the property of the talkers who describe it from a house on Ebury Street. Platonism, in the sense I mean, is the name of an impulse that is native to us all, frequent, tending to take a too complete possession of our minds. Why should the spirit of mortal be proud? The chief explanation is that modern mortal is probably a Platonist. We are led to believe that nature is rational and that by the force of reasoning we shall possess it. I have read upon high authority: "Two great forces are persistent in Plato: the love of truth and zeal for human improvement." The forces are one force. We love to view the world under universal or scientific ideas to which we give the name truth; and this is because the ideas seem to make not for righteousness but for mastery. The Platonic view of the world is ultimately the predatory, for it reduces to the scientific, which we know. The Platonic Idea becomes the Logos which science worships, which is the Occidental God, whose minions we are, and whose children, claiming a large share in His powers for patrimony.

Now the fine Platonic world of ideas fails to coincide with the original world of perception, which is the world populated by the stubborn and contingent objects, and to which as artists we fly in shame. The sensibility manifested by artists makes fools of scientists, if the latter are inclined to take their special and quite useful form of truth as the whole and comprehensive article. A dandified pagan worldling like Moore can always defeat Platonism; he does it every hour; he can exhibit the savor of his fish and wines, the fragrance of his coffee and cigars, and the solidity of the images in his favorite verse. These are objects which have to be experienced, and cannot be reported, for what is their simple essence that the Platonist can abstract? Moore may sound mystical but he is within the literal truth when he defends "pure poetry" on the ground that the things are constant, and it is the ideas which change—changing according to the latest mode under which the species indulges its grandiose expectation of subjugating nature. The things are constant in the sense that the ideas are never emancipated from the necessity of referring back to them as their original; and the sense that they are not altered nor diminished no matter which ideas may take off from them as a point of departure. The way to obtain the true *Dinglichkeit* of a formal dinner or a landscape or a beloved person is to approach the object as such, and in humility; then it unfolds a nature which we are unprepared for if we have put our trust in the simple idea which attempted to represent it.

The special antipathy of Moore is to the ideas as they put on their moral complexion, the ideas that relate everything to that insignificant centre of action, the human "soul" in its most Platonic and Pharisaic aspect. Nothing can darken perception better than a repetitive moral earnestness, based on the reputed superiority and higher destiny of the human species. If morality is the code by which we expect the race to achieve the more perfect possession of nature, it is an incitement to a more heroic science, but not to aesthetic experience, nor religious; if it is the code of humility, by which we intend to know nature as nature is, that is another matter; but in an age of science morality is inevitably for the general public the former; and so transcendent a morality as the latter is now unheard of. And therefore:

> O love, *they* die in yon rich sky,
>   *They* faint on hill or field or river;
> *Our* echoes roll from soul to soul,
>   And grow forever and forever.[5]

The italics are mine. These lines conclude an otherwise innocent poem, a candidate for the anthology, upon which Moore remarks: "The Victorian could never reconcile himself to finishing a poem without speaking about the soul, and the lines are particularly vindictive." Vindictive is just. By what right did the Laureate exult in the death of the physical echoes and call upon his love to witness it, but out of the imperiousness of his savage Platonism? Plato himself would have admired this ending, and considered that it redeemed an otherwise vicious poem.

Why do persons who have ideas to promulgate risk the trial by poetry? If the poets are hired to do it, which is the polite conception of some Hegelians, why do their employers think it worth the money, which they hold in public trust for the cause? Does a science have to become a poetry too? A science is the less effective as a science when it muddies its clear waters with irrelevance, a sermon becomes less cogent when it begins to quote the poets. The moralist, the scientist, and the prophet of idealism think evidently that they must establish their conclusions in poetry, though they reach these conclusions upon quite

---

5. Alfred Lord Tennyson, "The Princess."

other evidence. The poetry is likely to destroy the conclusions with a sort of death by drowning, if it is a free poetry.

When that happens the Platonists may be cured of Platonism. There are probably two cures, of which this is the better. One cure is by adversity, by the failure of the ideas to work, on account of treachery or violence, or the contingencies of weather, constitution, love, and economics; leaving the Platonist defeated and bewildered, possibly humbled, but on the other hand possibly turned cynical and worthless. Very much preferable is the cure which comes by education in the fine arts, erasing his Platonism more gently, leading him to feel that that is not a becoming habit of mind which dulls the perceptions.

The definition which some writers have given to art is: the reference of the idea to the image. The implication is that the act is not for the purpose of honest comparison so much as for the purpose of proving the idea by the image. But in the event the idea is not disproved so much as it is made to look ineffective and therefore foolish. The ideas will not cover the objects upon which they are imposed, they are too attenuated and threadlike; for ideas have extension and objects have intension, but extension is thin while intension is thick.

There must be a great deal of genuine poetry which started in the poet's mind as a thesis to be developed, but in which the characters and the situations have developed faster than the thesis, and of their own accord. The thesis disappears; or it is recaptured here and there and at the end, and lodged sententiously with the reader, where every successive reading of the poem will dislodge it again. Like this must be some plays, even some play out of Shakespeare, whose thesis would probably be disentangled with difficulty out of the crowded pageant; or some narrative poem with a moral plot but much pure detail; perhaps some "occasional" piece by a Laureate or official person, whose purpose is compromised but whose personal integrity is saved by his wavering between the sentiment which is a public duty and the experience which he has in his own right; even some proclaimed allegory, like Spenser's, unlikely as that may seem, which does not remain transparent and everywhere translatable into idea but makes excursions into the territory of objectivity. These are hybrid performances. They cannot possess beauty of design, though there may be a beauty in detailed passages. But it is common enough, and we should be grateful. The mind is a versatile agent, and unexpectedly stubborn in its determination not really to be hardened in Platonism. Even in an age of science like the nineteenth century the poetic talents are not so loyal to its apostolic zeal as they and it suppose, and do not deserve the unqualified scorn which it is fashionable to offer them, now that the tide has turned, for their performance is qualified.

But this may be not stern enough for concluding a note on Platonic Poetry. I refer again to that whose Platonism is steady and malignant. This poetry is an imitation of Physical Poetry, and not really a poetry. Platonists practise their bogus poetry in order to show that an image will prove an idea, but the literature which succeeds in this delicate mission does not contain real images but illustrations.

3. METAPHYSICAL POETRY

"Most men," Mr. Moore observes, "read and write poetry between fifteen and thirty and afterwards very seldom, for in youth we are attracted by ideas, and modern poetry being concerned almost exclusively with ideas we live on duty, liberty, and fraternity as chameleons are said to live on light and air, till at last we turn from ideas to things, thinking that we have lost our taste for poetry, unless, perchance, we are classical scholars."[6]

Much is conveyed in this characteristic sentence, even in proportion to its length. As for the indicated chronology, the cart is put after the horse, which is its proper sequence. And it is pleasant to be confirmed in the belief that many men do recant from their Platonism and turn back to things. But it cannot be exactly a *volte-face*, for there are qualifications. If pure ideas were what these men turn from, they would have had no poetry at all in the first period, and if pure things were what they turn to, they would be having not a classical poetry but a pure imagism, if such a thing is possible, in the second.

The mind does not come unscathed and virginal out of Platonism. Ontological interest would have to develop curiously, or wastefully and discontinuously, if men through their youth must cultivate the ideas so passionately that upon its expiration they are done with ideas forever and ready to become as little (and pre-logical) children. Because of the foolishness of idealists are ideas to be taboo for the adult mind? And, as critics, what are we to do with those poems (like *The Canonization* and *Lycidas*) which could not obtain admission by Moore into the anthology but which very likely are the poems we cherish beyond others?

The reputed "innocence" of the æsthetic moment, the "knowledge without desire" which Schopenhauer praises, must submit to a little

6. George Moore, *An Anthology of Pure Poetry* (New York, 1925), 25.

scrutiny, like anything else that looks too good to be true. We come into this world as aliens come into a land which they must conquer if they are to live. For native endowment we have an exacting "biological" constitution which knows precisely what it needs and determines for us our inevitable desires. There can be no certainty that any other impulses are there, for why should they be? They scarcely belong in the biological picture. Perhaps we are simply an efficient animal species, running smoothly, working fast, finding the formula of life only too easy, and after a certain apprenticeship piling up power and wealth far beyond the capacity of our appetites to use. What will come next? Perhaps poetry, if the gigantic effort of science begins to seem disproportionate to the reward, according to a sense of diminishing returns. But before this pretty event can come to pass, it is possible that every act of attention which is allowed us is conditioned by a gross and selfish interest.

Where is innocence then? The æsthetic moment appears as a curious moment of suspension; between the Platonism in us, which is militant, always sciencing and devouring, and a starved inhibited aspiration towards innocence which, if it could only be free, would like to respect and know the object as it might of its own accord reveal itself.

The poetic impulse is not free, yet it holds out stubbornly against science for the enjoyment of its images. It means to reconstitute the world of perceptions. Finally there is suggested some such formula as the following:

Science gratifies a rational or practical impulse and exhibits the minimum of perception. Art gratifies a perceptual impulse and exhibits the minimum of reason.

Now it would be strange if poets did not develop many technical devices for the sake of increasing the volume of the percipienda or sensibilia. I will name some of them.

First Device: metre. Metre is the most obvious device. A formal metre impresses us as a way of regulating very drastically the material, and we do not stop to remark (that is, as readers) that it has no particular aim except some nominal sort of regimentation. It symbolizes the predatory method, like a sawmill which intends to reduce all the trees to fixed unit timbers, and as business men we require some sign of our business. But to the Platonic censor in us it gives a false security, for so long as the poet appears to be working faithfully at his metrical engine he is left comparatively free to attend lovingly to the things that are being metered, and metering them need not really hurt them. Metre is the gentlest violence he can do them, if he is expected to do some violence.

Second Device: fiction. The device of the fiction is probably no less important and universal in poetry. Over every poem which looks like a poem is a sign which reads: This road does not go through to action; fictitious. Art always sets out to create an "aesthetic distance" between the object and the subject, and art takes pains to announce that it is not history. The situation treated is not quite an actual situation, for science is likely to have claimed that field, and exiled art; but a fictive or hypothetical one, so that science is less greedy and perception may take hold of it. Kant asserted that the æsthetic judgment is not concerned with the existence or non-existence of the object, and may be interpreted as asserting that it is so far from depending on the object's existence that it really depends on the object's non-existence. Sometimes we have a certain melancholy experience. We enjoy a scene which we receive by report only, or dream, or meet with in art; but subsequently find ourselves in the presence of an actual one that seems the very same scene; only to discover that we have not now the power to enjoy it, or to receive it æsthetically, because the economic tension is upon us and will not indulge us in the proper mood. And it is generally easier to obtain our æsthetic experience from art than from nature, because nature is actual, and communication is forbidden. But in being called fictive or hypothetical the art-object suffers no disparagement. It cannot be true in the sense of being actual, and therefore it may be despised by science. But it is true in the sense of being fair or representative, in permitting the "illusion of reality"; just as Schopenhauer discovered that music may symbolize all the modes of existence in the world; and in keeping with the customary demand of the readers of fiction proper, that it shall be "true to life." The defenders of art must require for it from its practitioners this sort of truth, and must assert of it before the world this dignity. If jealous science succeeds in keeping the field of history for its own exclusive use, it does not therefore annihilate the arts, for they reappear in a field which may be called real though one degree removed from actuality. There the arts perform their function with much less interference, and at the same time with about as much fidelity to the phenomenal world as history has.

Third Device: tropes. I have named two important devices; I am not prepared to offer the exhaustive list. I mention but one other kind, the ⌐

device which comprises the figures of speech. A proper scientific discourse has no intention of employing figurative language for its definitive sort of utterance. Figures of speech twist accidence away from the straight course, as if to intimate astonishing lapses of rationality beneath the smooth surface of discourse, inviting perceptual attention, and weakening the tyranny of science over the senses. But I skip the several easier and earlier figures, which are timid, and stop on the climactic figure, which is the metaphor; with special reference to its consequence, a poetry which once in our history it produced in a beautiful and abundant exhibit, called Metaphysical Poetry.

And what is Metaphysical Poetry? The term was added to the official vocabulary of criticism by Johnson, who probably took it from Pope, who probably took it from Dryden, who used it to describe the poetry of a certain school of poets, thus: "He [John Donne] affects the metaphysics, not only in his satires, but in his amorous verses, where nature only should reign. . . . In this Mr. Cowley has copied him to a fault."[7] But the meaning of metaphysical which was common in Dryden's time, having come down from the Middle Ages through Shakespeare, was simply: supernatural; *miraculous*. The context of the Dryden passage indicates it.

Dryden, then, noted a miraculism in poetry and repudiated it; except where it was employed for satire, where it was not seriously intended and had the effect of wit. Dryden himself employs miraculism wittily, but seems rather to avoid it if he will be really committed by it; he may employ it in his translations of Ovid, where the responsibility is Ovid's and not Dryden's, and in an occasional classical piece where he is making polite use of myths well known to be pagan errors. In his "amorous" pieces he finds the reign of nature sufficient, and it is often the worse for his amorous pieces. He is not many removes from a naturalist. (A naturalist is a person who studies nature not because he loves it but because he wants to use it, approaches it from the standpoint of common sense, and sees it thin and not thick.) Dryden might have remarked that Donne himself had a change of heart and confined his miraculism at last to the privileged field of a more or less scriptural revelation. Perhaps Dryden found his way to accepting Milton because Milton's miraculism was mostly not a contemporary sort but classical and scriptural, pitched in a time when the age of miracles had not given way to the age of science. He knew too that Cowley had shamefully recanted from his petty miraculism, which formed the conceits,

7. John Dryden, "A Discourse Concerning the Origin and Progress of Satire," in *Essays of John Dryden*, ed. W. P. Ker (Oxford, 1926), II, 19.

and turned to the scriptural or large order of miraculism to write his
heroic (but empty) verses about David; and had written a Pindaric ode
in extravagant praise of "Mr. Hobs," whose naturalistic account of nature seemed to render any other account fantastic if not contrary to the
social welfare.[8]

Incidentally, we know how much Mr. Hobbes affected Dryden too,
and the whole of Restoration literature. What Bacon with his disparagement of poetry had begun, in the cause of science and protestantism,
Hobbes completed. The name of Hobbes is critical in any history that
would account for the chill which settled upon the poets at the very
moment that English poetry was attaining magnificently to the fullness
of its powers. The name stood for common sense and naturalism, and
the monopoly of the scientific spirit over the mind. Hobbes was the ad-
versary, the Satan, when the latter first intimidated the English poets.
After Hobbes his name is legion.

"Metaphysics," or miraculism, informs a poetry which is the most
original and exciting, and intellectually perhaps the most seasoned,
that we know in our literature, and very probably it has few equivalents
in other literatures. But it is evident that the metaphysical effects may
be large-scale or they may be small-scale. (I believe that generically, or
ontologically, no distinction is to be made between them.) If Donne and
Cowley illustrate the small-scale effects, Milton will illustrate the large-
scale ones, probably as a consequence of the fact that he wrote major
poems. Milton, in the *Paradise Lost*, told a story which was heroic and
miraculous in the first place. In telling it he dramatized it, and allowed
the scenes and characters to develop of their own native energy. The
virtue of a long poem on a "metaphysical" subject will consist in the
dramatization or substantiation of all the parts, the poet not being required to devise fresh miracles on every page so much as to establish
the perfect "naturalism" of the material upon which the grand miracle
is imposed. The *Paradise Lost* possesses this virtue nearly everywhere:

> Thus *Adam* to himself lamented loud
> Through the still Night, not now, as ere man fell,
> Wholsom and cool, and mild, but with black Air
> Accompanied, with damps and dreadful gloom,
> Which to his evil Conscience represented
> All things with double terror: On the ground
> Outstretcht he lay, on the cold ground, and oft
> Curs'd his Creation, Death as oft accus'd
> Of tardie execution, since denounc't

8. Thomas Hobbes (1588–1679), British philosopher and political scientist.

> The day of his offence. Why comes not Death,
> Said he, with one thrice acceptable stroke
> To end me?[9]

This is exactly the sort of detail for a large-scale metaphysical work, but it would hardly serve the purpose with a slighter and more naturalistic subject; with "amorous" verses. For the critical mind Metaphysical Poetry refers perhaps almost entirely to the so-called "conceits" that constitute its staple. To define the conceit is to define small-scale Metaphysical Poetry.

It is easily defined, upon a little citation. Donne exhibits two conceits, or two branches of one conceit in the familiar lines:

> Our hands were firmly cemented
> By a fast balm which thence did spring;
> Our eye-beams twisted, and did thread
> Our eyes upon one double string.[10]

The poem which follows sticks to the topic; it represents the lovers in precisely that mode of union and no other. Cowley is more conventional yet still bold in the lines:

> Oh take my Heart, and by that means you'll prove
>   Within, too stor'd enough of love:
> Give me but yours, I'll by that change so thrive
>   That Love in all parts shall live.
> So powerful is this my change, it render can,
> My outside Woman, and your inside Man.[11]

A conceit originates in a metaphor; and in fact the conceit is but a metaphor if the metaphor is meant; that is, if it is developed so literally that it must be meant, or predicated so baldly that nothing else can be meant. Perhaps this will do for a definition.

Clearly the seventeenth century had the courage of its metaphors, and imposed them imperially on the nearest things, and just as clearly the nineteenth century lacked this courage, and was half-heartedly metaphorical, or content with similes. The difference between the literary qualities of the two periods is the difference between the metaphor and the simile. (It must be admitted that this like other generalizations will not hold without its exceptions.) One period was pithy and original in its poetic utterance, the other was prolix and predictable. It would

9. *Paradise Lost*, Book X, 845–56.
10. John Donne, "The Extasie."
11. Abraham Cowley, "The Change."

not quite commit itself to the metaphor even if it came upon one. Shelley is about as vigorous as usual when he says in *Adonais*:

> Thou young Dawn,
> Turn all thy dew to splendour. . . .

But splendor is not the correlative of dew, it has the flat tone of a Platonic idea, while physically it scarcely means more than dew with sunshine upon it. The seventeenth century would have said: "Turn thy dew, which is water, into fire, and accomplish the transmutation of the elements." Tennyson in his boldest lyric sings:

> Come into the garden, Maud,
> For the black bat, night, has flown,[12]

and leaves us unpersuaded of the bat. The predication would be complete without the bat, "The black night has flown," and a flying night is not very remarkable. Tennyson is only affecting a metaphor. But later in the same poem he writes:

> The red rose cries, "She is near, she is near";
> And the white rose weeps, "She is late";
> The larkspur listens, "I hear, I hear";
> And the lily whispers, "I wait."[13]

And this is a technical conceit. But it is too complicated for this author, having a plurality of images which do not sustain themselves individually. The flowers stand for the lover's thoughts, and have been prepared for carefully in an earlier stanza, but their distinctness is too arbitrary, and these are like a schoolgirl's made-up metaphors. The passage will not compare with one on a very similar situation in *Green Candles*, by Mr. Humbert Wolfe:

> "I know her little foot," gray carpet said:
> "Who but I should know her light tread?"
> "She shall come in," answered the open door,
> "And not," said the room, "go out any more."[14]

Wolfe's conceit works and Tennyson's does not, and though Wolfe's performance seems not very daring or important, and only pleasant, he employs the technique of the conceit correctly: he knows that the miracle must have a basis of verisimilitude.

12. Alfred Lord Tennyson, "Maud," XXII : 1.
13. "Maud," XXII : 10.
14. Anthologized in Louis Untermeyer's *Modern American and British Poetry* (New York, 1928), 394.

Such is Metaphysical Poetry; the extension of a rhetorical device; as one of the most brilliant successes in our poetry, entitled to long and thorough examination; and even here demanding somewhat by way of a more ontological criticism. I conclude with it.

We may consult the dictionary, and discover that there is a miraculism or supernaturalism in a metaphorical assertion if we are ready to mean what we say, or believe what we hear. Or we may read Mr. Hobbes, the naturalist, who was very clear upon it: "II. The second cause of absurd assertions I ascribe to the giving of names of 'bodies' to 'accidents,' or of 'accidents' to 'bodies,' as they do that say 'faith is infused' or 'inspired,' when nothing can be 'poured' or 'breathed' into anything but body . . . and that 'phantasms' are 'spirits,' etc."[15] Translated into our present terms, Hobbes is condemning the confusion of single qualities with whole things; or the substitution of concrete images for simple ideas.

Specifically, the miraculism arises when the poet discovers by analogy an identity between objects which is partial, though it should be considerable, and proceeds to an identification which is complete. It is to be contrasted with the simile, which says "as if" or "like," and is scrupulous to keep the identification partial. In Cowley's passage above, the lover is saying, not for the first time in this literature: "She and I have exchanged our hearts." What has actually been exchanged is affections, and affections are only in a limited sense the same as hearts. Hearts are unlike affections in being engines that pump blood and form body; and it is a miracle if the poet represents the lady's affection as rendering her inside into man. But he succeeds, with this mixture, in depositing with us the image of a very powerful affection.

From the strict point of view of literary criticism it must be insisted that the miraculism which produces the humblest conceit is the same miraculism which supplies to religions their substantive content. (This is said to assert the dignity not of the conceits but of the religions.) It is the poet and nobody else who gives to the God a nature, a form, faculties, and a history; to the God, most comprehensive of all terms, which, if there were no poetic impulse to actualize or "find" Him, would remain the driest and deadest among Platonic ideas, with all intension sacrificed to infinite extension. The myths are conceits, born of metaphors. Religions are periodically produced by poets and destroyed by naturalists. Religion depends for its ontological validity upon a literary understanding, and that is why it is frequently misunderstood. The

15. *The English Works of Thomas Hobbes of Malmesbury*, Vol. III (London, 1939), 34.

metaphysical poets, perhaps like their spiritual fathers the mediæval Schoolmen, were under no illusions about this. They recognized myth, as they recognized the conceits, as a device of expression; its sanctity as the consequence of its public or social importance.

But whether the topics be Gods or amorous experiences, why do poets resort to miraculism? Hardly for the purpose of controverting natural fact or scientific theory. Religion pronounces about God only where science is silent and philosophy is negative; for a positive is wanted, that is, a God who has his being in the physical world as well as in the world of principles and abstractions. Likewise with the little secular enterprises of poetry too. Not now are the poets so brave, not for a very long time have they been so brave, as to dispute the scientists on what they call their "truth"; though it is a pity that the statement cannot be turned round. Poets will concede that every act of science is legitimate, and has its efficacy. The metaphysical poets of the seventeenth century particularly admired the methodology of science, and in fact they copied it, and their phrasing is often technical, spare, and polysyllabic, though they are not repeating actual science but making those metaphorical substitutions that are so arresting.

The intention of Metaphysical Poetry is to complement science, and improve discourse. Naturalistic discourse is incomplete, for either of two reasons. It has the minimum of physical content and starves the sensibility, or it has the maximum, as if to avoid the appearance of evil, but is laborious and pointless. Platonic Poetry is too idealistic, but Physical Poetry is too realistic, and realism is tedious and does not maintain interest. The poets therefore introduce the psychological device of the miracle. The predication which it permits is clean and quick but it is not a scientific predication. For scientific predication concludes an act of attention but miraculism initiates one. It leaves us looking, marvelling, and revelling in the thick *dinglich* substance that has just received its strange representation.

Let me suggest as a last word, in deference to a common Puritan scruple, that the predication of Metaphysical Poetry is true enough. It is not true like history, but no poetry is true in that sense, and only a part of science. It is true in the pragmatic sense in which some of the generalizations of science are true: it accomplishes precisely the sort of representation that it means to. It suggests to us that the object is perceptually or physically remarkable, and we had better attend to it.

CRITICISM, INC.

 T IS STRANGE, but nobody seems to have told us what exactly is the proper business of criticism. There are many critics who might tell us, but for the most part they are amateurs. So have the critics nearly always been amateurs; including the best ones. They have not been trained to criticism so much as they have simply undertaken a job for which no specific qualifications were required. It is far too likely that what they call criticism when they produce it is not the real thing.

There are three sorts of trained performers who would appear to have some of the competence that the critic needs. The first is the artist himself. He should know good art when he sees it; but his understanding is intuitive rather than dialectical—he cannot very well explain his theory of the thing. It is true that literary artists, with their command of language, are better critics of their own art than are other artists; probably the best critics of poetry we can now have are the poets. But one can well imagine that any artist's commentary on the art-work is valuable in the degree that he sticks to its technical effects, which he knows minutely, and about which he can certainly talk if he will.

The second is the philosopher, who should know all about the function of the fine arts. But the philosopher is apt to see a lot of wood and no trees, for his theory is very general and his acquaintance with the particular works of art is not persistent and intimate, especially his acquaintance with their technical effects. Or at least I suppose so, for philosophers have not proved that they can write close criticism by writing it; and I have the feeling that even their handsome generalizations are open to suspicion as being grounded more on other generalizations, those which form their prior philosophical stock, than on acute study of particulars.

The third is the university teacher of literature, who is styled professor, and who should be the very professional we need to take charge

This essay first appeared in the *Virginia Quarterly Review*, XIII (Autumn, 1937), 586–602; later reprinted in *The World's Body*, copyright © 1938 by Charles Scribner's Sons; copyright renewed 1966 by John Crowe Ransom. Reprinted with the permission of Charles Scribner's Sons.

of the critical activity. He is hardly inferior as critic to the philosopher, and perhaps not on the whole to the poet, but he is a greater disappointment because we have the right to expect more of him. Professors of literature are learned but not critical men. The professional morale of this part of the university staff is evidently low. It is as if, with conscious or unconscious cunning, they had appropriated every avenue of escape from their responsibility which was decent and official; so that it is easy for one of them without public reproach to spend a lifetime in compiling the data of literature and yet rarely or never commit himself to a literary judgment.

Nevertheless it is from the professors of literature, in this country the professors of English for the most part, that I should hope eventually for the erection of intelligent standards of criticism. It is their business.

Criticism must become more scientific, or precise and systematic, and this means that it must be developed by the collective and sustained effort of learned persons—which means that its proper seat is in the universities.

Scientific: but I do not think we need be afraid that criticism, trying to be a sort of science, will inevitably fail and give up in despair, or else fail without realizing it and enjoy some hollow and pretentious career. It will never be a very exact science, or even a nearly exact one. But neither will psychology, if that term continues to refer to psychic rather than physical phenomena; nor will sociology, as Pareto,[1] quite contrary to his intention, appears to have furnished us with evidence for believing; nor even will economics. It does not matter whether we call them sciences or just systematic studies; the total effort of each to be effective must be consolidated and kept going. The studies which I have mentioned have immeasurably improved in understanding since they were taken over by the universities, and the same career looks possible for criticism.

Rather than occasional criticism by amateurs, I should think the whole enterprise might be seriously taken in hand by professionals. Perhaps I use a distasteful figure, but I have the idea that what we need is Criticism, Inc., or Criticism, Ltd.

The principal resistance to such an idea will come from the present incumbents of the professorial chairs. But its adoption must come from

1. Vilfredo Pareto (1848–1923), Italian sociologist and economist known for his theory on mass and elite interaction.

them too. The idea of course is not a private one of my own. If it should be adopted before long, the credit would probably belong to Professor Ronald S. Crane, of the University of Chicago, more than to any other man. He is the first of the great professors to have advocated it as a major policy for departments of English. It is possible that he will have made some important academic history.

II

Professor Crane published recently a paper of great note in academic circles, on the reform of the courses in English. It appeared in *The English Journal,* under the title: "History Versus Criticism in the University Study of Literature."[2] He argues there that historical scholarship has been overplayed heavily in English studies, in disregard of the law of diminishing returns, and that the emphasis must now be shifted to the critical.

To me this means, simply: the students of the future must be permitted to study literature, and not merely about literature. But I think this is what the good students have always wanted to do. The wonder is that they have allowed themselves so long to be denied. But they have not always been amiable about it, and the whole affair presents much comic history.

At the University of Chicago, I believe that Professor Crane, with some others, is putting the revolution into effect in his own teaching, though for the time being perhaps with a limited programme, mainly the application of Aristotle's critical views. (My information is not at all exact.) The university is an opulent one, not too old to experience waves of reformational zeal, uninhibited as yet by bad traditions. Its department of English has sponsored plenty of old-line scholarship, but this is not the first time it has gone in for criticism. If the department should now systematically and intelligently build up a general school of literary criticism, I believe it would score a triumph that would be, by academic standards, spectacular. I mean that the alive and brilliant young English scholars all over the country would be saying they wanted to go there to do their work. That would place a new distinction upon the university, and it would eventually and profoundly modify the practices of many other institutions. It would be worth even more than Professor Crane's careful presentation of the theory.

2. *English Journal,* College Edition, XXIV (1935), 645–67.

This is not the first time that English professors have tilted against the historians, or "scholars," in the dull sense which that word has acquired. They did not score heavily, at those other times. Probably they were themselves not too well versed in the historical studies, so that it could be said with honest concern that they scarcely had the credentials to judge of such matters. At the same time they may have been too unproductive critically to offer a glowing alternative. The most important recent diversion from the orthodox course of literary studies was that undertaken by the New Humanists.[3] I regret to think that it was not the kind of diversion which I am advocating; nor the kind approved by Professor Crane, who comments briefly against it. Unquestionably the Humanists did divert, and the refreshment was grateful to anybody who felt resentful for having his literary predilections ignored under the schedule of historical learning. But in the long run the diversion proved to be nearly as unliterary as the round of studies from which it took off at a tangent. No picnic ideas were behind it.

The New Humanists were, and are, moralists; more accurately, historians and advocates of a certain moral system. Criticism is the attempt to define and enjoy the æsthetic or characteristic values of literature, but I suppose the Humanists would shudder at "æsthetic" as hard as ordinary historical scholars do. Did an official Humanist ever make any official play with the term? I do not remember it. The term "art" is slightly more ambiguous, and they have availed themselves of that; with centuries of loose usage behind it, art connotes, for those who like, high seriousness, and high seriousness connotes moral self-consciousness, and an inner check, and finally either Plato or Aristotle.

Mr. Babbitt consistently played on the terms classical and romantic.[4] They mean any of several things each, so that unquestionably Mr. Babbitt could make war on romanticism for purely moral reasons; and his preoccupation was ethical, not æsthetic. It is perfectly legitimate for the moralist to attack romantic literature if he can make out his case; for example, on the ground that it deals with emotions rather than principles, or the ground that its author discloses himself as flabby, intemperate, escapist, unphilosophical, or simply adolescent. The moral objection is probably valid; a romantic period testifies to a large-scale

---

3. A group of conservative critics, including Irving Babbitt and Paul Elmer More, prominent in the late 1920s. They stressed the rational nature of man and the cultivation of all of his faculties.

4. In *Literature and the American College: Essays in Defense of the Humanities* (1908); *Rousseau and Romanticism* (1919); *On Being Creative* (1932).

failure of adaptation, and defense of that failure to adapt, to the social and political environment; unless, if the Humanists will consent, it sometimes testifies to the failure of society and state to sympathize with the needs of the individual. But this is certainly not the charge that Mr. T. S. Eliot, a literary critic, brings against romanticism. His, if I am not mistaken, is æsthetic, though he may not ever care to define it very sharply. In other words, the literary critic also has something to say about romanticism, and it might come to something like this: that romantic literature is imperfect in objectivity, or "æsthetic distance," and that out of this imperfection comes its weakness of structure; that the romantic poet does not quite realize the æsthetic attitude, and is not the pure artist. Or it might come to something else. It would be quite premature to say that when a moralist is obliged to disapprove a work the literary critic must disapprove it too.

Following the excitement produced by the Humanist diversion, there is now one due to the Leftists, or Proletarians, who are also diversionists. Their diversion is likewise moral. It is just as proper for them to ferret out class-consciousness in literature, and to make literature serve the cause of loving-comradeship, as it is for the Humanists to censure romanticism and to use the topic, and the literary exhibit, as the occasion of reviving the Aristotelian moral canon. I mean that these are procedures of the same sort. Debate could never occur between a Humanist and a Leftist on æsthetic grounds for they are equally intent on ethical values. But the debate on ethical grounds would be very spirited, and it might create such a stir in a department conducting English studies that the conventional scholars there would find themselves slipping, and their pupils deriving from literature new and seductive excitements which would entice them away from their scheduled English exercises.

On the whole, however, the moralists, distinguished as they may be, are like those who have quarrelled with the ordinary historical studies on purer or more æsthetic grounds: they have not occupied in English studies the positions of professional importance. In a department of English, as in any other going business, the proprietary interest becomes vested, and in old and reputable departments the vestees have uniformly been gentlemen who have gone through the historical mill. Their laborious Ph.D.'s and historical publications are their patents. Naturally, quite spontaneously, they would tend to perpetuate a system in which the power and the glory belonged to them. But English scholars in this country can rarely have better credentials than those which

Professor Crane has earned in his extensive field, the eighteenth century. It is this which makes his disaffection significant.

It is really atrocious policy for a department to abdicate its own self-respecting identity. The department of English is charged with the understanding and the communication of literature, an art, yet it has usually forgotten to inquire into the peculiar constitution and structure of its product. English might almost as well announce that it does not regard itself as entirely autonomous, but as a branch of the department of history, with the option of declaring itself occasionally a branch of the department of ethics. It is true that the historical and the ethical studies will cluster round objects which for some reason are called artistic objects. But the thing itself the professors do not have to contemplate; and only last spring the head of English studies in a graduate school fabulously equipped made the following impromptu disclaimer to a victim who felt aggrieved at having his own studies forced in the usual direction: "This is a place for exact scholarship, and you want to do criticism. Well, we don't allow criticism here, because that is something which anybody can do."

But one should never speak impromptu in one's professional capacity. This speech may have betrayed a fluttery private apprehension which should not have been made public: that you can never be critical and be exact at the same time, that history is firmer ground than æsthetics, and that, to tell the truth, criticism is a painful job for the sort of mind that wants to be very sure about things. Not in that temper did Aristotle labor towards a critique in at least one branch of letters; nor in that temper are strong young minds everywhere trying to sharpen their critical apparatus into precision tools, in this decade as never before.

It is not anybody who can do criticism. And for an example, the more eminent (as historical scholar) the professor of English, the less apt he is to be able to write decent criticism, unless it is about another professor's work of historical scholarship, in which case it is not literary criticism. The professor may not be without æsthetic judgments respecting an old work, especially if it is "in his period," since it must often have been judged by authorities whom he respects. Confronted with a new work, I am afraid it is very rare that he finds anything particular to say. Contemporary criticism is not at all in the hands of those who direct the English studies. Contemporary literature, which is almost obliged to receive critical study if it receives any at all, since it is hardly capable of the usual historical commentary, is barely officialized as a proper field for serious study.

Here is contemporary literature, waiting for its criticism; where are the professors of literature? They are watering their own gardens; elucidating the literary histories of their respective periods. So are their favorite pupils. The persons who save the occasion, and rescue contemporary literature from the humiliation of having to go without a criticism, are the men who had to leave the university before their time because they felt themselves being warped into mere historians; or those who finished the courses and took their punishment but were tough, and did not let it engross them and spoil them. They are home-made critics. Naturally they were not too wise, these amateurs who furnish our reviews and critical studies. But when they distinguish themselves, the universities which they attended can hardly claim more than a trifling share of the honor.

It is not so in economics, chemistry, sociology, theology, and architecture. In these branches it is taken for granted that criticism of the performance is the prerogative of the men who have had formal training in its theory and technique. The historical method is useful, and may be applied readily to any human performance whatever. But the exercise does not become an obsession with the university men working in the other branches; only the literary scholars wish to convert themselves into pure historians. This has gone far to nullify the usefulness of a departmental personnel larger, possibly, than any other, and of the lavish endowment behind it.

III

Presumably the departments of English exist in order to communicate the understanding of the literary art. That will include both criticism and also whatever may be meant by "appreciation." This latter term seems to stand for the kind of understanding that is had intuitively, without benefit of instruction, by merely being constrained to spend time in the presence of the literary product. It is true that some of the best work now being done in departments is by the men who do little more than read well aloud, enforcing a private act of appreciation upon the students. One remembers how good a service that may be, thinking perhaps of Professor Copeland of Harvard, or Dean Cross at Greeley Teachers College.[5] And there are men who try to get at the same thing

5. Charles Townsend Copeland, professor at Harvard 1893–1928; Ethan Allen Cross, professor and dean at Greeley Teachers' College 1906–1940.

in another way, which they would claim is surer: by requiring a great deal of memory work, in order to enforce familiarity with fine poetry. These might defend their strategy by saying that at any rate the work they required was not as vain as the historical rigmarole which the scholars made their pupils recite, if the objective was really literary understanding and not external information. But it would be a misuse of terms to employ the word instruction for the offices either of the professors who read aloud or of those who require the memory work. The professors so engaged are properly curators, and the museum of which they have the care is furnished with the cherished literary masterpieces, just as another museum might be filled with paintings. They conduct their squads from one work to another, making appropriate pauses or reverent gestures, but their own obvious regard for the masterpieces is somewhat contagious, and contemplation is induced. Naturally they are grateful to the efficient staff of colleagues in the background who have framed the masterpieces, hung them in the proper schools and in the chronological order, and prepared the booklet of information about the artists and the occasions. The colleagues in their turn probably feel quite happy over this division of labor, thinking that they have done the really productive work, and that it is appropriate now if less able men should undertake a little salesmanship.

Behind appreciation, which is private, and criticism, which is public and negotiable, and represents the last stage of English studies, is historical scholarship. It is indispensable. But it is instrumental and cannot be the end itself. In this respect historical studies have the same standing as linguistic studies: language and history are aids.

On behalf of the historical studies. Without them what could we make of Chaucer, for instance? I cite the familiar locus of the "hard" scholarship, the center of any program of advanced studies in English which intends to initiate the student heroically, and once for all, into the historical discipline. Chaucer writes allegories for historians to decipher, he looks out upon institutions and customs unfamiliar to us. Behind him are many writers in various tongues from whom he borrows both forms and materials. His thought bears constant reference to classical and mediæval philosophies and sciences which have passed from our effective knowledge. An immense labor of historical adaptation is necessary before our minds are ready to make the æsthetic approach to Chaucer.

Or to any author out of our own age. The mind with which we enter into an old work is not the mind with which we make our living, or enter into a contemporary work. It is under sharp restraints, and it is quite differently furnished. Out of our actual contemporary mind we have to cancel a great deal that has come there under modern conditions but was not in the earlier mind at all. This is a technique on the negative side, a technique of suspension; difficult for practical persons, literal scientists, and aggressive moderns who take pride in the "truth" or the "progress" which enlightened man, so well represented in their own instance, has won. Then, on the positive side, we must supply the mind with the precise beliefs and ways of thought it had in that former age, with the specific content in which history instructs us; this is a technique of make-believe. The whole act of historical adaptation, through such techniques, is a marvellous feat of flexibility. Certainly it is a thing hard enough to justify university instruction. But it is not sufficient for an English program.

The achievement of modern historical scholarship in the field of English literature has been, in the aggregate, prodigious; it should be very proud. A good impression of the volume of historical learning now available for the students of English may be quickly had from inspecting a few chapters of the Cambridge History, with the bibliographies.[6] Or, better, from inspecting one of a large number of works which have come in since the Cambridge History: the handbooks, which tell all about the authors, such as Chaucer, Shakespeare, Milton, and carry voluminous bibliographies; or the period books, which tell a good deal about whole periods of literature.

There is one sense in which it may be justly said that we can never have too much scholarship. We cannot have too much of it if the critical intelligence functions, and has the authority to direct it. There is hardly a critical problem which does not require some arduous exercises in fact-finding, but each problem is quite specific about the kind of facts it wants. Mountains of facts may have been found already, but often they have been found for no purpose at all except the purpose of piling up into a big exhibit, to offer intoxicating delights to the academic population.

To those who are æsthetically minded among students, the rewards of many a historical labor will have to be disproportionately slight. The official Chaucer course is probably over ninety-five per cent historical and linguistic, and less than five per cent æsthetic or critical. A thing of

6. *The Cambridge History of English Literature*, edited by A. W. Ward and A. R. Waller, 1907–1916.

beauty is a joy forever. But it is not improved because the student has had to tie his tongue before it. It is an artistic object, with a heroic human labor behind it, and on these terms it calls for public discussion. The dialectical possibilities are limitless, and when we begin to realize them we are engaged in criticism.

IV

What is criticism? Easier to ask, What is criticism not? It is an act now notoriously arbitrary and undefined. We feel certain that the critical act is not one of those which the professors of literature habitually perform, and cause their students to perform. And it is our melancholy impression that it is not often cleanly performed in those loose compositions, by writers of perfectly indeterminate qualifications, that appear in print as reviews of books.

Professor Crane excludes from criticism works of historical scholarship and of Neo-Humanism, but more exclusions are possible than that. I should wish to exclude:

1. Personal registrations, which are declarations of the effect of the art-work upon the critic as reader. The first law to be prescribed to criticism, if we may assume such authority, is that it shall be objective, shall cite the nature of the object rather than its effects upon the subject. Therefore it is hardly criticism to assert that the proper literary work is one that we can read twice; or one that causes in us some remarkable physiological effect, such as oblivion of the outer world, the flowing of tears, visceral or laryngeal sensations, and such like; or one that induces perfect illusion, or brings us into a spiritual ecstasy; or even one that produces a catharsis of our emotions. Aristotle concerned himself with this last in making up his definition of tragedy—though he did not fail to make some acute analyses of the objective features of the work also. I have read that some modern Broadway producers of comedy require a reliable person to seat himself in a trial audience and count the laughs; their method of testing is not so subtle as Aristotle's, but both are concerned with the effects. Such concern seems to reflect the view that art comes into being because the artist, or the employer behind him, has designs upon the public, whether high moral designs or box-office ones. It is an odious view in either case, because it denies the autonomy of the artist as one who interests himself in the artistic object in his own right, and likewise the autonomy of the work itself as existing for its own sake. (We may define a chemical as something which

can effect a certain cure, but that is not its meaning to the chemist; and we may define toys, if we are weary parents, as things which keep our children quiet, but that is not what they are to engineers.) Furthermore, we must regard as uncritical the use of an extensive vocabulary which ascribes to the object properties really discovered in the subject, as: *moving, exciting, entertaining, pitiful; great,* if I am not mistaken, and *admirable*, on a slightly different ground; and, in strictness, *beautiful* itself.

2. Synopsis and paraphrase. The high-school classes and the women's clubs delight in these procedures, which are easiest of all the systematic exercises possible in the discussion of literary objects. I do not mean that the critic never uses them in his analysis of fiction and poetry, but he does not consider plot or story as identical with the real content. Plot is an abstract from content.

3. Historical studies. These have a very wide range, and include studies of the general literary background; author's biography, of course with special reference to autobiographical evidences in the work itself; bibliographical items; the citation of literary originals and analogues, and therefore what, in general, is called comparative literature. Nothing can be more stimulating to critical analysis than comparative literature. But it may be conducted only superficially, if the comparisons are perfunctory and mechanical, or if the scholar is content with merely making the parallel citations.

4. Linguistic studies. Under this head come those studies which define the meaning of unusual words and idioms, including the foreign and archaic ones, and identify the allusions. The total benefit of linguistics for criticism would be the assurance that the latter was based on perfect logical understanding of the content, or "interpretation." Acquaintance with all the languages and literatures in the world would not necessarily produce a critic, though it might save one from damaging errors.

5. Moral studies. The moral standard applied is the one appropriate to the reviewer; it may be the Christian ethic, or the Aristotelian one, or the new proletarian gospel. But the moral content is not the whole content, which should never be relinquished.

6. Any other special studies which deal with some abstract or prose content taken out of the work. Nearly all departments of knowledge may conceivably find their own materials in literature, and take them out. Studies have been made of Chaucer's command of mediæval sciences, of Spenser's view of the Irish question, of Shakespeare's under-

standing of the law, of Milton's geography, of Hardy's place-names. The critic may well inform himself of these materials as possessed by the artist, but his business as critic is to discuss the literary assimilation of them.

V

With or without such useful exercises as these, probably assuming that the intelligent reader has made them for himself, comes the critical act itself.

Mr. Austin Warren, whose writings I admire, is evidently devoted to the academic development of the critical project.[7] Yet he must be a fair representative of what a good deal of academic opinion would be when he sees no reason why criticism should set up its own house, and try to dissociate itself from historical and other scholarly studies; why not let all sorts of studies, including the critical ones, flourish together in the same act of sustained attention, or the same scheduled "course"? But so they are supposed to do at present; and I would only ask him whether he considers that criticism prospers under this arrangement. It has always had the chance to go ahead in the hands of the professors of literature, and it has not gone ahead. A change of policy suggests itself. Strategy requires now, I should think, that criticism receive its own charter of rights and function independently. If he fears for its foundations in scholarship, the scholars will always be on hand to reprove it when it tries to function on an unsound scholarship.

I do not suppose the reviewing of books can be reformed in the sense of being turned into pure criticism. The motives of the reviewers are as much mixed as the performance, and indeed they condition the mixed performance. The reviewer has a job of presentation and interpretation as well as criticism. The most we can ask of him is that he know when the criticism begins, and that he make it as clean and definitive as his business permits. To what authority may he turn?

I know of no authority. For the present each critic must be his own authority. But I know of one large class of studies which is certainly critical, and necessary, and I can suggest another sort of study for the critic's consideration if he is really ambitious.

Studies in the technique of the art belong to criticism certainly. They

7. See, for example, Warren's "The Scholar and the Critic: An Essay in Meditation," *University of Toronto Quarterly*, VI (1937), 267–77, and "The Criticism of Meaning and the Meaning of Criticism," *Sewanee Review*, XXXVI (1938), 213–22.

cannot belong anywhere else, because the technique is not peculiar to any prose materials discoverable in the work of art, nor to anything else but the unique form of that art. A very large volume of studies is indicated by this classification. They would be technical studies of poetry, for instance, the art I am specifically discussing, if they treated its metric; its inversions, solecisms, lapses from the prose norm of language, and from close prose logic; its tropes; its fictions, or inventions, by which it secures "æsthetic distance" and removes itself from history; or any other devices, on the general understanding that any systematic usage which does not hold good for prose is a poetic device.

A device with a purpose: the superior critic is not content with the compilation of the separate devices; they suggest to him a much more general question. The critic speculates on why poetry, through its devices, is at such pains to dissociate itself from prose at all, and what it is trying to represent that cannot be represented by prose.

I intrude here with an idea of my own, which may serve as a starting point of discussion. Poetry distinguishes itself from prose on the technical side by the devices which are, precisely, its means of escaping from prose. Something is continually being killed by prose which the poet wants to preserve. But this must be put philosophically. (Philosophy sounds hard, but it deals with natural and fundamental forms of experience.)

The critic should regard the poem as nothing short of a desperate ontological or metaphysical manœuvre. The poet himself, in the agony of composition, has something like this sense of his labors. The poet perpetuates in his poem an order of existence which in actual life is constantly crumbling beneath his touch. His poem celebrates the object which is real, individual, and qualitatively infinite. He knows that his practical interests will reduce this living object to a mere utility, and that his sciences will disintegrate it for their convenience into their respective abstracts. The poet wishes to defend his object's existence against its enemies, and the critic wishes to know what he is doing, and how. The critic should find in the poem a total poetic or individual object which tends to be universalized, but is not permitted to suffer this fate.[8] His identification of the poetic object is in terms of the universal or commonplace object to which it tends, and of the tissue, or totality of connotation, which holds it secure. How does he make out the univer-

---

8. Ransom is arguing that the "irrelevant texture" of a poem is never completely assimilated into its logical structure.

sal object? It is the prose object, which any forthright prosy reader can discover to him by an immediate paraphrase; it is a kind of story, character, thing, scene, or moral principle. And where is the tissue that keeps it from coming out of the poetic object? That is, for the laws of the prose logic, its superfluity; and I think I would even say, its irrelevance.

A poet is said to be distinguishable in terms of his style. It is a comprehensive word, and probably means: the general character of his irrelevances, or tissues. All his technical devices contribute to it, elaborating or individualizing the universal, the core-object; likewise all his material detail. For each poem even, ideally, there is distinguishable a logical object or universal, but at the same time a tissue of irrelevance from which it does not really emerge. The critic has to take the poem apart, or analyze it, for the sake of uncovering these features. With all the finesse possible, it is rude and patchy business by comparison with the living integrity of the poem. But without it there could hardly be much understanding of the value of poetry, or of the natural history behind any adult poem.

The language I have used may sound too formidable, but I seem to find that a profound criticism generally works by some such considerations. However the critic may spell them, the two terms are in his mind: the prose core to which he can violently reduce the total object, and the differentia, residue, or tissue, which keeps the object poetical or entire. The character of the poem resides for the good critic in its way of exhibiting the residuary quality. The character of the poet is defined by the kind of prose object to which his interest evidently attaches, plus his way of involving it firmly in the residuary tissue. And doubtless, incidentally, the wise critic can often read behind the poet's public character his private history as a man with a weakness for lapsing into some special form of prosy or scientific bondage.

Similar considerations hold, I think, for the critique of fiction, or of the non-literary arts. I remark this for the benefit of philosophers who believe, with propriety, that the arts are fundamentally one. But I would prefer to leave the documentation to those who are better qualified.

THE ARTS AND THE PHILOSOPHERS

LEARLY the *International Encyclopedia of Unified Science*[1] is to be a philosophical enterprise, not a scientific one: *scientia scientiarum*. The editor of a literary journal follows it principally with this concern: will it include also *scientia artium?*

The editors seem to think it will, if perhaps somewhat incidentally. To me their theory means that the arts may be taken as quasi-sciences. In the terms of the Encyclopedia (or at least in Professor Morris' terms), the arts present us like the sciences with all the "dimensions" of meaning. Thus: with *semantical* (or objective) content which may be less systematic but is of the same sort as the semantical content of science; with *syntactical* relations which are ordinarily of a passing degree of rigor where the sciences require them to be perfectly rigorous; and especially, characteristically, with a great deal of unashamed *pragmatical* content, that is, free, direct, and frequent expression of personal interest, such as the pure sciences try their hardest to rule out. But I would suggest that to read the arts this way is to misread them, and that a much more radical approach is needed. Probably nowhere can there be a case where the "unification" of different sciences will seem so violent as the attempt to unify the arts under the same rule with the sciences.

As to the survival and prestige of the arts in the modern world, I find nothing but encouragement in the tone of the Encyclopedia, though there is room for a good deal more than I seem to see there.

The arts begin to stand today in the position which religion, an elder sister, was made to occupy during the last century: their disrepute in the intellectual circles increases almost at the rate at which philosophers find the time to attend to them. Philosophy in its public rôle has been likened to a sort of court to which science and art, or other natural disputants, may resort for "justice" for their claims. But this court is

This essay appeared in the *Kenyon Review*, I (Spring, 1939), 194–99. Reprinted by permission of Helen Ransom Forman.

1. *Foundations of the Unity of Science: Toward an International Encyclopedia of Unified Science* (Chicago, 1938–).

107

packed, and not with artists, or religionists, but with positivists and "naturalists," who are the proper attorneys for science. It has generally been packed in this sense; not often so decidedly. The court seems on the face of it to need an infusion of new blood. With or without great hope we must wait for the gradual accession of more jurists possessed of—of what equipment or learning, if we must be specific? Of a "literary" sense.

Philosophers need to "have everything" if they are to be really responsible. It is in default of literary sense that science-philosophers passing opinions upon the arts permit themselves to be foolish, and also to be harsh and destructive. Critically, their competence is for appraising discourse that is explicit, and it leads them to make many exemplary rejections in the name of scientific integrity. Coming to the arts, their puritan parsimony, killing eventually to all the arts, is applied most confidently to literature, in which they perhaps imagine themselves to be especially knowing because literature appears to employ language, and they employ it too. But it has become clear in our time, as probably not before, that literature is fully as esoteric and impenetrable a record for the mind of scientific cast as is any other art. Its language and that of science are two languages. A language that intends to be explicit, or literal, is not the same as one whose genius and incessant effort are for the implicit, or literary. There is little reason to expect that philosophers bred up to the one language would know how to speak, or even receive, the other language. Attainment in this second language is not made prerequisite to the investiture of the Doctors of Philosophy.

It is true that the arts, and literature not least, have sometimes gone far towards losing caste on their own motion. They have become explicit. Explicit is abstract and graphic; in science, it is the item which is formulated, therefore lifted out of the natural context, so that the context may be made invisible; in the half-hearted arts, it is the item which is too heavily underscored, and developed with systematic attention, so that the context may be subordinated and ignored. It is my impression that perhaps most of the poems which come to an editor's desk nowadays were condemned before they began because the impulse behind them was a conceptual rather than an artistic one. The Restoration and 18th Century in England constituted a whole literary period whose men of letters actually proposed to fall into step with the science-philosophers—Hobbes being the most eminent drill-sergeant—and to regard literature as nothing but science dressed in the costume of the period; as the pretty equivalent of science, suited to gentlemen and

ladies of breeding, and offering no real treason to the revelation which
was science. The consequence of this strategy was hardly, or barely, a
poetry, and for the most part a "bourgeois" document, in the odious
sense assigned to that term by radical political thinkers today. The 17th
and 18th Century poetries are existences almost in two different worlds
and the difference is, if an effective trope may be instituted to account
for it, that the 17th Century one had the difficult dimension of depth
and the 18th Century one succeeded only in being flat.

I invite attention to the kind of objection which Mr. Warren, in this
issue, takes to the art of Matthew Arnold; and to the ground of the criticism which is offered by some of the other reviewers.[2]

There have been plenty of "aesthetic systems" to go by, if we can go
by authority where none of the authorities seems right. The most familiar ways of construing art are two in number, and they equally regard it
as a thing which is nearly science. The first way, which was that of the
18th and generally the 19th Century critics, and as I think the one
given philosophical standing by Hegel, is to regard art as the *decorative*
or "sensuous" version of science; the truths are eminently discoverable
in this version, and it may well escape the censor if it does not try really
to hide them or subvert them. Technically, from the point of view of scientific purity, the arts in this version present good science trailing
clouds of glory which are made of—irrelevance. But as for a new and
right theory of art this one points undoubtedly in its direction; it is a
good lead. The second way is the more recent, and has been fancied by
the psychologists, especially those interested like Mr. I. A. Richards in
defending the creature's right to "expression" or "integration," and is to
this effect: art is the *emotional* version of science. I take it that this was
substantially Mr. Burke's understanding in his *Southern Review* essay
where he opposed a "poetic" meaning to the strict semantical one; he
was especially, and no doubt justly, interested in retaining the moral
resonances to go along with the pure objective presentations for the
benefit of good right-minded experiments.[3]

For these two views equally, art is permitted to save its neck on the
ground that it offers popular equivalents of science although, in strictness, science probably has, and need have, no equivalents. Intellectually its status is perfectly ignominious, for at least two reasons: (1) its

2. Robert Penn Warren, "Arnold vs. the 19th Century" (review of Lionel Trilling's *Matthew Arnold*), *Kenyon Review*, I (Spring, 1939), 217–21.
3. Kenneth Burke, "Semantic and Poetic Meaning," *Southern Review*, III (1938–39),
501–23.

semantic content, the net result in knowledge as hard science would define it, is in any work of art so trifling and commonplace that it is as if the artist were a second-rate parrot; and (2) while the artist complicates this content greatly, it is by diffusing it with stuff which, for the scientific thinker, and the occasion in hand, is nonsense.

The Encyclopedists are talking about the language of science. I imagine that now is a splendid time for the aestheticians, inside or outside the Encyclopedia, to make an assertion which would be round, bold, metaphysical, just, and tactically perfect. To this effect: art has a language of its own; it is not the same as the language of science; its semantical meanings cannot be rendered in the language of science. Art fixes a kind of knowledge of which science has no understanding, and which gentlemen too confined within the scientific habit cannot approach intelligently. Now it is not that these gentlemen look at art with intelligence, and then exclude some of its meaning with scorn; for they do not in the first place rise to a grasp of this kind of meaning, which is qualitatively unique and indivisible. And thinking of the trope by which I attempted above to describe this meaning, I believe it may be suggested that the linguistic achievement of art is, as we see very clearly in poetry, just the *trope*. Its object of knowledge, its *designatum* and *denotatum*, is an object in the round, a figure of three dimensions, so to speak; in technical language a singular and individual object. That is not an object which scientific knowledge has, or affects, or desires. Science with its propositions, art with its tropes. We are aware of how science abhors the figurative, the tropical, and that is significant. Art on its side abhors propositions, or it should. When the trope begins to reduce to a proposition, we are coming out of the solid world of art into the abstract plane of science. We are also relapsing further from the world of actuality, of which art is the closest fiction that we can have.

Literature is a very ambiguous procedure; it seems to mean business and turns out to mean something else. I must waive the analogies which the other arts may offer, or may not offer, and make a further remark about the language of literature. It employs the same words or "signs" for the most part as the language of science does. It employs the same syntax for the most part also. But not, I think, the same syntax in its widest sense as logic and method. A historical supposition seems important here. It would seem that science comes first, with its highly selective rendering of a given reality, which consists in attending to some single one of its aspects; art comes afterwards, in what mood we may imagine, and attempts to restore the body which science has emptied. On the surface it looks like a merely inconsequent and unbusinesslike science, but we have to read more closely than that, and indeed until we see that under its apparent conformity to the "syntactical rule" it is really repudiating the rule. It must increase the capacity of the language till it will entertain a *designatum* which theoretically, so far as I know, may be beyond the constitutional range of language. Its simplest trick, probably the staple one in its repertory, gives us such a piece of discourse as

> The trees stood up against the sky.

The difficulty in finding a scientific reading of this sentence is to discover a "dominant sign"; to determine whether a botanical discourse is being initiated, or one in physics, or one in optics. The succeeding lines so far as I recall them throw no light upon the problem, and it is never resolved. The line, and the poem, have improvised a successful immunity which preserves the object, a "total situation," from suffering siege and reduction. This is a tactic of simple stubborn obstruction.

A really definitive study of the tricks that poetry plays with syntax would be illuminating, and delicious. But I return to an easier topic: the future of the arts in a society in which science claims to be paramount. It was upon the exclusive motion and prosecution of natural science that the tropes of established religion were accused and convicted of uttering falsehood. That showed a wide failure of understanding, and, to be precise, of literary understanding, reflecting upon the intelligence of the attorneys, the court, and the jury. But art is much more protean and elusive than any established religion can be; they will find it harder to obtain conviction, and impossible to keep the prisoner long confined.

HONEY AND GALL

N 1922 Hardy published *Late Lyrics and Earlier,* a group of 152 poems entirely in his vein, and containing at least some of his finest pieces. In his vein: they show overwhelmingly his preoccupation with the irony of life, and ideologically as well as technically furnish authorization enough for a few general remarks about the poet.

I choose this volume for the sake of the Apology, the prose piece of about three thousand words which prefaces it. There he writes chiefly in protest against his critics' charge of "pessimism." He argues that this is indeed a very dark world, and in part as follows:

> If I may be forgiven for quoting my own old words, let me repeat what I printed in this relation more than twenty years ago, and wrote much earlier, in a poem entitled "In Tenebris":
>
> > If way to the Better there be, it exacts a full look at the Worst:
>
> that is to say, by the exploration of reality, and its frank recognition stage by stage along the survey, with an eye to the best consummation possible: briefly, evolutionary meliorism. But it is called pessimism nevertheless; under which word, expressed with condemnatory emphasis, it is regarded by many as some pernicious new thing (though so old as to underlie the Gospel scheme, and even to permeate the Greek drama); and the subject is charitably left to decent silence, as if further comment were needless.
>
> Happily there are some who feel such Levitical passing-by to be, alas, by no means a permanent dismissal of the matter; that comment on where the world stands is very much the reverse of needless in these disordered years of our prematurely afflicted century: that amendment and not madness lies that way. And looking down the future these few hold fast to the same: that whether the human and kindred animal races survive till the exhaustion or destruction of the globe, or whether these races perish and are succeeded by others before that conclusion comes, pain to all upon it, tongued or dumb, shall be kept down to a minimum by loving-kindness, operating through scientific knowledge, and actuated by the

This essay appeared in the *Southern Review,* VI (Summer, 1940), 2–19. Reprinted by permission of the Louisiana State University Press.

modicum of free will conjecturally possessed by organic life when the mighty necessitating forces—unconscious or other—that have "the balancings of the clouds," happen to be in equilibrium, which may or may not be often.

And the Apology concludes:

> It may indeed be a forlorn hope, a mere dream, that of an alliance between religion, which must be retained unless the world is to perish, and complete rationality, which must come, unless also the world is to perish, by means of the interfusing effect of poetry—"the breath and finer spirit of all knowledge; the impassioned expression of science," as it was defined by an English poet who was quite orthodox in his ideas. But if it be true, as Comte argued, that advance is never in a straight line, but in a looped orbit, we may, in the aforesaid ominous moving backward, be doing it *pour mieux sauter*, drawing back for a spring. I repeat that I forlornly hope so, notwithstanding the supercilious regard of hope by Schopenhauer, von Hartmann, and other philosophers down to Einstein who have my respect. But one dares not prophesy. Physical, chronological, and other contingencies keep me in these days from critical studies and literary circles
>
> > Where once we held debate, a band
> > Of youthful friends, on mind and art
>
> (if one may quote Tennyson in this century). Hence I cannot know how things are going so well as I used to know them, and the aforesaid limitations must quite prevent my knowing henceforward.[1]

We are probably not overly impressed with the poet's prose metaphysic. But through many poems we have won acquaintance with a poet whose character is homely, tender, honest, and magnanimous, so that we will demand an affection, if not a veneration, from the decent critic before he remark upon this poet's failure to recognize the bias of his own poems. By this mood we will distinguish ourselves from the harsher critics referred to in the text.

An unself-consciousness, such as belongs to a very individual and stubborn personality, prevented him from an objective appreciation of his eccentricity. "It is true," he says again in the Apology, "that some grave, positive, stark, delineations are interspersed among those of the passive, lighter, and traditional sort presumably nearer to stereotyped tastes." But if we turn through the volume we will find actually that about 132 poems of the grave sort are interspersed among about a score

---

1. In *Collected Poems of Thomas Hardy* (New York, 1923), 531–32.

of poems of the lighter sort, some of the latter far less light than they
might be. The most unquestionably light poem is the first one in the
volume, "Weathers," which I will quote:

I

This is the weather the cuckoo likes,
    And so do I;
When showers betumble the chestnut spikes,
    And nestlings fly:
And the little brown nightingale bills his best,
And they sit outside at "The Travellers' Rest,"
And maids come forth sprig-muslin drest,
And citizens dream of the south and west,
    And so do I.

II

This is the weather the shepherd shuns,
    And so do I;
When beeches drip in browns and duns,
    And thresh, and ply;
And hill-hid tides throb, throe on throe,
And meadow rivulets overflow,
And drops on gate-bars hang in a row,
And rooks in families homeward go,
    And so do I.

This pleasant poem might be said to claim that life is good enough in
any weather, the rainy as well as the sunny. But it is a deceptive beginning for the volume; it is refuted a hundred times, and, for example,
by the "Country Wedding," which I select because it too deals with
weathers, but much more in the Hardy mood. The poem has the subtitle, A Fiddler's Story. I quote the first two and last two stanzas:

Little fogs were gathered in every hollow,
But the purple hillocks enjoyed fine weather
As we marched with our fiddles over the heather
—How it comes back!—to their wedding that day.

Our getting here brought our neighbours and all, O!
Till, two and two, the couples stood ready.
And her father said: "Souls, for God's sake, be steady!"
And we strung up our fiddles, and sounded out "A."

. . . .

A grand wedding 'twas! And what would follow
We never thought. Or that we should have buried her

> On the same day with the man that married her,
> A day like the first, half hazy, half clear.

> Yes: little fogs were in every hollow,
> Though the purple hillocks enjoyed fine weather,
> When we went to play 'em to church together,
> And carried 'em there in an after year.

So the weather was equivocal, and was designed no better for the wedding than for the funeral. A special and very characteristic pointedness in the irony is provided in the circumstance that the lovers must be buried, as they were married, on the same day. For Hardy liked to tighten up the dramatic irony, as if to make it more imperative upon us, by his own violent contriving.

The author's philosophical remarks about his poetic intentions seem after the event, and unrelated to his actual poetic occasions. For what is evolutionary meliorism? It is the synthetic oleomargarine which stern Darwinians used to spread over the bread of doctrine when they denied themselves the old-fashioned butter of belief in a moral order. There may be some of it in the Hardy novels, I do not know; there is none in the verse, and there could scarcely be any way of its getting there. The ironic poems never tell us about evolutionary meliorism, nor do they exemplify this or anything evolutionary, but just continue to be ironic, as before, in a confused and unimproving universe. The poems of Hardy number close to a thousand, and all by themselves constitute a literature of irony which is solid perhaps beyond any parallel.

II

But there seems to be no absolute necessity requiring the quality of the poetic texture to deteriorate under the ironic thesis. It generally does not happen in Hardy's poetry.

Comparison suggests itself between Hardy and Housman. Both poets are ironists, and both use principally what we in America would call a "regional" material; respectively, life on all social levels in the rural counties of Wessex, and the humbler life of the farmer boy and soldier of the Queen, the Shropshire Lad. For the comparison I will take *Shropshire Lad* LIV:

> With rue my heart is laden
> For golden friends I had,
> For many a rose-lipt maiden
> And many a lightfoot lad.

> By brooks too broad for leaping
> The lightfoot boys are laid;
> The rose-lipt girls are sleeping
> In fields where roses fade.

And from Hardy I believe "The Garden Seat" will do:

> Its former green is blue and thin,
> And its once firm legs sink in and in;
> Soon it will break down unaware,
> Soon it will break down unaware.
>
> At night when reddest flowers are black
> Those who once sat thereon come back;
> Quite a row of them sitting there,
> Quite a row of them sitting there.
>
> With them the seat does not break down,
> Nor winter freeze them, nor floods drown,
> For they are light as upper air,
> For they are light as upper air!

These are not the best poems of their authors, but the former poem is much closer to Housman's best than the latter to Hardy's, so that I feel all the more assured in my comparative estimate of the two poets.

Both poets are celebrating mortality, and the ignominious ending of those who once were quick and beautiful. Housman's speech is much the more extravagant, but in trying to be heroic (if it tries) it succeeds only in being florid and insincere. Hardy, who is extremely ingenious and experienced in catching fresh perceptions of his brutal fact, commits himself to an odd but competent version of it, and does not even begin to let himself be led astray by the blandishments of rhetoric.

As for the Housman poem. That first line is painful, grandiloquent, incredible to the naturalistic imagination. And I think we must have misgivings as to the propriety of linking this degree of desolation with the loss of friends in wholesale quantities. Grief is not exactly cumulative, nor proportionate to its numerical occasions; it is the quality of a single grief rather than the total quantity of all the griefs that we expect to be developed in a poem, if the poem is in the interest of the deepest possible sentiment. The *golden* might pass without serious animadversion, except that the image needs a little specification: Shakespeare's golden lads and girls were in better order by virtue of the contrast with the chimney-sweepers. The more particular epithets which attend

Housman's lads and girls, *lightfoot* for the former and *rose-lipt* for the latter, receive a good deal of specification, and in fact the business developed out of these terms "makes" the concluding stanza, and therefore the ironical whole, if anything does. But what is this business? The lads for all their light-footedness lie by brooks too broad for their leaping; are they then buried beside broad streams? I think the poet means that they are buried beside mere brooks, but that any brooks now are too broad for them, and that lightfoot has become a misnomer in their present condition. Still I feel, without meaning to be too quarrelsome, that there is a failure of specification to account for the brooks; persons are not ordinarily buried beside brooks. And the rose-lipt girls sleep in fields where roses fade, but that does not seem so shameful an end. Roses fade in the best of fields—not in the fabulous fields where the amaranth grows, it may be, but those fields are not in question. What we require is an image to carry the fading of the rosy lips; to be buried in the ground involves this disgrace sufficiently for brutal logic but not for poetic imagination. The fading of the roses that grow out of the ground is really an image inviting a mitigation, and we must take care to remember at once that the rosy lips will not revive though we know the actual roses will bloom again; the item runs counter to the ironic intention. The ironical detail of this poem is therefore fairly inept. The imagination of this poet is not a trained and faithful instrument, or at least it does not work well for him here. That is not an additional charge, however, to saying that the poem as a whole is not very satisfactory, for it is the specific ground of the poem's failure. There cannot be a fine poetry without a fine poetic texture.

In Hardy's poem the living people have died and become ghosts. We have to concede Hardy's ghost-people early in our acquaintance with his verse. They are ubiquitous but they do not strain the will to believe unless we are very literal naturalists. Their behavior is wholly decorous, for they do nothing but haunt their former scenes and mouth their memories, they are invisible to all but the imaginative or the conscience-ridden among the living, and they never try to meddle in the workings of the natural world from which they have been severed. But here the ghosts of the dead persons are subordinate, so far as the text is concerned, to another instance of mortality: the imminent mortality of the rotting bench. The irony consists in remarking that the bench need not mind their sitting now, however many of them there be, since they are light as air; and we reflect that a circumstance which must be comforting for the bench is bleak for the human order of existence, and in the course of that reflection we find the subordinate item becoming the dominant. The parenthetic remark that the ghost-people are indifferent to winter and flood sounds as if it might be comfortable to have the ghosts' order of existence, and argues some superiority for them over the bench, but that is ironical too: this is the insensibility of death. In this little poem the poet does not give much evidence of remarkable powers of language—which would mean remarkable ranges, intensities, and delicacies of perception—but he gives evidence of craftsmanship. His invention works in the whole and in the parts; he does not spoil a projected business by unequal execution; and there is no disparity between an effect which is realized and another effect which we judge was intended. There are ambitious poems by other Victorians, and illustrious ones, of whom these statements would be too complimentary. I think some sense of the craft is shown in the repetition of the last lines of the stanzas. The repeated line is structural for the meter, but also for the logic: it does nicely in place of some sententious utterance which might have tried too hard to impress us with the grimness of the occasion.

But Housman and Hardy both philosophize sometimes, and both are pessimists, and another comparison might be made. I quote the latter half of *Shropshire Lad* XLVIII:

> Now, and I muse for why and never find the reason,
> I pace the earth, and drink the air, and feel the sun.
> Be still, be still, my soul; it is but for a season:
> Let us endure an hour and see injustice done.
>
> Ay, look: high heaven and earth ail from the prime foundation;
> All thoughts to rive the heart are here, and all are vain:
> Horror and scorn and hate and fear and indignation—
> Or why did I awake? When shall I sleep again?

The waking has been described earlier in the poem; it was out of the sleep in the womb, where "it was well" for the speaker, in "days ere I was born." From Hardy I pick for the comparison, "According to the Mighty Working":

I

When moiling seems at cease
In the vague void of night-time,
And heaven's wide roomage stormless

> Between the dusk and light-time,
> And fear at last is formless,
> We call the allurement Peace.
>
> II
> Peace, this hid riot, Change,
> This revel of quick-cued mumming,
> This never truly being,
> This evermore becoming,
> This spinner's wheel onfleeing
> Outside perception's range.

Comment upon Housman's poem will be remarkably like that upon his poem above. But here it is not so much that there is an inadequate image to specify the ironical situation, as that there is almost no image at all. To live is to see injustice done, and the acts of living are specified, if rather broadly, but the injustice is not. We are bidden to look, as if there were something to see; but there is nothing to see, there is only something to grasp conceptually, on the poet's authority, with the summary kind of understanding.

The language of Hardy's poem has the duality of most good "thoughtful" or philosophical poetry. It is not content with the concepts, but is constantly stopping to insert or to attach the particularity which is involved in images; a procedure which might be called the imaginative realization of the concepts. A genuine poetic energy will work with both these dimensions at once. It must be conceded that we do not find here a single extended image to bear the whole weight of the conceptual structure, as is the way of that precision method of poetic composition which flourishes in the "metaphysical" style. But the images come up now and again, to engage the sound reader's imagination; there is playing back and forth between the world of ideas and the world of images. There is *moiling*; there is the military (but probably trite) locution *at cease*; there is *vague void*, with at least enough phonetic interest to give a pause, and a quickening to the imagination; there is *night-time* and *light-time*, the latter just odd enough to justify the colloquial former; there is *heaven's roomage*, and *stormless*, and *allurement*, the last an image springing from the center of the irony and representing the elements as conspiring through their specious quiet to lull and mislead us, though their hostile processes are going on all the time. The second stanza probably is faster, with fewer image-stops. But the powerful first line reduces Peace to Change in very short order, by virtue of the *hid riot* intimated in the first stanza; and there is *quick-cued mumming*, a nice provincial and, for this poet, favorite image which is nearer than any other image in the poem to giving an adequate picture of the whole procedure; and there is a conclusion in terms of the Greek philosophy and the Greek figure of the spinner's wheel—and I deprecate a little the necessity of forgetting the mummer in order to introduce the spinner.

We observe that the metrical scheme of the Housman poem is ordinary, and satisfactory; that is, it has the syllabic sequences to make four formal lines, and to contribute a structural item to the poem which is in addition to the structure of the argument. The advantage would lie, doubtless, in heightening our metaphysical sense of a structured world; the most uneventful meters do this much. But in Hardy's poem the metrical value goes much further. It is so elaborate as to be tuneful, and to seem not only a symbol of structure but a structure of some little value in itself. It is almost Swinburnian—and Hardy admired Swinburne.

But we will feel—and here we abandon Housman—that the Swinburnian music will never in Hardy go along with a Swinburnian content. Swinburne writes:

> We are not sure of sorrow,
> And joy was never sure;
> To-day will die to-morrow;
> Time stoops to no man's lure;
> And love, grown faint and fretful,
> With lips but half regretful
> Sighs, and with eyes forgetful
> Weeps that no loves endure.[2]

There is more external music in Swinburne, but also more interior nonsense. Swinburne's idea was to assemble what pretty and gravely-sentimental words the rhyme and the meter allowed him, with them make some sort of syntax, and even keep to the general lines of a vague argument. Images, or halfway images, will turn up in this exercise, but he does not really expect us to scrutinize them, as if they could possibly have some close propriety. If we do so nevertheless, we see that they are factitious and childish; for example, where the lips of love are charged with registering the regret, and the eyes with registering the forgetfulness, when these responsibilities could obviously be transposed without injuring anybody or anything. With equal immunity could we prefer to have a whole regret and half a forgetfulness, instead of vice versa.

2. "The Garden of Proserpine."

I have the impression that Swinburne's peculiar poetics are now thoroughly appreciated, and also discounted.

In general, we may be sure that, the more determinate the metric, the more indeterminate will be the logical materials with which the meter is working. If the materials were entirely determinate, they would not permit a meter at all; the binomial theorem is an example, for it could never allow one syllable in its formulation to be changed to suit the meter. An elaborate metrical pattern (short lines, close rhymes) always invites the Swinburnian looseness of argument. Yet Hardy has a difficult metrical pattern here, and shows his very great addiction to short rhymed lines, yet does not allow the meter to determine him to rigmarole and nonsense. On the contrary, he keeps his sense as sharp and distinct as ever. The indeterminate element within which he has to range to make his meters is the *particularity* of his object; that is the principle I have been coming to. The particularity is inexhaustible, and if held under observation it offers plenty of apt images. These do not conflict with the thought, but only displace it momentarily or, even, *realize* it. No poet has a firmer sense of the function of a meter than Hardy has. I think of him as a poet who strains to make his meters without impairing his sense, and in straining succeeds. The signs of strain look like an honest effort, and I dislike to put a more unfavorable construction upon this aspect; we know that all poets must strain, and poetry is a laborious art. His maneuverings within the margins of the object's indeterminateness are visible somewhat like the brush-strokes on the painter's canvas.

III

Hardy is not one of the poets who have been much studied, and argued over, and finally assigned some rather fixed place in the line of poets, by the professional "scholars"; by the persons who canonize poets and put them into circulation officially through textbooks and classrooms. For that reason I cannot think of a better occupation for the literary scholars of 1940 than a careful appraisal of the poet born a hundred years ago. But the project is a delicate one.

His kind of poetry is so much his own, and so far from standard as that might be defined by nineteenth-century tradition, that it is difficult to find the place for him in a poetic "line." Either he was not influenced by the current styles of poetry that were admired in his lifetime, or else he was not adaptive and could not change from the style which he

came into at the outset, as into a style that suited him. For the one reason or the other he continued in it, though he widened its range. Either
reason does credit to his integrity, the difference being that in one case
the integrity is the character which is defined and defended by deliberate will, and in the other case it has a secret and even more powerful
seat, and is guarded from betrayal by a daimon, or an unconscious will.

I believe I am saying in effect, mostly, that he does not know how to
employ the tones of the laureate or public poet. He has very little of that
kind of virtuosity which the literate population waits to see, and expects to see from a more professional literary man. I have put poems of
his beside poems not only by Wordsworth, Tennyson, and Browning,
but by less oracular men such as Meredith, Arnold, Morris, Patmore,
and Francis Thompson; and his poems are on a lower level of self-
consciousness than theirs, and that appears to be a higher level of
freshness, innocence, and honesty. It would be a pleasure to document
this, but too laborious for this occasion.

And I am aware that this turns readily into a possible ascription of
"quaintness," and that presently it involves the question of a standard
of taste. Good taste is probably grounded less in metaphysics than in
the mores of the aristocrats, and the mores of the literary aristocrats are
the product of severe but conventional education. Hardy lacked a formal higher education. The fact in itself would have no disastrous consequences, unless in the one contingency that the self-educated man
might have to enter public life and permit comparisons with the highly-
trained and professional practitioners. But that is just what Hardy's
ghost now belatedly comes to, in the cool anniversary appraisal of his
genius as measured against all the other geniuses. He is not so much of
a "case" as was our Emily Dickinson, but he is a case. At any time in
Hardy's life there must have been twenty poets whose easiness with the
formal proprieties of theme and diction exceeded his own. And this is
not an observation which it would be a pleasure to document. I should
avoid it by recording in advance my consent to the charge that Hardy is
an uneven poet, and capable of marring fine poems by awkward and
tasteless passages; and even of writing whole poems that now are too
harsh, and again are too merely pedestrian. For some reason, however, I
must confess that these lapses have often seemed to endear the poet to
me, and to other readers I know, and I can think but of one way to rationalize so odd a reception: by the consideration that "bad form,"
though generally a thing to be reprehended, is possibly under one circumstance to be approved: where we feel that the ignorance behind it

is the condition of the innocence and spontaneity which we admire in the general personal context. Talents terrific by nature and consummate by profession and art, like Shakespeare and Milton, are not caught in error, but neither are they ever ingenuous, and among the pleasures of attending upon them is not the charm of the rare and unpredictable detail. The worst poetry that Hardy wrote, according to an impression many years old with me, was in his one long piece, the drama of *The Dynasts*, where he essayed the big Shakespearian style; he was not prepared to write that kind of poetry. He is a special poet, a great minor poet if the phrase is intelligible, and a poor major poet. He should rate well among English poets since Wordsworth, but that would be because in that span the greatest poets have had very disagreeable imperfections.

He was an amateur who did not have the professional equipment to see how provincial and honest his poetry was, nor how rare. He played boldly with syntax and lexicon, as Shakespeare had done, and he knew, if only from his acquaintance with Shakespeare, what the rights of poets were. But when he looked at his object the object was the actual one under his eye, not one out of Shakespeare, or out of literary conventions elsewhere. A superior metaphysical validity belongs to his lyrics and little narratives in that the particularity of their detail is sharp and local. I think highly of that kind of genuineness. It is an elemental virtue which is wanting—to our daily grief—in hundreds of well-groomed versifiers, who produce poems as smooth exteriorly as new Ford cars, and nearly as frequent; and in scores of publishing poets, though I should judge that their reward is not now what it used to be. As to its lack among the Victorians: that is their characteristic defect.

IV

In the volume under my hand occurs the poem which I like best of all those generated by the World War: "And There Was a Great Calm." The occasion is the signing of the armistice. There is more than common of Hardy's human tenderness in it, and, for once at least, the subject being what it was, we are not repelled by any sense of impropriety in the enveloping mood of ironic rage. It begins:

I

> There had been years of Passion—scorching, cold,
> And much Despair, and Anger heaving high,
> Care whitely watching, Sorrows manifold,

> Among the young, among the weak and old,
> And the pensive Spirit of Pity whispered, "Why?"

The Spirits are coming down again to earth, as they did in *The Dynasts*, to carry on their debate, and it is not too promising an opening; the allegory is literary and obvious, the mentality is too abstract. Yet the talking Spirits are integral to the philosophy of the poem, and there will be poem enough to sustain them before it is done. We pursue the course of the war, till presently we come to the line,

> And "Hell!" and "Shell!" were yapped at Lovingkindness,

and we are excited. The narrative gathers strength, somewhat in the degree that it improves in particularity, until suddenly, we are told, there sounded, "War is done!" I quote from this point on:

VI

> Breathless they paused. Out there men raised their glance
> To where had stood those poplars lank and lopped,
> As they had raised it through the four years' dance
> Of Death in the now familiar flats of France;
> And murmured, "Strange, this! How? All firing stopped?"

VII

> Aye; all was hushed. The about-to-fire fired not,
> The aimed-at moved away in trance-lipped song.
> One checkless regiment slung a clinching shot
> And turned. The Spirit of Irony smirked out, "What?
> Spoil peradventures woven of Rage and Wrong?"

VIII

> Thenceforth no flying fires inflamed the gray,
> No hurtlings shook the dewdrop from the thorn,
> No moan perplexed the mute bird on the spray;
> Worn horses mused: "We are not whipped to-day";
> No weft-winged engines blurred the moon's thin horn.

IX

> Calm fell. From Heaven distilled a clemency;
> There was peace on earth, and silence in the sky;
> Some could, some could not, shake off misery:
> The Sinister Spirit sneered: "It had to be!"
> And again the Spirit of Pity whispered, "Why?"

I will make little comment; it is obviously as sound as it is, in many respects, original. I like the honest locutions of the soldiers who murmur when they hear no more firing; of the first question smirked out by the Spirit of Irony, though his second sounds rather more suited to the well-lettered celestial; and of the worn horses who muse. I like the poplars, the flats, and the actions of the about-to-fire, the aimed-at, and the checkless regiment. Stanza VIII is beautifully compounded of locutions of several sorts; the last two lines belong exclusively to Hardy, and all are at home in his carefully modulated composition. The conclusion is conclusive.

V

We will say then that Hardy is a patient and honest workman, whose works frequently have complexity and power; and we will add that nowhere is he more consistent and honest than in the temperamental or philosophical bias of the works. I conclude by remarking upon the bias. It is a serious limitation.

I quote one more poem, quaintly characteristic in meter and diction but exceptional in its metaphysic, for the sake of asking the question, Why could not Hardy keep his ingenious imagination open to receive more occasions like this one? This very small poem is entitled "An Experience," and it is exceptional because there is no irony in the occasion:

> Wit, weight, or wealth there was not
> In anything that was said,
> In anything that was done;
> All was of scope to cause not
> A triumph, dazzle, or dread
> To even the subtlest one,
> My friend,
> To even the subtlest one.
>
> But there was a new afflation—
> That aura zephyring round
> That care infected not:
> It came as a salutation,
> And, in my sweet astound,
> I scarcely witted what
> Might pend,
> I scarcely witted what.
>
> The hills in samewise to me
> Spoke, as they grayly gazed,
> —First hills to speak so yet!
> The thin-edged breezes blew me

> What I, though cobwebbed, crazed,
> Was never to forget,
>   My friend,
> Was never to forget!

The philosophical tradition of the lyric—which Hardy so largely stood outside, by defect of education, or by defect of temper—would take this sort of experience as normal rather than exceptional. The mysterious particularity of nature does not oppose itself here to the rational or human order, but is quite agreeable, though not identical, with it. In something better than ninety per cent of Hardy's poems, I will suppose, nature is destructive of it—of that rational order which human beings count on when they plan and labor. The two worlds are in battle, and the issue is decided ordinarily with ridiculous ease in favor of nature's superior armaments. And as between Hardy and the tradition in this matter I think we are compelled on the most comprehensive aesthetic grounds to prefer the tradition.

Perhaps my terms are strange, and will bear a little repetition. A scientific formula exhibits pure structure, or entire rationality, and no contingency. The binomial theorem again, for instance; the expectation conveyed by it is that nothing in material nature will ever prevail against a piece of structure so perfect as this. But of course that expectation is cherished in abstraction from actual nature, whose contingency is perfectly unpredictable. An actual binomial would be, both inside and outside, within the realm of the energetic and unpredictable particularity of nature; the formula might hold up, or it might not. But, still more exposed, there are moral structures, and social structures, and planned human careers, admittedly less abstract and of less logical rigor than the binomial theorem, yet as rigorous and as resolute as they may be. All put their trust in a rational order; which is anything but secure against such natural irruptions as the impurity in the materials, the sickness and decay, or sin, or cataclysm. Their triumphs are short, if they triumph.

It is in art that we take interest, enormous and incessant interest, in the particularity of nature. But often, and perhaps strangely, this is a loving interest; not merely the interest of scientists and moralists attending to their practical business and remarking the hostile element with detestation. The latter sort of interest is for special occasions: it is for tragedy, where the issue is posed with a sense of crisis, with climaxes and dramatic resolution. It is not the staple interest of lyric.

For nothing is commoner knowledge than that we, each of us, shall, for example, die and revert to dust; before that time bear sickness, hurt, disappointment, and unkindness. And lyric need not spend itself on this topic, however ingenious its imagination of evil may be.

The search for evil belongs only to a fraction of Hardy; for he was a divided man. Nature was for him an insoluble ambiguity. From the philosopher in him it exacted the not-so-distinguished tribute of hateful indignation, and reiterated defiant "exposure." From the poet it usually got faithful perception, and love.

\

CRITICISM AS PURE SPECULATION

CHASM, perhaps an abyss, separates the critic and the esthetician ordinarily, if the books in the library are evidence. But the authority of criticism depends on its coming to terms with esthetics, and the authority of literary esthetics depends on its coming to terms with criticism.[1]

When we inquire into the "intent of the critic," we mean: the intent of the generalized critic, or critic as such. We will concede that any professional critic is familiar with the technical practices of poets so long as these are conventional, and is expert in judging when they perform them badly. We expect a critical discourse to cover that much, but we know that more is required. The most famous poets of our time, for example, make wide departures from conventional practices: how are they to be judged? Innovations in poetry, or even conventions when pressed to their logical limits, cause the ordinary critic to despair. They cause the good critic to review his esthetic principles; perhaps to reformulate his esthetic principles. He tries the poem against his best philosophical conception of the peculiar character that a poem should have.

Mr. T. S. Eliot is an extraordinarily sensitive critic. But when he discusses the so-called "metaphysical" poetry, he surprises us by refusing to study the so-called "conceit" which is its reputed basis; he observes instead that the metaphysical poets of the seventeenth century are more like their immediate predecessors than the latter are like the eighteenth and nineteenth century poets, and then he goes into a very broad philosophical comparison between two whole "periods" or types of poetry. I think it has come to be understood that his comparison is unsound; it has not proved workable enough to assist critics who have

This essay was first published in *The Intent of the Critic*, edited by Donald A. Stauffer (Princeton, 1941), 91–124. Reprinted by permission of Princeton University Press.

1. This essay was presented as a lecture at Princeton University in the winter of 1940–41 in a series of four lectures entitled *The Intent of the Critic*. The other participants were Edmund Wilson, Norman Foerster and W. H. Auden. The first two paragraphs referring to the local occasion of the discussion have been condensed into the present first paragraph by the editor with the author's permission. (Note in *The Intent of the Critic*, Princeton, 1941, when the essay first appeared.)

otherwise borrowed liberally from his critical principles. (It contains the famous dictum about the "sensibility" of the earlier poets, it imputes to them a remarkable ability to "feel their thought," and to have a kind of "experience" in which the feeling cannot be differentiated from the thinking.) Now there is scarcely another critic equal to Eliot at distinguishing the practices of two poets who are closely related. He is supreme as a comparative critic when the relation in question is delicate and subtle; that is, when it is a matter of close perception and not a radical difference in kind. But this line of criticism never goes far enough. In Eliot's own range of criticism the line does not always answer. He is forced by discontinuities in the poetic tradition into sweeping theories that have to do with esthetics, the philosophy of poetry; and his own philosophy probably seems to us insufficient, the philosophy of the literary man.

The intent of the critic may well be, then, first to read his poem sensitively, and make comparative judgments about its technical practice, or, as we might say, to emulate Eliot. Beyond that, it is to read and remark the poem knowingly; that is, with an esthetician's understanding of what a poem generally "is."

Before I venture, with inadequate argument, to describe what I take to be the correct understanding of poetry, I would like to describe two other understandings which, though widely professed, seem to me misunderstandings. First, there is a smart and belletristic theory of poetry which may be called "psychologistic." Then there is an altogether staid and commonplace theory which is moralistic. Of these in their order.

II

It could easily be argued about either of these untenable conceptions of poetry that it is an act of despair to which critics resort who cannot find for the discourse of poetry any precise differentia to remove it from the category of science. Psychologistic critics hold that poetry is addressed primarily to the feelings and motor impulses; they remind us frequently of its contrast with the coldness, the unemotionality, of science, which is supposed to address itself to the pure cognitive mind. Mr. [I. A.] Richards came out spectacularly for the doctrine, and furnished it with detail of the greatest ingenuity. He very nearly severed the dependence of poetic effect upon any standard of objective knowledge or belief. But the feelings and impulses which he represented as gratified by the poem were too tiny and numerous to be named. He never identified them; they seemed not so much psychological as infra-psychological. His was an esoteric poetic: it could not be disproved. But neither could it be proved and I think it is safe at this distance to say that eventually his readers, and Richards himself, lost interest in it as being an improvisation, much too unrelated to the public sense of a poetic experience.

With other critics psychologism of some sort is an old story, and one that will probably never cease to be told. For, now that all of us know about psychology, there must always be persons on hand precisely conditioned to declare that poetry is an emotional discourse indulged in resentment and compensation for science, the bleak cognitive discourse in its purity. It becomes less a form of knowledge than a form of "expression." The critics are willing to surrender the honor of objectivity to science if they may have the luxury of subjectivity for poetry. Science will scarcely object. But one or two things have to be said about that. In every experience, even in science, there is feeling. No discourse can sustain itself without interest, which is feeling. The interest, or the feeling, is like an automatic index to the human value of the proceeding—which would not otherwise proceed. Mr. Eliseo Vivas is an esthetician who might be thought to reside in the camp of the enemy, for his affiliations are positivist; yet in a recent essay he writes about the "passion" which sustains the heroic labors of the scientist as one bigger and more intense than is given to most men.[2]

I do not mean to differ with that judgment at all in remarking that we might very well let the passions and the feelings take care of themselves; it is precisely what we do in our pursuit of science. The thing to attend to is the object to which they attach. As between two similar musical phrases, or between two similar lines of poetry, we may often defy the most proficient psychologist to distinguish the one feeling-response from the other; unless we permit him to say at long last that one is the kind of response that would be made to the first line, and the other is the kind of response that would be made to the second line. But that is to do, after much wasted motion, what I have just suggested: to attend to the poetic object and let the feelings take care of themselves. It is their business to "respond." There may be a feeling correlative with the minutest alteration in an object, and adequate to it, but we shall hardly know. What we do know is that the feelings are grossly inarticulate if we try to abstract them and take their testimony in their own language.

2. See, for example, Eliseo Vivas, "The New Encyclopedists," *Kenyon Review*, I (Spring, 1939), 159–68.

Since it is not the intent of the critic to be inarticulate, his discriminations must be among the objects. We understand this so well intuitively that the critic seems to us in possession of some esoteric knowledge, some magical insight, if he appears to be intelligent elsewhere and yet refers confidently to the "tone" or "quality" or "value" of the feeling he discovers in a given line. Probably he is bluffing. The distinctness resides in the cognitive or "semantical" objects denoted by the words. When Richards bewilders us by reporting affective and motor disturbances that are too tiny for definition, and other critics by reporting disturbances that are too massive and gross, we cannot fail to grow suspicious of this whole way of insight as incompetent.

Eliot has a special version of psychologistic theory which looks extremely fertile, though it is broad and nebulous as his psychologistic terms require it to be. He likes to regard the poem as a structure of emotion and feeling. But the emotion is singular, there being only one emotion per poem, or at least per passage: it is the central emotion or big emotion which attaches to the main theme or situation. The feeling is plural. The emotion combines with many feelings; these are our little responses to the single words and phrases, and he does not think of them as being parts of the central emotion or even related to it. The terminology is greatly at fault, or we should recognize at once, I think, a principle that might prove very valuable. I would not answer for the conduct of a technical philosopher in assessing this theory; he might throw it away, out of patience with its jargon. But a lay philosopher who respects his Eliot and reads with all his sympathy might salvage a good thing from it, though I have not heard of anyone doing so. He would try to escape from the affective terms, and translate Eliot into more intelligible language. Eliot would be saying in effect that a poem has a central logic or situation or "paraphrasable core" to which an appropriate interest doubtless attaches, and that in this respect the poem is like a discourse of science behind which lies the sufficient passion. But he would be saying at the same time, and this is the important thing, that the poem has also a context of lively local details to which other and independent interests attach; and that in this respect it is unlike the discourse of science.[3] For the detail of scientific discourse intends never to be independent of the thesis (either objectively or affectively) but always functional, and subordinate to the realization of the thesis. To say that is to approach to a structural understanding of poetry, and to the kind of understanding that I wish presently to urge.

3. Ransom is reiterating the distinction between poetic and prose discourse.

III

As for the moralistic understanding of poetry, it is sometimes the specific moralists, men with moral axes to grind, and incidentally men of unassailable public position, who cherish that; they have a "use" for poetry. But not exclusively, for we may find it held also by critics who are more spontaneous and innocent: apparently they fall back upon it because it attributes some special character to poetry, which otherwise refuses to yield up to them a character. The moral interest is so much more frequent in poetry than in science that they decide to offer its moralism as a differentia.

This conception of poetry is of the greatest antiquity—it antedates the evolution of close esthetic philosophy, and persists beside it too. Plato sometimes spoke of poetry in this light—perhaps because it was recommended to him in this light—but nearly always scornfully. In the *Gorgias*, and other dialogues, he represents the poets as moralizing, and that is only what he, in the person of Socrates, is doing at the very moment, and given to doing; but he considers the moralizing of poets as mere "rhetoric," or popular philosophy, and unworthy of the accomplished moralist who is the real or technical philosopher. Plato understood very well that the poet does not conduct a technical or an original discourse like that of the scientist—and the term includes here the moral philosopher—and that close and effective moralizing is scarcely to be had from him. It is not within the poet's power to offer that if his intention is to offer poetry; for the poetry and the morality are so far from being identical that they interfere a little with each other.

Few famous estheticians in the history of philosophy have cared to bother with the moralistic conception; many critics have, in all periods. Just now we have at least two schools of moralistic critics contending for the official possession of poetry. One is the Neo-Humanist, and Mr. Foerster has identified himself with that. The other is the Marxist, and I believe it is represented in some degree and shade by Mr. Wilson, possibly by Mr. Auden. I have myself taken profit from the discussions by both schools, but recently I have taken more—I suppose this is because I was brought up in a scholastic discipline rather like the Neo-Humanist—from the writings of the Marxist critics. One of the differences is that the Neo-Humanists believe in the "respectable" virtues, but the Marxists believe that respectability is the greatest of vices, and equate respectable with "genteel." That is a very striking difference, and I think it is also profound.

But I do not wish to be impertinent; I can respect both these moralities, and appropriate moral values from both. The thing I wish to argue is not the comparative merits of the different moralities by which poetry is judged, but their equal inadequacy to the reading of the poet's intention. The moralistic critics wish to isolate and discuss the "ideology" or theme or paraphrase of the poem and not the poem itself. But even to the practitioners themselves, if they are sophisticated, comes sometimes the apprehension that this is moral rather than literary criticism. I have not seen the papers of my colleagues in this discussion, for that was against the rules, but it is reported to me that both Mr. Wilson and Mr. Foerster concede in explicit words that criticism has both the moral and the esthetic branches; Mr. Wilson may call them the "social" and esthetic branches. And they would hold the critical profession responsible for both branches. Under these circumstances the critics cease to be mere moralists and become dualists; that is better. My feeling about such a position would be that the moral criticism we shall have with us always, and have had always, and that it is easy—comparatively speaking—and that what is hard, and needed, and indeed more and more urgent after all the failures of poetic understanding, is a better esthetic criticism. This is the branch which is all but invariably neglected by the wise but morally zealous critics; they tend to forget their dual responsibility. I think I should go so far as to think that, in strictness, the business of the literary critic is exclusively with an esthetic criticism. The business of the moralist will naturally, and properly, be with something else.

If we have the patience to read for a little while in the anthology, paying some respect to the varieties of substance actually in the poems, we cannot logically attribute ethical character by definition to poetry; for that character is not universal in the poems. And if we have any faith in the community of character among the several arts, we are stopped quickly from risking such a definition for art at large. To claim a moral content for most of sculpture, painting, music, or architecture, is to plan something dialectically very round about and subtle, or else to be so arbitrary as to invite instant exposure. I should think the former alternative is impractical, and the latter, if it is not stupid, is masochistic.

The moralistic critics are likely to retort upon their accusers by accusing them in turn of the vapid doctrine known as Art for Art's Sake. And with frequent justice; but again we are likely to receive the impression that it is just because Art for Art's Sake, the historic doctrine, proved empty, and availed them so little esthetically, like all the other doctrines that came into default, that they have fled to their moralism. Moralism does at least impute to poetry a positive substance, as Art for Art's Sake does not. It asserts an autonomy for art, which is excellent; but autonomy to do what? Only to be itself, and to reduce its interpreters to a tautology? With its English adherents in the 'nineties the doctrine seemed to make only a negative requirement of art, that is, that it should be anti-Victorian as we should say today, a little bit naughty and immoral perhaps, otherwise at least non-moral, or carefully squeezed dry of moral substance. An excellent example of how two doctrines, inadequate equally but in opposite senses, may keep themselves alive by abhorring each other's errors.

It is highly probable that the poem considers an ethical situation, and there is no reason why it should repel this from its consideration. But, if I may say so without being accused of verbal trifling, the poetic consideration of the ethical situation is not the same as the ethical consideration of it. The straight ethical consideration would be prose; it would be an act of interested science, or an act of practical will. The poetic consideration, according to Schopenhauer, is the objectification of this act of will; that is, it is our contemplation and not our exercise of will, and therefore qualitatively a very different experience; knowledge without desire. That doctrine also seems too negative and indeterminate. I will put the point as I see it in another way. It should be a comfort to the moralist that there is ordinarily a moral composure in the poem, as if the poet had long known good and evil, and made his moral choice between them once and for all. Art is post-ethical rather than unethical. In the poem there is an increment of meaning which is neither the ethical content nor opposed to the ethical content. The poetic experience would have to stop for the poet who is developing it, or for the reader who is following it, if the situation which is being poetically treated should turn back into a situation to be morally determined; if, for example, the situation were not a familiar one, and one to which we had habituated our moral wills; for it would rouse the moral will again to action, and make the poetic treatment impossible under its heat. Art is more cool than hot, and a moral fervor is as disastrous to it as a burst of passion itself. We have seen Marxists recently so revolted by Shakespeare's addiction to royal or noble *personae* that they cannot obtain esthetic experience from the plays; all they get is moral agitation. In another art, we know, and doubtless we approve, the scruple of the college authorities in not permitting the "department of fine arts" to direct the collegians in painting in the nude. Doctor Hanns Sachs, successor to

Freud, in a recent number of his *American Imago*, gives a story from a French author as follows:

> He tells that one evening strolling along the streets of Paris he noticed a row of slot machines which for a small coin showed pictures of women in full or partial undress. He observed the leering interest with which men of all kind and description, well dressed and shabby, boys and old men, enjoyed the peep show. He remarked that they all avoided one of these machines, and wondering what uninteresting pictures it might show, he put his penny in the slot. To his great astonishment the generally shunned picture turned out to be the Venus of Medici. Now he begins to ponder: Why does nobody get excited about her? She is decidedly feminine and not less naked than the others which hold such strong fascination for everybody. Finally he finds a satisfactory answer: They fight shy of her because she is beautiful.[4]

And Doctor Sachs, though in his own variety of jargon, makes a number of wise observations about the psychic conditions precedent to the difficult apprehension of beauty. The experience called beauty is beyond the powerful ethical will precisely as it is beyond the animal passion, and indeed these last two are competitive, and coordinate. Under the urgency of either we are incapable of appreciating the statue or understanding the poem.

IV

The ostensible substance of the poem may be anything at all which words may signify: an ethical situation, a passion, a train of thought, a flower or landscape, a thing. This substance receives its poetic increment. It might be safer to say it receives some subtle and mysterious alteration under poetic treatment, but I will risk the cruder formula: the ostensible substance is increased by an x, which is an increment. The poem actually continues to contain its ostensible substance, which is not fatally diminished from its prose state: that is its logical core, or paraphrase. The rest of the poem is x, which we are to find.

We feel the working of this simple formula when we approach a poetry with our strictest logic, provided we can find deliverance from certain inhibiting philosophical prepossessions into which we have been conditioned by the critics we have had to read. Here is Lady Macbeth planning a murder with her husband:

4. "Beauty, Life and Death," *The American Imago*, I (December, 1940), 95.

> When Duncan is asleep—
> Whereto the rather shall his hard day's journey
> Soundly invite him—his two chamberlains
> Will I with wine and wassail so convince,
> That memory, the warder of the brain,
> Shall be a fume, and the receipt of reason
> A limbec only; when in swinish sleep
> Their drenched natures lie as in a death,
> What cannot you and I perform upon
> The unguarded Duncan? what not put upon
> His spongy officers, who shall bear the guilt
> Of our great quell?[5]

It is easy to produce the prose argument or paraphrase of this speech; it has one upon which we shall all agree. But the passage is more than its argument. Any detail, with this speaker, seems capable of being expanded in some direction which is not that of the argument. For example, Lady Macbeth says she will make the chamberlains drunk so that they will not remember their charge, nor keep their wits about them. But it is indifferent to this argument whether memory according to the old psychology is located at the gateway to the brain, whether it is to be disintegrated into fume as of alcohol, and whether the whole receptacle of the mind is to be turned into a still. These are additions to the argument both energetic and irrelevant—though they do not quite stop or obscure the argument. From the point of view of the philosopher they are excursions into particularity. They give, in spite of the argument, which would seem to be perfectly self-sufficient, a sense of the real density and contingency of the world in which arguments and plans have to be pursued. They bring out the private character which the items of an argument can really assume if we look at them. This character spreads out in planes at right angles to the course of the argument, and in effect gives to the discourse another dimension, not present in a perfectly logical prose. We are expected to have sufficient judgment not to let this local character take us too far or keep us too long from the argument.

All this would seem commonplace remark, I am convinced, but for those philosophically timid critics who are afraid to think that the poetic increment is local and irrelevant, and that poetry cannot achieve its own virtue and keep undiminished the virtues of prose at the same

5. *Macbeth*, Act I, Sc. vii, 61–72.

time. But I will go a little further in the hope of removing the sense of strangeness in the analysis. I will offer a figurative definition of a poem.

A poem is, so to speak, a democratic state, whereas a prose discourse—mathematical, scientific, ethical, or practical and vernacular—is a totalitarian state. The intention of a democratic state is to perform the work of state as effectively as it can perform it, subject to one reservation of conscience: that it will not despoil its members, the citizens, of the free exercise of their own private and independent characters. But the totalitarian state is interested solely in being effective, and regards the citizens as no citizens at all; that is, regards them as functional members whose existence is totally defined by their allotted contributions to its ends; it has no use for their private characters, and therefore no provision for them. I indicate of course the extreme or polar opposition between two polities without denying that a polity may come to us rather mixed up.

In this trope the operation of the state as a whole represents of course the logical paraphrase or argument of the poem. The private character of the citizens represents the particularity asserted by the parts in the poem. And this last is our x.

For many years I had seen—as what serious observer has not—that a poem as a discourse differentiated itself from prose by its particularity, yet not to the point of sacrificing its logical cogency or universality. But I could get no further. I could not see how real particularity could get into a universal. The object of esthetic studies became for me a kind of discourse, or a kind of natural configuration, which like any other discourse or configuration claimed universality, but which consisted actually, and notoriously, of particularity. The poem was concrete, yet universal, and in spite of Hegel I could not see how the two properties could be identified as forming in a single unit the "concrete universal." It is usual, I believe, for persons at this stage to assert that somehow the apparent diffuseness or particularity in the poem gets itself taken up or "assimilated" into the logic, or produce a marvellous kind of unity called a "high unity," to which ordinary discourse is not eligible. The belief is that the "idea" or theme proves itself in poetry to be even more dominating than in prose by overcoming much more energetic resistance than usual on the part of the materials, and the resistance, as attested in the local development of detail, is therefore set not to the debit but to the credit of the unifying power of the poetic spirit. A unity of that kind is one which philosophers less audacious and more factual than Hegel would be loath to claim. Critics incline to call it, rather esoterically, an "imaginative" rather than a logical unity, but one supposes they mean a mystical, an ineffable, unity. I for one could neither grasp it nor deny it. I believe that is not an uncommon situation for poetic analysts to find themselves in.

It occurred to me at last that the solution might be very easy if looked for without what the positivists call "metaphysical prepossessions." Suppose the logical substance remained there all the time, and was in no way specially remarkable, while the particularity came in by accretion, so that the poem turned out partly universal, and partly particular, but with respect to different parts. I began to remark the dimensions of a poem, or other work of art. The poem was not a mere moment in time, nor a mere point in space. It was sizeable, like a house. Apparently it had a "plan," or a central frame of logic, but it had also a huge wealth of local detail, which sometimes fitted the plan functionally or served it, and sometimes only subsisted comfortably under it: in either case the house stood up. But it was the political way of thinking which gave me the first analogy which seemed valid. The poem was like a democratic state, in action, and observed both macroscopically and microscopically.

The house occurred also, and provided what seems to be a more negotiable trope under which to construe the poem. A poem is a *logical structure* having a *local texture*. These terms have been actually though not systematically employed in literary criticism. To my imagination they are architectural. The walls of my room are obviously structural; the beams and boards have a function; so does the plaster, which is the visible aspect of the final wall. The plaster might have remained naked, aspiring to no character, and purely functional. But actually it has been painted, receiving color; or it has been papered, receiving color and design, though these have no structural value; and perhaps it has been hung with tapestry, or with paintings, for "decoration." The paint, the paper, the tapestry are texture. It is logically unrelated to structure. But I indicate only a few of the textural possibilities in architecture. There are not fewer of them in poetry.

The intent of the good critic becomes therefore to examine and define the poem with respect to its structure and its texture. If he has nothing to say about its texture he has nothing to say about it specifically as a poem, but is treating it only insofar as it is prose.

I do not mean to say that the good critic will necessarily employ my terms.

V

Many critics today are writing analytically and with close intelligence, in whatever terms, about the logical substance or structure of the poem, and its increment of irrelevant local substance or texture. I believe that the understanding of the ideal critic has to go even further than that. The final desideratum is an ontological insight, nothing less. I am committed by my title to a representation of criticism as, in the last resort, a speculative exercise. But my secret committal was to speculative in the complete sense of—ontological.

There is nothing especially speculative or ontological in reciting, or even appraising, the logical substance of the poem. This is its prose core—its science perhaps, or its ethics if it seems to have an ideology. Speculative interest asserts itself principally when we ask why we want the logical substance to be compounded with the local substance, the good lean structure with a great volume of texture that does not function. It is the same thing as asking why we want the poem to be what it is.

It has been a rule, having the fewest exceptions, for estheticians and great philosophers to direct their speculations by the way of overstating and overvaluing the logical substance. They are impressed by the apparent obedience of material nature, whether in fact or in art, to definable form or "law" imposed upon it. They like to suppose that in poetry, as in chemistry, everything that figures in the discourse means to be functional, and that the poem is imperfect in the degree that it contains items, whether by accident or intention, which manifest a private independence. It is a bias with which we are entirely familiar, and reflects the extent to which our philosophy hitherto has been impressed by the successes of science in formulating laws which would "govern" their objects. Probably I am here reading the state of mind of yesterday rather than of today. Nevertheless we know it. The world-view which ultimately forms itself in the mind so biassed is that of a world which is rational and intelligible. The view is sanguine, and naïve. Hegel's world-view, I think it is agreed, was a subtle version of this, and if so, it was what determined his view of art. He seemed to make the handsomest concession to realism by offering to knowledge a kind of universal which was not restricted to the usual abstracted aspects of the material, but included all aspects, and was a concrete universal. The concreteness in Hegel's handling was not honestly, or at any rate not fairly, defended. It was always represented as being in process of pointing up and helping out the universality. He could look at a work of art and report all its substances as almost assimilated to a ruling "idea." But at least Hegel seemed to distinguish what looked like two ultimate sorts of substance there, and stated the central esthetic problem as the problem of relating them. And his writings about art are speculative in the sense that he regarded the work of art not as of great intrinsic value necessarily, but as an object-lesson or discipline in the understanding of the world-process, and as its symbol.

I think of two ways of construing poetry with respect to its ultimate purpose; of which the one is not very handsome nor speculatively interesting, and the other will appear somewhat severe.

The first construction would picture the poet as a sort of epicure, and the poem as something on the order of a Christmas pudding, stuffed with what dainties it will hold. The pastry alone, or it may be the cake, will not serve; the stuffing is wanted too. The values of the poem would be intrinsic, or immediate, and they would include not only the value of the structure but also the incidental values to be found in the texture. If we exchange the pudding for a house, they would include not only the value of the house itself but also the value of the furnishings. In saying intrinsic or immediate, I mean that the poet is fond of the precise objects denoted by the words, and writes the poem for the reason that he likes to dwell upon them. In talking about the main value and the incidental values I mean to recognize the fact that the latter engage the affections just as truly as the former. Poetic discourse therefore would be more agreeable than prose to the epicure or the literally acquisitive man; for prose has but a single value, being about one thing only; its parts have no values of their own, but only instrumental values, which might be reckoned as fractions of the single value proportionate to their contributions to it. The prose is one-valued and the poem is many-valued. Indeed there will certainly be poems whose texture contains many precious objects, and aggregates a greater value than the structure.

So there would be a comfortable and apparently eligible view that poetry improves on prose because it is a richer diet. It causes five or six pleasures to appear, five or six good things, where one had been before; an alluring consideration for robustious, full-blooded, bourgeois souls. The view will account for much of the poem, if necessary. But it does not account for all of it, and sometimes it accounts for less than at other times.

The most impressive reason for the bolder view of art, the speculative one, is the existence of the "pure," or "abstractionist," or non-representational works of art; though these will probably occur to us in other arts than poetry. There is at least one art, music, whose works are all of this sort. Tones are not words, they have no direct semantical function, and by themselves they mean nothing. But they combine to make brilliant phrases, harmonies, and compositions. In these compositions it is probable that the distinction between structure or functional content, on the one hand, and texture or local variation and departure, on the other, is even more determinate than in an impure art like poetry. The world of tones seems perfectly inhuman and impracticable; there is no specific field of experience "about which" music is telling us. Yet we know that music is powerfully affective. I take my own musical feelings, and those attested by other audients, as the sufficient index to some overwhelming human importance which the musical object has for us. At the same time it would be useless to ask the feelings precisely what they felt; we must ask the critic. The safest policy is to take the simplest construction, and try to improvise as little fiction as possible. Music is not music, I think, until we grasp its effects both in structure and in texture. As we grow in musical understanding the structures become always more elaborate and sustained, and the texture which interrupts them and sometimes imperils them becomes more bold and unpredictable. We can agree in saying about the works of music that these are musical structures, and they are richly textured; we can identify these elements, and perhaps precisely. To what then do our feelings respond? To music as structural composition itself; to music as manifesting the structural principles of the world; to modes of structure which we feel to be ontologically possible, or even probable. Schopenhauer construed music very much in that sense. Probably it will occur to us that musical compositions bear close analogy therefore to operations in pure mathematics. The mathematicians confess that their constructions are "non-existential"; meaning, as I take it, that the constructions testify with assurance only to the structural principles, in the light of which they are possible but may not be actual, or if they are actual may not be useful. This would define the mathematical operations as speculative: as motivated by an interest so generalized and so elemental that no word short of ontological will describe it.

But if music and mathematics have this much in common, they differ sharply in their respective world-views or ontological biases. That of music, with its prodigious display of texture, seems the better informed about the nature of the world, the more realistic, the less naïve. Perhaps the difference is between two ontological educations. But I should be inclined to imagine it as rising back of that point: in two ontological temperaments.

There are also, operating a little less successfully so far as the indexical evidences would indicate, the abstractionist paintings, of many schools, and perhaps also works of sculpture; and there is architecture. These arts have tried to abandon direct representational intention almost as heroically as music. They exist in their own materials and indicate no other specific materials; structures of color, light, space, stone —the cheapest of materials. They too can symbolize nothing of value unless it is structure or composition itself. But that is precisely the act which denotes will and intelligence; which becomes the act of fuller intelligence if it carefully accompanies its structures with their material textures; for then it understands better the ontological nature of materials.

Returning to the poetry. It is not all poems, and not even all "powerful" poems, having high index-ratings, whose semantical meanings contain situations important in themselves or objects precious in themselves. There may be little correlation between the single value of the poem and the aggregate value of its contents—just as there is no such correlation whatever in music. The "effect" of the poem may be astonishingly disproportionate to our interest in its materials. It is true, of course, that there is no art employing materials of equal richness with poetry, and that it is beyond the capacity of poetry to employ indifferent materials. The words used in poetry are the words the race has already formed, and naturally they call attention to things and events that have been thought to be worth attending to. But I suggest that any poetry which is "technically" notable is in part a work of abstractionist art, concentrating upon the structure and the texture, and the structure-texture relation, out of a pure speculative interest.

At the end of *Love's Labour's Lost* occurs a little diversion which seems proportionately far more effective than that laborious play as a whole. The play is over, but Armado stops the principals before they disperse to offer them a show:

ARMADO. But, most esteemed greatness, will you hear the dialogue that the two learned men have compiled in praise of the owl and the cuckoo? It should have followed in the end of our show.

KING. Call them forth quickly; we will do so.

ARMADO. Holla! approach.

(*Re-enter Holofernes, etc.*)

This side is Hiems, Winter, this Ver, the Spring; the one maintained by the owl, the other by the cuckoo. Ver, begin.

THE SONG

SPRING. When daisies pied and violets blue
    And lady-smocks all silver-white
    And cuckoo-buds of yellow hue
    Do paint the meadows with delight,
    The cuckoo then, on every tree,
    Mocks married men; for thus sings he,
            Cuckoo;
    Cuckoo, cuckoo: O word of fear,
    Unpleasing to a married ear!

    When shepherds pipe on oaten straws,
    And merry larks are ploughmen's clocks,
    When turtles tread, and rooks, and daws,
    And maidens bleach their summer smocks,
    The cuckoo then, on every tree,
    Mocks married men; for thus sings he,
            Cuckoo;
    Cuckoo, cuckoo: O word of fear,
    Unpleasing to a married ear!

WINTER. When icicles hang by the wall,
    And Dick the shepherd blows his nail,
    And Tom bears logs into the hall,
    And milk comes frozen home in pail,
    When blood is nipp'd and ways be foul,
    Then nightly sings the staring owl,
            Tu-who;
    Tu-whit, tu-who, a merry note,
    While greasy Joan doth keel the pot.

    When all aloud the wind doth blow,
    And coughing drowns the parson's saw,
    And birds sit brooding in the snow,
    And Marian's nose looks red and raw,
    When roasted crabs hiss in the bowl,
    Then nightly sings the staring owl,
            Tu-who;
    Tu-whit, tu-who, a merry note,
    While greasy Joan doth keel the pot.

ARMADO. The words of Mercury are harsh after the songs of Apollo. You
that way,—we this way. (*Exeunt.*)

The feeling-index registers such strong approval of this episode that
a critic with ambition is obliged to account for it in terms of the weight
of its contents severally.

At first glance Shakespeare has provided only a pleasant little carica-
ture of the old-fashioned (to us, medieval) debate between personified
characters. It is easygoing, like nonsense; no labor is lost here. Each
party speaks two stanzas and concludes both stanzas with the refrain
about his bird, the cuckoo or the owl. There is no generalized argument, or dialectic proper. Each argues by citing his characteristic exhibits. In the first stanza Spring cites some flowers; in the second
stanza, some business by country persons, with interpolation of some
birds that make love. Winter in both his stanzas cites the country business of the season. In the refrain the cuckoo, Spring's symbol is used to
refer the love-making to more than the birds; and this repeats itself,
though it is naughty. The owl is only a nominal symbol for Winter, an
"emblem" that is not very emblematic, but the refrain manages another
reference to the kitchen, and repeats itself, as if Winter's pleasure focussed in the kitchen.

In this poem texture is not very brilliant, but it eclipses structure.
The argument, we would say in academic language, is concerned with
"the relative advantages of Spring and Winter." The only logical determinateness this structure has is the good coordination of the items
cited by Spring as being really items peculiar to Spring, and of the Winter items as peculiar to Winter. The symbolic refrains look like summary or master items, but they seem to be a little more than summary
and in fact to mean a little more than they say. The argument is trifling
on the whole, and the texture from the point of view of felt human importance lacks decided energy; both which observations are to be
made, and most precisely, of how many famous lyrics, especially those
before that earnest and self-conscious nineteenth century! The value of
the poem is greater than the value of its parts: that is what the critic is
up against.

Unquestionably it is possible to assemble very fine structures out of
ordinary materials. The good critic will study the poet's technique, in
confidence that here the structural principles will be discovered at
home. In this study he will find as much range for his activities as he
desires.

Especially must he study the metrics, and their implications for structural composition. In this poem I think the critic ought to make good capital of the contrast between the amateurishness of the pleasant discourse as meaning and the hard determinate form of it phonetically. The meter on the whole is out of relation to the meaning of the poem, or to anything else specifically; it is a musical material of low grade, but plastic and only slightly resistant material, and its presence in every poem is that of an abstractionist element that belongs to the art.

And here I will suggest another analogy, this one between Shakespeare's poem and some ordinary specimen of painting. It does not matter how old-fashioned or representational the painting is, we shall all, if we are instructed in the tradition of this art, require it to exhibit along with its represented object an abstract design in terms of pure physical balance or symmetry. We sense rather than measure the success of this design, but it is as if we had drawn a horizontal axis and a vertical axis through the center of the picture, and required the painted masses to balance with respect to each of these two axes. This is an over-simple statement of a structural requirement by which the same details function in two worlds that are different, and that do not correlate with each other. If the painting is of the Holy Family, we might say that this object has a drama, or an economy, of its own, but that the physical masses which compose it must enter also into another economy, that of abstract design; and that the value of any unit mass for the one economy bears no relation to its value for the other. The painting is of great ontological interest because it embodies this special dimension of abstract form. And turning to the poem, we should find that its represented "meaning" is analogous to the represented object in the painting, while its meter is analogous to the pure design.

A number of fascinating speculative considerations must follow upon this discovery. They will have to do with the most fundamental laws of this world's structure. They will be profoundly ontological, though I do not mean they must be ontological in some recondite sense; ontological in such a homely and compelling sense that perhaps a child might intuit the principles which the critic will arrive at analytically, and with much labor.

I must stop at this point, since I am desired not so much to anticipate the critic as to present him. In conclusion I will remark that the critic will doubtless work empirically, and set up his philosophy only as the drift of his findings will compel him. But ultimately he will be compelled. He will have to subscribe to an ontology. If he is a sound critic his ontology will be that of his poets; and what is that? I suggest that the poetic world-view is Aristotelian and "realistic" rather than Platonic and "idealistic." He cannot follow the poets and still conceive himself as inhabiting the rational or "tidy" universe that is supposed by the scientists.

WANTED: AN ONTOLOGICAL CRITIC

POEM differentiates itself for us, very quickly and convincingly, from a prose discourse. We have examined some important new critics who sense this fact but do not quite offer a decisive version of what the differentia is.[1]

It is not moralism, for moralism conducts itself very well in prose, and conducts itself all the better in pure or perfect prose. And the good critics who try to regard the poem as a moral discourse do not persuade themselves, and discuss the poem really on quite other grounds.

It is not emotionalism, sensibility, or "expression." Poetry becomes slightly disreputable when regarded as not having any special or definable content, and as identified only by its capacity for teasing some dormant affective states into some unusual activity. And it is impossible to talk definitively about the affections which are involved, so that affective criticism is highly distinct.

Much more promising as a differentia is the kind of structure exemplified by a poem. The good critics come round to this in the end. But it is hard to say what poetry intends by its odd structure. What is the value of a structure which (a) is not so tight and precise on its logical side as a scientific or technical prose structure generally is, and (b) imports and carries along a great deal of irrelevant or foreign matter which is clearly not structural but even obstructive? This a- and b-formulation is what we inevitably come to if we take the analysis our best critics offer. We sum it up by saying that the poem is a loose logical structure with a good deal of local texture.

It is my feeling that we have in poetry a revolutionary departure from the convention of logical discourse, and that we should provide it with a bold and proportionate designation. I believe it has proved easy to work out its structural differentiation from prose. But what is the sig-

This essay first appeared in *The New Criticism* (1941) and is reprinted from Ransom's *Beating the Bushes*, copyright © 1972 by New Directions Publishing Corporation. Reprinted by permission of New Directions Publishing Corporation.

1. In previous chapters of *The New Criticism* Ransom has discussed I. A. Richards, William Empson, T. S. Eliot, and Yvor Winters.

nificance of this when we have got it? The structure proper is the prose of the poem, being a logical discourse of almost any kind, and dealing with almost any suitable content. The texture, likewise, seems to be of any real content that may be come upon, provided it is so free, unrestricted, and extended, that it cannot properly get into the structure. One guesses that it is an *order* of content, rather than a kind of content, that distinguishes texture from structure, and poetry from prose. At any rate, a moral content is a kind of content which has been suggested as the peculiar content of poetry, and it does not work; it is not really peculiar to poetry but perfectly available for prose. I suggest that the differentia of poetry as discourse is an ontological one. It treats an order of existence, a grade of objectivity, which cannot be treated in scientific discourse.

This should not prove unintelligible. We live in a world that must be distinguished from the world, or the worlds, for there are many of them, which we treat in our scientific discourses. They are its reduced, emasculated, and docile versions. Poetry intends to recover the denser and more refractory original world which we know loosely through our perceptions and memories. By this supposition it is a kind of knowledge which is radically or ontologically distinct.

II

I have failed to find a new critic with an ontological account of poetry. But I almost thought I had found a new philosopher, or aesthetician, with one. It would have been Mr. Charles W. Morris, of the University of Chicago and the *Encyclopedia of Unified Science*. I had his name at first in the title at the top of this paper. But I could not study his aesthetic achievement very long without seeing that, though he got to the point where one further step would have taken him into an ontological conception of poetry, he held back and did not take that step; either as if he lacked the speculative curiosity to go further, or as if the prospect ahead of him impressed him vaguely as dangerous, probably threatening some disparagement of the paramount prestige of science.

The writings of Mr. Morris which bear on our discussion are, first, the presentation of his now-famous semantic system, *Foundations of the Theory of Signs*, in Vol. I, No. 2, of the *Encyclopedia*; and, applying his new semantics to art, the two essays, "Science, Art and Technology," in *The Kenyon Review* of Autumn, 1939, and "Aesthetics and the Theory of Signs," in *The Journal of Unified Science*, Vol. VIII.

Mr. Morris as a semanticist finds that all discourse consists in signs, and that any sign functions in three dimensions. There is the *syntactical* dimension, involving all of what we should call its logic; there is the *semantical* dimension proper, involving the reference of the sign to an object; and finally the *pragmatical* dimension, involving whatever reference there may be in the sign, implicit or explicit, to its psychological, biological, and sociological uses. I cannot here enlarge upon this outline. There is no short cut to Mr. Morris's knowledge; his own account will need to be read, and then reread. I think it will appear to the reader that he had a genius for fixing sound distinctions, and imposes order on a field that has hitherto been filled with confusion. I have but one source of hesitation. I do not quite sense the coördinate equality, as a component in the sign-functioning, of the pragmatical dimension with the other two. It is like according a moral dimension to poetry because there are some poems which not only present their own content but in addition moralize about this content. We may reflect that they need not do so, and that many other poems do not, and that the moral value we may find for the poem seems somewhat external to the poem itself. But at any rate Mr. Morris makes the pragmatical dimension quite distinct from the others, if not subsidiary, and that is something. Science, in Mr. Morris's view, need not be very conscious of any pragmatics; and so it may be, in our view, with art; really it is technology, or applied science, that is decidedly pragmatical.

For Mr. Morris not only distinguishes three irreducible dimensions of meaning, but finds as well three irreducible forms of discourse: science, art, and technology. These seem to him to emphasize respectively the semantical, the syntactical, and the pragmatical dimensions. To us, as I have just remarked, art may seem specially affiliated with science, and further away from technology, in not having any necessary concern with pragmatics or usefulness. But in another sense it is closer to technology and further from science. We recall our old impression, or perhaps we recall our knowledge of the Greek philosophers, to the effect that art, like technology, is concerned with making something, as well as knowing something. And what poetry makes—and the word means a making—is the poem, which at least in respect to its meter is a peculiarly novel and manufactured form, and obviously a rather special unit of discourse.

With regard to the credibility of aesthetic discourse, Mr. Morris pronounces handsomely enough: like scientific discourse, it is objective, and knowledge-giving. He says:

It is true, I believe, that the aesthetic sign, in common with all signs, has all three dimensions of sign-functioning; such a position seems a wise corrective to the common but too simple view that the artist simply "emotes" or "expresses himself" without any concern for actuality.[2]

But if art as knowledge seems to Mr. Morris capable of the same sort of validity that science has, and at times to be indistinguishable from science in this respect, it has a remarkable differentia, and is forever unlike science, in the following respect. The sign which science employs is a mere sign, or "symbol," that is, an object having no other character—for the purpose of discourse at least—than that of referring to another object which is its semantical object. For example, symbols are algebraic characters; or words used technically, as defined in the dictionary, or defined for the purpose of a given discourse in the discourse itself. But the aesthetic signs are "icons," or images. As signs they have semantical objects, or refer to objects, but as iconic signs they also resemble or imitate these objects.

The significance of this distinction that immediately flashes upon us, though it does not seem to be noticed by Mr. Morris, is that the object symbolized by a scientific sign would seem to be abstract, as, for example, a single property or aspect of objects, whereas the object symbolized by an iconic or aesthetic sign must be a whole object. And even if both seem to refer to the whole object, and the same object, there is a difference; if, for example, the scientific sign is of "man," the iconic sign is of "this particular man." By general convention the man of scientific discourse is the definable and "essential" man, whose definition involves a single set of values which are constant and negotiable for logical discourse. The man of the iconic sign is evidently imitable, or imaginable, but not definable. In brief, under the iconic sign the abstract item is restored to the body from which it was taken.

The iconic character of aesthetic signs is given by Mr. Morris in a rather matter-of-fact sort of testimony; yet it is almost the more impressive just because he does not draw the exciting implications. It amounts to a late restoration of the old doctrine of art as "imitation," to which Plato and Aristotle adhered, but which most modern aestheticians have abandoned as something absurdly simple. "Imitation" is a commonplace locution, but may be thought unworthy of the aesthetic occasion; yet I can imagine our aestheticians solemnly accepting the doctrine of "icons" because it sounds technical; actually of course it is one of the two ordi-

2. "Science, Art and Technology," *Kenyon Review*, I (Autumn, 1939), 421.

nary terms in which the Greeks rendered the idea of imitation. And since Mr. Morris is affiliated in the project of the *Encyclopedia* with naturalist, positivist, and pragmatist philosophers, I think of this enlightened testimony as another evidence of what I have hoped for: the capacity of radical modernist philosophy to apprehend and testify to kinds of truth that do not necessarily suit its own preoccupations, which are scientific ones.

It is sometimes difficult to say what is being "represented" by an aesthetic icon; in music, for example, or in a poem which makes discourse without very often referring specifically to concrete material objects. We think of "reflective" poetry which is truly poetry, and is imaginative, and yet probably a little deficient in brilliant object-images. Mr. Morris makes no question but that any variety of poetry employs iconic signs. (He offers at one point an analysis of "abstract" painting for the purpose of showing that it denotes ultimately the structure of the natural world.)

It is less difficult, and I believe Mr. Morris does not remark this problem, to see how the poem, which is a discourse in words, may offer icons as easily as painting does. The icons here are in the mind, they are the mental images evoked. The technical use of language by the poet is one that lifts words out of their symbolic or definitive uses into imaginative or image-provoking uses.

III

And that is almost as far as Mr. Morris goes. He claims that art is especially interested in the syntactical dimension of discourse, but offers almost no study of how art makes a syntax out of its peculiar mixture of pure symbols and liberal iconic signs. That would become a study of almost monumental significance. Is its validity comparable with that of science? Is its syntactical validity comparable with its own semantical validity, which Mr. Morris is good enough to accept as beyond question?

Science deals exclusively in pure symbols, but art deals essentially, though not exclusively, in iconic signs. This makes at once a sharp formal or technical distinction between the two forms of discourse; but one would think it must become also a philosophical distinction. Mr. Morris elicits chiefly the consequence that no treatment of the arts can be included within the *Encyclopedia of Unified Science*. Only semeiotic, the theory of signs, which makes its own entry as prefatory to the body of the work, may remark for the sake of formal exclusion upon the contrasted arts. But one might think that semeiotic required a closer and therefore surer study of the arts than that; for example, a study of the question why science did not choose, or had not the constitutional capacity, to employ iconic signs also; and, of course, of the ontological question itself, respecting the grades of content that the two discourses handled through their different sorts of signs, and the elemental or categorical nature of scientific knowledge as determined through the comparison with aesthetic knowledge.

In the independent essays outside the *Encyclopedia* Mr. Morris does offer some results of his own study. They seem to me inadequate. For example:

> The view proposed is that the aesthetic sign designates the value properties of actual or possible situations and that it is an iconic sign (an "image") in that it embodies these values in some medium where they may be directly inspected (in short, the aesthetic sign is an iconic sign whose designatum is a value). To give content to this statement it would be necessary to analyze in detail the notion of value and the characteristics of iconic signs, but this is neither practical nor advisable in the present context. For whatever theory of value be maintained, it must be recognized that objects have value properties among their total set of properties (an object can be insipid, sublime, menacing, oppressive, or gay in some contexts just as it may have a certain mass or length or velocity in other contexts) and that aesthetic media, since they themselves are objects, can embody certain value properties (a small piece of cork could hardly be sublime, but it could be insipid or even gay).[3]

Here it seems to me that Mr. Morris in effect is about to recant from his doctrine of the icons. The icon here is only a medium denoting, by embodying, a value; but that is more than a symbol does; he should say that the icon is a body imitating some actual embodiment of the value. And what value? I do not think he makes it clear, even with the help of his illustrations, how an icon embodies a value-property, or what sorts of values aesthetic discourse ordinarily is interested in. Certainly it sounds as if the aesthetic value-properties were quite different from the scientific ones; gaiety and sublimity, among others, for aesthetic value-properties, mass and velocity for scientific ones. It is rather suspicious that several of the aesthetic value-properties mentioned might be said to be affective ones, whereas the scientific value-properties mentioned are objective physical ones; so that Mr. Morris's aesthetic theory looks

3. Morris, "Science, Art and Technology," 415.

at this point like another version of affective or psychologistic theory. But we require much more detail from him about all this.

Briefly, may we say that the observations of Mr. Morris are promising, and even exciting: aesthetic discourse is objective knowledge, and its constituent signs have the remarkable character of being icons. But the sequel is disappointing. An icon merely embodies some certain value-property or other; that is all we are told about its operation. And as to the human significance, the usefulness or pragmatical function, Mr. Morris's imagination is again very timid. For example:

> . . . the scientists may be helped in the scientific study of values by the vivid portrayal of the value whose conditions he endeavors to trace.

And similarly:

> The technologist in turn can only be grateful for the vivid presentation of the values whose status in nature he attempts to control.[4]

The artist is pictured here as furnishing the icons which embody the precise and single scientific values, not the values causing the massive affective states referred to in the previous quotation. But his virtue seems to lie solely in the technical assistance, or else the moral encouragement, which his icons lend to the scientist and technologist in their need.

The aesthetic project has turned out rather small and ignominious after its fine beginnings in Mr. Morris's hands.

We might sketch here, though tentatively and rudely, a really ontological argument, such as Mr. Morris's preliminaries seemed to invite.

The validity of a scientific discourse depends in part, we should say, on its semantical purity. That is, each symbol should refer to an object specifically defined, or having a specific value-aspect, for the discourse; and throughout the discourse it should have exactly that reference and no other. The reference of a single symbol is limited, and uniform.

In aesthetic discourse, however, we replace symbols with icons, and the peculiarity of an icon is that it refers to the whole or concrete object and cannot be limited. As Mr. Morris says, an icon "embodies" the value-property that is the object of discourse. But "embodies" is a great word, and Mr. Morris ought to accept its consequences. Certainly he offers no rule as to how the value-property may be isolated in the body of the containing icon, or placed in the center, or otherwise made to

---

4. Morris, "Science, Art and Technology," 419.

stand out so that we shall be sure to attend to it rather than to the containing book.[5]

The icon is an individual, therefore indefinable; that is, it exceeds definition. In the play, the icon is our image of Prince Hamlet, and it is never twice the same, so that the rule of consistent definitive reference is abrogated with each reappearance. An individual has too many properties, and too many values. If a kind of discourse is accredited (and given a semantical bill of health) which proposes to deal in particulars, as one must propose to do which deals in icons, then it is removed far indeed from scientific discourse; it decidedly invites philosophical attention, and one must be prepared to make dispositions which are heroic, because in the present state of theory they will be novel.

The syntactical dimension is imperiled, upon the introduction of icons into discourse, along with the semantical. It will be impossible for discourse to compel its icons to function in the strict logic which we have learned to expect from the symbols. The logic of art will probably be variable in the degree of its validity, but always in degree lower than that of science. At the same time we shall probably incline to assert that it will have no validity at all unless it holds itself together at least in part by scientific symbols. So the aesthetic discourse will be discovered, one expects, making digressions from its logic with its icons at local points; or perhaps maintaining itself on the whole in terms of valid symbols, but occasionally and suddenly building a routine symbol out into the icon denoting the full body of the object of which the symbol denotes only a single value-property. But the semantics and the syntactics of art together invite the most exacting study if we care to identify them really.

In scientific discourse we deal with a single value-system at a time. In art only the paraphrase, of which Mr. Morris gives an adequate account, and which is the "moral," the theme, or the argument of the discourse, offers the single-value system; the work itself goes beyond its paraphrase into the realm of the natural objects or situations themselves, which are many-valued.

5. It is true that in one context he talks about the icon as representing a "consummatory" or final value, as if constituting the image of a body so obviously meant for consumption, so ripe for immediate consumption, that nobody could resist knowing the value it meant to put forward. But even so I do not know what the body is for. The body is an impediment, and has to be waived, in order to attend to the value that interests the consumer, or even the strict discourser. But it is much easier to suppose that the body is there to be attended to as much as the value; and that attention to the body may not be characteristic of scientific discourse, but is the distinguishing characteristic of aesthetic discourse. (Ransom's note)

Art as a discourse, indeed, is anomalous, and all but incredible; a discourse which looks legitimate so long as it looks merely scientific, but every moment or so turns up its icons, in which it hardly seems that discourse could take place.

Science, as Mr. Morris says, is statemental, and its statements have predictive value. But art employs icons, which being individual are contingent and unpredictable. Art seems to permit us to predict only some order of unpredictability.

But principles of this sort are ontological. The world of predictability, for example, is the restricted world of scientific discourse. Its restrictive rule is: one value at a time. The world of art is the actual world which does not bear restriction; or at least defies the restrictiveness of science, and offers enough fullness of content to give us the sense of the actual objects. A qualitative density, or value-density, such as is unknown to scientific understanding, marks the world of the actual objects. The discourse which tries systematically to record this world is art.

As to the pragmatics of the poetic act, or its "psychological, biological, and social" motivation, I have almost nothing to suggest. It seems very idle to assume, as Mr. Morris does in effect, that the pragmatical intention of art is the same as that of science; we would ask him why scientists should not commit themselves then to aesthetic as well as scientific discourse. But the psychologists have not furnished us with decisive motivations for this as for many other acts. It is an act of knowledge. The scientific and aesthetic ways of knowledge should illuminate each other; perhaps they are alternative knowledges, and a preference for one knowledge over the other might indicate an elemental or primary bias in temperament. But even if the pragmatical sanction behind the act has to be improvised, and psychologically is less than regular, nevertheless it seems certain that the act is imperative.

IV

At this point I venture to abandon the framework of Mr. Morris's speculations. They have provided considerable moral reinforcement for the inquiry. I wish to start a little further back in the ontological analysis of the poem.

The critic of a poem knows that the labor of composing it was, at the least, a verbal exercise in search of a language which on the one hand would "make the sense," and on the other hand would "make the rhythm," and if it liked would even "make the rhyme." He knows it so well that perhaps he is past being curious about the fact.

But it is still strange to us, who are not agreed on any standard version of the natural history of the form, that poetry should ever have coveted a language that would try to do not one hard thing but two hard things at once. Extravagant exercises with language are not the rule by which the logical men have arrived at their perfections of thought. But the composition of a poem is an operation in which an argument fights to displace a meter, and the meter fights to displace the argument. It would seem that the sacrifices made on both sides would be legible forever in the terms of peace, which are the dispositions found in the finished poem, where the critic must analyze them if he thinks they further the understanding of poetry. Most critics seem to think it does not, for they do not try the analysis, nor the philosophical speculations it might suggest. On the contrary, it is common for critics to assume that a good poet is in control of his argument, and that the meter has had no effect on it, or if anything points its logic all the better, and that the form of the argument is perfect.

If the unsatisfactoriness of poetic theory, which strikes us so painfully, is due to the absence from it of radical philosophical generalities, the fault must begin really with its failure to account for the most elementary and immediate aspect that formal poetry wears: its metrical form. The convention of the metrical form is thought to be as old as the art itself. Perhaps it is the art itself. I suggest that the meter-and-meaning process is the organic act of poetry, and involves all its important characters.

Let us suppose a lady who wishes to display a bowl of fruits upon her sideboard and says to her intelligent houseboy: "Go to the box of apples in the pantry and select and bring me a dozen of the biggest and reddest ones." The box contains a hundred apples, which vary both in bigness and in redness. And we will suppose, as it is easy to suppose, that there is no definable correlation between the bigness and the redness; a big apple is not necessarily a red one, and vice versa. The boy interests himself in the curious problem, and devises the following solution.

He ranges the apples first in order of their bigness, and denotes the biggest as B_1, the next as B_2, and so on down to B_{100}. Then he ranges the apples in order of their redness, and denotes the reddest as R_1, the next reddest as R_2, and so on down to R_{100}. Then for each apple he adds the numerical coefficient of its bigness and the numerical coefficient of its redness; for example, the apple which is tagged B_1 is also tagged R_{36}, so that its combined coefficient is 37. He finds the twelve apples with lowest combined coefficients and takes them to his mistress.

She will have to concede, as he has conceded, that objects systematically valued for two unrelated properties at once are likely not to be superlative in both properties. She will not secure the perfection of her object in one aspect if she is also trying to secure its perfection in another aspect. She has committed herself to a two-ground basis of selection, and her selections on the one ground have to accommodate themselves to her selections on the other ground. It is a situation in which some compromises are necessary.

But she may find an unexpected compensation. In regretting the loss of certain nearly solid-red apples, which are denied to her because they are little, she may observe that the selected apples exhibit color patterns much more various, unpredictable, and interesting. She finds pleasure in studying their markings, whereas she would have obtained the color-value of her solid-red apples at a glance.

I am sorry to think that no such compensation appears for her putting up with second-best apples in the respect of size; which is a stupid category. But I am afraid the analogy of the bigness-redness relation in apples does not represent sufficiently the meter-meaning relation which we are to examine in poetry.

V

Much more difficult than the selection of apples that shall be both big and red is the composition of a poem on the two-ground basis of (1) an intended meaning and (2) an intended meter. In theory the feat seems impossible, unless we are allowed to introduce some qualifications into the terms. It is true that language possesses two properties, the semantic and the phonetic; that is, respectively, the property of referring under fairly fixed conventions to objects beyond itself, which constitute its meaning, and the property of being in itself a sequence of objective physical sounds set to an elementary music.

I assume that there is hardly necessity for an extended argument to the effect that a perfect metrical construction, of which the components were words selected from the range of all actual words, and exclusively for phonetic effects, would not be likely to make noteworthy sense. It would be nonsense. Nor for another argument to show that a pure logical construction would not be likely to make meter. The latter case we have with us always, in our science, in the prose of our newspapers and business correspondence, in our talk. Even so, there might be some instruction in considering for a moment such a little piece of mathematical discourse as this:

$$(a + b)^2 = a^2 + 2ab + b^2$$

Here the mathematician is saying exactly what he means, and his language is not metrical, and we can discover if we try that he does not want any poet to meter it, on the matter-of-fact ground that the poet would have to take liberties with his logical values. At once a question or two should present themselves very vexingly to the nebulous aesthetician: What sort of liberties does the poet take with a discourse when he sets it to meter? And what sort of discourse is prepared to permit those liberties?

An argument which admits of alteration in order that it may receive a meter must be partly indeterminate. The argument cannot be maintained exactly as determined by its own laws, for it is going to be undetermined by the meter.

Conversely, a metrical form must be partly indeterminate if it proposes to study an argument. It is useless to try to determine it closely in advance, for the argument will un-determine it.

The second principle, of the two just stated, may seem the less ominous. To most poets, and most readers, the meaning is more important than the meter.

Let DM stand for determinate meaning, or such of the intended meaning as succeeds in being adhered to; it may be fairly represented by the logical paraphrase of the poem. IM stands for indeterminate meaning, or that part of the final meaning which took shape not according to its own logical necessity but under metrical compulsion; it may be represented by the poem's residue of meaning which does not go into the logical paraphrase. DS stands for the determinate sound-structure, or the meter; and IS stands for whatever phonetic character the sounds have assumed which is indeterminate.

In theory, the poem is the resultant of two processes interacting upon each other; they come from opposite directions. On the one hand the poet is especially intent upon his meter, DS, which may be blocked out as a succession of unaccented and accented syllables arranged in lines, perhaps with rhyme endings; but there is DM, a prose discourse, which must be reduced into the phonetic pattern; his inclination is to replace its words with others from the general field of words which suit the music, and without much regard for their logical propriety. But he is checked on the other hand where he starts with firm possession of DM, a prose meaning, but has to assimilate it to DS, the sound-pattern that he has chosen; his inclination is to replace the required metrical sounds with others that suit his logic and are not quite so good for the sound-structure.

Actually, a skillful piece of composition will have many stages of development, with strokes too subtle and rapid to record, and operations in some sort of alternation from the one direction and the other. The poet makes adaptations both of sound to meaning (introducing IS) and of meaning to sound (introducing IM). Both adaptations are required for the final version of the poem.

VI

The most interesting observation for the critic, perhaps, is that the poem is an object comprising not two elements but four; not merely a meaning M, but DM, that part of a meaning which forms a logical structure, and IM, a part which does not belong to the structure and may be definitely illogical, though more probably it is only additive and a-logical; and not merely DS, a sound-pattern, but IS, a part of the total sound-effect which may be in exception to the rule but at any rate does not belong to it. These elements are familiar enough to the poet himself, who has manipulated them. Frequently they are evident to the critic too. They should be, very substantially; they can be distinguished to the extent that he is capable of distinguishing them. Logically they are distinct elements, now, in the finished poem, though it may not be possible to trace back the precise history of their development under the tension of composition.

I cannot but think that the distinction of these elements, and especially of DM and IM, is the vocation par excellence of criticism. It is more technical than some other exercises which go as criticism, but more informed. It brings the criticism of poetry to somewhat the same level of professional competence as that of the discussions which painters sometimes accord to paintings, and that which musicians accord to music; which means, I think, an elevation of our normal critical standard.

If a poet is a philosopher, explicitly or implicitly, treating matters of ethical or at least human importance—and it is likely that he is that—the discussion of his "ideology" may be critical in every sense in which one may be said to criticize systematic ideas; but the ideas of the poet, struggling but not quite managing to receive their really determinate expression, are only his DM, and a better version is almost certain to be found elsewhere in prose, so that their discussion under the poem is likely to be a tame affair. Few poets serve, as Wordsworth and Shelley may be thought to do, as texts for the really authoritative study of ideas; mostly they serve amateur ideologists for that purpose, or serve distinguished critics who fall back upon this sort of thing because nothing is quite prescriptive in their vocation. The more interesting thing to study is the coexistence and connection of DM and IM—the ideas and the indeterminate material in which they are enveloped. This kind of study is much severer, but its interest is profounder and more elemental than the merely ethical; it is an ontological interest.

Possibly an examination of poetry along these lines might finally disclose the secret of its strange yet stubborn existence as a kind of discourse unlike any other. It does not bother too much about the perfection of its logic; and does bother a great deal, as if it were life and death, about the positive quality of that indeterminate thing which creeps in by the back door of musical necessity. I suggest the closest possible study of IM, the indeterminate meaning.

But there are two kinds of indeterminacy in IM, and I wish to show how the poet in metering his argument yields reluctantly to the first, as to an indeterminacy that means only inaccuracy and confusion, and then gladly to the second, as to an indeterminacy that opens to him a new world of discourse.

First, he tries to shift the language within the range of a rough verbal equivalence, and to alter DM no more substantively than necessary. A given word will probably have synonyms. The order of words in a phrase may be varied. A transitive predication may be changed to a passive; a relative clause to a participial phrase. In the little words denoting logical connections and transitions a good deal of liberty may be taken without being fatal; they may be expanded into something almost excessively explicit, or they may be even omitted, with the idea that the reader can supply the correct relations. A single noun may become a series of nouns, or nearly any other element may be compounded, without introducing much novelty. Epithetical adjectives and adverbs may be interpolated, if they will qualify their nouns and verbs very obviously. Archaic locutions may be substituted for contemporary ones. A poet is necessarily an accomplished verbalist, and capable of an almost endless succession of periphrases that come nearer and nearer to metered language until finally he achieves what he wants; a language that is metrical enough, and close to his intended meaning.

Mr. C. D. Abbott at the library of the University of Buffalo is collecting a very large number of work sheets from living poets, with the idea of securing an objective exhibit of the actual process of perfecting poems by revision. The most immediate use of these manuscripts that will suggest itself will surely be the critical study of the way poets tinker with given phrases in order to adapt them to the metrical pattern. Presently there should be a voluminous bulk of evidence on this point. But anybody who has tried versification can predict the sort of evidence that will turn up. Meanwhile we may see what evidences there are in the final poems themselves.

Wordsworth would probably be cited by the historian as one who metered his language with more method than inspiration, especially in his longer work. Here is a passage from the *Prelude*, where he is talking about the power of poetry, and its habitation in a place called "the mystery of words":

> . . . there,
> As in a mansion like their proper home,
> Even forms and substances are circumfused
> By that transparent veil with light divine,
> And through the turnings intricate of verse
> Present themselves as objects recognized
> In flashes, and with glory not their own.[6]

It is easy to find disagreeable lapses of logic here. There are the painful inversions of order, clearly in the interest of metric: *light divine* and *turnings intricate*. The line *As in a mansion like their proper home* is certainly a curious involution for *As in a mansion which is their proper home*. The third and fourth lines are not transparent for us like the veil talked about: Does the veil possess and give off the divine light? And if not, how does it circumfuse the forms and substances with it? The brevity of statement is either a laziness on Wordsworth's part, or it is a recourse to elliptical expression invited by metrical exigencies. But at this point all our little objections pass into a big and overwhelming one: there is really in this passage scarcely any specific discourse of respectable logical grade. We do not know what any of these pretty things is, or does. No prose would be cynical enough to offer so elusive a content.

6. *The Prelude*, Bk. V, 599–605.

The mansion, the forms and substances, the magic veil, the divine light, the movement of the turnings, the flashes and the borrowed glory—these look like responsible and promising objects, but none of them establishes a sufficient identity when they all assemble together. The poet became a little paralyzed, we may imagine, when he took pen in hand to write a poem; or got that way after going a certain distance in the writing of a long one. I go beyond the direct evidence here, but I assume that making distinguished metrical discourse was such a job, and consisted in his own mind with so much corruption of the sense at best, that he fell into the habit of choosing the most resounding words, and stringing them together as the meter dictated. This is not unusual in Romantic poetry. The point to make about Romantic poetry now is not the one about its noble words, but a negative and nasty one: the noble words are almost absurdly incoherent. (But I realize that my tone is too severe.)

Pope was not a Romantic, and I suppose the language has known no poet more nice in his expression. I quote:

> Close by those meads, forever crowned with flowers,
> Where Thames with pride surveys his rising towers,
> There stands a structure of majestic frame,
> Which from the neighboring Hampton takes its name.
> Here Britain's statesmen oft the fall foredoom
> Of foreign tyrants and of nymphs at home;
> Here thou, great Anna! whom three realms obey,
> Dost sometimes counsel take—and sometimes tea.[7]

With so great a master of language, it is a little dangerous to insist on the exact place where the meter coming in drove some of the logic out. But the superiority of his logic over Wordsworth's is not so overwhelming as it seems; for the most part it is merely that his improvisations are made to look nearly natural, as if he thoroughly intended them all the time, and meter had nothing to do with them. The *flowers* is arrived at gracefully, but the chief source of any "inevitability" claimed for it is the fact that it rhymes with *towers*, which is more important to the discourse. In four lines we come to Hampton Court, where will presently appear Belinda, whom we have left traveling in her boat on the Thames. Hampton Court has a location with respect to the Thames which we need to know, under the principles of the logical or narrative argument; and at Hampton Court assemble the royalty and the fashionable gentry,

---

7. *The Rape of the Lock*, Canto III, 1–8.

whom we must know too; these are among the necessary moves. Hampton Court is close by those *rising towers* which are London-on-Thames, and that is enough as to its location; it is a matter of course that it will be close by the meads, since the towers will rise out of the meads by the river rather than rise out of the river. If we should invert the two lines, as follows,

> Near where proud Thames surveys his rising towers,
> And where are meads forever crowned with flowers,

something would happen not only to the euphony of the language but to the respectability of its logic, for then it would be plain that the meads-and-flowers line is chiefly useful for filling up a couplet. But the next couplet lacks honest logical economy too. The *structure of majestic frame* is nothing but a majestic structure, with a rhyme tag added, and the account of the naming of Hampton Court is a metrical but logically gratuitous expansion of the simple recital of its name. The other two couplets both employ rhyme words, and contexts to assimilate them, which are so incongruous that they have to be employed in discourse as the occasions of wit. As logicians we need not take much stock in wit as forwarding argument, even when it is free from suspicion as a device to look after difficult rhyme pairings; it supposes such a lack of an obvious logical relation between two things that any technical bridge of connection must be accepted. No honest "argument" prefaced to a poem would cover the poet's witticisms. We condemn Romantic poets for injecting their burning sentiments into an objective argument, but other poets are given to wit, which is likewise at the expense of argument and logic.[8] A final remark will sound a little captious. Hampton Court is in mind, but the word "Court" is not used and possibly its absence troubles the poet; at any rate if he does not have a court he supplies the short passage with three royalties. There is the lady of the meads, a figurative queen, with a crown of flowers. Thames, a figurative patriarch, and at least a prince with all his rising towers

---

8. Mr. Cleanth Brooks reproves the sentimentality of simple poets, but puts himself rather off guard by his blanket counterendorsement of the wit of university or sophisticated poets. If we had an aesthetician's version of Horace's fable of the town mouse and the country mouse, we would be sure to find the latter uttering countrified sentimental discourse, and scorned by the other; but the discourse of the town mouse not only would be smart, it would presently become oversmart and silly; so that in the long run we should smile at her as at the country cousin, and for much the same reason; naïveté, as plain in personal vanity as in simplicity. Elizabethan comedy finds its butt in the smart town character as readily as in the country simpleton. (Ransom's note)

(though a little while earlier there was a feminine character of the same name upon whose "silver bosom" Belinda rode in her boat); and actual Queen Anne. It seems an excessive profusion of royalties.

There are certainly readers of the Binomial Theorem who are prohibited by conscience from the reading of poetry; we have just been looking at some of the reasons. On these terms meter may be costing more than it is worth. Milton thought of the possibility, and went so far as to renounce its most binding device, the rhyme; it is employed by

> Some famous modern Poets, carried away by Custom, but much to their own vexation, hindrance, and constraint to express many things otherwise, and for the most part worse, than else they would have expressed them.[9]

But greater purists might apply this logic to all the rest of the metrical devices. We turn to Milton's own unrhymed verse, and find:

> Thus, while he spake, each passion dimm'd his face
> Thrice chang'd with pale, ire, envy and despair,
> Which marr'd his borrow'd visage, and betray'd
> Him counterfeit, if any eye beheld.[10]

The argument of this narrative passage would explain how Uriel, deceived once by Satan in his "stripling cherub's" disguise, perceives now his identity through the satanic passions registered in his face, and initiates the next cycle of action by informing the angels guarding Paradise. But the language, as is not uncommon with Milton, from the point of view of logic is almost like a telegraphic code in its condensation, and omission of connectives; it is expansible to two or three times its length in prose, and readable only with difficulty by unaccustomed readers. Yet it also lapses from strict logic in precisely the opposite direction, by the importation of superfluous detail. The three successive increments of pallor and their respective causes would seem beyond the observation of Uriel, in the sun, and in fact we learn presently that what Uriel actually marked was Satan's "gestures fierce" and "mad demeanor." Milton is aware of this, and gives himself a technical alibi in our passage by being careful to say that the pallor stages betrayed the fraud not necessarily to Uriel but to any good eye that might be close enough to see them. Still, if Uriel did not see them they do not matter.

9. This quotation is taken from Milton's note, "The Verse," which precedes Book I of *Paradise Lost.*
10. *Paradise Lost*, Bk. IV, 114–17.

It would have been hard to persuade Milton out of this passage, with its deficiencies and superfluities; but suppose we might have proposed an alternative version, which would seem safely eclectic and within the traditional proficiencies of poetry; and I shall not mind appearing ridiculous for the sake of the argument:

> Speaking, rank passion swelled within his breast
> Till all the organism felt its power,
> And such a pallor in his face was wrought
> That it belied the angelic visage fair
> He had assumed. Uriel, unsleeping guard,
> With supernatural vision saw it plain.

But Milton in his turn would instantly have gibed at it, and on our terms; at the dangling participle and the poetic inversion, as violations of good syntax; and then at the constant tendency, perhaps proceeding from our nervous desire to come with some spirit out of an embarrassing situation, to exceed the proper logic content, as shown in all four first lines by the verbs, *swelled, felt, was wrought,* and *belied.* They are ambitious, and start our minds upon little actions that would take us out of the plane of the argument.

Returning to rhymed verse, there is this passage from a poem which deserves its great fame, but whose fabulous "perfections" consist with indeterminacies that would be condemned in the prose of scientists, and also of college freshmen; though I think in the prose of college seniors they might have a different consideration:

> Had we but world enough, and time,
> This coyness, lady, were no crime.
> We would sit down, and think which way
> To walk, and pass our long love's day.
> Thou by the Indian Ganges' side
> Should'st rubies find: I by the tide
> Of Humber would complain. I would
> Love you ten years before the flood,
> And you should, if you please, refuse
> Till the conversion of the Jews;
> My vegetable love should grow
> Vaster than empires and more slow.[11]

I will use the pedagogical red pencil, though I am loath. World, as distinguished from time, is not space, for the lovers already have all the

---

11. Andrew Marvell, "To His Coy Mistress."

space in the world, and long tenure would not increase it. It is a violent condensation meaning, I think, "the whole history of the world before us," and combining with the supposal of their having time to live through it; it supports the historical references which follow. *We would, thou should'st, my love should*: the use of the auxiliaries is precise, varying according to rule from person to person, and uniformly denoting determination or command: "we would arrange it so." But it is remarkable that in so firm a set of locutions, which attests the poet's logical delicacy, the *thou should'st* is interchangeable with *you should*; the meter is responsible for the latter version, since otherwise we should have the line, *And thou should'st, if thou pleased'st, refuse*; or, taking the same liberty with tenses which we find actually taken (again for metrical reasons), *And thou should'st, if thou pleas'st, refuse*; but either line clogs the meter. *Which way* is one phrase, but language is an ambiguous thing, and it has two meanings; *in which direction* as applied to *walk*, and *in what manner* as applied to *pass our day*. The parallel series in lines 5–7 is in three respects not uniform: *Ganges* has little need of a defining adjective, except the metrical one, but when once it has become *Indian Ganges* there is every right on the part of its analogue to be styled *English Humber*; and *Ganges' side* calls for *Humber's side*, or for merely *Humber's*, with *side* understood, but rhyme produces for Humber a *tide*; and the possessive case in the first member would call for the same in the second member, but is replaced there actually by an *of*-phrase. *Refuse* brings out of the rhyming dictionary the *Jews*, which it will tax the poet's invention to supply with a context; but for our present purposes the poet has too much invention, for it gives him the historical period from the Flood to the conversion of the Jews, which is a handsome way of saying ten thousand years, or some other length of time, and seems disproportionate to the mere ten years of the same context, the only other period mentioned. *Vegetable* is a grotesque qualification of love, and on the whole decidedly more unsuitable than suitable, though there are features in which it is suitable. *Vaster* would correlate with *slower*, but not with *more slow*; but they would not be correlatives at all after *grow*, for *vaster* is its factitive complement and *slower* can only be for *more slowly*, its abverb. Finally, there is the question of how the vastness of the poet's love can resemble the vastness of empires; the elegance of the terms seems to go along with the logic of a child.

VII

But the important stage of indeterminacy comes, in the experiment of composition, when the imagination of the poet, and not only his verbal mechanics, is engaged. An "irrelevance" may feel forced at first, and its overplus of meaning unwanted, because it means the importation of a little foreign or extraneous content into what should be determinate, and limited; but soon the poet comes upon a kind of irrelevance that seems desirable, and he begins to indulge it voluntarily, as a new and positive asset to the meaning. And this is the principle: the importations which the imagination introduces into discourse have the value of developing the freedom which lurks in the "body," and under the surface, of apparently determinate situations. When Marvell is persuaded by the rhyme consideration to invest the Humber with a tide, or to furnish his abstract calendar with specifications about the Flood, and the conversion of the Jews, he does not make these additions reluctantly. On the contrary, he knows that the brilliance of the poetry depends on the shock, accompanied at once by the realism or the naturalness, of its powerful individuality. But the mere syllabic measure, and not only the rhyme, can induce this effect. When the poet investigates the suitability of a rhyme word for his discourse, he tries the imaginative contexts in which it could figure; but the process is the same when he tries many new phrases in the interest of the rhythm, for their suitability, though his imagination has to do without the sharp stimuli of the rhyme words. And by suitability I mean the propriety which consists in their denoting the proper effect which really belongs to the object. In this way what is irrelevant for one kind of discourse becomes the content for another kind, and presently the new kind stands up firmly if we have the courage to stand by it.

The passages cited above were in support of the negative and corrupt IM, but they illustrate also the positive IM, which is poetic texture, for the critic, and ontological freedom for the philosopher. Wordsworth has the most abstract argument, but instead of pursuing it closely and producing a distinguished logical structure—it might have come to a really superior version of the argument we are here trying to build up, something about the meaning of poetry—he wavers toward some interesting concrete objects, producing a mansion, a veil, a light, and a set of intricate turnings; but here too he is stopped, as if by some puritan inhibition, from looking steadily at his objects to obtain a clear image;

so that his discourse is not distinguished either for its argument or for its texture. Pope unquestionably has the narrative gift, which means that he has access to the actual stream of events covered by the abstract argument; he is perhaps one of many poets prefiguring our modern prose fiction, and knows that he may suspend his argument whenever he pleases, provided he may substitute another equally positive content, namely, a subnarrative account of the independent character and history of its items. Milton looks principally like a man out of a more heroic age than Pope, in the casualness and roughness of his indeterminacy, but he is bolder also in the positive detail: nothing in Pope's passage compares with his stopping to name the three specific passions in the mind of Satan, and to imagine each one as turning Satan's visage paler than the one before had left it. As for Marvell, we are unwilling to praise or to condemn the peccadilloes of his logic, and here is a case where we take no account of the indeterminacy of the bad sort that results from the metering process, and distresses so many hardheaded readers. This is all overshadowed, and we are absorbed, by the power of his positive details.

Indeterminacy of this positive or valuable sort is introduced when the images make their entry. It looks as if there might be something very wise in the social, anonymous, and universal provision of metrical technique for poetry. The meter seems only to harm the discourse, till presently it works a radical innovation: it induces the provision of individual icons among the hard-and-fast logical symbols. This launches poetry upon its career.

VIII

The development of metrical content parallels that of meaning. As the resonant meter un-determines the meaning and introduces IM, so in turn the likely meaning un-determines the meter and introduces the variations of IS.

The usual minimum of a meter, in English practice, is a succession of lines having a determinate number of determinate feet, and a foot is some syllabic combination having one accented syllable. The most general consequence is that a unit of phonetic structure—a few lines of blank verse, a stanza of rhymed verse, a sonnet or whole poem sometimes—is super-imposed upon a unit of meaning-structure; within it the foot may not coincide with the word or small logical unit, but the two structures use precisely the same constituent language in the long run, and come out at the end together; and this is a summary feat of remarkable coördination, when we approach it with the prejudice of a person used to working in pure structures, that is, in one structure at a time. In reading the poem we have our ear all the time immediately upon the progress of the meter, just as we have our discursive mind all the time on the course of the argument; so that the two structures advance simultaneously if not by the same steps, and every moment or so two steps finish together, and two new steps start together. And what we call a "phrase" is at once a period in the argument and a definable element in the metrical structure, and "phrasing" means to the poet the act of grouping the words to serve the two purposes as simultaneously as possible.

We may suppose that the phonetic effect and the meaning-effect are, in theory, perfectly equal and coördinate. But probably we all have much more interest in the meaning than in the sound. Therefore it is convenient to say that the phonetic effect serves as a sort of texture to the meaning. This is to assign to the meaning an ontological addition.

But within the phonetic effect considered for itself alone we find the poet developing for his meter, which is the regular phonetic structure, its own kind of texture, which consists in the metrical variations. He is driven into this course by considerations exactly the same, except in reverse, as those we have seen compelling him to develop within the meaning a texture of meaning. The latter was forced upon him by the necessity of adapting his meaning to the meter; and this is forced upon him by the necessity of adapting his meter to the meaning. When he cannot further reduce his meaning to language more accurately metrical, he accepts a "last version" and allows the variations to stand. These variations of course present the contingency and unpredictability, or in one word the "actuality," of the world of sound. Many phonetic effects are possible really; and here and there a foot or a phrase holds stubbornly to its alien character and is not quite assimilated to the poet's purpose.

But the texture that is realized within a meter is under conventional restrictions, the like of which have not been formulated for the texture within the meaning. Variations from the meter are permissive, but they must be of certain kinds. I suppose experience has shown, or else there is a strange consent of feeling, that the phrasing of the determinate meaning can always be roughly accomplished if allowed a few permissive variations; that the metrical effects, plus the effects allowed in the variations, make language sufficiently flexible to carry any meaning. Take iambic verse, for example, which is the staple for English. Elizabethan dramatic verse became somewhat loosened up or "Websterized" before it finished; and later Coleridge very nearly got the anapaestic foot adopted as a legitimate variation for the iambic within short rhymed lines. But with such exceptions the poets have confined their metrical departures from iambic verse to the permissive variations with remarkable unanimity. So at least until our own period. There have been many poets recently, including the lettered as well as the unlettered, who have cast off the "bondage" of the meters, and employ them only as they find it convenient, or else make it their rule on principle not to cultivate anything approaching metrical determinateness. But I am talking here about the traditional practice. The critic must take it into account if he cares to discuss the traditional poets; there can be no dispute about that.

Shakespeare wrote,

> Whén to | the sés | sions of | swéet sí | lent thóught
> I sum | mon úp | remém | brance of | things pást,

but we may safely suppose that he was aware of the possibility of many other versions, as for example,

> When síts | my pár | liamént | of sí | lent thóught
> To trý | afrésh | the swéet | remém | bered pást.

The assumption that this version entered his mind is of course improbable for more reasons than one, but at least it represents a common situation: the option between a fairly determinate meaning consisting with a variant or indeterminate meter, and a revised and less determinate meaning leading to a more determinate meter. Decision is in favor of the former alternative, but it is in the light of the fact that the metrical variations are all permissive and conventional. Here they consist in the following substitutions: a trochaic for the first iambic of the first line; a double foot or ionic for the third and fourth iambics of that line; and a double foot or ionic for the fourth and fifth iambics of the second line. But the meaning is slightly more severe than the alternative meaning, and Shakespeare does not care to tinker with it. In the alternative version the boldness of the figure may be too odd; and even in that version the third foot of the first line would have in *párliamént* an extra syllable, unless we take advantage again of the permissions and say it is "accounted for by elision."[12]

In Donne, unless it is in Wyatt, whose meters are very difficult to construe, we have the feeling that we should find indeterminacy of metric carried furthest, sometimes almost to the point of unseating the iambic principle:

> Twó graves | must híde | thine and | my córse;
> If óne | might, déath | were nó | divórce.

The difficulty of the first line is that every one of the monosyllables, except possibly *and*, is capable of taking a strong logical accent. We do not in fact know how to read it; we do know that the line from which it is in variation is iambic tetrameter; see the following line, completing the couplet, which is dutifully regular. We assign therefore some reading, almost arbitrary, which perhaps metrifies the line sufficiently and respects its structural logic, and we think of that perverseness in Donne which led him so often to mock the law without technically breaking it. Perverseness, that is, as Ben Jonson construed it; and by any account an insubordinacy, or an individualism, which was reluctant to conform, and seemed to offer the pretense that a meaning was involved which was too urgent to tamper with in the interest of meter. But we can defend the substantive orthodoxy of this poet's metrical technique if we should hear complaint against the following line; it has ten syllables, and is shown by its context to be intended for an iambic pentameter:

> Blásted | with síghs, | and súr | róunded | with téars.

The parallelism of *with sighs* and *with tears* suggests that the participles on which they depend are also closely coupled; if we are blasted by the sighs, as by winds, we ought to be fairly drowned by the tears, as by floods. But this last is precisely what *surrounded* means. It is from the French *suronder* (Lat. *superundare*), to overflow. The verb in its weak modern sense could hardly find room for two logical accents, and the iambic structure might collapse; but then the logical structure would be impaired too, because it would come in this word to a foolish anticlimax. The only proper reader of the line is the one who trusts the integrity of Donne's metrical intention and looks to see how it can pro-

12. The three permissive variations in iambic verse have now all been named: Trochaic for iambic, ionic for two iambics, and extra syllable accounted for by elision. (Ransom's note)

pose to conform here. To this reader the metric is informative. It is strictly the meaning of the line which has determined the variations in the meter, but we have found a meaning which does not destroy the meter, and it is decisive.

Milton is bold in his metric, but his conscience is exacting, and his irregularities come under the conventions. He writes:

Weep nó | more, wóe | ful Shép | herds, wéep | no móre.

The brilliance of this line consists in its falling eventually, and after we have tried other readings in vain, into the entire regularity which was the last thing we expected of it. We are used to receiving the impression, which he likes to give, and which represents a part of the truth, that his determinate meaning produces an indeterminateness in the local meters of nearly every line, even if we understand that this indeterminateness stops at the limits of the permissive convention. Under that impression we were inclined to scan the line this way:

Wéep no | móre, woe | ful Shép | herds, wéep | no móre,

which is a metrical line found many times in Milton; but we were troubled over what happened to the logic of the accentless *woeful*. We said to ourselves, however, that the first *weep no more* had precisely the same logical values as the second one. All the same, the *woeful* is really not up to Milton's level as a workman, and we are not content with it. We finally try the normal meter, and we see that Milton intended us to come to it, and thought we must come to it if we believed in his technical competence. In the phrase *weep no more* it is difficult to say that one word has a heavier logical accent than another; yet we cannot accent them all, as we should like to do, and would do in prose. Or can we? The fact is that, reading the line as we finally do, we not only accent all three words but are obliged to: first *no*, then *weep*, then *more*; for the phrase occurs twice. Again the meter is informative. It could not be so if there were not the most minute give-and-take between the meaning and the meter as principles trying to determine each other, and arriving every moment or so at peace with honor, which means careful adjustments by means of reciprocal concessions.

And now I must make an admission that my readers will surely have anticipated. It is not telling the whole truth to say that Shakespeare and other accomplished poets resort to their variations, which are metrical imperfections, because a determinate meaning has forced them into it. The poet likes the variations regardless of the meanings, finding them essential in the capacity of a sound-texture to go with the sound-structure. It is in no very late stage of a poet's advancement that his taste rejects a sustained phonetic regularity as something restricted and barren, perhaps ontologically defective. Accordingly he is capable of writing smooth meters and then roughening them on purpose. And it must be added, while we are about it, that he is capable of writing a clean logical argument, and then of roughening that too, by introducing logical violence into it, and perhaps willful obscurity. We have therefore this unusual degree of complexity in the total structure: the indeterminate sound or the indeterminate meaning, IS or IM, may have been really come to independently, by a poet who senses the aesthetic value of indeterminateness and is veteran enough to go straight after it. But nothing can be introduced into the meaning without affecting the meter, and vice versa; so that IM, and not only DM as was represented in the beginning, un-determines the meter again and produces IS; and, conversely, IS, and not only DS, may un-determine the meaning again and produce IM. It will sound very complicated, but good poets will attest it if we ask them, and I think they will also offer the objective evidences in their poetry if we are skillful enough to read them.

It is necessary to offer some sort of formal disposition of one very large and vague character in the poetic effect: the euphony of the language. Under that head will come the liquidity of the consonantal sequences, which is much more marked in poetry than in prose; the elimination or reduction of harsh consonantal combinations, such as arise naturally in the juxtaposition of words selected on any pure meaning-principle; and the fixing up of the succession of vowel sounds, by way of ensuring variation, or at least avoiding sequences of flat or light vowels. These are working principles of composition also, and naturally they are of effect in un-determining the meaning. To that extent they are structural principles. Doubtless we think of euphony ordinarily as a principle striving for pure luxury of sound; it pleases the musical ear, and we may be sure it pleases also the articulatory sense, even when we read the poem silently. But that is not our kind of argument. Euphony is a sort of last textural refinement within the phonetic dimension of poetry. I believe that in evaluating it we must give "refinement" precedence over "textural." To refine the texture is to make it less perceptible, to make it smoother, to subtract from its private character, and that is to make it consist better with the structure. I incline therefore to think of euphony as a determinate phonetic principle, like meter, though much less binding and interfering in relation to the meaning. Theoretical complications present themselves when we think of it as coming into conflict with meter as a rival structural principle. But I believe we have seen complications enough in this section.

IX

And finally we must take account of a belief that is all but universal among unphilosophical critics, and flourishes at its rankest with the least philosophical. It is this: the phonetic effect in a poem not only is (a) metrical and (b) euphonious, but preferably, and very often actually, is (c) "expressive"; that is, offers a sort of sound which "resembles" or partly "is" or at least "suggests" the object that it describes. It is necessary to say rather flatly that the belief is almost completely fallacious; both theoretically on the whole, and specifically in detail, for most of the cases that are cited to prove it. The single word does not in fact resemble appreciably the thing it denotes. The notion that it does is fully disposed of by Mr. I. A. Richards in Chapter III of his *Philosophy of Rhetoric*, assisted by Mr. Leonard Bloomfield's *Language* and Aristotle's *Poetics*, on which Mr. Richards draws for authoritative support. Furthermore, the phrase, or sustained passage, does not in its "movement" resemble the denoted situation at all closely. I do not know any authoritative analysis to cite against this latter form of the fallacy, and I shall not try to improvise one here. I am content—though not all my readers may be—to say that the resemblance usually alleged turns out to be, for hardheaded judges, extremely slight and farfetched; and, to make up for default of argument about this, to offer a little ontological speculation which might make the popular error intelligible by showing what it is really trying to say. There is some sort of truth in even a misstatement.

A wonderful "fitness," harmony, or propriety, even an enduring stability, seems to obtain in the combination of the semantic property and the phonetic property into a fine poetic phrase. It is something we all feel, and I believe it is the fact we need to account for here. But what is the law of its corporate existence? The law is an ontological one: the two properties shall not be identical, or like, homogeneous; they shall be other, unlike, and heterogeneous. It is the law of the actual world everywhere; all sorts of actual things are composed on this principle. It is only the naïve prejudice of our first way of thought, our Eleatic stage of thought, that makes us conceive that the properties must unite by virtue of their sameness. The passage from that stage into the riper stage of thought has its first and most famous description in the discourse of the Eleatic Stranger in Plato's *Sophist*; it has systematic exploitation in Hegel and many other logicians. Red and red will not cohere with each other to make anything but an aggregate of red, nor even do red and yellow make anything astonishing; but red and big, along with a multitude of other properties, heterogeneous properties, cohere into an apple, which is a One formed out of the Many. I suppose we do not understand in any rational sense a particular object, such as an apple, holding together not by mathematical composition but by its own heterogeneity. But we recognize it perceptually. The World of Appearance (or opinion) seemed to Plato inferior to the World of Pure Being (or reason), but he acknowledged that the former was the world which our perceptions took hold of, and indeed was the world of nature.[13]

The poetic phrase is not very much like an apple, and we must concentrate upon that. In what world of discourse does it have its existence? As a thing of sounds it exists in the words; as a thing of meanings it exists in a world beyond the words. The heterogeneity is rather extreme. We recall the old puzzle, the debate on whether the poem resides in the physical words uttered or in the interpretation that is given them. But it exists in both at once; and for fear we forget about the words, they are metered, so that they may be forced upon our attention. One of the "touchstones" used by Matthew Arnold, and fancied by Mr. Eliot and many others, is Dante's line,

> In la sua volontade è nostra pace

But the English translation is only,

> In His will is our peace,

which is not a poetic touchstone at all. The meaning is not combined now with the sounds; the words have become mere symbols, used but not incorporated into the object. The line in its English version has suffered ontological annihilation: it has lost one of its worlds. But it seems rather irresponsible to claim that Dante's own version has its superior virtue in the fact that its sound seems to "express" or "suggest" its meaning; though I think I know critics who might be prepared after a little time to argue it, with much circumstance.

The triumphant citations from poetry, the "proofs" that we offer of its

13. For the sake of accuracy I should say that the preference was that of Socrates, or of the Plato of the early dialogues. (Ransom's note)

power, the touchstones, are always phrases, not single words nor little groups of words; they may be lines, or passages of some lines each. I find more significance in this fact than, merely, that a distinguished piece of logical discourse has to have extension in order to have complexity. It is even true that a compelling phonetic character cannot be imposed upon the words unless there are enough of them to organize into a recognizable meter. Furthermore, and beyond that, the meaning employs the words, but the meter employs the syllables. There is no point-to-point coördination between the development of the semantic structure and that of the phonetic structure. The relation between the two in a poetic phrase seems something like the relation between two melodies in counterpoint, except that our two structures originally look much more heterogeneous than the melodies. Perhaps the aesthetic import of the semantic-phonetic combination is also like that of counterpoint. But I am not sure what profit there is in saying this. It is not obvious that musical aesthetic is much more articulate than literary aesthetic, even allowing for the genius of Schopenhauer. I should think it true of the counterpoint, but at any rate I should judge of the double structure of the poetic phrase, that its force is in its speculative or ontological intimations. The semantic structure alone, like the melody in the treble, may be an aesthetic structure, for it is a logical structure which at the same time admits body, or texture, as pure logical structures do not; yet the phonetic structure, which would seem perfectly unrelated to it, is made to combine with it. It seems a tighter job, stronger, and more wonderful, than the counterpoint can be, for the melodies are two, though they are simultaneous, while the poetic phrase is a single event. Ontologically, it is a case of bringing into experience both a denser and a more contingent world, and commanding a discourse in more dimensions.

X

This has probably gone far enough as an ontological brief in the study of poetic discourse in English. I am aware of its insufficiencies. It is the ontological sense of the traditionalist poets, and their readers, that I have wished to discover. It feels congenial for me.

But what should the ontological critic say about the moderns? Much of our own poetry is conspicuously other than traditional. Not, I believe, the poetry of Robinson, Frost, Bridges, Yeats, perhaps even Hopkins; who have adhered, or almost adhered, or intended to adhere, to the tradition. The poetry I am talking about is written by such poets as Pound, Eliot, Tate, Stevens, perhaps Auden, though I do not mean to list them formally, nor suggest that any of them is uniformly accountable to a critique. These poets are generally known to have high regard for traditionalism, but they make wide and deliberate departures from it for the sake of their own poetry.

The superficial marks of our modernist poetry are very well known. An excellent brief assemblage of them into a list is in "A Note on Poetry," by Mr. Randall Jarrell, prefacing his own verses in *Five Young American Poets*. He considers modernist poetry to be substantially "romantic," and lists its marks, as follows:

> I have no space for the enormous amount of evidence all these generalizations require; but consider some of the qualities of typical modernistic poetry: very interesting language, a great emphasis on connotation, "texture"; extreme intensity, forced emotion—violence; a good deal of obscurity; emphasis on sensation, perceptual nuances; emphasis on details, on the part rather than the whole; experimental or novel qualities of some sort; a tendency toward external formlessness and internal disorganization—these are justified, generally, as the disorganization required to express a disorganized age, or alternatively, as newly-discovered and more complex types of organization; an extremely personal style—*refine your singularities*; lack of restraint—all tendencies are forced to their limits; there is a good deal of emphasis on the unconscious, dream-structure, the thoroughly subjective; the poet's attitudes are usually anti-scientific, anti-commonsense, anti-public—he is, essentially, removed; poetry is primarily lyric, intensive—the few long poems are aggregations of lyric details; poems usually have, not a logical, but the more or less associational structure of dramatic monologue; and so on and so on.[14]

My notes on this poetry are provisional and unsure, but I shall risk them in order to come down to date. The following account will be the merest sketch of a criticism, and will not even cite any of this poetry specifically.

The fundamental consideration is that the moderns are well instructed in the practice of the traditionalists. But this is what has happened: they find the old practice trite, and ontologically inadequate for them. Yet they lack any consistent conception of what a new practice might be—and a new practice that would be radical enough is probably not possible—and therefore they work by taking liberties with the old practice, and irregularize and de-systematize it, without denying it.

14. *Five Young American Poets* (Norfolk, Conn., 1940), 87–88.

They do not find sufficient profit in that traditional poetic labor which consists in the determinate metering of a determinate discourse. I have argued that some ontological triumph, something impossible for pure discourse, may be secured in this way. They are acquainted with the technique, and find it too easy. The well-metered discourse is impaired for them because it is transparently artful; they want a more direct and less formal knowledge.

They will not tolerate the experience of having the meaning brought by the meter into an indeterminateness of the compelled variety, with the only half-concealed irregularities such as those of Pope and Marvell above, or the resonances like those of the Romantic Wordsworth. Their disaffection is rather advanced. I suppose it is due fundamentally, though paradoxically, to their revulsion against scientific discourse. In seeking a discourse of greater ontological competence they do not propose to exhibit faults that are beneath the enemy standard of performance; and with the rapid and visible perfection of scientific discourse, occurring for the most part since the poetic achievements of the great traditionalists, indeterminateness of the ragged sort can be detected by the literate public everywhere, and is too disreputable. The age of prose, they might argue, has made obsolete the faltering logic of old-fashioned metered poetry. The disabilities of the procedure are too obvious; the advantages promised in it they propose to secure otherwise.

Being technically experienced, they have commanded of their own imagination, and when they seek indeterminateness of the positive sort, such as is denoted by the iconic signs, they do it directly. They have the power. They manage without the suggestion that comes in the verbal manipulations of metering. Perhaps their imagination, which might otherwise be confined by scientific discourse, has been in the long run released by precisely the kind of poetic exercise described above as elementary in the traditional technique, with meter working functionally in the composition. If so, the moderns might be called the products of a poetic tradition; but they are only its end products; or their status is even posttraditional: they are only the heirs of a tradition.

They have no enthusiasm for the meters, with the result that their poetry is far gone in its natural indeterminateness on that side. But they are committed on principle to an unprecedented degree of indeterminateness in the meaning, and their poetry is let down on that side too. This latter indeterminateness yields brilliant images; but it tends to logical inconsequence. The inconsequence does not come from haggling with the meter but from the intractable energy of the images. Evidence of this is that the mode of the inconsequence is chiefly ellipsis: the crowding of the images together without the terms for their logical relations; but also, as we think in view of the honesty of the work, the crowding together very largely without the logical relations themselves. The effect is an ontological density which proves itself by logical obscurity.

The dense and brilliant yet obscure world of the modern poets may reflect a certain initial ontological sense. Their most actual world, as they sense it, resists mastery, is more mysterious than intelligible, perhaps is more evil than good. It is a world of appearances, and suggests, for example, the world of Heraclitus; as if they had knocked the bottom out of history and language and become early Greeks again. They are antipathetic to the modern everyday world of business, science, and positivism, which ontologically disconcerts them. Their early Greek is pluralist, relativist, and irrational.

Their poetry is the manifest of such a skepticism, and virtual if tacit abjuration, as to seem to subject this generation to the category of decadence—if we know enough about the cycle of a culture to apply the term responsibly.

But, for that sense, it probably does not give quite the necessary impression of spent energies. And in that sense it is not quite thorough. A thing that is in startling exception occurs now and then in the practice of every one of the poets: the perfect poetic phrase. This phrase, which may well stand isolated in the context of indeterminacy, will lack nothing that is achievable of realizing the virtue intended by the traditional technique. It is a touchstone. The occasion of so sudden a flight may be simple nostalgia, looking backward.

But also it may be a reluctant testimony to real ontological efficacy, very much as it has been arrived at in the past experience of the race with its language; and to the impatience of spirited modern youth who will probably come eventually to sobriety and to power.

ARTISTS, SOLDIERS, POSITIVISTS

EMEMBERING our Winter discussion, I return to those great difficulties which disturb Mr. Ames, or any other man interested in art's good name. Let us call them the moral difficulties, or the political and public difficulties, which art always encounters when it begins to manifest its curious luxuriance.[1] The time scarcely comes when there is enough of dedicated public service to fight the evil in the world, and improve the lot of the citizens; when is there a time for art? How can we ever do less than ask to see the artist's service stripes, and certificate of honorable discharge from duty? In war time, the indulgence which the public extends to the artist, if he would have his person deferred in the draft, is that he may enlist his art. But at any time: what is the public service which art renders, that it should hope for reputation and favor?

I find a text by quoting from a letter of a kind which frequently comes to the office of this *Review*. This one came recently by photostat from a soldier in foreign service:

> I'd like to be perfectly honest and report that while both pieces interested me greatly, they also managed to infuriate. I hope sincerely that at this late date one can express legitimately a feeling of horror at the continuing preoccupation with Eliot in the pages of the *Review*. Fascinating as he has always been, and in a sense always will be, to the practising poet as well as the committed aesthete, the unrelenting dragging of his name and fragments of his poems and critical dicta into so many of your papers begins to pall—even on a once-ardent disciple. . . . Granted that there is always a needed clarification by sensitized critics of the nature and function of poetry, concomitant with the writing of *vital* poetry. . . .
>
> What *are* we after in poetry? Or, more exactly, what are we attempting to rout? The commandos of contemporary literature are having little to do with Eliot and even poets of charming distemper like Wallace Stevens

This essay first appeared in the *Kenyon Review*, VI (Spring, 1944), 276–81. Reprinted by permission of Helen Ransom Forman.

1. Van Meter Ames, "Art and Science," *Kenyon Review*, VI (Winter, 1944), 101–113, and John Crowe Ransom, "Art Needs a Little Separating," 114–22; Van Meter Ames, "The Novel: Between Art and Science," *Kenyon Review*, V (Winter, 1943), 34–48.

(for whom we all developed considerable passion). Not necessarily a poetry of time and place, either. The question of poetry as in life (and in the
Army) is one of survival, simply. . . . Men like Karl Shapiro (his "Anxiety,"
in *Chimera* recently, is notable), John Berryman, Delmore Schwartz tran-
scend the aesthetic of poetry—thank God! I find the poetry in *Kenyon
Review* lamentable in many ways because it is cut off from pain. It is intellectual and it is fine, but it never reveals muscle and nerve. It does not
really matter whether poetry of men in war, or suffering the impact of
communiques, has a large or small "frame of reference." It must, I feel,
promise survival for all who are worth retrieving—it must communicate
a lot of existence; an overwhelming desire to go on. (There's a hell of a lot
of work yet to do—postwar—even if one doesn't resolve as a poet.)

I'm waiting for an American poem of the forties called "The Quip
at the Heart of the Debacle." Not magnificent in its "orchestration of
themes," Ransom! Dialectics and self-appointed emendators of the poem
will have to go by the board. The condition for approach to the poem will
be baptism by fire. I believe there are minds and emotions ripe for that
poem. Will they be found in the editors and readers of the *Review*?

The communication is still unanswered; but consider how difficult it
is for an editor to find the suitable reply to such a letter. Should he argue that its author is too much in earnest, and has no right to hold an
art so strictly to account? It would seem too rude, as well as lacking in
understanding, inasmuch as no view of art other than this could suggest itself to a soldier risking his life at the front. Survival is the issue
with that soldier, though not merely his own survival. Yet the only reply
that could have any validity would have been that the editor, and most
of the contributors and readers, were not at the front as the soldier was,
and saw little to gain by pretending they were at the front, and felt that
a normal literary activity such as they were still trying to maintain
could not occur at the front, nor be directed from the front.

I do not mean to discuss the state of the arts in war, since my views
would be only commonplace, but their state in peace. And the first thing
to say is that in peace the arts are often held to account as if in war. This
is an old story, and my acquaintance with it goes back through the recent peace, and leads me now to tell a little personal history. Soon after
the other war I became painfully aware not of a literary soldier at the
front but of two journals in New York—the *Nation* and the *New Republic*. Their sense of art seemed to me to be just the one which is now
revealed in the soldier's letter; and this was only confirmed as it grew
steadily more explicit, and as these powerful journals seemed to communicate it to nearly the whole colony of American letters. If to my pro-

vincial sense of the times no front existed then, they were evidently under a different impression. But anybody who is fighting fiercely enough, and sometimes unscrupulously too (for that is the realism of hard fighting, as if survival hung upon every trifle), might be said to be making a front of his own. Theirs was a social and political one, but they made it very active, and turned many first-rate literary men into commandos. The tone was likely to be portentous, and the import "vital" in some elemental way. I think now it need not be said that these journals made up their own war rather than that their editors and contributors were redoubtable men, and went to the very forefront of a long and submilitary kind of war that was already on. And I have long since adapted my feelings to that reality. My idea of the policy for a literary art was not theirs, but it would have been if I had been under the conviction that a big fight was being waged, and I ought to be in it; then I should have been grim and dedicated too, and thought no more about it.

It is clear that there is a powerful illusion which runs throughout society to the effect that art is accountable as a public utility. I should not desire to oppose myself to it, nor do I think illusions are without their truth. In keeping with Mr. Ames's sense of the natural history of art, it would seem altogether probable that art came into existence for primitive man, and pleased him, long before he knew it was art, or had a name for it. The art-work was a utility first; it was a piece of art only second; and, in the lack of an explicit public sense of how it differed from a mere utility, it was a piece of art almost furtively, or *sub rosa*. And this has been very nearly the status of art, as a public institution to which the whole society consented, throughout our Occidental civilization. That is to say, the illusion of its being a mere utility has dominated, and prevented much consciousness of its being anything else. But there must have been uproar when its guilty secret at one time or another was publicly exposed. This was the noise made by the proto-aestheticians, full of glory and defiance as they pronounced the complete separatism of their art and its emancipation from public responsibility; augmented by that of the men of conservative habit who immediately retorted to them that these so-called objects of art were nothing new, but perfectly familiar objects, whose utility was obvious.

Mr. Ames contributed to these pages earlier an essay on fiction: "Between Art and Science." The zeal of the current novelists for their social and political causes, he thought, kept them from realizing fully the now well-explored possibilities of a fine art. And now Koestler's novel, as Mr. Rahv reports it, tells of the disillusionment of a political revolutionist whose ideals have been smashed, a sore situation.[2] But this man, and this author, ought to go on with the fight, says the reviewer; one cannot retire into a stale domestic life. And there is a requisite of honor in happiness, or in art. But I should like it if a poor soldier might be allowed to retire in good conscience eventually, with his causes sufficiently gained; and I am troubled by a sense that Mr. Rahv is scarcely prepared for this event, and that to a veteran of the wars life looks insupportable if not involved in the "panic" and the "promise" of revolutionary movements.

Art is addicted to peace. Its contribution is not very large if measured by its plea for the military or revolutionary cause, or in general the moral and/or scientific causes which are the Positives of human life. It is something at least next in importance, but hard to define. (The older writers referred to it as a *je ne sais quoi*, yet had a good enough recognition of it.) In these days I believe it can be said that this characteristic effect has been identified, as indeed it was by the Greeks. Along with its Positive, which is probably presented with only low-grade effectiveness, the work of art makes rich displays of a content which we had better call *naturistic*. Art practices a different economy from that of science; not content to remain in the strictly humanistic world of action, it plays with nature. I wish to show what I think that means; but I would remark first, against possible misunderstanding, that art does convey its Positives; they are its argument, or "design," and therefore either the direct expression of valuable ideals, or else paradigms of rational human process. It is this Positively which secures to it a public patronage.

The concern which artists have for nature, unless all signs fail, is a soft or sentimental one: a tender regard, or—why should we not say as the poets do—a love for nature. But how can that be? It seems out of character, if man is still a biological organism as the other animals are. It is probably in the English Romantic poets that we find naturism most explicit, like a profession of faith, and also closest to absurdity. But I will cite a romantic of our own century, Rupert Brooke, who proceeds in a manner slightly shocking to the sober reader to advertise the artist as "the great lover," in his poem of that name. (If he be taken as representing the man of private sensibility merely, it makes no difference, for the argument is the same.) In this poem Brooke's turn for detached and extrabiological affairs of the heart (which is strongly Keatsian, as is the diction) does not attest an animal vitality, nor constitute a human ca-

2. Philip Rahv, "Lost Illusions" (a review of Arthur Koestler's *Arrival and Departure*), *Kenyon Review*, VI (Spring, 1944), 288–92.

reer. In the prelude he makes extravagant protestation of the depth of his passion, but in the recital it seems that it may attach to such objects as "feathery, faëry dust," "rainbows," "blue-massing clouds," "furs to touch," "footprints in the dew," and "the flowers themselves"—for even this last item is too slight, too isolated. There is unreality in reading love into one's casual relations with these objects; and, if that is so, there is fallacy in imagining that love must in any case obtain for their grand aggregate, though it might then amount literally to a "love of nature." Real love, we must suppose, is the well-known biological business; or, by a figurative and legitimate extension, it is desire—desire for its focussed, its specific object. And this is our fundamental concern with nature. But the experience becomes involved and massive, and in that degree imperfect logically, and the less immediately effective, as aesthetic elements are imported into it; which happens as we manage to project our attention upon the whole concretion of the object and not merely its desirable part. At this stage we may assert all the more stoutly—being tutored by polite usage—that we love the object, which is now the big loose object; but there would seem to be a slight slipping in our logic, for it is not quite true. The tender sentiment replaces the greedy desire as Psyche replaces Eros. But we may be very sure that the affair must not quite become "platonic," or the whole relation will collapse. The marginal items are bathed in the gentle glow which is the lurid blaze diffused; a borrowed light. In this fact, if we like, there is evidence that it takes a first-rate Positive passion, and I think also a well-assured and habitually triumphant one, to survive the assimilation of a great mass of naturistic increment. But we are aware when the evidence is abused, by some pale aesthete; who generally meets with the harsh critic to tell him that his laborious aesthetic masses are out of any common psychic relation to us, and cannot give us an active concern. In justice to Brooke it must be conceded that many neutral items (in his catalogue of some forty) become eligible for his love because their Positive occasion suggests itself, or is actually cited. Thus "the strong crust of friendly bread," and "the cool kindliness of sheets that soon/ smoothe away trouble."

Aesthetic, then, is an adjective which imputes to its nouns a rather remarkable history: the times it qualifies would be neutral, and lacking of human interest for the given occasion, but that there is an item nearby in which the interest is very real, and powerful enough to spread over them too. They are not accessory to this interest though they seem to be, and take care not to conflict with it; they receive it.

We might define nature also; and first as we become aware of it locally in our casual experience. Nature is a contingent and heterogeneous lot of objects which we have to define principally by exclusion: it comprises those items which we perceive outside the focus of the desire-process. For strictly Positive experience, it is hostile to this process and has to be overcome, or it is irrelevant and has to be overlooked. For aesthetic experience its status is very different: it appears to participate in the Positive process and therefore to be valuable, or, what is still more wonderful, to participate in the object of desire and therefore to be desirable. The two impressions of nature are in high contrast. One or the other will probably color our impression of the total world, the aggregate of all objects; which also is called nature.

The value of the aesthetic increment, so very promiscuous in its naturism, is entirely illusory according to the Positivists, from whom Mr. Ames seems to diverge. But it is evident that, if desire is our great preoccupation with nature, the desire-process undergoes a transformation, and our steady occupation with nature cannot be defined by the exclusive logic of desire. Nor can our civilization, if we have one. How does any civilization record itself to us better than by its characteristic arts? These, with a little translation, denote the occupations which the citizens have developed in their dealing with nature, and which are very different from the mere animal drives, including the struggle for survival. Let the basic satisfactions be secured by total war if necessary, or by total Positive technology. We will assume that they are already assured to the citizens at the stage where the arts begin.

ART AND THE HUMAN ECONOMY

HIS ESSAY refers to two preceding ones, by Mr. W. P. South-ard and Mr. T. W. Adorno: there is some editorial presump-tion on my part in collating them and commenting [on] them together.[1] Special disservice is done to Mr. Southard, whose essay in the first place is a literary appreciation of Robert Penn Warren's poetry, and of a quality permitting us to think the poet is lucky in having found his exegete so soon. But Mr. Southard in the course of his thesis, and Mr. Adorno immediately, embark upon the same topic, and it is one that has a great urgency for us: the unhappy human condi-tion that has risen under the modern economy, and the question of whether religion and art can do anything about it. It is true that the writers do not have quite the same diagnosis of this condition, but it will be noticed that they make cross references to each other unknowingly.

Mr. Adorno is evidently for collectivism in politics, but not with all the potential ferocity of a partisan, i.e, fanatically. His social ideal has no room for religion yet provides a special asylum for art. But art is curi-ously close to religion in his very original and engaging description of it, as a concrete monad representing the universal concretion itself; that is to say, as a construction from which the experient receives cosmic or ontological vision. What else is it for? It is not attached to the practical life which falls under the overall survey of the political economy. It is free, and Mr. Adorno awards to it an *imperium in imperio*. That is a handsome concession which many collectivists have not made.

The marvelous concretions of Proust's novel are principally of hu-man beings in relations too tangled ever to be resolved intellectually. The element of external nature—the scene or the natural object—is never excluded, for Proust has the sensibility of a poet as well as that of a modern novelist, but for our attention it is certainly not dominant.

This essay first appeared in the *Kenyon Review*, VII (Autumn, 1945), 683–88. Re-printed in Ransom's *Beating the Bushes*, copyright © 1972 by New Directions Publishing Corporation. Reprinted by permission of New Directions Publishing Corporation.

1. W. P. Southard, "The Religious Poetry of Robert Penn Warren," and T. W. Adorno, "Theses Upon Art and Religion Today," *Kenyon Review*, Vol. VII, No. 4 (Autumn, 1945). (Ransom's note)

Proust does not follow the lead of Wordsworth, returning to external nature to find God, returning there also to find—by an indirection that Wordsworth scarcely succeeded in making clear—man himself. It would seem to be a bad logical error, and I do not know that Mr. Adorno commits it, to think that God was a term of discourse which referred to the mystery of nature as long as nature was mysterious, but for the moderns who have "conquered" nature can have no particular exigency. But it would be a form of the same error—and Mr. Adorno distinctly is free of this one—to think that art deals with the "magic" of external nature but that there is nothing equally magical in a human concretion, which therefore only needs to be understood and disposed of by political science. There is mystery everywhere, as we hear it said in pious quarters; and let us say that there is mystery for the intellect in every concretion, and no possibility of thinking it out of existence.

Has art then no effect upon action, and does it not modify in any way one's commitment to action? I am inclined to think that it is in more or less ironic reaction from the fury of the practical life, and might be called "pietistic" in its mildly disparaging effect upon agents. Mr. Adorno seems to think that religion was repressive upon one or another developing form of practice, but I wonder if art does not register a disaffection with all practice. If it does not oppose something in advance, it seems at any rate to record the transaction afterward in the strangest manner. It takes us back into the concretion from which action has already delivered us.

At any picnic we have the politeness to remark for the host's benefit the local concretions of nature to which he has conducted us, but it may be that we will regard our fellow picnickers as simple and understandable creatures. The history of that might go back a long way, and even to the famous division of labor of which Mr. Adorno speaks. The division of labor made action effective by limiting sharply the apparent concretions of the natural materials which the laborer manipulated. It is true that modern life must come to terms either here or there with the whole of nature, and indeed modern life confronts a denser nature than the ancients could possibly know. But the divided laborer does not entertain this vision, nor does he know nature professionally as other than the humble if stubborn set of materials assigned him. (It might be said that the productive society at large confronts the whole concretion of nature, but so far as this purpose is concerned society is principally a fiction.) Now his own labor is not sufficient to maintain his life, but has to be integrated with all the other labors which likewise are divided and dependent. He is in daily or even hourly relation with the other laborers if he cares to live. But the explicitude of these relations tends to limit the depth of his acquaintance, and to induce the feeling that the laborer in the other field has merely a kind of functional existence, or is in fact principally the other "party" to a contract. It was at the stage of the loose agrarian society, where the laborer dealt individually with his local microcosm, and did not need to relate himself incessantly to the other laborers, that acquaintance was more spontaneous and went deeper. The basis of relations then might be the curious reciprocal exploration of their human concretions, on personal or aesthetic grounds. Friendship or brotherly love, in Aristotle's account, ripens between economically independent and fully rounded men. And, even now, it is not Proust the machine-tender or Proust the draper who can dwell so long on a human history without exhausting it, but Proust the free citizen, the man of means and leisure, and even the voluptuary of human relations. He knows the human heart because his own vision, his own experience, is complete. And it is because there will be in any society men strong enough to complete their experience eventually, and no society able to repress them permanently, that we say art has an eternal vitality.

But when we say there will be men strong enough for art, we are conscious that we are saying also, men weak enough, that is, men backward enough; engaged upon the progressive division of labor yet given to hideous lapses of zeal and faith; going to the length of art by way of looking back. Is not there a kind of weakness in all this Remembrance of Things Past? I wonder that we have not heard about the "failure of nerve" on the part of artists as such, and not merely of particular writers. When I was a boy we used to say that somebody had "gone back on" somebody else. We were describing a kind of renegade, who couldn't after all go through with his pledge, and the novel individuation demanded. But in art we do not go back with any such finality.

Now we come to the terms of Mr. Southard's argument. We are far gone in our habit of specialized labor, whether we work with our heads or our hands; it has become our second nature and nearly the only human nature that we can have, in a responsible public sense. We have fallen, as Mr. Southard would say, and henceforth a condition we might properly call "decadence" is our portion; guilt and repentance, guilt followed by such salvation as can be achieved. In the forms which this salvation takes, we do go back into our original innocence, but vicariously or symbolically, not really. We cannot, actually go back, and if we try it the old estate becomes insupportable; a little trial will show that. It was the estate of good animals opposing nature with little benefit of rational discourse, therefore of abstraction (the splitting off of the concept from the total image) and special effectiveness. We would not like it now. So we manage as we are with the help of salvation, an excellent thing though only for a guilty species. Salvation is simple as picnics, or games, it may be; but for superior sinners it must take a higher form, such as individual works of art, or religious exercises which are institutionalized and rehearsed in ritual. All these are compensatory concretions—they return to primitive experience but only formally; by no means do they propose to abandon the forward economy.

I find myself in the fullest sympathy with Mr. Southard's argument—up to the unexpected jump he makes at the end. It seemed that we had taken our constitutional and predestined development, and our progress was irreversible; but suddenly Mr. Southard proposes to found an agrarian community within which innocence may be recovered. I can reproach him for his phantasy with a better conscience inasmuch as I have entertained it too, as one of the Southern agrarians. And it seems to be in order to offer a brief notice about that, though I will not pretend to be representing Mr. Warren, or Mr. Tate, or others of the group.

Mr. Southard taxes the Southern agrarians for not having practiced what they preached, and that is a hit in a place where they have been hit before, though rarely by critics of his philosophical caliber. But I am struck by a slight dampness of spirit in his abjuration of the world. He says the young would seem to have made sacrifices enough in these days, as if that would be almost the greatest one yet. And it would be; it is a sacrifice which I hope he would not make. For without consenting to a division of labor, and hence modern society, we should have not only no effective science, invention, and scholarship, but nothing to speak of in art, e.g., *reviews* and contributions to *reviews*, fine poems and their exegesis; and on both sides of the line he has already given achievement. The pure though always divided knowledges, and the physical gadgets and commodities, constitute our science, and are the guilty fruits; but the former are triumphs of muscular intellect, and the latter at best are clean and wholly at our service. The arts are the expiations, but they are beautiful. Together they comprise the detail of human history. They seem worth the vile welter through which homeless spirits must wade between times, with sensibilities subject to ravage as they are. On these terms the generic human economy can operate, and they are the only terms practicable now. So the Southern agrarians did not go back to the farm, with the exceptions which I think were not thoroughgoing. And presently it seemed to them that they could not invite other moderns, their business friends for example, to do what they were not doing themselves. Nor could they even try to bring it about that practicing agrarians, such as there might still be in the Old South, should be insulated from the division of labor and confined securely in their gardens of innocence. An educator or a writer cannot abandon the presuppositions behind his whole vocation, nor imagine that they have less than a universal validity for the region, and ought to be kept out of the general circulation as beyond the common attainment. I find an irony at my expense in remarking that the judgment just now delivered by the Declaration of Potsdam[2] against the German people is that they shall return to an agrarian economy. Once I should have thought there could have been no greater happiness for a people, but now I have no difficulty in seeing it for what it is meant to be: a heavy punishment. Technically it might be said to be an inhuman punishment, in the case where the people in the natural course of things have left the garden far behind.

But I think the agrarian nostalgia was very valuable to the participants, a mode of repentance not itself to be repented. It matured their understanding of the forward-and-backward rhythm of the human economy. And now, for example, whatever may be the politics of the agrarians, I believe it may be observed that they are defending the freedom of the arts, whose function they understand. Not so much can be said for some intemperate exponents of the economic "progress."

As a formal definition of the art-work I have nothing to offer that would compete with Mr. Adorno's adaptation of the Leibnitzian monad. But as a natural history of the event, giving a sense of its background and its participation in the total human economy, it leaves something to be desired, and in conclusion I will try to sketch this area of meaning as it might be revealed upon a public occasion. It will be a historic occasion, but I am improvising the detail, since I do not know my facts. Let us say that it is time to unveil the statue of an eminent public man, and let it be Bismarck. His program has been notably strenuous, and it has succeeded. His very physiognomy and carriage when rendered by the faithful sculptor will betoken the audacity of his conceptions, his per-

2. Result of Inter-Allied conference of World War II held at Potsdam, Germany, July 17 to August 2, 1945, among Truman, Churchill, and Stalin, to discuss the peace settlement in Europe.

sistence with them, and even the habit of success. The citizens do not let their rites wait upon his death, and it is to be emphasized that these are not death rites, and in no sense exult in his mortality but in the grandeur of his career at its prime. It is only 1879, but everybody now can see his greatness, and he is already in history, a firm instance of those uncompromising human spirits who travel far from their origins and make their mark.

But there is an ambiguity in the event. In that act of turning him to stone and planting him immovably in the earth, there is a question of what these people really mean to celebrate on their festal occasion. It is as if they were not honoring the efficacious Bismarck any more than they are honoring the Nature to whom they now commit him, like a truant returned to the parental bosom. In the mound and in the pedestal upon the mound that support the stone Bismarck the earth seems to rise a little way, but still with an inscrutable dignity, to welcome him; as if his willful alienation had always been conceded, had in nowise been mortal for her, and now, if he liked, was over. The golden Rhine flows past evenly, as if he did not mind having upon his bank a thing even so sternly individuated as a Bismarck. By the art of the statue Bismarck himself is invested with a beauty whose conditions he would not and could not have fulfilled in his own person. And all who are present understand these things, perhaps without knowing it. Let us say: Those who are supposed to commemorate action are commemorating reaction; they are pledged to the Enlightenment, but, even in Its name, they clutter It with natural piety.

POETRY

I, THE FORMAL ANALYSIS

OR TWENTY or twenty-five years we have lived with a kind of literary criticism more intensive than a language has ever known. But a revulsion is setting in against it. The new criticism probably is most at home today in the academy where it flourishes as a lively "minority" movement. The literary enthusiasms of the academy are sometimes tardy, however, and it is common for a given taste to have run through its period among professional men of letters at about the time it establishes itself among the students and instructors. From these it receives a second start in life, and if the taste is an intelligent one this will doubtless be a long life. But at the moment the new criticism appears to have been slightly disappointing to the expectations it had aroused.

It has achieved a linguistic revolution in its reading of poetry. Its emphasis is upon the total connotation of words. Approached from this point of view a poem discovers to the critic a kind of centrifugal energy, whereby its meaning expands with a little encouragement, and can be followed by the sympathetic imagination. The detailed phrase is honored with the spread of its own meaning, though this meaning may be away from that of the poem as a whole. And the critic goes straight from one detail to another, in the manner of the bee who gathers honey from the several blossoms as he comes to them, without noticing the bush which supports all the blossoms. The poem is more generous than the bush in its capacity for bearing blossoms which are not alike but widely varied, in size, fragrance, hue, and shape. So poetry has waited for our age to recognize and publish a sort of irresponsible exuberance in the energy of its materials, which constantly imperils its sober order. In fact the new critics, careless of the theoretical constitution of poetry, have contrived to create a sense of its disorder. But at last this has become embarrassing. We have grown familiar with many exciting turns

This essay first appeared in the *Kenyon Review*, IX (Summer, 1947), 436–56. Reprinted by permission of Helen Ransom Forman.

of poetic language, but we begin to wonder if we are able to define a poem.

Mr. Cleanth Brooks has done as much as any critic except of course William Empson, to establish the new criticism. His new book, *The Well Wrought Urn*, exhibits all the ingenuity we should expect of him for reading the obscure meanings of many well known poems, and something else besides. He is seriously attempting now to see poems as wholes, and to conceive that difficult object, the unitary poem. But how will he reassemble and integrate the meanings when he has made it his first duty to dissipate them? I can scarcely think he succeeds in the new role, and for me that is a good evidence of its exceeding difficulty.

He has various formulations for the poem as a whole, but usually they employ terms as undefined as their definiendum, and confuse us. Perhaps he means them to. But if there is one formulation which seems to him more suitable than others, for it recurs oftenest, it is that which asserts that the unity of poetic language has the form and status of a verbal paradox. He has always liked to stand and marvel at paradox— "with its twin concomitants of irony and wonder"—while I think it is the sense of the sober community that paradox is less valid rather than more valid than another figure of speech, and that its status in logical discourse is that of a provisional way of speaking, therefore precarious. We do not rest in a paradox; we resolve it.

Mr. Brooks is encouraged by the stream of paradoxes in "The Phoenix and the Turtle," where Shakespeare in praise of married love declares by means of the most extravagant figures that the lovers become one and cease to be two. Shakespeare may not repeat himself, but in this instance he finds many different ways, I dare say too many ways, of saying the same thing; his poem is a *tour de force*. Mr. Brooks quotes three of the stanzas:

> So they loved as love in twaine,
> Had the essence but in one,
> Two distincts, division none,
> Number there in love was slaine.
>
> Hearts remote, yet not asunder;
> Distance and no space was seene,
> Twixt this Turtle and his Queene;
> But in them it were a wonder. . . .
>
> Property was thus appalled,
> That the selfe was not the same;

> Single Natures double name,
> Neither two nor one was called.

He comments:

> Precisely! The nature is single, one, unified. But the name is double, and
> today with our multiplication of the sciences, it is multiple. If the poet is
> to be true to his poetry, he must call it neither two nor one: the paradox is
> his only solution.[1]

But I am afraid of this "Precisely!" It might seem humorous to some
minds nurtured in logical positivism, for there are few locutions so notorious as paradoxes for having imprecision as their essence. If we do
not resolve a paradox by correct statement, it is because we sense the
correct statement intuitively and immediately, and do not require it formally. So I believe we sense it here; the sober truth of the matter does
not fail to occur to us, and I will risk the vulgarity of writing it out as we
are likely to see it, namely, that "Turtle and Phoenix in their wedded life
ideally become one in certain respects which are not beyond determination, but in other respects remain two." They can easily be both one
and two if we understand that they are "One-as-respects-abc" and
"Two-as-respects-$defn$." The terms of the paradox seemed to contradict
and exclude each other, but do not really if we state them correctly;
however, in that event we come to the end of the paradox.

Mr. Brooks is not realistic in wanting us not to resolve his paradoxes.
But I can readily suppose that the situation seems desperate, and he
feels impelled to offer on behalf of poetry some fairly impenetrable esoteric quality and even—for he uses this word once or twice—some
"magic." As a literary critic he has a hollow scorn for the procedures of
"science"; and he advises the scientists in effect that they cannot understand poetry and had better leave it alone. But this is to underestimate the force of logic in our time and, for that matter, the great weight
of the rational ideal in Western civilization. The logical positivists can
take poetry apart as they take theology apart, and the defense of poetry
in the last resort, like the defense of religion, will have to be a defense of
its human substance, and on the naturalistic level. That is the prospect
which faces the critic. And there can be little doubt that this defense
will be made and that it will succeed. Meanwhile, it is the poet's in-
stinct, or his uncanny innocence, or some strategic wisdom deeper
in him than he can sound, to keep the warm human substance half-

1. Cleanth Brooks, *The Well Wrought Urn: Studies in the Structure of Poetry* (New
York, 1947), 20.

hidden in his technical poetic language; sometimes under paradoxes, but better under simpler and sturdier linguistic staples. For some reason or other, poetry guards itself against being handled by logicians, to whom it must not wish to answer. But in all societies the poet has enjoyed his special "license" of speech, and probably he has conferred his human benefits. It is the critic who must explain him and defend him when he is brought to trial, lifting his guard of secrecy if necessary. And I dare say Mr. Brooks feels, as I do, that this event is imminent in an age of logical positivism.

On the strength of this general understanding I think that mystification, at the level of literary criticism, is no longer a good strategy. And, for example, it is mystifying if we wish to go along with Coleridge's honest confusion of more than a century ago. The famous Coleridge statement about poetry is imbedded in a passage by Mr. Brooks as follows:

> . . . For that fusion [of mutually exclusive terms, by paradox] is not logical; it apparently violates science and common sense; it wields together the discordant and the contradictory. Coleridge has of course given us the classic description of its nature and power. It "reveals itself in the balance or reconcilement of opposite or discordant qualities: of sameness, with difference; of the general, with the concrete; the idea, with the image; the individual, with the representative; the sense of novelty and freshness, with old and familiar objects; a more than usual state of emotion, with more than usual order. . . ." It is a great and illuminating statement, but is a series of paradoxes. Apparently Coleridge could describe the effect of the imagination in no other way.[2]

But the effect can be described in other ways. These paradoxes about poetry can be resolved. Probably the emotion has to be located at one place in the poem, the order in another; likewise the general, as distinguished from the concrete; and so forth. The pairings are Kantian, for Coleridge had the considerable distinction in his time of being equal to absorbing Kant and Schelling. They are obtained by insights which took genius, I have no doubt, and are good insights for analysis to begin with. They constitute an early monument of insight, it may be; but it is not helpful of Mr. Brooks to intimidate us with the reminder that this monument of insight is a "classic." I cannot but think that the recent revival of Coleridge's involved critical language has been obfuscating, and there is little doubt that it has been dull, and against the grain of the living language.

2. Brooks, *The Well Wrought Urn*, 18–19.

If the so-called new criticism has power it is because the new meanings which it discovers in the poetic text are profound and moving. But the new critics, on the whole, have not stopped to explain how that should be so. It is not the new criticism but the old criticism which insists upon discovering the perennial "human values." The old criticism is emotive and passionate. But it has not failed to have some development of its own. I do not identify it with the new criticism even when, at the very height of the period of the new criticism, it has been busily applying the Freudian psychology to literature, and finding some strange and well hidden grounds for its obvious force. (This criticism has acquired sensibility, for instance, for the horrors of frustration, anxiety, and despair motivating many modern works which have a surface of gaiety, or fantasy.) On the other hand the new criticism has been as weak in its psychology as it has been brilliant in its semantical effort. The idea has been that the expanded meanings which the text of poetry yields under the willing hands of the new critics are rewarding enough in themselves; but it depends on what the meanings are humanly worth.

The rise of the new criticism has been due to advances in our understanding of language, and the old criticism has renewed itself by reason of advances in our psychology. Perhaps these considerations permit us to think there is now a chance which did not previously exist for a successful theory of poetry. We still hold with Aristotle that our acquaintance with an action is perfect, humanly speaking, when we have obtained its formal cause and its final cause. But the formal analysis of poetry is a linguistic exercise; and the determination of its use and motive is a psychological one. At the same time we should avoid thinking that the two researches are entirely separate. The only formal cause which we care to consider is one with which we can associate some standard human purpose, and the only final cause that does any good is one which can realize itself in the formal fact. The two studies have to be in consultation together at every step.

II

One of the chapters of Mr. Brooks's new book is entitled, "The Heresy of the Paraphrase." There is always a distinction between the poetic text and its logical paraphrase. They are in different languages. We do not expect the poetry to come trimmed to a perfectly logical form, and when we put it into the form we paraphrase it. Mr. Brooks is perfectly right in abhorring the popular idea that the meaning of the text and the meaning of the paraphrase are the same. The paraphrase "reduces" the text; even if it should employ more words than the text it leaves out some of the meaning. I should think the implication is that the logical mind, or let us even say the logical life or the life of reason, cannot find this residue pertinent to its program.

For our analysis, this is a crucial implication. For we will take it that the poem has two kinds of meaning, somewhat as Brooks, Coleridge, and Kant have intimated. One is the ostensible argument, which we can render by paraphrase, and which is entirely useful and reputable. The other is the tissue of meaning which resists rendering, and does not really intend to be rendered because its human usefulness would be brought into question. And at this point it occurs to us to regard the poem as a work on the order of a Freudian dream, having not only a "manifest" and permissible content but a "latent" and suspected content. We shall keep firm hold of that possibility.

Paraphrase straightens out the text and prunes the meaning down to its own purposes, and in general corrects the "faulty thinking." But the quoted term is Freud's; Freud has the gift for linguistic analysis just as logical positivists have it. Indeed, his gift is greater in the sense that Freud looks for human significance where the logical positivists are content with noting technical "nonsense." In any case a logical discourse is one whose terms have respective referents which are definitive and unchanging in content, and whose syntax keeps them in explicit relatedness without a breach. On the other hand, a poetic text is probably inconsistent as to the meanings of its terms; and surely it is over-inclusive in that it gives them meaning which goes beyond the logical occasion; and therefore, if not on principle, it is loose as to its syntax. The syntax approaches the vanishing point with the phenomenon which Freud calls "regression"; he finds it in dreams, and it is the limiting case almost reached in many modern poems, where we go back upon the train of the definitive ideas till we come to the whole images or substances which gave rise to them, whereupon we drop the ideas. It might be beneath the dignity of the logical positivist to paraphrase a document in such condition, but it is precisely according to Freud's taste to try to recover the ideas and make sense appear again out of nonsense; it is cardinal with him that any mental behavior will make sense if we can only get into it. It is not the Freudians who are the enemies of poetry unless it is *per accidens*: by reason of some personal or professional vagary of interpretation which restricts the freedom of their analysis. But there are many varieties of dystax. And even upon the friends of poetry there devolves the obvious task of paraphrase, and they perform interpretation, or *explication de texte*, in which is recovered a related or syntactical "sense" that was by no means given explicitly. Paraphrase is a critical function.

For there are two summary propositions here which seem to need putting. Sometimes I find myself thinking that one of them is primary, and the other is secondary; but at another time I think the reverse. A. The poem is not included in its paraphrase. B. But the poem must include its own paraphrase, or else a logical argument capable of being expressed in a paraphrase. There are several reasons for the B, if anyone should object. An easy one is that the poem has its reputation to consider. One of the elemental facts about poetry is that it is *public*, just as Freud asserts repeatedly that the whole character of wit depends on the understanding that it is public; it must make contact with its auditors, and therefore it must be decent enough to make formal sense.

There are many occasions when a critic feels called to make the paraphrase. But probably they all have one simple condition in common: that the sense of the text is made out with some difficulty, and needs an exposition. The literary work may be so long, and have so many parts, that laborious paraphrase is necessary for the sake of perspective and proportion. The argument of the long poem has to be summarized by books, cantos, stanzas; the play has to be plotted, by act and scene; the whole has to be comprehended. Or the argument is difficult, for some part of a long work, for the part or whole of a short work. "Sailing to Byzantium" is a difficult poem, so that most of its critics have undertaken to explain the drift of its argument on the whole and within the several stanzas.

One familiar and curious consequence of paraphrasing a difficult text is the common critic's feeling that with this labor his responsibility has been fully discharged; and the general public is pretty sure to have that feeling. It is as if the poem were a truth done up in an anagram, waiting only to be deciphered. That which is behind the paraphrase, and does not get translated into the paraphrase, receives very little more of the reader's conscious attention. We may continue to read the text, and even come to appreciate it more and more, but we do not seem to need to think further about it. Perhaps we believe we prefer the text to the paraphrase at so late a stage because it is pleasant to look at those knots and gnarls of language which resisted our understanding; they are like the fanged head of the slain lion which the hunter keeps. But doubtless this is illusory. It is too likely that we relish the text for itself, for what it actually is apart from the reduction we have in the paraphrase. But in that case we receive it unconsciously, whereas we received the paraphrase by conscious and virtuous effort.

And what are we to say about the text which we never think of paraphrasing, and nobody asks us to paraphrase? It is in the same position as the text which we have paraphrased already, and therefore think we have disposed of. The text which does not invite paraphrase is one whose logic we obtain intuitively and at once; it is logically transparent. And what do we find to say about it? I will suggest an easy paradox, whose two terms do not exclude each other but fit together with perfect nicety: Analysis of the difficult text is easy, and analysis of the easy text is difficult. Mr. T. S. Eliot remarked sagely that the argument of a poem is sometimes like the biscuit which the burglar takes along for the dog. Mr. Eliot does not approve of psychological speculation about poetry, and that is a strategic position which is respectable though in the present juncture of affairs I do not share it. But it is significant that he should liken the poet to a burglar, placing the public censor with a logical argument as the burglar placates the dog with the biscuit, and then, we must suppose, going on with the business which is also like the burglar's; business done better in the dark, and not for the public eye. On the occasion we are considering now, however, the faithful watchdog is confident that the burglar carries no equipment besides the biscuit, and the public censor basks in the belief that the poet does not intend anything but his argument.

But even the friend of the poet is embarrassed if we ask him to paraphrase the easy text; that is, to put a "proper" text directly beside the given one, whereupon he will have on his hands two texts instead of one.

Matthew Arnold was indignant with the young man in one of the new English "training colleges" who was asked to paraphrase Macbeth's question,

> Can'st thou not minister to a mind diseased?

and rendered it,

> Can you not wait upon the lunatic?

It caused Arnold to rail upon what we should call the decline of the humanities in education, because of people like Professor Huxley who had filled up the curriculum with natural sciences. But the paraphrase of the young student is intelligent; what did Arnold think a paraphrase was for? What would the young man's teacher have done by way of paraphrase, and what would Arnold himself do? If it were not for Mr. Eliot we might say that no great critic has been so averse as Arnold to the intensive analysis of the texts he admired. But the fact is that only a person with the undeveloped sensibility of a schoolboy would care to paraphrase Macbeth. He is sure to be trapped. On the one hand there is the warmth and fulness of Shakespeare, slightly gratuitous for the occasion and perhaps illicit, and yet one feels oafish not to covet that. On the other hand there is the perfect language which carries the logic of the occasion, pointed, and admirable for its uses precisely because it is cold and bare. He does not like to expose this distinction in public, as if to make a choice between the two, or even discuss the grounds of choice.

Presently I shall propose the analysis of a longer passage from Shakespeare, in order to see how radically the language of poetry differs from the prose of its occasion. It will be a sort of preview of what we shall see there if I try to show here how Macbeth's question differs from the schoolboy's paraphrase; at least in part. Macbeth is not thinking of a mere lunatic or medical "case" but of the dis-ease of mind of a person, who is his dear wife the Lady Macbeth. And he wants the physician not merely to "take the patient" as we should say and give her the specific treatment, but to give her also a warm personal consideration; though we may remark that, the better the physician, the less likely he would be to accept the patient on this basis. Both *mind diseased* and *lunatic* are in syntax nouns, but the one is substantial in meaning, with a referent already known and held in affection for many adjectival qualities, while the other is limited to a referent consisting of one adjectival essence which is functional to the occasion. Both *minister to* and *wait upon* are in syntax verbs, but the one has a spread of meaning over many adverbial nuances, while the other denotes only the technical act which determines the event.

III

Modern poems engage the critic readily and pleasantly, because they are difficult, and the project of establishing the canonical paraphrase is a dignified critical responsibility. And that is true for some old poems. But I have chosen for study a passage from Shakespeare, and it is a popular passage which most schoolboys know and "understand." It is the second of the three parts of Antony's funeral oration over Caesar, the one which marks the turning-point of the orator's persuasiveness.

The occasion is where Antony brings the populace round the body of Caesar to witness the rents in the garment and to receive the detailed account of the killing. It follows upon an opening part in which Antony has harped upon the official account of the act as one performed for patriotic reasons by honorable men. In Shakespeare's play this is represented as a very strong account. We should have had no play, because there would have been no hero, if Brutus had not held by it sincerely and intelligently. Brutus is a patriot and an honorable man. Antony has not subscribed to the argument as yet, and will not; but in order to deliver the funeral oration he has had to promise Brutus that though he will praise Caesar he will by no word question the authorized statement upon Caesar's killing.

So the passage is part of an oration which is official, and from this point of view we may act on behalf of the logical positivist and determine the kind of logic it would be expected to have. Let us suppose, in modern fashion, that the robe with the rents in it is going to be permanently displayed in the state museum; beside it will be a notice identifying the rents by the names of the conspirators whose blades respectively made them; the order will be chronological, and the items will be accompanied where possible by statements about the effect of the blows upon Caesar's resistance, till finally we come to the account of the rent through which Brutus administered the death-blow. The citizens are entitled to their facts. The speech of Antony would be an oral documentary exposition of these data, and would confine itself scrupulously to treating them as bearing on the purpose in hand. Such would be the paraphrase. It would belong to an order of logical construction for which there is not only precedent, but considerable use.

But it is notorious that Shakespeare's Antony does not stick to the rules. Shakespeare's historical source was Plutarch, whom he knew through North's translation of the current French version of the *Lives*. Two of the Lives, those of Brutus and Antony, indicate that Plutarch, himself a historian of orderly documentary habit, was well aware of Antony's crucial departure and of its intention. Thus, in the life of Brutus according to North:

> Antonius making his funeral oration in praise of the dead, according to the ancient custome of Rome, and perceiving that his words moved the common people to compassion, he framed his eloquence to make their hearts yearn the more; and taking Caesar's gowne all bloodie in his hand,

he layd it open to the sight of them all, shewing what a number of cuts and holes it had upon it.[3]

Antony's documentation in Shakespeare's play is careless and incomplete, and so it must have been if Plutarch had given it, but the speech explicitly follows North's Plutarch in being *moving* and *eloquent*, qualities which indicate an intrusion of content alien to the documentary style. But North misses in Plutarch a locution that records almost technically Antony's departure from the style. The North phrase, *he framed his eloquence to make their hearts yearn the more*, is far better rendered in our standard modern translation, which is that of Dryden and others as revised by Clough; it becomes there *passing into the pathetic tone*. This is closer to the Greek, but it is even better than the Greek, and sounds like the work of Dryden, with his genius for critical prose. (I am unable to say whether it is actually Dryden's or Clough's.) We could do worse than say summarily, even today, that Antony at this point of his oration passes from the "logical mode" into the "pathetic mode." Poetry is language in the pathetic mode, which is the mode not of logic but of feeling. It is in the light of this principle that I wish in a moment to exhibit our text.

Feelings do not belong in a thought-work; they are exiled from technical science, for instance, as everybody knows. In the serial progress of a piece of thinking we may be treating a great many objects about which we have stored-up feeling-responses, but we do not release the feelings. Freud is as well aware of this as are the logical positivists; he says that thought "inhibits" feelings; that is why it is painful, and beyond the power of infants and primitive men, and even of those civilized men who in the pinch cannot accept the responsibility for being rational but must revert to infantile habits. Thinking is a game of suspense, like holding one's breath when we dive, in which we postpone feelings and attend to our undertaking, at least until we have achieved the specific goal and can relax.

The feelings, at any rate those in the area of our present discussion, are responses to objects and situations. If feelings define the poetic language on its subjective side there must be a correlative definition for it on the objective side. The feelings we are talking about are local or incidental ones which we stop to indulge as we pass from one object to another in the over-all progress of the argument. The feelings engage

---

3. *The Lives of the Noble Grecians and Romans*, translated out of Greek into French by James Amiot and out of French into English by Sir Thomas North (London, 1676), 824.

with these objects not in their straight functional sense but in a substantival sense. For it is not for the subsidiary object in its limited aspect
as we use it in the argument that we have any particular feeling, but for
this object as it is known to our experience and affections as a whole;
that is, substantively. It is a point of logical principle that our terms
must denote limited referents. The same point is made when it is said
that in logic there are no proper nouns; if there are singular nouns they
denote single but indifferent instances of the logical type. But in poetry
we have proper nouns and substantival referents. Poetry is therefore a
discourse in the "pathetic mode" if we emphasize the feelings which
attend it, but let us say loosely that it is in the "substantival mode" if we
emphasize the character of the referents.

That is half the truth. But we are not to forget the other half. When
we say that we expect of any poem that it will yield a paraphrase, we are
saying that poetry is still a discourse in the logical mode. Its referents
may have for us their various underlying or substantival meanings, but
they do not fail to have also their functional or logical meanings as required of discursive language. Poetry is therefore a logical discourse but
an impure one. It will occur to us to ask if we may not refer to it as a
compound discourse on the ground that this description would be better suited to its dignity. That would be assigning to the impurity represented by the substances a consistent character, as we should be doing
if we pronounced ab a compound formed of a and b. It is premature to
argue that question, but I think eventually the answer will be affirma-
tive. In that case we shall be able to hope for an inclusive logic that is
really competent for the analysis of poetry, something that is true of no
logical system today; and for an orderly kind of poetic analysis. And it
would be strange if a discourse answering to such a staple form of language as poetry should have to remain indeterminate in status, as the
messy present state of poetic theory would suggest that it is.

Before we proceed to analysis there is one more preparation to make.
The text has been chosen not quite at random. It is not only a poetic
discourse but a rhetorical discourse. In either case it is in the pathetic
or substantival mode. I am taking the rhetoric of Antony in the meaner
sense of the word. It is the art of the crafty speaker, aiming at effective
persuasion rather than logical conclusion. He makes the worse appear
the better cause by setting the feelings against the force of the true
logic. What other instrument is eligible for Antony when he is sworn
not to dispute the argument of Brutus openly? For that matter, what
other instrument works so fast? As to the feelings evoked by poetry,

they cannot be said to be exactly in the service of the argument which is proceeding, for they are diversions, and impede the argument, necessarily—there is no use in pretending for a moment that it is otherwise. But they are innocent diversions; it is not the intention of the poet to destroy his own argument. With the rhetorician it is different. The feelings which he evokes bear intentionally against the critical steps in the argument: they are destructive. They are the very feelings which need to be inhibited first by the thought-work. The speaker evokes them as if by inadvertence. Or he may even invoke them, by naming them directly, and tease them into activity by reminding them that they are inhibited, and must not be excited. In our text the argument in question is the official one offered by the conspirators, and it is a logical argument. Shakespeare has had the insight to show Brutus, who precedes Antony in the same pulpit, as delivering this argument in prose. But the common feelings which are released in Antony's rhetorical version testify that one step in the process of the conspiracy feels to the primitive mob like ingratitude and murder, and that is enough. The feelings surge up, and the argument is overwhelmed.

I am not a technical Freudian, not knowing the system closely though I have read some of the fundamental texts repeatedly. And I am not an orthodox Freudian, since I do not feel impelled to embrace the precise teachings of Freud, nor some "official" set of doctrines approved by a circle of Freudians. Freud liked to disparage his own qualifications for indulging in aesthetic theory, and he has nothing which could fairly be called a theory of poetry. But it is clear that Freud would have relished the psychic bearings of Antony's rhetorical substances and feelings. Antony's feelings must rate as id-feelings which would have been expressly forbidden by the ego presiding over the argument; so a specific guilt attached to their indulgence. Freud had the professional interests of a doctor of medicine, and he followed the conflict of the ego and the id at the clinical level, where he could translate the id's furtive expression into flagrant guilt and obscenity. It is for that reason, if any, that he was disqualified for the poetic analysis. The offenses of poetry against reason are very curious and in bulk they are massive, but taken individually they must have seemed to him short of being drastic enough for the doctor's attention. The rhetoric of Antony, like wit and satire and other destructive forms of art, would come closer to his interest.

But I will list the pathetic or substantival lapses in our passage indifferently, not trying to distinguish between rhetorical and poetic. There will be enough of both. There will be enough of the standard usages of poetry to establish pretty clear, as I think, its addiction to substances, and to some peculiar substantival locutions.

IV

We come to our text. It is a rounded unit of verse, found in Act III, Scene ii, lines 173–198, of the play.

> If you have tears, prepare to shed them now.
> You all do know this mantle: I remember
> The first time ever Caesar put it on;
> 'Twas on a summer's evening, in his tent,
> That day he overcame the Nervii:
> Look, in this place ran Cassius' dagger through:
> See what a rent the envious Casca made:
> Through this the well-beloved Brutus stabb'd;
> And as he pluck'd his cursed steel away,
> Mark how the blood of Caesar follow'd it,
> As rushing out of doors, to be resolved
> If Brutus so unkindly knock'd, or no;
> For Brutus, as you know, was Caesar's angel:
> Judge, O you gods, how dearly Caesar lov'd him!
> This was the most unkindest cut of all;
> For when the noble Caesar saw him stab,
> Ingratitude, more strong than traitors' arms,
> Quite vanquish'd him: then burst his mighty heart;
> And in his mantle muffling up his face,
> Even at the base of Pompey's statue,
> Which all the while ran blood, great Caesar fell,
> O what a fall was there, my countrymen!
> Then I, and you and all of us fell down,
> Whilst bloody treason flourish'd over us.
> O, now you weep; and I perceive you feel
> The dint of pity: these are gracious drops.

For convenience I will list the comments numerically. But it needs to be remarked that they are not intended to be exhaustive.

(1) The opening line, *if you have tears*, is a sort of prologue advertising a passage likely to be in the pathetic mode. But Antony is not yet sure that it will reach his auditors and make them weep. The two concluding lines, *O, now you weep*, etc., make an epilogue. The auditors

weep, the rhetoric has succeeded, and Antony has dropped his guard and broken his promise to Brutus. Considering its brevity, his speech has had perhaps the most astonishing success recorded for us anywhere in the annals of oratory, whether history or imaginative literature. It is followed presently, after another prompting, by evidences in the Roman style of its triumph, as the citizens start severally shouting,

> O piteous spectacle!
> O noble Caesar!
> O woeful day!
> O traitors, villains!
> O most bloody sight!
> We will be revenged.
> Revenge! About! Seek! Burn! Fire! Kill!
> Slay! Let not a traitor live!

(2) The passage is masterfully metered, in a blank verse which is firm yet always is kept alive and compelling to the auditors' attention by the permissive variations. Meter is another and subtler advertisement of the intention of this kind of discourse. Unmetered words, as in common prose, may be said to have only external referents since their intrinsic sounds are not noticed except as identifying the external referents. But metered words force upon us their own phonetic character, to go along with their usual referents, and the referents become at once substantival; that is, they comprise each one adjective which does not participate in the logical argument. They furnish us with at least a little substance, and that is usually for us a token that we shall have more. For we know very well how, when we come to a body of language which is obviously metered, we have to get our minds ready at once to make a different adaptation from that which we make for prose; or turn away from it if we will not make this adaptation, on the ground that we are not in the mood for poetry. In the recent admirable number of the *Quarterly Review of Literature* honoring the late Paul Valéry, Mr. William Troy writes very well by way of discussing this poet's pronouncements upon his art.[4] We are told that Valéry shared with the Symbolists the ideal of a poetry of incredible involution, which could never be paraphrased; and it is certainly true that his poetry, like theirs, resists our logic. But they required of themselves the scrupulous provision of at least the sort of logic that goes into the formation of meters, a logic on

---

4. William Troy, "Paul Valery and the Poetic Universe," *Quarterly Review of Literature*, III, No. 3 (1946), 232–39.

the musical order, which is entirely determinable. Mr. Troy translates a writing of Valéry's upon the distinction prose vs. poetry, in which we read:

> The essence of prose is to perish—that is to say, to be "understood," which is to say to be dissolved, destroyed without hope of return, entirely replaced by the image or the impulse which it signifies in linguistic terms.[5]

This strong language seems to mean what has just been asserted: that the phonetic character of a word in prose is dropped from attention as soon as we have used it to obtain its common referent, but in poetry is tightly secured to this referent, and shares in its survival. The metered word denotes a low-grade substance. And I think from our experience that we will say it is also the sign of a freely substantival discourse.

(3) The mantle is not the logical mantle, the any and indifferent mantle which, worn on the body of Caesar, must have been pierced by the conspirators' daggers and thereby have supplied the given documentation but nothing else. This is a substantival mantle. It is a recognizable mantle, and when it is seen it evokes its own history in the spectator's imagination, and the appropriate feelings. It must be about ten years old if Shakespeare's audience cares to reckon its age, since Caesar first wore it on the evening of the battle with the Nervii. That was perhaps the most brilliant feat of arms in his conduct of the Gallic wars, and certainly it caused the greatest triumph to be voted him. Antony remembers when Caesar first put it on. That is a good item psychologically but it is false historically, since Antony could not have been then in Gaul with Caesar. But Shakespeare's historicity is not our topic, nor does it much concern the auditors. We will not go outside the play to question Shakespeare about Antony's remembrance; nor to ask if it was likely that Caesar, who was foppish, had the habit of publicly wearing robes that were ten years old. In the play he is given to wearing this mantle, and doubtless each time the citizens see him in it they think of his service to the state and feel a gush of affection. So they do now.

(4) Only three rents are noted in the garment though earlier in the play we have seen six conspirators striking at Caesar. (In Plutarch there were even more conspirators, and the wounds they inflicted numbered twenty-three.) But perhaps it is fortunate. It is not upon the quantity of bloodshed that Antony is about to enlarge. Besides Antony

5. Troy, "Paul Valery," 233.

in his substantival style makes the gesture of individualizing each of
the strokes mentioned, a policy which would grow very tiresome if the
list should be long. Thus (a) one conspirator's *dagger ran through this
place*, but (b) another conspirator *made this rent, see!* and (c) a third
conspirator *stabbed through this one*.

(5) At this point Antony becomes bolder. He begins to provoke feelings toward persons and objects by using directive adjectives or epithets. These denote, or pretend to denote, stock classifications of the
persons as good or bad, liked or disliked, and invite stock responses. So
we have *the envious Casca, his cursed steel, the noble Caesar, his
mighty heart, great Caesar, bloody treason*. We also have *the well-
beloved* Brutus, and that is on the way to being assumed as a stock
classification but its affective status will not be clear till we dwell on it a
little; it initiates the passage about Brutus and Caesar which develops
that this *well-beloved* man who stabs the friend who loves him is unkind.

(6) The metaphor under which we are made to see Caesar's blood,
and think of it pouring out after Brutus' stroke, is remarkable. The
blood flowing from the blood-vessels which have been punctured becomes the page or houseboy rushing out of Caesar's body, the house, in
order to make certain that this is really Brutus who is making such a
rude disturbance to gain entry where he is always welcome. And what
is the use of such pretense? The fact from which our metaphor starts,
or the "tenor" if we will use Richards' admirable term, is simply the
flowing of the blood. It might seem that this would be enough to make
the citizens weep, and hate Brutus if they loved Caesar. But the mechanical flowing of the blood does not tell enough; it would have flowed
just the same if Casca, or Cinna, had struck instead of Brutus. Human
blood can very well be effective as a poetic substance, but a still richer
substance is wanted here. So we are shifted to the "vehicle," which substitutes the page for the blood; the page is better than the blood in that
he seems to do what the blood does but in addition bears the knowledge
of Caesar's love for Brutus. For the stroke of Brutus' dagger we are
given in substitution a mere pounding at Caesar's door. Is it not worse
to shed blood than to be rude to a loving friend? Shakespeare thinks
not, in this instance. Antony flatters the citizens, but calculates that he
will win them, by assuming that they will think not. In this metaphor
the terms of the given tenor do not give the poet occasion for enough
substance, so he makes his occasion, and tries by way of analogy a vehicle which holds more substance. The feelings which it prompts would

be justified, we may think, if they should be the same feelings which respond to the facts of the tenor elsewhere. But technically they are responses to a fiction.

(7) Two lines drop quite out of the category of documentary or formal exposition.

The first one,

> Judge, O you gods, how dearly Caesar lov'd him!

is an interruption by apostrophe. The rhetorician makes use of apostrophe, for one reason, because its implications are safe from rebuttal by the person apostrophized, who is absent. Antony has called Brutus Caesar's angel; this is mildly metaphorical, and through its theological connotation seems to have suggested that the rich context of Roman religion might be introduced into the human situation. The substance receives a considerable thickening through this addition, though it is not dwelt upon in words. But the manner and intent of its introduction are rhetorical. Antony assumes not only that the gods pronounce as they are requested in favor of Caesar's goodness, but that his auditors will assume it.

The other line,

> O, what a fall was there, my countrymen!

is an exclamation; therefore it is perhaps a pure instance of affective as opposed to logical language. An exclamation shortcuts a great deal of inconvenient factual evidence. It intimates that the speaker has judged the evidence and is moved, and it communicates his emotion without his evidence. But displayed emotion is contagious. The thing exclaimed on is the disastrous reach, the mysterious potency, of Caesar's fall, as if it were something beyond the speaker's power of description.

(8) One of the boldest lines of the passage both metrically and meaningfully is,

> That was the most unkindest cut of all.

In *most unkindest cut* we have five syllables about equally capable of receiving the logical prose stresses, but two have to be subordinated to the rank of unstressed syllables. The metrical problem is soluble, but the line remains memorable. However, it is memorable anyway, having not only its double superlative but its combination of simplicity and gravity. It is one of those lines which might be read as a mere logical

paraphrase but in its context is substantival. It concerns the unkindness of Brutus. If we feel that somehow we do not analyse out of it quite
as much meaning as it appears to have, it may be because we do not
grasp the enormity of unkindness for the Elizabethan mind. The adjective *kind* was still close to the noun *kind* from which it took its meaning. To be kind was to be natural, and not unnatural, according to the
standards of one's kind; then it was to have a powerful group sense of
loyalty and consideration towards others of one's kind. To be unkind
was to be an unnatural monster who lacked this sense for others of his
kind. He was the more unnatural when they had been kind to him; the
word subsumed ingratitude. In its full sense—which has not survived—
there was scarcely anything worse to be than unkind. Unkindness
summed up and covered great crimes. Thus in *Hamlet* when the King
addresses the Prince,

> But now, my cousin Hamlet, and my son—

Hamlet's aside takes the form,

> A little more than kin, and less than kind.

meaning that Claudius may be a member of Hamlet's own family in
more ways than one, but he is not even true to the obligations a man
owes to members of human kind; kinship has not stopped him from
murdering his virtuous brother. In our own play, Antony charges Brutus with unkindness perhaps ambiguously, wanting the word to carry
its strong moral feeling, but willing for the sake of his promise to Brutus to let it carry its weaker feeling, with which we are well acquainted,
as going with a breach of tact or a selfishness of less than statutory importance. Of course we prefer the greater meaning to the lesser, and so
did the populace. Whatever Antony's right to take this moral position, in
view of his official commitment, we cannot hold that the hypocritical
rhetorician is not going to work for a righteous cause. He converts his
auditors to a fierce righteousness, and it is almost as if he had completed his oration too soon. In a moment they will want to hurry off to
their righteous vengeance, and he will have to beg them to wait and
learn of their benefits from Caesar's will. After that their morality will
have a vested interest, and to our way of thinking may be on a lower
because less disinterested plane. But technically they will feel gratitude
to Caesar which should make them all the more kind to his memory,
and resentful of Brutus' unkindness.

(9) There are several quick instances of personification, or—since the word is not capitalized like the name of a person—half-personification, which we might call reification, or perhaps substantivalism. An essence is promoted to a mythical and semi-religious substance embodying the essence. But this substance is entirely fictional.

The first one is *ingratitude*. The noun is properly abstract, that is, it denotes an essence abstracted from individual persons possessed each of many adjectives. But in becoming substantival the essence does not revert to the human individual from whom it came, for example to the ungrateful Brutus, but takes a new kind of expansion into an embodied "spirit of ingratitude," as we should say. But embodied; for ingratitude becomes physical in order to be stronger than *traitors' arms*—if it were simply the ungrateful Brutus it could have no other arms than his— and also in order to cause the physical heart of Caesar to burst. I should agree with the logical positivists that this is semantically a poor sort of term for discourse. It would be very arbitrary if it were not vague. Fortunately it is brief. Shakespeare did not spend himself, as Spenser and many another poet had done, with building such abstractions into substances as incredible as they were elaborate. A rhetorical intention is behind the figure here: to intimate that Caesar had the physical constitution and prowess of a great hero, and could not have been vanquished by a few assassins. In North's Life of Caesar Shakespeare found the occasion:

> . . . then Brutus himself gave him one wound about his privities. Men report also, that Caesar did still defend himself against the rest, running every way with his body; but when he saw Brutus with his sword drawne in his hand, then he pulled his gowne over his head, and made no more resistance. . . .

The second instance is even less developed: the mysterious potency of Caesar's *fall*. The *O, what a fall* saves Antony some embarrassment as well as labor; the affective trick of exclamation. Doubtless we are led to think of Adam's Fall, and its malignity and continuing potency. Here we are told only that Caesar fell, and that his fall shook the Roman world, or at least was an exclamatory occasion, and extended its influence so far that

> Then I, and you, and all of us fell down.

And this brings us to the third instance, in the next line:

> Whilst bloody treason flourish'd over us,

which is more commonplace than either of the others, and even less developed.

(10) The passage about Caesar's falling

> Even at the base of Pompey's statue,
> Which all the while ran blood,

is irresolute in its intention. Why the *even*? It is too late for Antony to use it meaning *exactly*, or *just*, in order to render his documentation precise. Perhaps the line is simply the easy metrical version of *at the base of even Pompey's statue*. Plutarch saw a great irony in this detail. For Pompey too had been Caesar's enemy, the greatest enemy who had opposed him till now, but had been vanquished; yet Caesar falls at the feet of the stone Pompey, and his blood is spilled as if to perform a sacrifice to Pompey. It would have been easy for Antony to make a lugubrious point of this, and to reinforce hatred of the conspirators with the old hatred of Pompey. It was still fresh, for the play had opened with the tribunes of the people, men of Pompey's old party, trying to keep the people from making holiday in Caesar's honor. Shakespeare was very conscious of Plutarch's note, for he kept North's phrase in saying that the statue *ran blood*, which was a bad way of saying that it ran with Caesar's blood. But if Caesar's relation to Pompey is not built into the situation it is probably just as well. Antony's oration had had shifts and surprises and excitements enough. With a wealth of substances and a continuous play on feelings he had produced many complications, and if he should be immoderate and want to push them further he might produce confusion.

POETRY

II, THE FINAL CAUSE

I. SENTIMENTS OF ALL SIZES

 N ANTONY'S SPEECH there is quite a cluster of substantival objects for affections; the well-known mantle, the vision of Caesar resting after his battle with the Nervii, the blood rushing out like the houseboy to see if this is really Brutus, the tough fighter whom only the sense of ingratitude can vanquish, the falling Caesar. But all are facets of one great substantival object, which is the person of Caesar. So in two ways the passage is something special. In the first place the object is a very great one, and the feeling it invokes is of overpowering intensity. Furthermore, we have seen that the feeling for this object works in rhetorical fashion against the speaker's own official argument; it does not accompany the thought-work but counters it and destroys it.

But feeling is not restricted in poetry to a role either so single or so destructive. Human affections are vastly and inconspicuously diffused among the objects of poetry, as among those of common experience. We need to look at another poetry—again it will be a Shakespearian and "popular" passage—in order to sense the wider but lower range of its substantival-affective usages. Let it be the passage where Oberon plans for himself and Puck to make use of the magic flower. Smeared on the eyes of the sleeping victim, its juice will put him in love with *the next thing he espies*. The joke seems harsh, but it is "practical" in more ways than one. We have little sympathy with the victim Demetrius, who has scorned the love of the worthy Helena, but we have misgivings against Oberon's playing the joke on his queen Titania. It goes against his own sensibility. But he and Titania already get along badly together, for we have just seen them quarreling with high words, and the plan will justify itself by its consequence: Titania will concede to her husband's side of their dispute, and incidentally will return to her husband's bed. Oberon's speech is in *Midsummer Night's Dream*, II, i, 249–267:

This essay first appeared in the *Kenyon Review*, IX (Autumn, 1947), 640–58. Reprinted by permission of Helen Ransom Forman.

> I know a bank where the wild thyme blows,
> Where oxlips and the nodding violet grows,
> Quite overcanopied with lush woodbine,
> With sweet musk-roses and with eglantine:
> There sleeps Titania sometime of the night,
> Lull'd in these flowers with dances and delight;
> And there the snake throws her enamell'd skin,
> Weed wide enough to wrap a fairy in:
> And with the juice of this I'll streak her eyes,
> And make her full of hateful fantasies.
> Take thou some of it, and seek through this grove:
> A sweet Athenian lady is in love
> With a disdainful youth: anoint his eyes;
> But do it when the next thing he espies
> May be the lady: thou shalt know the man
> By the Athenian garments he hath on.
> Effect it with some care that he may prove
> More fond on her than she upon her love:
> And look thou meet me ere the first cock crow.

We will attend first to the paraphrase element. Oberon is rehearsing for his own benefit the location of Titania, and the action he intends when he finds her. After that he is directing Puck as to the where, when and how of the action against Demetrius. It is notable that this thought-work is not dogged by much substantival-affective diversion in its latter half which is for Puck's benefit. Oberon gives matter-of-fact or prosy commands to his servant, and does not invite him to indulge with his master in feelings. Oberon has a monopoly in the feelings both in his own right as a man of sensibility with a distasteful chore to perform, and in the right of his victim the dainty Titania. Attended by her elves, she keeps woodland court in the very best style, but rather as if she were the virgin Diana instead of a wife with a husband at home. But the plan against her is really going to be carried out. Nothing will stop it, not even the gentle diversions of Oberon on his errand; on the contrary, these seem to take the curse off the action and redeem it.

We are struck by superfluity in the detail of locating Titania's bower; this is substantival detail. The place of her sleeping is not merely "determined," in the way of practical identification for Oberon's guidance. It is "overdetermined," as Freud would say; that is, determined to a degree that goes beyond conscious purpose. So we have one of those dense little "nature" passages which are constantly irrupting into poems and slowing up the action. A bank serves Titania for a bed, and it is overdetermined in respect to the three named wildflowers which make the bedcovering. Above it is the canopy, likewise overdetermined in respect to three named wildflowers of which it is composed. Of the first three flowers, two receive adjectives which are gratuitous and overdetermining; of the second three, two, again, are overdetermined by adjectives. Then we proceed to Titania herself, who scarcely needs special identification for Oberon, but who in passing before his imagination is overdetermined in that, though she will be found sleeping, the manner of her going to sleep is pictured: *lull'd in these flowers with dances and delight.* That this is really the manner of it we can see in detail in the next scene: she goes to bed and her fairies dance and sing her to sleep. Eventually, upon finding her sleeping, Oberon will do his dirty work, as promised in much terser language: *And with the juice of this I'll streak her eyes, And make her full of hateful fantasies.* The poetic preliminaries do not prevent the final action. But if he bears the ugly juice in his right hand, so to speak, with his left hand he gathers posies; for his own benefit of course, because he is fond of them, and no doubt also because they suit his extralogical thoughts about Titania. He is a fussy and plaintive man yet in his taste a proper husband, and we do not fear but that under his management of the conjugal relation Eros will be "replaced by Agape," so that the ceremony of civilization may be maintained. But we have one more item. In the bower not only do the flowers offer themselves for bed and canopy, but there also *the snake throws her enamell'd skin.* Oberon seems to like the handsome snake as he likes the flowers, but does Titania? We are later to see her fairies on her behalf singing a spell to keep *snakes, hedgehogs, newts,* and many other disagreeable beasts away from her bed. He has the tact to present the skin as of a female snake, *enamell'd,* and vested in pure verbal luxuriance as *weed wide enough to wrap a fairy in.* And his chief consideration in the matter is after all for the fairy who will have the snake skin for sleeping bag. This he may have learned from Titania, who elsewhere bids her elves hunt the rere-mice *for their leathern wings, To make my small elves coats.*

Shakespeare's fantasy of the fairy people is not for his readers' every mood, for we may be too preoccupied with the difficulties of human concerns. But the chief characters are of unmistakable humanity. In Oberon's speech we have the picture of a common pattern of human behavior. We go about our business, but even if it is fairly urgent we have more energy of mind than we need to attend to it; and this energy proceeds to diffuse itself freely upon the context of our enterprise.

There is scarcely a homely enterprise that does not need to be filled out, so that it will engage us fully, by certain local diversions. But these we can analyse, and they appear to consist in taking spontaneous and affectionate notice of minor objects which we are handling or passing, and of course of the images that readily come to us of the principal or goal object.

The trouble with this kind of poetic analysis, which makes these affective diversions public, is not in any inherent logical difficulty, for none is involved, but in the fact that we have looked for something much more distinguished, and perhaps more esoteric, in the representations of poetry, and do not like to see it performing an office so homely. But it is now a commonplace that usually we do not exactly know what we are doing; so it would not be strange if we do not realize what poetry is doing.

2. PRECIOUS OBJECTS

Whether we respond to the substantival objects by grand passions (as to the person of Caesar) or by moderated and even casual affections (as to the absent wife of whose graces we are mindful even when she is being punished, as to the boudoir or the glade which is furnished with flowers): they occupy for us a position which I shall indicate by calling them "precious objects." By precious I mean: beyond price, or valued at more than the market value of such objects. Our affective life spends so much energy on them that they must be regarded as important in our personal if not in our professional economy. And the wide range of precious objects is indicated in any casual listing of common ones, such as the following: father and mother, husband or wife, child, friend; one's own house, "view," terrain, town; natural objects "at large" which familiarly invest our lives, such as sun and moon, sky and sea, mountain and forest, river, plain; and even objects that are far less tangible when we try to comprehend them as wholes, though we must have had many tangible experiences within them, such as one's nation, church, God, business, "causes," and institutions.

And now, under a few headings, we should examine the character in which precious objects present themselves to us.

A precious object is a familiar one, yet it is always capable of exhibiting fresh aspects of a substance which is contingent and unpredictable. That is to say, it is what is denoted in logic by a proper noun, or one that cannot be exhausted by definition. It is what certain philosophies now

call an "existent"—though not an odious one, as some of them prefer to
have it. It is a sizable object, and a comparatively permanent one; we
leave it and come back to it; we may even call it, speaking comparatively, an absolute object, since it persists full-bodied and unchanged in
the midst of what is confused and shifting. We cherish it precisely in its
absoluteness and inviolability. This is clear if we consider the case
where the object is personal, for we extend to that person in full equality all the rights that we claim ourselves in our own absoluteness. The
precious object is of course most complete, most perfect, when it is a
personal object, for then it not only extends its favors but replies to our
communications. But we may easily find that surreptitiously we refer a
degree of personality even to impersonal precious objects though we
may "know better."

Now a negative mark. The precious object which is "loved" must be
distinguished from the ordinary object which is "used." The loved object is surely substantival, but it is no less certain that the used object is
merely "specific." A specific object is one that has been abstracted from
substance by the technical reason for employment in a desire-process.
(Specific means: having the properties of a species or class object without surplus or contingent properties.) Now it is theoretically possible
for us to put all our energies into desire-processes, and therefore to entertain none but specific objects. But it is not too soon to have heard a
good deal of disparagement of that view of life in our time. For example,
to Gabriel Marcel, the Catholic Existentialist, Miss Marjorie Grene in
the last issue of this Review attributes a description of it. Of all the imperfect modern philosophies we learn that Marcel criticizes most the
"technical" one; in Miss Grene's words it

> seems to him most important and most dangerous. As Marcel sees it, the
> principal characteristics of a technical view of the world are: that it un-
> derstands things only in terms of some hold (*prise*) that human agents
> have on them, some way of manipulating them; that such techniques of
> manipulation, and consequently the world itself, appear perfectible—
> even natural catastrophes are looked on as unaccountable flaws in the
> machinery which we have not rectified, but of course will ultimately rec-
> tify; and that in the light of this way of regarding things man himself be-
> comes for himself only an object of such techniques, knowing himself
> only by reflection as another object to handle—and to perfect, when he
> fails to run right. The moral results of this world view are, for Marcel,
> conspicuous and deplorable. The "interior life" being minimized by such
> an externalizing attitude, human aspirations are reduced likewise to their

minimum: *i.e.* to the mechanical pursuit of instantaneous pleasures—
which Marcel calls "le Anglo-Saxon having a good time."[1]

But we put this in our own terms by saying that for the technical view
of life there are no precious objects but only specific objects. We had
better not belittle either the desire-processes or the specific objects
which they employ; they constitute life primarily; and so obviously do
they define the main economy of living that it is difficult in theory to
find a place for precious objects and their affects. Nor do we need to
deny to specific objects their "reality." The properties specified are
really there, but they do not comprise the "existents" from which they
have been abstracted by thought. And it is even true that in any practical process we actually handle substantival objects, for there are no
other objects in existence; but we do so without attending to the substance enveloping the specific objects—unless, of course, it irrupts into
the operation and spoils it. But if it be said that we attend to substantival objects only for the sake of finding and clearing our specific objects, it is our view here that we attend to substantival objects also for
the sake of obtaining precious objects.

The precious objects contain specific objects; they have their uses;
they do attach themselves therefore, if only partially, to the material
economy. The relation of the precious object to the specific object
within it is thus precisely the same as the relation of the art-work to its
own thought-work, the poem to its paraphrase. Again, it is the same
relation as that of Agape to Eros in the myth of sex; for Agape does not
deny the erotic principle, and there is not one chance that she could
win the pragmatical citizens if she opposed it with a principle of denial.
And the relation is also that of the god, that large-scale substantival
"personification" which becomes a precious object, to the providence
he exerts on behalf of the worshippers. Though he may represent
the whole world as absolute existent, he would scarcely be loved if
the world did not seem to contain a dispensation favorable to human
happiness.

It follows that the use precedes the love; and it seems likely that the
love arises spontaneously in the course of many uses, and develops unconsciously more than consciously. It is along this line that we must
look for the "natural history" of a given precious object. Otherwise we
should be committing ourselves to the thesis that we regard reason as

1. "Two More Existentialists: Karl Jaspers and Gabriel Marcel," *Kenyon Review*, IX
(Summer, 1947), 382.

concerned organically with specific needs and specific objects, but regard sensibility as aimless and parasitic. Sensibility is at the service of
reason, reporting to it the substantival situation within which reason
has to work specifically, but this service is finished when reason has
found the specific process and stabilized it. It is only then, as we employ the process by rote, and "without noticing," that the idle sensibility
goes back to its substantival objects and recovers them. This might be
very gradual; and in this connection we have a curious phenomenon.
Replace the familiar useful object with a new object, and let the new
one be even superior in its utility to the old one; at once we feel the pain
of deprivation, yet we had not known we had any personal interest
there. This is the well-known pain of nostalgia.

Finally, the precious object has to be distinguished, as I think, from
the love-object of the Freudians. Freud was a gentle and cultured man,
who did not propose to betray the values of his civilization. It seemed to
him desirable that love in the wider sense, as having a diffused object,
should replace love in the narrow sense, as having a specific object. But
love for Freud is a restricted term; it refers to sex. Thus he mentions
"beauty" only when it resides in a sex object, and then to this effect:
beauty is the affective aspect which the loved object wears for us in its
secondary sexual characteristics. But we may prefer to judge that this
beauty, when attributed to a person actually or potentially our love-
mate, may refer to characteristics beyond the secondary sex characteristics as well as beyond the primary. And what is to be said of the
beauty of other objects? For the Freudians, love is tied to sex even in
childhood, before sex becomes focussed in the sexual organs; but at
this stage sex expresses itself actually, in part, in "feelings of tenderness and affection." Now Freud finds that the first "rich" development
of sex occurs in children at the age of three to five. Accordingly, Dr.
Brill, the American translator of Freud, is perfectly regular when he reports (in his Introduction to the Modern Library edition) the case of a
four-year-old child as follows:

> An apparently normal girl of about four became very nervous, refused
> most of her food, had frequent crying spells and tantrums, with conse-
> quent loss of weight, malaise, and insomnia, so that her condition be-
> came quite alarming. After the ordinary medical measures had been
> found of no avail, I was consulted. The case was so simple that I could not
> understand why no one had thought of the cure before I came on the
> scene. The child had begun to show the symptoms enumerated above,
> about two months after her mother was separated from her. . . . [It] was

really a disturbance in the child's distribution of libido. When the mother
was forced to leave her home, the libido which the child ordinarily trans-
ferred to the mother became detached and remained, as it were, floating
in the air. She was unable to establish any new transference with the
mother-substitutes which were offered to her, and was cured as soon as
her love object was restored.[2]

But two questions occur to us concerning the little girl's trouble. First,
whether it is not an ordinary though severe case of nostalgia, such as
might be caused by the loss of any precious object, though undoubtedly
the mother was a very important one; and second, whether it had to
wait for the "rich" sexual period of the fourth year before it could occur.
Without being a child-psychologist, it seems to me that I have observed
certain almost hysterical behaviors in a child of scarcely a year's age,
and they seemed to be manifested nearly as much over being taken to
live in a strange house as over the mother's absence. The inference
would be that the formation of precious objects is a more versatile behavior than the Freudians have chosen to think, and that it occurs as
soon as the suitable objects develop in experience.

3. ADVANCE TO GENERAL SENSIBILITY

A unit of Shakespeare's verse, as we have seen, may be well punctuated
with locutions denoting precious objects, which stop us long enough
for us to make prepared responses. But this is not the whole story. It
must be acknowledged that poetic language is not tied to this practice,
as if it were the only possible practice; it does not have to evoke the
precious objects in the familiar, rounded, and absolute form. Probably it
may be said that, the more "advanced" a poetry is, the better it is able to
dispense with them. In that case it will be substantival freely, everywhere, and inconclusively. In the sister art of painting we have something very like this. The old painters elected, and were employed, to
represent famed and precious objects to which the whole public would
respond whether it "understood" painting or not. According to the
usual analysis of the classic painters, they did not fail to have their
thought-work, their structure, which was in the "balance" of the color-
masses, according to geometrical or dynamic design. Evidently in that
art the patrons can go directly to their substantival objects without
passing through the thought-work to which the objects are pinned; and

2. A. A. Brill (ed.), *The Basic Writings of Sigmund Freud* (New York, 1938), 17.

a special kind of logical expertness is required to "paraphrase" the painting in terms of its over-all design. However that may be, the painters eventually came to the point where they refused to their illiterate public the sop of common sentiment; they elected to represent objects which were substantival enough, but not associated in experience with any standard affects. (Later still, the painters elected not to represent any natural objects at all, in their "abstractionist" art; but that is another topic, and might not have much relevance to developments in poetry.) But good poets no less than good painters can manage without precious objects, or with very few of them. They animadvert constantly to substance, darting away from the thought-work to find quick, fresh configurations of it, yet these are nothing for us to cherish, to live with; they are not our precious objects. The public for these poets is scarcely going to be that general public which, when it reads seriously, proposes to take solid substantival staples from literature for its nourishment; but a special public conditioned to the need of the substantival as a world, as a principle; "lovers of nature" who love it any time they see it vivid, and do not have to wait till they have appropriated it and got used to it. This conditioning implies some adventurousness, and of course a good deal of experience. And this poetry addresses itself to sensibility rather than to sentiment.

Let us examine the passage where Claudius addresses his Queen just after Ophelia has delivered her mad songs and retired. It is *Hamlet*, IV, v, 77–96:

> O Gertrude, Gertrude,
> When sorrows come, they come not single spies,
> But in battalions. First, her father slain:
> Next, your son gone: and he most violent author
> Of his own just remove: the people muddied,
> Thick and unwholesome in their thoughts and whispers,
> For good Polonius' death; and we have done but greenly,
> In hugger-mugger to inter him: poor Ophelia
> Divided from herself and her fair judgment,
> Without the which we are pictures, or mere beasts:
> Last, and as much containing as all these,
> Her brother is in secret come from France;
> Feeds on his wonder, keeps himself in clouds,
> And wants not buzzers to infect his ear
> With pestilent speeches of his father's death;
> Wherein necessity, of matter beggar'd,
> Will nothing stick our person to arraign

> In ear and ear. O my dear Gertrude, this,
> Like to a murdering-piece, in many places
> Gives me superfluous death.

Here again the paraphrase is simple enough. Claudius remarks that troubles do not come singly. Then he lists in one long sentence his five recent troubles; a colon marks the end of each item up to the last, which has the period; but some of the items are compounded, or attended with comment, the separation of the parts being accomplished by a semicolon. (In Shakespeare the colon is chiefly for indicating a stop too big for the semicolon and not big enough for the period.) Finally, he remarks that any one of the five troubles by itself is enough to ruin him.

Now there is a well-formed sentiment presiding over even this lively and unsentimental passage. *O Gertrude, Gertrude*, begins the first sentence, and *O my dear Gertrude*, begins the last one. We may not like Claudius, who is the villain in the play if there is one, but he shares his troubles with Gertrude, and that confers a humanity upon him. Perhaps in a poetic drama every character has to have a core of sentiment if the dramatist expects to give him poetic speech. But outside of Claudius' affection for Gertrude in the background, I believe the whole quality of this speech is sensibility, and not sentiment.

We notice quickly how very "figurative" is the passage. And this suggests a good form for our analysis to take. We are accustomed to concede to the poet the right to depart considerably from the grammar and idiom of the prose language. Yet it is a strange concession. The great public which has been making it since the beginnings of historic literature can scarcely have known the ground for making it. It will be said that it is to enable the poet to keep his meters. But the explanation is unsophisticated. At most it may be that the difficulty of keeping meters was the cause of his linguistic irregularities when he was a tyro; later he learned to keep tolerable meters without using disordered language, but continued to use it anyhow because now he liked it for its poetic effect. (I used to write that the young poet went over his poem to smooth out the language, and the old poet went over it to roughen the language up.) However that may be, the poets do have their poetic "license." Its latitude is wide, yet it falls readily into certain types or categories of aberration. These are what we call the "figures of speech." The Greek grammarians had a keen sense for this sort of thing, far keener than ours; they identified and named more tropes, or figures, than succeeding nations have cared to keep in their literary lexicons. In the passage before us we may regard every flaw in the thought-work as a lapse from the norm of language, and every lapse from the norm of language as a figure. But instead of listing the score or so of cases as we come to them, we shall be content to remark most of them under the headings of important figures. It will not be necessary for us to find a technical name for every figure.

I. We may even group figures together. And first those that fall into a group of what we may call syntactical figures, or, more properly, dystactical figures; those that do not make substantival additions to the content directly, but only indirectly, by distorting the grammar of the discourse. In this sense we have mention of Hamlet as *most violent author Of his own just remove.* Our slight difficulty in obtaining the sense of this causes us to review the previous behavior of Hamlet, and this is actually to make substantival addition if we review more than we need to use in order to be sure that we review enough. Any difficulty in a reading, any "obscurity," is to the same effect. Here we do not know whether *remove* is active or passive. But, if active, its author is so clearly Hamlet that we should not require the given emphasis; so we take it as passive, it is Hamlet's being removed to England. How is he the author of that? But here we have the *violent*; being violent, Hamlet was removed, and he brought it upon himself. The figure would be called condensation, or ellipsis. The poetic strategist would calculate—perhaps intuitively—that elliptical statement would lead not only to filling in the parts omitted but also to exploring the substantival situation in order to find the right parts; a case where parsimony is really for the sake of excess.

Ophelia is said to be *Divided from herself and her fair judgment.* A sententious imprecision of some kind. The young lady has become schizophrenic, a split personality. One of her personalities, perhaps the one who sings bawdy songs, is named Ophelia, the other is named *herself*; the status of the *her fair judgment* is uncertain. Ridiculous consequences flow if we care to play with these terms. Even so, I doubt if we want the line otherwise; a foolish, pompous line about madness. I will suppose that it would have been idiomatic for Shakespeare to say, as we should say now, that Ophelia was not herself, and had lost her mind or judgment.

As much containing, and *our person to arraign*: wrong word-order. Modern poets have nearly surrendered their license to this figure. It does not lead to much recovery of substance.

In ear and ear: elliptical, nearly foolish, yet still impressive; as if the world were too crowded, and time too short, for precision.

In many places Gives me superfluous death. We sense some kind of incoherence here. One point may be that not all the many deaths (there are only five) are superfluous, since one must be counted in order to make the others so. Then we question whether the other four are really deaths if Claudius is already dead. But the dystax of poets is a paradise for schoolmasters if they are provided with red pencils, and not particularly dedicated to sensibility.

II. The other great group of figures is composed of those which introduce substance directly, by naming it; and also illegitimately, in the sense that it is foreign substance, and not merely the substance recovered to the given situation. (When a given specific object, such as the-Caesar-who-was-killed, is expanded into "great Caesar" or "noble Caesar" or Caesar-wearing-this-mantle, that is still within the context and not a departure, and might by comparison be called a legitimate substantival expansion; and we can have that without resorting to a figure.)

The sorrows *come not single spies, But in battalions*: metaphor. They come actually in multitudes, but that is not enough; let them come in vivid multitudes, and why not in multitudes of soldiers, or battalions? They are certainly "inimical" to happiness. But given the battalions for the way they come, the way they do not come will be as single soldiers; and single soldiers would best come in, if they came in, as spies, to "spy out the land." So they *come not single spies*, a locution even more vivid than that about battalions. It contributes to battalions, however, in making us think of the attack of an unprincipled enemy who without warning is suddenly at the stage of full-blown war with us.

Greenly: metaphorical for childishly or hastily.

It is said that without judgment *we are pictures, or mere beasts.* Metaphors. Without judgments we have "percepts without concepts," if that is possible, in respect to our knowledge; *i.e.* we have pictures, in our thought, and nothing else; or we are pictures. And in respect to our conduct we have animal rather than moral motivations; we are as animals, or we are animals.

Ophelia's brother *Feeds on his wonder, keeps himself in clouds, And wants not buzzers to infect his ear With pestilent speeches of his father's death.* A series of metaphors. The last one contains metaphors. The *buzzers* are the scandal-mongers whose whispering is like the buzzing of flies in the ear. What they do is to *infect* not his mind but his

ear with *pestilence*; but at this point we swing back into the tenor with
pestilent speeches.

As to the buzzers' speeches we learn that in them *necessity, of matter beggar'd,* arraigns the king's person. As I understand it: some people
are bound to arraign my person even when they have no material evidence against me. *Necessity* and *matter* are metaphorical in a sense
the reverse of usual; the vehicles are not more but less substantival
than the given tenors—*necessity* as compared with the-people-who-
needs-must, and *matter* as compared with material evidence—and
therefore might be thought to be less vivid. But our impression of actual
effect here must be very different. And we consider that the rule of metaphor is to replace the less vivid with the more vivid, but the rare exception will have the value of surprise, and may be even more effective
than the rule. Certainly the phrase here requires imagination, participation, on our part.

Like to a murdering-piece: simile. The simile says *like*, or *as*, the
metaphor does not go through that formality. Metaphor therefore would
seem to be the more concealed, the more effective; simile publishes its
intention and may look too artificial, inviting resistance.

III. Under separate heading I bring the figure of mixed diction, one
of Shakespeare's finest and most individual usages. I am not sure
whether it belongs properly under I or II above; perhaps it would go
under I. The Greeks knew the figure, but in no language is its opportunity quite so brilliant as in English. The two dictions which are mixed,
or juxtaposed, are the native, primitive, or folk speech, generally constituting the larger element or context, and latinical speech, generally
in the position of an elegant or foppish condensation dropped into the
context. The usage originated, as I think, in the reluctance of English
to domesticate its Renaissance adoptions from the Latin, which would
have been to lose their foreign and aristocratic tone; Shakespeare's own
practice was important if not determining in the resistance.[3]

One of the most arresting places in the entire passage, for the sensitive reader, has this kind of mixed diction for its chief distinction;
we have done but greenly, in hugger-mugger to inter him. The *greenly*
and the *hugger-mugger* strike us as highly vernacular and countrified
speech but they lead us straight to the prim latinity of *inter*. The common English word would have been bury; in the graveyard scene of

3. An essay of mine, "On Shakespeare's Language," discussed this topic in the Spring
1947 number of the *Sewanee Review*. (Ransom's note)

this play that word occurs seven times, by my count, while *inter* does not occur once. We may say that for the *greenly* and *hugger-mugger* sort of taste *inter* is absurd, but no more than *greenly* and *hugger-mugger* are absurd for the *inter* taste. The absurdity is of the kind which results in laughter, if we are prepared for it by the context; and even here, where we are following a good thought-sequence, we sense something nearly comic. Shakespeare is very daring with his latinical locutions in this style. But we can go even further in our analysis. The *hugger-mugger* taste is an id sort of taste, and the *inter* taste is an ego sort of taste; by every character which we are inclined to attribute to these entities. Consequently in this form of mixed diction we have repeated for us on a very small scale, on a microcosmic scale, the fundamental conflict which divides the poem between the interests of the ego and the interests of the id.

As to the classification of Shakespeare's mixed diction, we have a substantival usage perhaps on the order of meter. It induces the sense of a certain character in the medium itself (the medium is language) when the medium ought to have no character of its own, and be gone as soon as it delivers its referent.

Other instances are a little less decisive: latinical *infect* and *pestilent* in their pure English context; and *superfluous* in its context.

4. TELEOLOGY OF SUBSTANCE

Even though we must have omitted some of the substantival usages of Shakespeare, and mistaken others, yet we cannot come to this point in the poetic analysis and postpone any further the teleological speculation. How are we to conceive the poet's interest in the substantival object when it would seem that the organic processes are regularly and perfectly accomplished through specific objects? It looks like a perverse interest; the logical positivists might well scorn it, with their ideal of rational perfection; and the pragmatists, and naturalists, with their concern for positive human goals. They would be wrong, as I think, on the whole; but not for reasons which have yet been shown; nor for reasons which will always be withheld from their peculiar orders of intelligence. I am horrified by the horror which is still being professed toward these new philosophies by apologists of poetry, as of religion. But I think it too intransigent of us, and I am afraid it will be quaint, to deny all recent ways of thinking. I should say that logical positivism is a rather specialized philosophy, but that is not true of naturalism. In naturalistic speculation, a man is nothing less than a biological and psychological organism. I cannot see why he should be more; provided of course the whole man can be figured organically, including the poet in man.

We have had a great deal of poetic theory in the past, but it has not been argued with that understanding. It has been based of course on some sort of poetic analysis, and this did not fail to disclose the wealth of "sensibilia" or "percepts" that found its way into the poem; it was evident even to the cursory observer in the form of vivid coloration, the local energy, and the general "decorative" element in the discourse. Nor was effort spared to account for so strange a feature. One type of explanation said—it still says—that the sensibilia are not so irreconcilable, so ultimate, as they look. They are in the poem, but they make no great difference; the logic of the argument is so powerful that it takes care of them, absorbing them, assimilating them, without a residue; which means that the poem only looks like a poetic discourse but to the careful reader is only a prose. But this explanation seems dogmatic. It is not accompanied by detailed demonstration.

Another explanation has been that the sensibilia are in the poem for the most obvious of reasons: for the benefit of certain "faculties" which needed to exercise themselves with them; the faculties in question being set down variously as the senses, perception, imagination, the feelings, the attitudes. In one form or another this position has been argued by such thinkers as Kant and Coleridge, Richards and Brooks. But it is scarcely eligible in these days. If there are "faculties," they have not been accepted into the organism in order to transact their own private business but in order to help with the organic business. To logical positivists the form of the argument is "tautological." To the naturalists it is simply "unreal"; that is, not according to the psychical formations as we know them.

The teleology of the thought-work, if we care to isolate that, as the prose-value of the poem, is transparently clear; that of the substantival excrescences is hidden. Their purpose is hidden, and even the thing itself is not always conceded. But this looks like the description of a Freudian situation of somewhat low-grade intensity. And that is precisely what I have been preparing to propose. Let us see what we can do if at once we take the thought-work to be the ego's, the play upon substance to be the id's. Our task is then, if possible, to rationalize the id-motive; that is, to see what there might be in the situation of the organism, unknown to immediate consciousness, which would justify the peculiar interest of the id if the id could speak for itself.

The id, in Freud's doctrine, is that part of the psyche which initiates behavior. It is the seat of the instincts which determine the human goods, or at any rate the directions or goals of human behavior. The instincts are compulsive upon the id, no doubt, yet it is a truly psychic or purposive entity, having pleasure for its motivating principle and accepting the instinctive patterns because they bring their pleasures. Unfortunately for the id, it is situated so deep in the physiological organism—this is why Freud's is called the "depth" psychology—that it is blind, and does not know how to obtain its desires from the outer world. But that is because it has set up a deputy, or agent, to manage its public affairs; this is consciousness, the ego, which has the double duty of being a sensory organ, in contact with the outer world, and a reasoning or technological organ to work out the uses of this world for the id's benefit.

All goes well until some erratic, persistent, and unintended behavior indicates to the observer that a compulsion is coming through from the id which the ego cannot control. Presumably there is a wish which the id will not surrender and the ego, wiser than the id and engaged in long-range planning, will not perform. Is the id for all its blindness meddling in the faithful stewardship of the ego? Or does the id assert itself because the ego has betrayed its dearest interests? Freud studied these disorders—they were precisely the phenomena which drove him to the first systematic concept of the unconscious psyche or id—and as an arbiter pronounced rather in favor of the ego and against the id. He developed the technique called psychoanalysis, by which the childlike and inarticulate id could be made to talk after all, and to reveal its secret wish. But upon the revelation the wish evaporated, it was too absurd even to talk about in the wiser language of the ego, and the id knew it; the id had been talked out of its wish. In the course of Freud's career of speculation, however, he seemed to become more and more sympathetic with the id in its conflicts with the ego. The ego with its principle of reason was too enterprising, too ambitious; it involved the whole psyche in adaptations which brought anxieties and deprivations too great to be borne. In a late work such as *Civilization and Its Discontents*, Freud is fully sensitive to the burden that rests upon the modern spirit and threatens civilization with collapse. And since his death we have had the issue of orthodoxy mooted between two schools of Freudians: the sociological one, which believes that the ego must keep the ascendancy, and repress the id; and the biological, which believes that this policy is too dangerous and the id must come nearer to having its way. It suits our present interest, as apologists of poetry, to incline decidedly towards the biological view.

Of course I have given a reduced and simplified version of Freud's doctrine, and it may well be abhorrent to a good Freudian. For instance I have neglected to tell of Freud's frequent excursions into "meta-psychology," in which he carefully blue-printed the possible neural mechanisms which would support the conscious-unconscious compounds of behavior as he liked to figure them on the psychological level.

But on the strength of my representations we can at least figure something of the responsibilities we undertake if we improvise a speculation which Freud never fully and systematically made: about the apparent "sentimental attachment," or "fixation," of the psyche with respect to certain natural objects, going beyond practical interest in these objects as the source of gratifications for the id. It would look as if we must promise to do several things. One thing we may pass over without bothering: the attitude of the brisk managerial ego, the practical reason, to this attachment; it is devoted to aggression against the environment, and the best it can do with the objects in question in their strange new status is to make sure that they do furnish their plain uses. But among the things we seem to undertake is, first, to identify the kind of pleasure which the fixation brings to the id, though this may not be quite what the notoriously libidinous id is supposed to want. Freud's own psychology is hedonistic with respect to psychical motivation, but on the other hand his hedonism must be the most comprehensive and most versatile on record. Then we ought to be able to know that there is a possible physiological mechanism enabling the supposed fixation to work; but so far as I am concerned this provision will have to be waived. The only comfort I can take is from the general understanding that the psychical mechanisms always precede the neural mechanisms in the order of our speculations, and often have to wait for them. Finally, since a speculative psychologist must also be a biologist, we must see how our psychic fixation serves the long-range needs of the biological organism. This last would be ultimate motive, or final cause proper. It seems not really to matter very much whether we regard some mechanism as instituted by a natural providence—such as we denote by Mother Nature, or just Nature, capitalized—which we can never isolate and identify; or regard it as arrived at in the course of the mutations of species and stabilized because those creatures who had it were the ones "calculated"—though there was nobody to make these calculations—to survive on the strength of it. Either way, we are accustomed to think of the "purpose" of the mechanism; and of course the term itself is teleological if we go back to the Greek, where mechanism is something contrived. But given the mechanism, we see at once its relation to the id's pleasure; the latter provision is a sort of immediate cause, or sanction, which pulls the level and puts the mechanism into operation.

5. PURPORT OF A MYTH

The installation of our mechanism in the species would be prehistoric, and it is beyond our grasp for even better reasons than that. But there have been many mythical accounts of the sort of thing, and sometimes they help to give us a teleological perspective. Freud himself was myth-opoeic in his representations, and he was like Plato and Paul in the character of his constructions, if not like Moses; he gave us Id, Ego, Super-ego, and certain Censors at the gates of these sovereignties. (Freud resorted to the figure of personification.) So I will repeat a very famous myth, but will venture to make one elaboration upon it.

When the creation of the species was otherwise finished, it was as if the Creator, speaking in the language of Moses, had sped the young Adam upon his career in these words. *Thou shalt have dominion over the earth and all that is upon the earth; but in ruling them to thy desires thou shalt not escape from loving them; for thou art created from the dust.*

That would seem a supreme irony, as Mr. Brooks would say. The creature is invited to boundless empire over nature, but just in the degree of his success he will be softened by scruples that he would not have willed. Thus he can never become, for example, a god, since he is a creature of earth and at any moment will catch himself being a loyal participant in the earth-community. However aggressive in his pride of dominion, and progressive in the development of his techniques, he will be impeded as fast as he advances. But the irony of the provision will be turned round if we are able presently to reflect that perhaps it is at our own expense, for having thought it was at Adam's expense. The probability rises too strong in our minds, as we reflect, that the provision was for Adam's safeguard and blessing.

At any rate, it is worth remarking, how consonant the purport of this myth would be with the intention which we read between the lines of Moses' stern decalogue. The commandments do not explain themselves, and for the most part they are in the harsh negative, they are "forbidding" commandments, and therefore pedagogically poor. But what is forbidden is chiefly the overriding of love and sensibility. The following objects are marked for love: God, a most embarrassing object to handle logically even in a commandment, but here an object whose mercies are represented as flowing already, therefore to be thankfully accepted but scarcely to be enforced against his fictitious and intangible person; parents; husband and wife; human beings; and objects of bourgeois existence which one may think to steal or covet but which for this purpose have to be earned. We should remember that those instructions which had been given Adam originally had had to receive before long an addition. Adam had eaten of the fruit of the tree of knowledge, and had been promptly intoxicated, becoming in his own thought as a god; foreseeing the division of labor, the development of technology, and acquisition of the means of instant satisfaction of all the desires. So he was warned by his Creator that his vision was illusory: *In the sweat of thy face shalt thou eat bread.* But this was a wholesome notice, which may be taken to mean that cheaply acquired objects, or other men's objects coveted as the commandment forbids them to be coveted, may not be loved though indeed they may be used, and in that case the safeguard of love will not be operative. And now, in Moses' time, here are the commandments, and they are graven on stone tablets. It is good provision for a people already admirably conditioned in their personal habits, but gravely imperilled because they wander through the wilderness, still lacking the elemental security of a "home" on the face of the earth.

THE LITERARY CRITICISM
OF ARISTOTLE
(RECONSIDERATIONS, NO. 10)

I F THERE were a subtitle, I should like it as follows: The literary criticism of a man of letters who had become a pedagogue, and of an idealist who had become a naturalist.[1]

We are present upon an academic occasion, at which it is an honor to assist. Let me begin by recalling a handsome consideration which is cited by intellectual historians. The Lyceum which Aristotle founded late in life, and directed for thirteen years, was the first university to exist according to the pattern which Europeans and Americans now know so familiarly. The Aristotle with whom we are acquainted is the Aristotle of the Lyceum, an academic man, dedicated to a career of oral teaching, despiteful of the glory which awaits the literary man, and, as I think the saying goes in the administrative offices of the modern academy, "unproductive" in the public sense. What he left to posterity was the ferment of his ideas in the heads of his old pupils, plus the lecture-notes from which he had taught them, and which some of them might edit and publish later if they liked. (No mention is made of these notebooks in the author's will, which as such documents go is a model of modesty as well as kindly personal consideration.) The *Rhetoric* and the *Poetics* contain his literary criticism, and both have precisely this history; they are Aristotle's private lecture-notes.

We feel an irony when we reflect that the idealistic Plato never overcame his intellectual distaste for the "world of appearances," which was nothing else but this actual and sensible world, yet gave to his public writings such a literary beauty as subsequent philosophers have not repeated. We may be very sure that every literary stroke of Plato's pen

---

This essay first appeared in the *Kenyon Review*, X (Summer, 1948), 382–402. Reprinted by permission of Helen Ransom Forman.

1. This paper was read at the symposium on "The Great Critics" at Johns Hopkins University on April 13. (Ransom's note)

bears testimony to the fascinating configurations of this world. We are glad of his condescension, for it relieves us of what might have been the impression of a poverty of substance greater than we could bear. On the other hand it was Aristotle's part to emerge slowly from Plato's ambitious and puritanical discipline, and undertake to point the human career to such happiness as the ample natural world provides; yet he had the identical inconsistency of Plato, only in reverse. He turned from the stiff Platonic doctrines, but also from the literary form of the Platonic dialogue, in spite of some brilliant early successes in it, and was content to seek and tell the specific, the naked truth. This is a man whom I must hold in extraordinary honor. Yet his habit of delivery is not that of the literary critic according to our own convention. What is more important, at that stage in the thinking of Europe the time for a mature theory of literature had not arrived, so that in his own theory we have much of solid rightness, but at crucial places it goes along with a scantness, almost a wilful withholding, as in the deliverances of the oracle of Delphi—indicating hard labor for the interpreters.

A schoolmaster's literary criticism cannot be quite the thing we now find ourselves coveting. There is a criticism which is literary in the double sense; the literary quality attaches to the object of criticism of course, but it attaches to the work of criticism too. The indubitable art-work invites a low-grade and lesser art-work to celebrate as well as judge it. The critic never ceases to be impressed with his fine object. He starts with a spontaneous surge of piety, and is inducted by the contagion of art into a composition of his own, which sustains the warmth unashamed, and probably manages a rounded literary effect having a beginning, a middle, and an end. All that is delightful, it is what we need, it must be according to the deepest proprieties. But the procedure is likely to seem unprofessional to the academic critic, for it is his virtue to have made the choice of Aristotle, and to be seeking but the one thing: to deliver the critical judgment with justice and precision.

On the other side, there are advantages for us in the academic commodity. And the first one is that the academic man, at least if his scruple is of Aristotelian grade, does not shake several bushes at once and confuse the categories, but attends to one category at a time. That is the way to obtain definitive findings. Today we shall spend our time on the *Poetics*, waiving the *Rhetoric*; and on that larger part of the *Poetics* which deals with tragedy, waiving the part about epic, and not speculating as to the part about comedy which is missing. So let us first remark that Aristotle does not mix the literary or poetic issues of drama with its moral issues; I had almost said, does not adulterate them. He could have discoursed about morals if he liked, and with what we are tempted to call an Aristotelian authority, which here was very great; the tragic heroes are morally above the average, as he says, while their moral consciousness is acute; but it is also vocal, and articulate, easily to be taken by the critic at its face value, and that is not the thing which makes the heroes' delivery poetical; if it is the thing which makes it moral, still this is the *Poetics*, not the *Ethics* according to Eudemos or according to Nikomachos. Nor does he indulge in religious theory under color of discussing poetic theory. It is always commented that he never mentions what must have been even more familiar to his public than to us: the fact that the Attic tragedies originated in the holy festival of Dionysos. If they were full of allusions to judgments which ubiquitous Greek gods passed upon offending heroes, and heroines, these must have seemed symbolic determinations to Aristotle, whose naturalistic cast of thought was always gaining upon his transcendental training; and since the natural world, to all intents and purposes, means "everything in the world," it is certainly well provided with sequences, and consequences, which even the hero's strength is not going to controvert; these will take their course, they will humble his spirit sufficiently for anybody's taste, and if he is a hero the sign is that he will accept them with a certain style, which his poet will know how to render. Aristotle got the tragedies into simpler dramatic perspective by secularizing them, naturalizing them. Do religious persons find that the tragedies have thereby been robbed of their religious interest? That would be odd. We must stop on that a moment; Aristotelianism, the naturalistic way of thinking, is at stake. The movement from ritual to romance, and from romance to naturalism seems to be according to the line of the human progress, and perhaps on the whole the line can be traversed in only one direction. Doubtless this is just about as bad as it is good. But it is a linguistic phenomenon; a matter of translating from an earlier language into a later. In the course of this translation nothing that is valid need be given up for lost, for the value was always that of a symbol whose referent was something that "took place" in the natural world.

There is another advantage in the criticism which comes out of the academy, a double one. The area of literary judgment has two margins, which might be called a nether margin and an upper, and there is always a good deal of exploration to be done in both the marginal areas. Let the nether area be the one to which the academic man devotes his professional "scholarship." He must be learned in the culture and lan-

guage of the period, the biography of the author, the bibliography of the
works, and all that, which could easily be rehearsed on some other academic occasion. It is enough that Aristotle was of exemplary erudition,
and prodigious in research. It was he who recovered to the Greek world
the list of the tragic trilogies which had taken the three prizes in each
of the years since the time of Aeschylos when this Apollonian entertain-
ment, which Aristotle liked very much, had come to follow upon the
primitive Dionysian revels, which could not have been much to his
taste. The list had a coverage of many hundreds of single plays. Nor is
there any doubt that he knew the plays, if the texts were still available,
and the illustrations in the *Poetics* cite many which are unknown to us.
Our own stock is of about thirty tragedies, all by Aeschylos, Sophocles,
and Euripides, out of about two hundred and fifty which are ascribed to
these authors alone. Incidentally, they have great individual differences
for us, yet belong so uniformly to a single genre, highly perfected and
sustained over an almost unbelievable period in a changeful age, that
we know we do not run a big risk, nor are the first to run it, if we judge
that our critic was lecturing upon the finest national achievement in
our Western literature. He had his data in hand.

At the other margin of critical judgment we enter a speculative region. Here the academic critic must furnish a philosophical equipment.
Aristotle's was the kind of naturalistic philosophy which inquires into
functions or final causes. What is poetry good for, if it claims a place in
the crowded psychic economy? What passion have we in mind if we
profess a passionate concern with poetry? As the race becomes increasingly self-conscious, that is to say philosophical, and psychological, we
require the fine behaviors as well as the gross or common ones to disclose their human significance, and we include the behavior of rev-
erence, which is religious, and the behavior of sensing beauty, which is
aesthetic.

Now we have come to the essential synoptic shape of the thought of
Aristotle the critic. You will have anticipated me. We must figure *mimesis* or imitation, and *katharsis* or purgation, and I do not doubt that the
reporter will stand or fall according as he pronounces upon these cardinal Aristotelian usages.

Imitation is Plato's mocking term for the poetic procedure as compared with what he regarded as better procedures. Aristotle took it over
without remark as a correct technical description. It is the use of language to denote natural objects as given, contingent, today as "existential"; to be received in their fulness, which is their giveness; to be dis-

tinguished from those abstract or working objects which we employ in practical operations without having to notice them except to see whether they answer to the specifications we have laid down. And the peculiar linguistic device which accomplishes this feat is a kind of mimicry; Aristotle cites for example the picture which conveys the object through a configuration of lines on the paper just like the object's own. Mimicry is strictly a human gift, but it is scarcely affected with magical powers, or metaphysical ones. In the literary art the words are mimetic indirectly; they evoke images of the natural objects, and the images are mimetic. And there is no great trick to that. But let us enforce the term beyond possible misunderstanding. We are speaking mimetic or poetic language, we are evoking the whole or natural object, the moment we qualify the common noun by a single adjective or association which is not contained in its definition. To take a homely illustration, we hear that a lady has gone to the butcher's with her shopping-basket. We know what a butcher is; a species of economic agent with whom housewives deal, the instances being indifferent, i.e. one just like another, unless perhaps they may have been graded, and given numerical coefficients to indicate their economic ratings. But suddenly it is said that the lady finds her butcher *slumped over his chopping-block and weeping*; immediately we are transported into a world of contingencies, surprises, local excitements, possible dangers; more intractable than we were prepared for. That is an ambiguous example, since it may lead to action or to aesthetic contemplation. A literary example, which involves the technical device of figure of speech and is cited by Aristotle under the head of poetic diction, is where Aeschylos represents Philoctetes as saying of his ancient wound: "The ulcer eats the flesh of this foot of mine." And Euripides, altering things as usual to his taste, stretches the figure and has Philoctetes say: "The ulcer is feasting upon my foot."[2] The common situation turns exotic, and vivid. One poet casually makes the ulcer into a devouring monster. The other poet says to himself that we may not choose to see it so, for we have had it put this way before—for example, Aristotle's own father, the physician, might carelessly have remarked that some ulcer was "eating" into the flesh—but he will compel us, so he turns the monster into a decadent Corinthian epicure making a banquet on flesh he should never have eaten. But a third example is needed to show the gentle side of the tragic imagery, though the English translation is execrable. It is where the unhappy

2. See *Aristotle's Art of Poetry*, ed. by W. Hamilton Fyfe (London, 1940), 61.

Trojan women listen to the lamentation which fills their ruined city. But the object is too large and obsessive for them, and their sensibility must be freshened, and gentled, so that a humble image from bird life is imported:

> The sea-washed shores around
> With cries and shrieks resound,
> As when the poor bird for her young complains,
> And anguish swells her strains.

The technique always works by citing some excess of natural quality which removes the object from classification and disposition, as a particular always qualitatively exceeds the universal. I labor this a little, but the distinction is crucial. Without the excess, which is not every time though perhaps normally a "fine" excess, the particular collapses into the familiar universal, the language of imitation returns to the language of logic and use.

But what is the service of these imitations? What do we want with objects realized in their fulness when the uses of the appetitive life are satisfied with any objects that meet the respective qualifications, and the excess of the proper noun over the common noun comes to us, if we are attending to our own business, as an inordinate claim upon our attention? Aristotle had his answer to these questions, but at first sight it comes close to quibbling. Thus: we value an imitation because it gives us pleasure. That is almost a tautology. If we ask somebody, Why do you do this? and he replies, Because I like to do it, we are offended, feeling that we knew as much already. But in strictness Aristotle's answer is not a tautology. Frequently he remarked, though perhaps not in the *Poetics*, that we do some things for no other reason than the pleasure of doing them, and these activities are ends in themselves; but do other things which are laborious and painful, not pleasant at all, because they are the means to pleasure eventually. Therefore when he says that we value imitation because of the intrinsic pleasure, he means that there is no ulterior reason. It is the first occurrence so far as I know of the doctrine of art for art's sake. Yet Aristotle as a naturalist ought never to stop being concerned with ulterior reasons. Plato said readily enough that poetic imitation was pleasant, but argued that this was a vicious pleasure, and ought not to be indulged, since its consequence was vulgarizing, and discouraging to real intellectual attainment. Aristotle does not seriously take up that argument. Putting the best construction upon his silence, we may say that he is a good naturalist insofar as he accepts on

principle all the staple behaviors of the species, not rejecting some because they are considered vulgar but thinking that their human universality presents them in compelling dignity. Yet a modern naturalist cannot stop there. He does not believe for a moment in isolated faculties, in
behaviors that have no relation to the general psychic economy. The
notion of a behavior for the behavior's sake is not one that a post-
Darwinian naturalist, for example, will entertain; for I think it must be
a postulate of the doctrine of biological evolution that within the evolved
species every established pattern of activity, whether psychological or
physiological, is one which has proved its case as a true organic function. With all his genius, Aristotle was unacquainted with Darwin. But
just as a special salvation has to be arranged by Christian theologians
for Abraham and the heroes of the Old Testament, so we must have a
saving clause for Aristotle the pre-Darwinian naturalist. Let it be only
for modern poetic theorists that we denounce art for art's sake as an
evasive slogan, an abrogation of biological responsibility. Unless, of
course, it should happen to be a mere Bohemian brashness, to tease the
moralists with; and we will not make a quarrel with the wits.

But the doctrine became difficult of application when Aristotle must
pass upon the specific art of Attic tragedy. The intrinsic pleasure would
seem insignificant there. It is true that the poetic imitations keep going
at the usual rate, on the periphery so to speak of the principal action, as
if the poet were saying to the dramatist, My show must go on too. But
what is their force against the human sufferings portrayed in the tragic
action, heightened steadily, protracted clear to the moment of death,
which is the obscene stroke itself, and must not be included directly in
the action but only reported, or rendered by a noise from the wings,
offstage? Aristotle insists of course that the little pleasures, which luxuriate in the poetic diction, are there to be received, though he maintains
brazenly that the tragic plot is overwhelmingly the thing that counts.
We can see him putting himself on guard early about the poetry of poetic drama when the drama is tragic. Before he goes into tragedy, when
he is only pointing out our natural pleasure in imitations, he is careful
to remark that sometimes this pleasure is taken chiefly in admiring the
technical achievement of the imitator, so that we may even enjoy the
picture of a corpse if it is done skilfully. We would remark that there
may be pleasure in it, but there is also a good deal of pain; which is
precisely what Aristotle is compelled presently to emphasize. The plot
of a tragedy, he says flatly, and repeats many times, must be such as to
cause us plain pity and terror; these are unpleasant emotions. Pity is a

wretched business, which not only distracts us from our duties of the moment but incapacitates us, by destroying our animal faith in the goodness of the natural world; and terror is disordering and needs no comment. He would have the playwright steel himself constantly to his endeavor, never relaxing his severity and feeding us with a turn of action which would mitigate these emotions. It is my impression that the gentle and idealizing critics do not fancy Aristotle's toughness about this, but then it is hard to believe that they have assimilated the horror of the actual tragedies which he is reporting. It was sheer good luck, says Aristotle, that the Attic playwrights found a grand source for their tragic plots, as if made to order for them, in the stock of common legends about the ancient royal houses. The legends are improbable, and for tragic purposes almost too good to be true, but they were well known, and could be repeated as if they were true. The great families of the legends would seem to have been highly specialized in domestic horrors.

> Let us see, then, [says Aristotle] what kinds of incident strike us as horrible or piteous. In a deed of this sort the parties must necessarily be either friends, or enemies, or indifferent to one another. Now when enemy does it on enemy, there is nothing to move us to pity either in his doing or in his meditating the deed, except so far as the actual pain of the sufferer is concerned; and the same is true when the parties are indifferent to one another. Whenever the tragic deed, however, is done within the family—when murder or the like is done or meditated by brother on brother, by son on father, by mother on son, or son on mother—these are the situations the poet should seek after. The traditional stories, accordingly, must be kept as they are, e.g., the murder of Clytaemnestra by Orestes and of Eriphyle by Alcmaeon.[3]

It is grim. Yet these murderers must be represented as good men, indeed a little better than ourselves, not so much depraved as given to errors of judgment, or we should not identify ourselves with them by sympathetic imagination, and must fail to experience the pity.

It is clear that our absorption in such tragedies indicates a behavior of the second sort which we noted just now; they are not so much for the trifling intrinsic pleasure which comes from the steady flow of the poetic diction, but for the sake of the eventual happiness to which they are the means. Tragedy for tragedy's sake is hardly the name of a ra-

3. The translation is Bywater's in Principal W. Hamilton Fyfe's *Aristotle's Art of Poetry* (Oxford). (Ransom's note)

tional motivation, and if there is such a thing we call it masochistic and
destructive. Aristotle's position is a good functional or even Darwinian
one. And the function which he specifies is *katharsis*: the purgation of
all the pity and fear from the psyche through the technique of tapping
them by means of the horrors of the play. That will be a healthy relief
when it comes, and most certainly a pleasant one.

He repeats this formulation a good deal too, like a paradigm which
the teacher writes upon the blackboard. With what oral elaboration in
this instance we do not know, but none is incorporated in the written
text for us now. Katharsis is a gross physiological metaphor out of *mate-
ria medica*, whereby the draining of the poisonous slops from the body
is made to stand for the subtle psychic relief under the fourth figure of
metaphorical substitution, which proceeds by analogy; this would be
according to Aristotle. He does not miss in his linguistic analysis, but
he is not so proficient in the psychic mysteries. If he is sometimes a
pre-Darwinian naturalist, he makes it all too clear that psychologically,
for all his shrewdness, he dwells in an untechnical pre-Freudian night.
For my part I cannot help but find this figure of purgation inept; it is too
hard to apply it and see how the clearing out of the painful emotions
must follow from artificially prompting them; there must be subtler
mechanisms at work. Yet who will disagree with him, once the point is
made, and deny that somehow composure is restored to the auditors of
proper drama, and even to its readers? And what an excellent thing that
must be! A recent work is entitled, *The Age of Anxiety*.[4] But history repeats itself, and it must have been Aristotle's notion that his was that
age. Pity for misfortune greater than the victim has deserved, at a time
when such misfortune is endemic in our community, and terror because it happens to people as good as we are,—these emotions are
vicious company for the vital and constructive thoughts in our heads.
They sap our courage, they paralyse our initiative, while actual defeat
and frustration are brought only the nearer by our inaction. And living
in apprehension, we will try anything that promises to restore the equa-
ble temper which conditions a good vital effort.

We must think of Aristotle as a true humanist, a Greek very close to
his racial culture, and beyond Plato in his responsiveness, for having
the noble and improbable insight that the tragic art purges men of their
fears and makes them better men. But to grasp the technique of this
purging we have to make a configuration of our own, and go beyond

4. W. H. Auden, *The Age of Anxiety: A Baroque Eclogue* (New York, 1947).

Aristotle. I think the trick to try will be something like this: to see if the lavish, the all-but-incessant poetry with which the Greek dramatists invest their tragedy does not throw a decent obscurity over the terrible events; and though of course it does not promise to avert these, if at least it does not immunize us against our terror. Incidentally such a strategy would be most agreeable to the careful critical sense, in that it would bring the tragic plot and the poetic diction back into reciprocal working relation, and not leave them separated and at cross-purposes as Aristotle does. Now the terror we feel is not wholly stupid, it is not born of total blindness, for our eyes may be fastened precisely upon the shapes of doom. But that is all we shall see if we are terrified, it is all we can think about, and we freeze from staring at the Gorgon's head. So at the lowest estimate it may be by a mere technique of diversion from the obsessive horror that we are restored to sanity. To recover presence of mind is to make the mind resume its most gallant and extravagant activities, and so to put off again the season when it must revert, if it ever reverts, to primitive monomania under the pain. All this will seem indirect, and casuistical; but in these days we do not discount the psyche's capacity for improvization.

According to Aristotle, a logical intellect must preside over the manipulation of the tragic plot. At any rate that is what we conclude from his emphasis upon the probability of the events, and the suitable and common types of character in the *dramatis personae* who enact them. He says the plot deals with universals rather than particulars. The poetic diction in the meantime is imitating busily, that is to say it is going away from the universals of the plot a thousand times to evoke its particulars. And so we have an anticipation of that very opposition of reason and sensibility which characterizes the world of art and beauty for Immanuel Kant, in that modern work which is regarded as the foundation of systematic aesthetics. But in Aristotle the two components do not work together, and the human drama of their opposition is not made clear.

We are later than Aristotle culturally and, as it would follow, philosophically. Aesthetic historians, severally, tell us why the *Critique of Judgment* could not have appeared before its actual date of 1790. A grossly simplified and lay version of this why would be as follows.

The Greek philosophers our ancestors were motivated by a pride of intellect and a contempt for free sensibility. The Eleatics gave the cue when they renounced the sensible world, at least up to the limits of human strength, and occupied themselves in the contemplation of pure determinate being. And presently there is a theology which sets up a "divine" world of pure being as actual, though invisible, and allows the human soul, as a rational being divinely implanted in the natural body, partly to inhabit it. This dogma was in the grand style, and formed a great stream of the European tradition, and its force is not spent yet. Plato, however, had too much resourcefulness, and healthy worldly interest, to stop long in the arid otherworld of pure intellection. The Platonic Idea is his invention. The rational principle comes down to earth; it grips the matter of common nature and transforms it into what is orderly and rational yet still existent, till this existential world itself partakes of the nature of the divine world. Naturally the Ideas must take on more and more complexity if they want to grip the natural objects in the whole manifold of their concretions; naturally Plato did not go a great way in developing them. But we will make a long jump and come to his successor Hegel, who extends the range of the Ideas brilliantly, and with so much success that he is able to talk of the Concrete Universal. And what is that? The Concrete Universal is the common or abstract universal, the bare concept, prodigiously improved internally; so elaborated and organized that now it hopes to take into its grip *all* the qualities that sensibility discovers in the concretions of nature; till reason and sensibility shall have identical objects, and logic and aesthetics become one. But Hegel's success with this project was specious; the analytical intelligence of the last century has been in painful revolt against it, and the latest revolt is that harsh and tormented movement, the current "existentialism."

If Hegel is Plato's pious and dutiful successor, his unwitting successors have been legion. They are the men who have seen what intellect was really good for, and made it pay; men of the last three or four centuries, whose intellectual formations have been close, persistent, and specialized, aggregating into what we call our modern science; who produced the industrial revolution. By the time of Kant, but scarcely before then, it was possible to say a very simple thing about the faculty of specialized reason, or intellect, for it had been empirically established. Thus: it is the instrument of our appetitive life. Kant made the identification clearly though he did not surrender all the aspirations he entertained on behalf of reason; Schopenhauer and Bergson repeated it with the indignation of disillusioned men; and it is Freud's basic assumption that reason is the technical organ by which the human creature reacts to environment and secures his desires. The Concrete Universal or Idea did not have the comprehensive grip it tried for, and the intellectualists have reverted to the abstract or common universal. The latter's grip is very effective indeed for its own purposes, but these do not include anything like a comprehension of nature; and nature is still as "infinite" or boundless as the ancients hatefully called it, inviolable in its contingency and plenitude.

Not for one minute is this reporter tempted by ambition, neither is he inclined by temperament, to "reject" the scientific achievement. He understands that reason is the *differentia* of our species, the organ which raises it above the others in effectiveness, gives it the dominion over nature which was promised in our story of creation. We have used it well, to obtain more and better goods from nature. We are still, or rather we are again, an animal species, for which the appetitive life has every priority, being the condition prior to all those aspirations which are not appetitive, if there are such aspirations. But just now the predicament of high-minded persons is slightly embarrassing. A human aspiration is probably the strangest and most characteristic of the human behaviors, since it is a move away from the line of the common economy, and covets what would not seem quite possible, a reckless and pointed suspension of animal interest. It is evidently a *proprium* of the species, if not the essential *differentia*. The form which aspiration once liked to take was intellectual, as with Plato. But at the moment this is not so good, now that intellectual attainment is scarcely the rarity it once seemed, and now that it is so firmly identified with common animal motivation.

I imagine that the general topic of this Symposium, upon which we concentrate soberly for three full days, tempts us all into magnificent secret strategies. Perhaps, for example, we find ourselves supposing that our aspiration, the thing which will best certify our humanism by essaying what is slightly superhuman, is now going to be under the aesthetic form. I believe this will require of us behaviors that are not for the sake of dominion over nature, of which the technical organ is reason, but for the sake of something so impractical as gentleness, or love, whose organ is sensibility. It is difficult to describe it behavioristically. What we love we can look at, we can crave the presence of, or if we are absented we can "imitate" in the way of imagination and art, we can explore continually for fresh insights—but what can we really, adequately do? There is singularly little in the way of overt action that we can do to express the diffuse and massive excitement that comes over us from love. The term of course will refer to Agape rather than Eros. In its full range it will mean simply our love for our own kind, as in happy families, though that is an admirable attainment, but what is still more quixotic, the love of nature. This last extension is not necessary for the ethical aspiration. But it is necessary for religion, if nature means "everything in the world," and it is necessary for art; in these aspirations the achievement is finer than ethical, though not more heroic.

The easiest perspective upon such aspirations comes from the naturalistic description. The creature was formed within nature; but immediately nature became his environment, external to him; whereupon self-preservation depended upon enforcing his needs and uses against environment. A risk is run in the formation of any organic species, lest it fail to establish its vital economy firmly against an environment horribly unresponsive to the creature's poor techniques. But suppose he is man, the technologist himself, and does establish his economy, and comes to feel secure in it, well assured that the environment will yield him its favors when he demands them, and that its bounty is not going to be exhausted—what then? It is my impression that the complete naturalist, with whatever reservations when it comes to interpreting it, must attest the thing as follows. The creature begins to devote some of his leisure and unexpended energy—his technique has earned them—to reversing the normal attitude to environment, so that where there was only dominion and use there develops a sentimental fixation upon certain natural objects, which is conspicuously disproportionate to their utility. These become his "precious objects," the objects which he prizes at more than their utility-value, for he loves them. In this role, as we have seen, he is capable of only redundant and nondescript behaviors. There is little he can do for the object, which after all is an alien and inviolable natural object; nor is there anything he can do for himself, since fixation started where the utility of the object left off; so that it is no wonder that his sentimental exhibitions in the eyes of a sardonic naturalist may seem slightly absurd. But presently, as if because he is tired of repeating the same little endearments, yet is still under the compulsion of his tender feelings, while he cannot invent actions forceful enough or various enough to express them, the sentimentalist employs his wits and transforms himself into the man of sensibility; and now he has infinite resources. Poetry lies before him, and the future of poetry is immense. Now the whole of nature, rather than its obvious and familiar concretions, becomes the object of his affection, so that he will be ready to stop wherever he may be traversing it, and make observations and imitations *en passant*; for there is nature always and everywhere. He is on the watch for natural effects which are not useful but brilliant and vivid, i.e. notable, as for a man carrying a notebook. With experience his perceptions become constantly more acute, and they improve still further as he becomes proficient linguistically, i.e. in the language, or medium, of imitation.

This is the crude sketch of a natural history of sentiment and sensibility, and of the arts which exist for their most perfect expression. It might easily prompt the satirical treatment if it tells the truth, and does not disguise the illogic, and a certain promiscuity, which obtain in these formations. It deals with an odd sort of behavior; but there is so much of it that the naturalist may be led to take it professionally, that is to say seriously. He would have to speculate upon the function of a gratuitous behavior; the economy of an attitude which seems determined to be out of economic character. Its real motivation will have to be an unconscious one.

As speculations go, this one is probably not too hard. If the creature's natural adaptations are successful, then the awkward honors that are being paid to nature have a festal character, and festivals look quite serious, lending themselves as they do to the greatest public occasions. With respect to the given adaptation to which the festival logically refers, we should expect that the festal effect must be strongly confirmatory, or conservative; it would confirm the adaptation which has succeeded, whose success is the occasion and public content of the festive art; and surely a good adaptation is entitled to some confirmation. The arts will scarcely know that they exert a conservative influence, though this has often been said about religion; it is the naturalist who would know it; he might think it important. Furthermore, or perhaps this is a corollary principle, the arts will induce the sense of security, and they will be tonic for the apprehensive or timid. Here we have worked back to the old topic of the *Poetics*. But now we are dealing with successes, not tragedies, and the fearful do not exactly pass their nights in wakefulness and trembling when the times are easy and the feeling about things is a feeling of success. Let us say at the least that the temperamentally fearful obtain through art a proper confidence. What they think they do is to attach themselves in joy, and perhaps with a mystic sense of communion, to the alien form of nature, and it is as if they had never a care of their own in the world; but there is more than coincidence in the fact that they have negotiated successfully with nature for their needs. Joy in beauty is wonderfully spontaneous, and it is impossible for us ever to feel more innocent, or, as aestheticians put it, "disinterested." Many critics of art are willing to stop uncritically upon that note, and it does well enough for them if they are not Aristotle. It is the duty of the naturalist to look a little further. According to my own guess, he will conclude that a certain exhilaration or exuberance of spirit has been achieved, such as must signify a sound and sturdy foundation of animal faith, and is, considering the peril of the animal predicament in the world, propitious.

In art we are conditioned through the spectacle of success to the habit of sensibility, and among other services it will serve us in the evil hour. The tragic drama, devoted to unsuccess, shows the way. So we come back finally to our starting point. The tragic Greek plots which Aristotle studied move at nearly all times with a great train of free and energetic imagery, and to the handsomest phonetic or musical accompaniment. These are the forms of the sensibility which the heroes use in actual speech when they fall upon adversities. With my small Greek I seem at least here and there to verify these effects, to which the scholars have testified. To an audience which was as Greek as the play itself, the plight of the heroes though mortal was not too terrible, since the heroes themselves were not terrified out of their wits but continued in easy exercise of the most liberal powers of mind; and by sympathy the auditors became for the time being as the heroes. As public affairs the tragedies of course were exemplary, and normative; the spectators were a little more enabled to go through with their own vile occasions.

Tragedy is the literary form where the strength of sensibility is really tested. It is a great *tour de force* in art, the work of the virtuoso. The heroes fail of success, and know they are failing. No practical adaptation is possible, and the animal struggle ceases, though not for the reason that it ceases in the arts of success. But sensibility operates all the same; the focus of dramatic interest is turned altogether upon sensibility; the issue is known, and the plot is not the thing now, the heroic style is the thing. We are reminded of the situation of the religious man when he says: "Though he slay me, yet will I trust him." This religious man must have had a long conditioning. We may be sure that his aspiration did not begin with so immoderate a leap of animal faith, but started modestly in the flush of his early experiences of God's goodness; these repeated themselves, till they confirmed his courage and formed his religious character; this now is irreversible, and the time is past when he could denounce God and die in stony hatred or in terror.

In conclusion I will quote from the talk in a scene where a famous hero dies. But perhaps no one of us now has the ear to follow those remarkable Greek meters sensitively, certainly not I; while it would only

defame the masterpieces to read from our miserable English translations. In the spirit of Aristotle I resort to that fourth figure of metaphor
which is the substitution by analogy. It will be Shakespeare's scene
where Antony dies. There are differences between the classical and the
Shakespearian, but perhaps they are outweighed by the analogies.

Antony's war against Caesar has come to grief, and if he does not
wish to be taken captive it is time for him to die. He appeals to his servant Eros, who is pledged to kill him when the moment comes:

> Thou art sworn, Eros,
> That when the exigent should come—which now
> Is come indeed—when I should see behind me
> The inevitable prosecution of
> Disgrace and horror, that, on my command,
> Then thou would'st kill me. Do't; the time is come.
> Thou strik'st not me, 'tis Caesar thou defeat'st.
> Put color in thy cheek.[5]

Antony's rich poetic vein does not show diminution. The verse flows
easily from it, not muddied or thickened by emotion. But Eros will not
strike, and Antony has to direct to him an argument suitable to his
intelligence:

> Eros,
> Would'st thou be window'd in great Rome and see
> Thy master thus with pleach'd arms, bending down
> His corrigible neck, his face subdued
> To penetrative shame, whilst the wheel'd seat
> Of fortunate Caesar, drawn before him, branded
> His baseness that ensued?[6]

A reader is obliged to suppose that Antony folds his arms as he speaks,
and bends his neck, to suit the words; his lively imitation tries two me-
dia at once, for the benefit of an auditor who is not only stubborn but a
little bit unimaginative. The poetry is of the highest inventiveness, and
of a veteran sensibility.

We stop here. Though there are several ingenious and beautiful
turns to come before Antony actually dies, I assume that the point has
been made. Antony is purged of terror by his own poetry, and we are
purged. Even Cleopatra will show that she has been affected by his example, when she invites her own death in these words:

5. *Antony and Cleopatra*, Act IV, Sc. xiv, 62–69.
6. *Antony and Cleopatra*, Act IV, Sc. xiv, 71–77.

> We'll bury him; and then, what's brave, what's noble,
> Let's do it after the high Roman fashion,
> And make death proud to take us.[7]

But we must quarrel a little with her aesthetics, which does not exactly take into account the technical *katharsis*. She did not hear the speeches I have quoted, and seems to think that Antony merely fell upon his sword like any simple Roman soldier. It would have been excellent for Antony to be an antique Roman, and a Stoic. It would have taught him to die decently, if that means to die dumbly, in a constriction of sensibility, as by a feat of virtual anaesthesia; for that is possible too. But that is not the line of the tragic hero. It is better for him to finish when he is in full character, when the world is beautiful to his sensibility. He is then perfect in his fidelity to the human career, and ought to be approved by the naturalist as he is loved by the aspiring spectator.

7. *Antony and Cleopatra*, Act IV, Sc. xv, 86–88.

WILLIAM WORDSWORTH

NOTES TOWARD AN UNDERSTANDING

OF POETRY

UR POET was one of the giants. We cannot say less, for Wordsworth did what Burns and Blake could not do: he reversed the direction of English poetry in a bad time, and revitalized it. But in order to do this he had to speculate upon what was possible, and what was advantageous, by virtue of the very constitution of a poetic action; he had to study poetry as well as write it. He was driven to a conception of poetry which was more radical, or thoroughgoing, than that of any of his predecessors, but it justified itself in his own poetic production. It is Wordsworth's innovations in the theory upon which I should like to offer some notes, as my tribute to the poet: in the theory, because he theorized as well as practised; and notes, because my impressions are speculative and imperfect, and in what has always been an area of speculation do not aspire anyway to be demonstrative.

The first notes have to do with the famous doctrine of poetic diction as laid down in the Preface. I had written, the "notorious" Preface, for it was a monstrous indiscretion, such as no other important poet ever committed so far as I know: giving his enemies two targets instead of one. There was a saving rightness in it, but its valor was that of an innocent, while the stubbornness which kept on republishing it indicated a man with a philanthropic intention.

In the Preface Wordsworth declares that the language of poetry is not different from the language of prose. He enters qualifications, however. He calls it once the language of "good" prose, and again the language of prose "when prose is well written." Nor does he claim that this neutral language is the language of all poetry, but that it is the language

This essay first appeared in the *Kenyon Review*, XII (Summer, 1950), 498–519. Reprinted by permission of Helen Ransom Forman.

of much of the best poetry, and especially the language which he has made the staple of his own poetry. I mention these reservations, because I would not have it thought that Coleridge, who ridiculed the statement, must be in the right because he had the last word. Coleridge writes about it in the *Biographia Literaria* just after Wordsworth, in 1815, had finally published a new edition without putting the famous Preface in front of it; and Coleridge reads Wordsworth a long and weary lecture about an unqualified identification of the languages of prose and poetry which Wordsworth had not made. One is tempted to feel that Coleridge is determined to praise Wordsworth's poetry, as he had always done, but in the matter of poetic theory is pretty confident that the honors will lie with himself. And indeed Coleridge's critical writing was much more supple and professional, better organized and documented, than Wordsworth's. It has been of permanent influence upon poetic theory. Nevertheless, he did not write like an acute critic about poetic diction; and, for that matter, when it came to the point of discovering the three occasional faults in Wordsworth's poetry, and the six excellences which were frequent, we do not find Coleridge using incisive critical principles, but perfunctory and academic ones which scarcely convey the sense that this poetry was revolutionary.

Wordsworth documents his contention about prose diction skimpily, by citing a single poem and disposing of it quickly. But if we will consider what he does not say along with what he says, it will give us a good deal of Wordsworth's mind. To find the diction he approves he takes an eighteenth-century poem, so that we are not surprised if his approval does not extend to the whole poem. It is Gray's sonnet on the death of Richard West, which contains in some form the Wordsworthian tender feelings toward nature, and by all means a Wordsworthian "elementary" passion of grief for a friend. Here is the poem:

> In vain to me the smiling mornings shine,
> And reddening Phoebus lifts his golden fire:
> The birds in vain their amorous descant join,
> Or cheerful fields resume their green attire.
> These ears, alas! for other notes repine;
> A different object do these eyes require;
> My lonely anguish melts no heart but mine;
> And in my breast the imperfect joys expire;
> Yet morning smiles the busy race to cheer,
> And new-born pleasure brings to happier men;

> The fields to all their wonted tribute bear;
> To warm their little loves the birds complain.
> I fruitless mourn to him that cannot hear,
> And weep the more because I weep in vain.

In this sonnet the octet composes nicely by having its base-lines AB rhymed three times, while the sestet composes by having its base-lines CD rhymed twice: ABABABAB, CDCDCD. In the first half of the octet the speaker represents the morning with its sunshine, the birds, and the fields, as trying by turns to cheer him with their small joys. In the second half of the octet he resists them, on the ground that his ears are listening for other sounds and his eyes looking for other sights, while his heart has an anguish they cannot understand, so that their imperfect joys expire within his breast (perhaps before they reach his heart of hearts). In the first four lines of the sestet the amiable objects try him again, perhaps with more spirit, and in almost the original order: the morning, the fields, and the birds. In the concluding two lines he dismisses them once more with the important specification that he mourns to "him that cannot hear" and weeps to one who is not there to comfort him. This is about as graceful in design as the elegiac mode can well afford to be.

In printing the poem Wordsworth italicizes certain lines as follows: all the speaker's words about himself which make the second quatrain, except its first line, so that we have:

> *A different object do these eyes require;*
> *My lonely anguish melts no heart but mine;*
> *And in my breast the imperfect joys expire;*

and all the speaker's words about himself at the end:

> *I fruitless mourn to him that cannot hear,*
> *And weep the more because I weep in vain.*

His comment is in a single sentence: "It will easily be perceived, that the only part of this Sonnet which is of any value is the lines printed in Italics; it is equally obvious, that, except in the rhyme, and in the use of the single word 'fruitless' for fruitlessly, which is so far a defect, the language of these lines does in no respect differ from that of prose."

Now the italicized lines are not a bad illustration of his point, though Coleridge picks at them. It is something for Wordsworth to have found them in a poem by Gray, whom he introduced as "more than any other man curiously elaborate in the structure of his own poetic diction." Really there was "flesh and blood," as Wordsworth required, in the academic young poet who, at twenty-six, mourning for his old friend and schoolmate, was like Milton, at twenty-nine, mourning for Henry King; though the later poet's *Lycidas* turns out to be a very small affair. The lines in which he expresses his grief are "manly," to use another Wordsworthian term, and especially, as compared with the lines about the natural objects, they are plain. Undoubtedly it is Wordsworth's principle that the situation has such dignity in itself as not to need the elaborate eighteenth-century diction to support it, nor the handsome reinforcements furnished by simile and metaphor as recommended by the rhetorics. In this particular poem the dead friend's character is not explored, but there is no time for it, and at any rate we have in every line of the speaker about him the expression of his own feeling; for the subject's feeling belongs in this style as well as the treatment of the object. The one line which Wordsworth rejects from this part is where the subject's ears are said to "repine"; the tropology is foolish there, though in the next line it seems proper for his eyes to "require."

And now the reasons for Wordsworth's dissatisfaction with the other lines. The Phoebus business of course is out. But otherwise it is touching, in some degree, that the natural objects seem to solicit the mourner to partake of their joy, and in saying "joy" the poet is in the heart of Wordsworth's own vocabulary. But the objects are too pretty, they are too petty, and the fact is that they are too meanly regarded altogether. In one of the happiest moments of his life—and it was in 1800, the very year of the first publication of the Preface—we find Wordsworth come to live at last at Grasmere to pursue his dedicated career, and writing a passage about the surpassing beauty of the region in which he declares solemnly: "On Nature's invitation do I come." But this was the opening of a long poem in which the poet assigns to nature the most magnificent attentions to man; we shall see something of this.

We will imagine also that he did not like the idea of Gray's having his speaker decline the solicitations of the natural objects, poor though they might be; that was "sullen" of him, as Wordsworth would have said. In the poem *Ruth*, the English girl who has been won by the "Youth from Georgia's shore" is abandoned by her husband even before embarkation for America, and left to lead the life of a vagrant; and what is her response to nature now? She was won originally by her husband's account of the charms of his country, being sensitive to those of her own; and now we read:

> The engines of her pain, the tools
> That shaped her sorrow, rocks and pools,
> And airs that gently stir
> The vernal leaves—she loved them still;
> Nor ever taxed them with the ill
> Which had been done to her.

It was likewise with Michael himself, in that finer poem which tells how the old shepherd had seen his son Luke go out to seek his fortune, but not till he was sworn to return with means to save the humble estate, and strength to help his father complete the building of the stone sheepfold; and how finally the old man has the news that Luke has plunged into the dissolute ways of the city and fled for his misdeeds beyond the seas. Nevertheless

> among the rocks
> He went, and still looked up to sun and cloud,
> And listened to the wind; and, as before,
> Performed all kinds of labour for his sheep,
> And for the land, his small inheritance;[1]

so that perhaps we feel meanly relieved, a little easier in the presence of such magnanimity, when we are told that though he went as usual to the sheepfold,

> 'tis believed by all
> That many and many a day he thither went,
> And never lifted up a single stone.[2]

The plain diction or prose-poetry diction which Wordsworth defends on principle, and adopts for himself, is evidently that which registers factually a human passion for a concrete object. It is time to introduce that word "concrete." It is an ill-favored word, but I cannot think that as critics we can do without it. Modern philosophy has no other word which stands so squarely for the natural object in its fuller character. It is valuable for ontologists to have the word to denote that plenum of the natural world which is so much denser than our appetites need it to be, and denser than our intellect can grasp when it would lay down in science the laws of nature. It has even become corrective of modern science, which would otherwise attach too absolute a reality to these laws. The name to cite here, I should think, is that of Alfred North White-

---

1. *Michael*, lis. 455–59.
2. *Michael*, lis. 464–66.

head, whose *Science and the Modern World* shows how far the science of the eighteenth century had failed to be an account of the world which we familiarly sense. His name is the better for my purpose because it is well known to Wordsworthians; he has a chapter that pays great honor to Wordsworth as the man who broke through the Great Chain of Being which was becoming more and more the attenuated or abstracted being of a mechanistic universe. And his word for the object of Wordsworth's vision is concreteness; he might have preferred to say "prehensive unity," but that would probably have estranged the Wordsworthians. Wordsworth knew that the poet always seeks concreteness. He knew also that it is the animal or appetitive faculties, and science and business their instruments, which deal with the abstractions, and a faculty quite different which is interested in concretions. Our appetitive business with a concretion is to find some use to abstract from it, and then to abandon it; but when we are out of the dominion of our appetitive urgencies we engage with a concretion by fixing upon it our passion, or our affections large and small. And thus a considerable part of our history is written round concreteness as such. It is in exception to our animal economy, to all appearances, but this is our actual behavior.

In choosing to deal directly with the natural concretions, and with the feelings which engage with them, Wordsworth was willing to throw away most of the tropology with which poetry was commonly identified. But we may put this quite clearly in terms which we owe to Professor I. A. Richards; they are now in wide usage. Wordsworth proposed to stick to the *tenor* of his situation, and have little recourse to extraneous *vehicles*.[3] This defines the "good prose" which he liked. It would not be the merely utilitarian prose, but the prose to be found in sermons, in literary essays, above all in our time in prose fictions, and wherever else the style develops the "concretions of nature" rather than the lean "concretions of discourse." For some two years I have felt deeply grateful to Wordsworth for giving his authority to this special kind of language. Perhaps it will improve our perspective on the linguistic performance of the poet, and not to be a mere impertinence, if I list the several general devices which I find peculiar to the poetic language, including of course the prose-poetry language favored by Wordsworth. The list is crude, but I have been testing it over several years, and the devices seem really distinct.

1. This is the one in which I feel confirmed by Wordsworth. The de-

---

3. *The Philosophy of Rhetoric*, London, 1936. (Ransom's note)

vice consists in using Singular Terms, or perhaps we might call them Spreaders; i.e., words and phrases which explore the vivid concreteness in the objects and events, even while seeming to prosecute a discourse in logical terms which would refer only to their uses. This is the primary device in any stylebook, and it richly deserves study. It is the way in which sensibility is put to work. I name it first, because its reference is entirely within the tenor. But I came to it last.

2. Dystactical Terms, or Rufflers; where a logical confusion is deliberately cultivated. The terms would be such as inversions, alterations in the idiom, ambiguities and obscurities, faulty series, condensations and ellipses, omission of rational connectives. They too stick to the given or tenor in a sense, but they return it to its original inchoate state of nature, so to speak, where we have to look to find the logical connections. Perhaps the assumption is that while doing so we will have to receive a substantial sense of the original concretions. This device has perhaps as many varieties named in the rhetorics as the one which follows; and Longinus is a critic who knows how to pin them down.

3. Metaphorical Terms, or Importers; where vehicle is introduced. By way of analogy or association of ideas, foreign objects are brought into the situation. This is the most spectacular of the linguistic devices, and easiest to remark. Doctor Johnson enunciated the rule of practice: "A simile, to be perfect, must both illustrate and ennoble." That is to say, the vehicle must have good logical excuse to get in, and its objective content must have the same sense with respect to its powerful affects as the tenor into which it is introduced; so that it both extends the concretion and fortifies our feelings toward the original object.

4. Meters. Fundamentally, we must believe, they mean to enlarge the poetic concretion by introducing the phonetic values which belong to the medium and are independent of the semantic referent. Wordsworth said good things about the functions of meter without saying this primary thing; but he did not employ our terms concreteness and concretion.[4]

4. Linguistic devices such as I have listed seem well within the repertory of every accomplished poet. Wordsworth made use of importers (3) and even a low grade of rufflers (2) when he wished; and of course there is that large chapter of his achievement which consists in the five hundred sonnets, which began with his listening one day (it was May 21, 1802) to Dorothy's reading of Milton's sonnets; in the sonnets there is a great extension of Wordsworth's tropology, and also of the topical range of his verse.

I should like to remark at least in a subnote that Santayana has given us the term "concretion of nature" to mean the natural object itself as given to the sensibility; and the term "concretion of discourse" to mean the operational rule by which we abstract from the sensible objects those aspects that are fitted logically for our use. I think there must also be

Wordsworth is able to compose many lyrics and longer poems by employing spreaders (1) and meters (4) alone. It is the first of his great innovations. Poetry of that kind was not unheard of before Wordsworth, but it did not exist in important poetry on this scale. Many readers are repelled by the shortage in rufflers (2) and importers (3), which they have learned to expect of poets, and which in other poets they have found giving to verse its greatest brilliance. They regard Wordsworth's poetry as too plain; and indeed we must think of it as the plain style. Probably it is not so plain absolutely as comparatively. The plain style sticks to its tenor, but there may be a great range of sensibility carrying it on and establishing vivid and abundant content. The stylist can achieve his distinction here as well as anywhere else. If there is still a tendency to flatness, comparatively speaking, it will incline to relieve this impression by registrations of feeling which the showy styles do not commonly like to affect. And Wordsworth himself attached great importance, evidently greater than other poets have done, to the meters, as a wonderful instrument of concretion. My own idea is that many of us for the first time, when we were young, discovered in the poetry of Wordsworth what poetry was; but turned from him as we became experienced in other poetry of greater virtuosity; and through some need felt in our maturity have finally come back to him with admiration for the purity of his style. The test poem for me is *Michael*. No part of it is less plain or more plain than the lines I have quoted. I have wavered between resistance and participation till at last it has (at this writing) won me. It has a kind of virtuosity of its own, which consists in its relentless understatement (by poetical standards) of the occasion, where other poets are virtuosos by overstatement, over-writing, aiming perhaps to overwhelm us with their "fine excess." In *Resolution and Independence* the style is less severe, the imagination is stirring as if about to spring into metaphor though it stops short, and the musical effect is especially luxurious. *The Old Cumberland Beggar* is on the order of *Michael*. The shorter and more lyrical poems do not exercise us so much by their denial. Yet *I wandered lonely as a cloud, The Solitary Reaper*, and *To the Cuckoo* are almost entirely in plain style. And among the Lucy poems I will quote the brief last one:

---

distinguished a third concretion of discourse and certain concretions of nature as established within the field of operation by spreaders (1) and rufflers (2), plus an increment of exotic foreign content as established by importers (3); plus a completely new dimension of content as established by meters (4). The poetic concretion is of maximum comprehensiveness in the kinds of content, and probably must be regarded as a concretion which can be unified only within the spread of the imagination. (Ransom's note)

> A slumber did my spirit seal;
>   I had no human fears:
> She seemed a thing that could not feel
>   The touch of earthly years.
>
> No motion has she now, no force;
>   She neither hears nor sees;
> Rolled round in earth's diurnal course
>   With rocks, and stones, and trees.

This is technically very different from those other lines about Lucy, where she was

> A violet by a mossy stone
>   Half hidden from the eye!
> Fair as a star, when only one
>   Is shining in the sky.

It is finer; of more powerful concretion. And it has a tone most unusual in Wordsworth, if I am not mistaken. The language of the second stanza, with its "motion," "force," and "earth's diurnal course," is very close to the language of Newtonian physics against which, at least as a description of man's relation to his universe, Wordsworth is said by Whitehead to have been the chief rebel. In that case we have here a savage irony. Professor Cleanth Brooks is most adept among critics in spotting ironies, and has even found them in Wordsworth's *Ode*, though I imagine this poet at large must offer lean hunting in that species of game; but I should covet his remark on this second stanza. To me it seems to say: How right are these mechanic philosophers, for Lucy herself is in the grip of their forces and revolutions—now that she is dead! Irony and satire would be well within the scope of the poetry of the tenor or fact. But the greatest locus of the plain style, of course, must be *The Prelude*. Whether we read it for psychological narrative, or natural description, or philosophy, we find a magnificence which many times is sustained at great length.

The remaining notes will have to do with another originality of Wordsworth's: his doctrine concerning the love of nature as the poetic theme. We must look now not at the Preface but at the formidable *Prelude*, which is poetic theory in verse. Does a man really love nature, and how may that be, and what good comes of it? *The Prelude* of course is a long spiritual autobiography in which Wordsworth memorizes with great fullness his own encounters with nature and comments on them. He had grown up in the love of nature; he had gone out into the world of affairs and come to grief; he had attended with a young man's generous fervor upon the French Revolution, and suffered disillusionment; he had tried to work his way out of his sickness by intellectual decisions, and failed; and in the end it took a return to the nature of the early days to heal him. That is the point to which the narrative of *The Prelude* brings him, at age thirty-five, after an unusual range of vital experience.

There are some commonplaces of knowledge which I shall not argue. Evidently it is natural enough for a child to love nature, and there is no reason for him to outgrow it. It is natural too, and important, to love man, but Wordsworth for the unity of his doctrine prefers to think that this comes about as one of the consequences of loving nature—in whose tone he thinks he can catch "the still, sad music of humanity." I agree with Professor Lionel Trilling that it is natural for the child to love man even in the first place, especially man in the person of his mother. Wordsworth would not deny this. But it is especially from the love of nature that the peculiar Wordsworthian benefit accrues to child and man; it is an experience having the most beneficent consequences upon the pursuit of happiness. For Wordsworth is a practical humanist, an anthropocentrist in the long run, and it is his idea that we win our individual happiness not by challenging the opposing natural element but by embracing it. If we can obtain the sense of community with the infinite concretion of the environing world, we may cease to feel like small aliens, even though busy, cunning, and predatory ones. In our cultural paradigms we have a saying about the peace which passeth understanding, and one about the security of that perfect love which casteth out fear; and Wordsworth had deeply assimilated these biblical phrases. Such values, if we accept them, must be of even greater moment to us today than in the time of Wordsworth, in the degree of our increased alienation from nature and, I think, our increased anxiety. I shall assume that as Wordsworthians we are able to verify them in our own experience.

Wordsworth meant always to display the affections in their purest or most elemental form; therefore to treat the affections as they fixed themselves upon nature, and nature in her wild or original state, such as that of his Cumberland region—an advantage incidentally that most of his readers in their daily lives can never match. If our experience of nature is confined to enjoying the suburban lawn or garden, or the public park landscaped for the edification of our modern societies, there is always the possibility that a narcissistic element may creep into the experience and restrict it: we may be admiring man more than nature.

And our occasional jolly picnics into the heart of nature somewhere may not take us decisively out of the consciousness of our confederated kind, and certainly do not give us time to develop the required feelings. Perhaps when we theorize about the great passions we will remark that it is possible for the boy or the man to fix his affections upon his human mother, but possible also in some sense to fix them upon the elemental mother who is nature. That would be an experience of ontological dignity. In the instructive mythology of Freud we learn a great deal about the one mother, but nothing about the other. But let me offer a modern or post-Wordsworthian fable. Its parts may be found, though isolated and not much developed, in John Dewey's writings, for example. There was a time when man with his principle of individuation had not emerged from the matrix, the maternal womb, of nature, nor had his problems emerged with him. But in due time he was brought forth, the umbilical cord was severed. Then began that long torture in which he now throve upon his aggressions, and now stood fixed in guilt and fear, toward that nature who no longer contained him but indifferently confronted him; the subjective-objective duality so bitterly felt in our modern philosophers. Very well. But the fable says that man nevertheless discovered in himself a wonderful gift for what is called "aesthetic" experience; and that in this aesthetic experience the hateful distinction between subject and object is for once obliterated. In this experience man returns to nature, his mother, yet in his own character, and without suffering death. This is fable or myth. The first part, about man's birth out of nature, is evidently suggested by the hypothesis of biological evolution; the second part, about his salvation, goes back most directly to the idealistic German philosophers. This second part would have made quick sense to Wordsworth. He possessed the principle of it through the conversations with Coleridge, at the time when their friendship was perfect, when each required the other to give his whole thought, and the other withheld nothing.

We think of *The Prelude* as the sequential account of scores of occasions where some given natural concretion presents itself to the boy and elicits his response. Nature is not offered by the poet, and could not be offered, in the visual fullness which is recorded by the painter. The concretion tends to be massive yet individualized, and its presence is likely to enter unexpectedly and dramatically into the consciousness of a boy who is about the business of a boy. The response of the boy's feelings will generally persuade us; it is good drama, and we have been boys.

But I am afraid we have to consider something in the response of that boy after all which we feel like resisting, or more probably feel like reading very carelessly or even skipping in order not to resist. A heavy overlay of religious experience is added to the spontaneous joy of the boy's simple affections. A more or less uniform religious doctrine is adhered to throughout the poem, and brought to consciousness within the boy's response almost every time before the poet will leave him alone. (And of course there are the systematic doctrinal meditations interpolated at many places by the poet himself.) The doctrine has been studied by many scholars. Here is probably the hardest as well as the last understanding of Wordsworth which they have had to master.

It is a doctrine of pantheism, or natural religion, or pan-psychism, or Boehmenism: Professor Stallknecht shows conclusively, so far as I am concerned, how closely at many points Wordsworth follows the teachings of Jacob Boehme.[5] Of course he follows others of similar teaching, and with all his eclecticism may still at many places put the doctrine in his own words. But as I understand it, by the least statement of this religion of nature we must conceive the boy's experience under color of the following beliefs: (a) That the spirit of the natural universe focusses all its terrific power in the given concretion; and (b) that this is expressly for the purpose of aggressively seeking him out and making itself known to him and giving him its joy. I say "it" rather than "he" for the sake of keeping to Wordsworth's thought. This is according to a theory of religion which is on the order of his theory of the poetic diction: an experience that sticks close to its tenor, while that tenor consists in the pure natural concretions, and does not intend to offer the presence under the figure of "personifications," which would convert it into a human image and perpetrate the pathetic fallacy. How can he avoid it? Now I should not wish to scorn a cosmic compassion which resorts by such tricks, such very human tricks, to these philanthropic aggressions. But in the name of David Hartley,[6] who is another of Wordsworth's heroes, I suggest that pragmatically, psychologically, it is more usual for us to regard the cosmic constructs of religion as fashioned afterwards, and indeed upon the base of those spontaneous affective responses which people make to nature; so that in the ordering which Wordsworth authorizes, the cart is before the horse. We have a mystical experience which precedes its own empirical technique. The indepen-

5. *Strange Seas of Thought*, Durham, 1945. (Ransom's note)
6. David Hartley (1705–1757), British philosopher who argued that all human knowledge is based on sense experience and the association of ideas.

dent lyrics of Wordsworth are not burdened with all this significance, and those readers who do not know *The Prelude* can think of him as a lyric poet who is content on the whole with his *métier*. Of course the early appearance of *Tintern Abbey* may startle them, for that was the prelude to *The Prelude*. I think they may respond to it by regarding its eloquence as that of a kind of straining, muddled Protestant theologism; for so William Empson regarded it; he was not aware that its terms were those of an already stated theology, and perhaps regular enough in that kind of orthodoxy. *The Prelude* is a religious poem, and unquestionably means much to many Wordsworthians in that sense. Even so, we cannot but wonder if he does not read back into the boy's mind some of the matured configurations of his own. And I think we may prefer to take our poetry as an experience which is local, and plural, rather than cosmic, and one. It will still give the quick joy, and the instant sense of community with the natural objects, and we can go a long way on that.

For me the important successors to Wordsworth in the poetry of nature have been Keats, and Hopkins, and our own Robert Frost. Of these Hopkins is the only analogue of the Wordsworth of *The Prelude*; Hopkins subsumed the love of nature under a religious dispensation. But Hopkins was a Roman, and even the militant order of the Society of Jesus was a comfortable dispensation which, so to speak, laid down once for all the stipulations of an all-embracing faith, and did not mean that afterwards the common believer should compel every spontaneous experience to disclose its dogmatic bearings. The doctrine of Scotus[7] gave to Hopkins his special charter. It allowed him to seek the "dapple" in things, where we are challenged by a natural effect that surely cannot be contained by the intellect. In the poem *Pied Beauty* this priest is uninhibited in his presentation of the humblest natural beauty. He crosses himself at the beginning, as it were, where he says, "Glory be to God for dappled things"; and at the end, where he ascribes this beauty to God's creation though God's own beauty is past dapple and change. I think this must be the version of religious nature-poetry which in our literature is the classical one. The believer has embraced the faith, attended his masses, performed his tithes; it is assumed that his spontaneous activities now will not have to be too careful doctrinally. Including his making of verses, and even making them about nature, if that is one of them; the father confessor will neither question their inno-

7. John Duns Scotus (ca. 1266–1308), Franciscan philosopher who attached a great importance to the individuality ("thisness") of things as opposed to St. Thomas Aquinas' abstractions.

cence, nor induce a fatal self-consciousness in the poet by showing him how they lead the philosophic mind toward God. There is no indication that Hopkins' superiors offered any reproach against his *Wreck of the Deutschland*, where he permitted himself to lay a daring interpretation upon the action of the tall nun who called out from the deck of the foundering ship to Christ to "Come quickly." Was she asking Christ to give her crown to her now, and to let it be though in heaven just the familiar landscape of springtime in place of those winter seas? Already she can sense the dreadful fog lifting:

> For how to the heart's cheering
> The down-dugged ground-hugged grey
> Hovers off, the jay-blue heavens appearing
> Of pied and peeled May!

But of course the fertile Hopkins can think of other interpretations for her cry, all of them more orthodox. Death is after all an official occasion for the priest. Let us hope that dogma will keep its dignity upon that tempting and infinitely delicate occasion.

I am ignorant in these matters. But I should like in the concluding note to offer the speculation that Wordsworth himself may have repented of the dogmatic zeal of his *Prelude*, or at any rate allowed it to worry him endlessly. The evidence is chiefly in the *Ode on Intimations of Immortality*, that poem of Wordsworth's which beyond all the others is splendid, beyond them confused in its argument, and destined to be mooted.

Wordsworth has told us that the first four stanzas of the *Ode* were composed at one time (and it was while the composition of *The Prelude* was under way), but that a period of several years intervened before the other seven stanzas were added (by which time of course *The Prelude* had been finished and laid away till its author could make up his mind to publish it). In the early part of the *Ode* the speaker mourns because nature does not now wear for him the celestial light, the glory, in which it was once arrayed. It still has its loveliness. A certain personal episode is mentioned in the third stanza:

> Now, while the birds thus sing a joyous song,
> And while the young lambs bound
> As to the tabor's sound,
> To me alone there came a thought of grief:
> A timely utterance gave that thought relief,
> And I again am strong.

What was the timely utterance? Professor Trilling suggests that it was *Resolution and Independence*, the poem about the aged leech gatherer composed near this time.[8] But the trouble which is healed by the meeting with the leech gatherer can hardly be the trouble which is the burden of the *Ode*. In the pertinent part of the smaller poem we read:

> I heard the sky-lark warbling in the sky;
> And I bethought me of the playful hare:
> Even such a happy Child of earth am I;
> Even as these blissful creatures do I fare;
> Far from the world I walk, and from all care;
> But there may come another day to me—
> Solitude, pain of heart, distress, and poverty.

He goes on to wonder how he can expect others to provide for his livelihood, and the thought of Chatterton and Burns reminds him how poets "begin in gladness; But thereof come in the end despondency and madness." Then as if providentially he meets the leech gatherer, who is decrepit and poverty-stricken but has no fear, and he is comforted. The animal or economic discouragement represented here is unusual with Wordsworth, whether in his poems or in his life so far as we have it. The Wordsworth of our impression is about as tough as a leech gatherer. We are tempted to think he offers himself in this weakness mostly in order to make a dramatic foil to the leech gatherer. But this assumption is not necessary. What we are sure of is that the mood would not fit the *Ode*, where the poet's complaint is that he no longer obtains from natural objects the religious intimations which he ascribes to his youth; that is to say, the overwhelming sense of the presence of God. So I prefer to follow the usual opinion which identifies the "timely utterance" with the little poem, *My heart leaps up when I behold*. The last lines of this poem are placed by the poet under the title of the *Ode* as a text, and the complete poem is as follows:

> My heart leaps up when I behold
>   A rainbow in the sky:
> So was it when my life began;
> So is it now I am a man;
> So be it when I shall grow old,
>   Or let me die!
> The Child is father of the Man;

8. *The Liberal Imagination*, New York, 1950, 138–41. (Ransom's note)

> And I could wish my days to be
> Bound each to each by natural piety.

For me this perfect little poem seems to say by indirection that the important thing in the child's experience was the spontaneous joy of
seeing the rainbow; and the full sense of God which belongs to the man
with his laborious dogma may not really have been there. The joy was
enough, and it is enough now if the man has never lost the gift for joy.
The idea of the "natural piety" is not according to Boehme, I believe,
but quite according to Hartley, ancestor perhaps of our contemporary
psychology with its habit of associations and derivations. Parentheti-
cally, however, we do have to notice that the locution itself is somewhat
foreign to our psychological jargon. To know what piety is we have to
have read Virgil and seen how Aeneas was pious because he honored
his father Anchises, and bore him upon his own back from burning
Troy. That was a piety symbolic of how each day a man must take up
the life of yesterday, so that no human gift or possession will be allowed
to fail.

The gift for responding to the rainbow had not failed for Wordsworth. But at the end of stanza four he is still troubled: the fact remains
in spite of the "timely utterance" that he cannot instantly read from his
present experience what his big work has been so confidently attribut-
ing to the youthful experience. He tests it in laboratory fashion by crucial experiments, with a tree, a field, and a pansy:

> Oh evil day! if I were sullen
> While Earth herself is adorning,
> This sweet May-morning,
> And the Children are culling
> On every side,
> In a thousand valleys far and wide,
> Fresh flowers; while the sun shines warm,
> And the Babe leaps up on his Mother's arm:—
> I hear, I hear, with joy I hear!
> —But there's a Tree, of many, one,
> A single Field which I have looked upon,
> Both of them speak of something that is gone:
> The Pansy at my feet
> Doth the same tale repeat:
> Whither is fled the visionary gleam?
> Where is it now, the glory and the dream?

We gather that he is not yet prepared to fall back upon the satisfactions of natural piety. He will let the poem wait in order to see if he can recover the visionary gleam.

In the long concluding part of the *Ode* he tries a desperate dogmatic expedient. He compounds his dogmas now; or perhaps he waives the old one while he tries the new one. The new one is the Platonic dogma of recollection, whereby the freshly incarnated soul of the child recalls its pre-migrationary dignities. Perhaps the religious overtones of the child's vision as Wordsworth thinks of them can be accounted for more simply in that way. But he is honest enough to indicate in his preface to the finished poem that this dogma is not particularly congenial to him, and that a religious system will scarcely find in it a very firm support. And in the latter stanzas the man is no more able than before to have the experience which he imputes to the child. He still wavers between mourning for his disability and making the most of the natural piety. For his conclusion it is practically as well as artistically needful for him to be content with what he has. He concludes quietly:

> To me the meanest flower that blows can give
> Thoughts that do often lie too deep for tears.

I believe this means that the flower addresses him as a lyrical object, and that he can then *think* himself into full religious consciousness very much as a priest will turn any spontaneous experience by his dialectic into occasion for glorifying God. But this is a process of intellect not given in the original intuition. The idea that the child saw God in the flower surely and intuitively is the ground on which Wordsworth has pronounced him "Mighty Prophet," "Seer blest," and "best Philosopher." But in that case the man has simply not inherited fully from the child's estate. Natural piety has not worked.

The concern which Wordsworth registers in the *Ode* will perhaps have for us not only its face value there, but another which we can infer: a disillusionment with the achievement of the great *Prelude*. In that poem he has read off to his adult readers the intuitive religiousness of the child as if it were a universal and exemplary experience. But what if the adult mind cannot have this experience? Wordsworth came to the melancholy conviction that it lacked the power. And what if the child's mind lacked it too, if Wordsworth in the excess of his prodigious memory had given it more power than it had had? I think we will imagine that his question harrowed the poet.

What we do know is that Wordsworth did not take pleasure in the completed *Prelude*, with all its magnificence, and the sense of its having taken the best labors of his life. While he was writing it, his intimates and he spoke of it as part of the broad philosophical project, *The Recluse*, as Professor Garrod has shown.[9] But he published the middle third part of *The Recluse* in 1814, under the title *The Excursion*; and in its preface he referred to another work, evidently *The Prelude*, as only "preparatory," and concerned with the author's development and credentials as a poet and philosopher. Even so, he withheld its publication, and that came about only after his death, and the title as we have it was supplied by his widow.

What we lose by finding this significance in the *Ode*, and in *The Prelude* in the light of the *Ode*, is a certain epistemology, or psychology, of the religious experience. A man does not seem to have a complete version of it in the intuitive manner with which Wordsworth endowed the child. And perhaps the child did not really have it that way, either. But what we are left with is a very full account of Wordsworth's religious experience itself at a certain period, however it may have been achieved; and what seems even more essential, because it would be the condition of a religious experience, always the spontaneous and lyrical joy in nature which is aesthetic experience. The short poems which Wordsworth wrote are rarely affected by our present discussion. He referred to them as the "little cells, oratories, and sepulchral recesses" which flowered out from the sacred "edifice" of his intended great poem. But the figure is misleading. They are the fundamental earth, or they are the foundation stones, upon which if there is to be a religious edifice it must rise.

9. H. W. Garrod, *Wordsworth: Lectures and Essays* (London, 1923), 194.

HUMANISM AT CHICAGO

HE AMERICAN UNIVERSITY works with both hands, and the right hand hardly knows what the left hand is doing. The right hand discharges its obvious duty, directing the strenuous and ever-enlarging courses in the sciences called "social" and "natural," getting the younger generations ready to enter the world of affairs. The left hand directs the "humanities," and that is something different. I do not know if many humanists would care to tell what they mean by the term intellectually, and if they would not we may think the left hand is not so sure what itself is doing. But the humanists at the university can tell at once what they mean by the term professionally. The humanities at the university are simply the studies of English and other literatures. Now American education is such a huge and sprawling affair that it is difficult to know where the central intelligence is located. But there is clearly effective in it somewhere a fixed intention to make large provision for literary studies at the highest level. It is not that a person has to go to the university in order to have the literary experience, but it will be bigger and richer if he has it as the university has it. And I have to tell of that as I know it. He will be made to learn about certain technical practices in this art, for one thing; but they are word-practices, this being the art which employs language, the commonest and most intimate medium possible, and he ought to be put at home with them. Then, and possibly in consequence, he will be able to ask and answer more intelligently the questions about its mysterious power; about how the experience of a literary object works in the mind of the experient, and what it does for him as a poor creature with strange and almost inarticulate needs.

This is the most self-conscious of ages. We seem specially devoted to the pursuit of truth by self-knowledge. Socrates might have delighted to live in it; and even younger persons who do live in it are likely to arrive at the university already fixed in the idea that they are entitled to know, really, how things affect them; which is according to the modern

This essay first appeared in the *Kenyon Review*, XVI (Autumn, 1952), 647–59. From *Poems and Essays*, by John Crowe Ransom, copyright © 1955 by Alfred A. Knopf, Inc. Reprinted by permission of the publisher.

temper, and the Socratic. I have noticed that it makes them a little difficult, it makes them critical of the studies at which they are put to work.
It makes the humanists who stand over them a little nervous. Many
humanists that I know are given to worrying over their responsibility;
they have to assign lessons in literature, of all subjects; they have to
induce a degree of speculative fury in the discussions, and make it do
work; and to set the modest goals, which must not be too modest, of
literary understanding. But the chances are, as I believe, that good humanists just in the degree they feel ill-prepared to give the courses will
actually offer them the more cheerfully, because they can go along with
their students, put themselves into the attitude of inviting a fresh experience of literature, and have it in the flush of their speculative consciousness. The humanists whom I esteem never stop being learners.

Perhaps the last sentence brings me to the topic; I am not quite sure.
It is to be presumed that the humanists at the University of Chicago,
some fifteen years ago, had their painful indecisions as to how to direct
the literary studies when their own speculations were not exactly coming through on schedule. They were academic humanists, and exposed
to the hazard of the profession. But it appears that suddenly they made
a clean sweep of their difficulties, not by taking the plunge (into renewed speculations) but by turning to authority; by appropriating a
program of studies not their own, and waiving the hard questions.[1] The
program. But from time to time they have written individually to dedi-
cate to it all their industry, and certainly now it must be said that they
executed it faithfully, for they worked like beavers, or like scientists.
But it was a rigid program, allowing little freedom for the discussions to
develop something in their own context and out of their own fury. And
since it was a program which had to be recovered from antiquity, it was
antiquated. This inference is hard to escape even though it was the *Poetics* of Aristotle himself which the Chicago humanists adopted for
their handbook.

I know almost nothing about the academic operation of their program. But from time to time they have written individually about their
doctrine. And now the older papers are published along with new ones
in *Critics and Criticism* (University of Chicago Press: $6.00), edited
with an introduction by R. S. Crane; a book which will serve as the official version of the intellectual activity of these humanists. It runs to
some 300,000 words and contains twenty essays by six authors: R. S.

1. Ransom feels that this program is a successor to the "One Hundred Great Books"
concept, which the University of Chicago had offered as a "fresh experience of literature."

Crane, W. R. Keast, Richard McKeon, Norman Maclean, Elder Olson, Bernard Weinberg. It would seem that Crane initiated and led the movement. In the introduction he explains some of the background of their thinking. They observed that the program of literary studies ordinarily breaks down into four special disciplines: language, analysis of intellectual ideas, history, and criticism. Without abandoning the other three, which are always in order, they elected as their special interest to work at criticism, the most neglected of the four; that is why they are here. There is no indication of how it went with them before they embraced Aristotelianism. Perhaps Richard McKeon, in the department of philosophy, had something to do with that decision. He is a leading Aristotelian in our time, and has clarity of mind as well as learning. In the writings here he seems less committed than his associates. In the essay, "The Philosophic Bases of Art and Criticism," the perspective is wide, and there is a relativism in his acceptance of different critical systems at face value. I should imagine that his influence in the group has been a broadening one. Perhaps it has made for what urbanity there is in the tone of the polemical essays. Sometimes the reader feels that a rather abusive tone is followed almost too quickly by a conciliatory one, as if according to plan. But it should be said that these critics conduct themselves with as much politeness as we are used to in such controversies. We can sniff an exciting air as of something momentous when men of character and conviction debate the meaning of literature; perhaps a little show of plain passion is only what was to be expected.

(The rivalry of critical schools is in this respect no worse than that of religious sects. And it would anyhow be a set of *humanists* which would be listed as the school or the sect, according to my understanding. If humane letters do not perform the peculiar offices of religion, one reason would be that they do not do what Arnold said religion had done: "attach themselves to the fact, to the supposed fact." But they refer to the same order of reality, and they do it incessantly, though they may do it discreetly, and principally by way of implication or symbol. Their effect is pervasive enough, and it might conceivably be said that the effect of literature is comparable to that of religion, and in the same sense. These remarks are indeed parenthetical, but they do say that literature is taken seriously, and its apologists are likely to show fight.)

I can find no reservations in their commitment to the critical theory of the *Poetics*. They are pure Aristotelians, if we will allow for a little necessary supplementation of the handbook; but perhaps this suggests that we should call them neo-Aristotelians. The *neo* will cover those extensions of the rules which have to be made if we consider that

Aristotle's treatise is occupied with laying down the laws for poetry at large—a thing he does much too easily—and then with examining at length the appropriate structure of Greek drama and more briefly that of Greek epic; but now they have to look into Shakespeare and modern drama and fiction, where Aristotle through no fault of his own was unacquainted, and into lyric poetry where Aristotle's treatment is missing. The program has to work now; it has to work in Chicago, U.S.A. But they made the adaptations scrupulously, and did not exceed their authority so far as I can see. Reading the historical essays in their book, we have the conviction that there has not been a group of scholars in the whole intellectual history of Europe who have possessed their Aristotle so firmly and used him so uncritically; at least in this particular field. Theirs has been a great piety, and perhaps even the most disapproving humanist must concede, How touching!

And there was a time when I, for example, like a good many young men I knew, could not endure to listen to disparagement of my philosopher. I knew the Nichomachean *Ethics*, and used it for years as a sort of Bible. But when I got seriously into the *Poetics*, my veneration was a little chilled. The work did not seem commensurate with my literary speculations; by that time I had at least read Kant and Croce. And now that my own age has witnessed a flood of importunate writings by spirited critics, I do not turn back and sound Aristotle upon certain of our stock preoccupations with literature without making the depressing discovery that he is unfamiliar with them; and presently, that if I try to force from him some pronouncement by implication, the starch starts going out of the whole business; clearly this is not the way to proceed in it. We still have to search out the mysteries as they offer themselves, and from where we stand.

But it is quite worth our while if we need a work-out, and for me at the moment it is a point of honor, that we should see what we can make of the *Poetics*. That was an extraordinary passion, we like to say, which Aristotle had for making a single systematic disposition of things which went together yet seemed to be tangled hopelessly. The enormous tangle of values in the literary object challenged him. Common language suggested that a poem after all was a single made object, a *poieton*. So he asked, What was the human purpose in making it? and how then is it put together? The two questions really make one question; the second is not worth asking till the first is asked and answered. The famous definition of the tragic play is in answer to both questions; according to Butcher it reads:

> Tragedy, then, is an imitation of an action that is serious, complete, and of a certain magnitude; in language embellished with each kind of artistic ornament, the several kinds being found in separate parts of the play; in the form of action, not of narrative; through pity and fear exciting the proper purgation of these emotions.[2]

It is very full, as exhaustive as a definition had better try to be. There are a fair number of balls here for the poet (or the critic) to keep in the air at the same time. But still there are two omissions which have to be supplied from context. The crucial purgation (*katharsis*) of the painful pity and fear is the form which the pleasure takes; pleasure is always the purpose of art, and had as well be named in a treatise on one of the literary genres; it is named many times in the discussion which follows. The other omission is from the constructive part of the definition, but it is supplied immediately. Aristotle proceeds to name four major "parts" in the play which have to be maneuvered in proper relation to each other constantly as composition goes on: Plot, Character, Thought, and Diction. Nor does he delay to declare that Plot (*muthos*) is the main part, the "soul" of the play so to speak, while the other parts are subsidiary, working only for the plot, and diminishing in comparative importance in the order in which they are named.

Almost any literary critic is aware that Aristotle was exacting in his demands upon the plot. He was expert in his sense of the plotting of the Greek plays. He talked about the playwright's "invention" in giving the novel turn to the stock actions which came from the familiar legends of the old Greek houses; about "recognition" scenes and "reversals" of fortune; about "probability" in the actions as a better rule than factuality; about complication and unravelling, and the tragic ending. The discussion of plot is the largest and most lucid block of writing in the *Poetics*, and perhaps insofar as the Greek plays are strange to modern students it is required reading for that particular course. But what carries over into the study of any drama (or for that matter of fictions and lyric poems) is something else: the tight organization he would force upon the various actions composing the single plot. Each action must be effect of the previous action and cause of the following one, by logical necessity. Of course the causal sequence is not one of merely mechanical actions, since the human agency is guaranteed every moment by character, thought, and diction. But as to the close economy of the system, Aristotle is a perfectionist. One wonders if this necessarily follows

2. S. H. Butcher, *Aristotle's Theory of Poetry and Fine Art* (London, 1902), 23.

from the purpose of the play as given in the definition. It is Aristotle who likes his plotting tight, but what the spectator or reader is supposed to like is the kind of plotting which provokes the right emotional response. Who is to say that he may not actually be better served by a loose plotting? Perhaps *he* will say, and I am not sure what it would be. Or if it is a matter of pleasure in general, which Aristotle often appeals to, even when he is officially limited to the pleasure of purgation, the spectator again may say, and now he may even have a certain distaste for what is most relished by Aristotle. It really does not seem too important; except that perhaps a dismal prescience may weigh upon us here, and cause us to think of those odious critics to come whose whole vocation will be in seeking the "well-made" play, or story.[3]

We come to the subordinate parts of the play. The terminology is a little strange for us. Character is *ethos*, ethical character; the auditors of the play are good men, and the protagonist must be an even better one, the embodiment of a virtue which is almost but not quite perfect. *Ethos* is not equivalent to the Latin *dramatis persona*, and our own "character" does double duty for both; a character in the play may very well *have* character in the sense of habitual goodness. But I do not see here any sense of still a third kind of character: the Shakespearian, modern, passionately cherished, almost religious sense of the total individuality of a person who is rich in vivid yet contingent traits, even physical traits, that are not ethical at all. This kind of character engages an auditor's love, and that is more than his ethical approval. It also engages a critic's psychological powers, and more deeply than *ethos* does. But on this point the reader of the *Poetics* must be admonished that Aristotle is dealing with a stern Greek kind of play. He must emphasize the "universal" in character as the plot-material for these ethical plays— though probably all plays are ethical, whatever else they may be—and he would object to the particularity or accidents of personality as something which history was better prepared to relate than drama.

Thought (*dianoia*) is likewise not quite what it might seem. The word means a thinking through, and names the power to articulate one's thought throughout a whole speech and over a variety of speeches; a virtue of large-scale discourse. The agents in the play must express their thought and feeling forcefully, not once but through a sustained effort; otherwise it will not be clear how they think they are affected by the other actions, nor why they perform their own actions.

3. The "well-made" play refers to a type of drama originated by Eugene Scribe (1815–1887) that stressed mechanical and arbitrarily contrived patterns of plot structure and suspense.

Finally there is Diction (*lexis*), or the power to use language for the small-scale effects which are produced by the words themselves, and the grammatical phrases in which the words are put together. Every discourse has its own diction, but Greek plays are in the "poetic" diction, and that has to be accounted for. For me it is impossible to say that Aristotle has accounted for it. Poetic diction means two things to him. One is its metered language. Aristotle knows his meters, and in one place appears to be thoroughly enjoying himself as he substitutes other words for the given words in several lines to see how the sense would be altered, but refrains easily from altering the meters. The advantage he finds in metered language is that everybody likes rhythm. But some one may object, for this must occur to every one: Not so much as that; why not leave the play to its plot and wait for your rhythm another time, when you can listen to music? I cannot see that Aristotle has any important use for the meters in a play or epic; or that the Chicago people have use for them in Shakespeare or lyric poems. Critics generally never offer much of a theory about the meters so far as I know; there seems to have been a singular lapse of the critical imagination. But the other characteristic of poetic diction as Aristotle treats it is its fondness for unusual words and word-uses; or what we call its figurative language. Aristotle knows the kinds of words, and of figures, and gives examples with the utmost cheeriness, defending some of them from certain named critics who felt outraged by them. These tricks make the language striking and hold the auditor's attention, or they sweeten or ornament the language and delight him. But does that not mean, in either case, that they divert attention from the plot? I should think there is significance in Aristotle's remark that the poetic diction is best used "in the pauses of the action"; is this not equivalent to saying that it will interfere with the action when that is at its height? Shakespeare's rule seems rather opposite to this; in his plays the diction is least lively when there is transition from one action to another, but in the midst of action the whole power of his poetry is working. Somebody might conceivably argue that Shakespeare was preeminently a poet (in the sense of being a master of poetic language) though also a playwright, and used the play to provide him with plenty of poignant occasions for the poetry. But it does not seem advisable to put the plot and the poetry into rivalry, or bother as to which had the honor to come first in his intention. Both are there, and both engage with our emotions, though apparently not quite with the same ones. Aristotle does handsomely by the plot, and has nothing very impressive to say for the poetry.

I could not if I tried find anything more shocking to say of Aristotle than this. It is a good place to stop. What will his gentle reader in these times think of a critic who prefers the plot to the poetry and mentions the poetry only at the end as if it were a small gratuity or bonus? Here, I believe, is the biggest issue separating the ancient philosopher and the Chicago restorationists, on the one hand, and the modern critics on the other. But there is a little more to be said about it. At Chicago they are entirely aware of this issue; they do not evade it. They have five hundred words to say about it where Aristotle had ten, and say them perspicuously in our own idiom, though in the substance about as we can imagine Aristotle saying them if he could have addressed himself to the moderns. The place where their argument is closest and clearest is the latter part of Elder Olson's essay, "William Empson, Contemporary Criticism, and Poetic Diction."[4] Olson, by the way, is their best man in a long hard fight at close quarters. The critic who identifies poetry with a special language is under obligation to read this essay and see if his confidence is shaken. Olson undertakes to show in detail that there is little of consequence left in the language of the play after we have allowed for what it does by way of plain denotation in getting the dramatic elements of the action before us; that is to say, after we have used up the substantial prose base upon which the fineries of diction are mounted.

There is no sign of yielding on either side, and my report seems to conclude with an implacable quarrel. I am scarcely of Mr. Olson's side, and I would not have my bravery impugned, yet I cannot but wonder if the critics of the future may not find a quaintness in this feuding. For a year or so I have been taking occasional notes on a possible critical program which, though conciliatory, will doubtless prove bold beyond my strength. It looks a little better to me at the moment, now that I have seen Chicago critics, with a temperamental predilection for plot, being so zealous against poetry; and vice versa, other critics, with a temperamental predilection for poetry, being so zealous against plot. Both are right about the thing they want, but as to the other thing they are narrow, exclusive, "monistic" (to use the hieratic epithet which the Chicago critics hurl against their enemies), or "monolithic" (the cultural epithet which various and other critics have hurled sometimes against theirs). I do not like to let the occasion slip. But my ideas are tentative, unproved, and till now, even in brief form, unwritten.

I suggest that we think of a poem as constructing and realizing not

4. *Critics and Criticism,* 45–82.

one poetic object, but three objects at once. Two are familiar to us, though a given critic is likely to think that one or the other is to be found in the poem, not both. The third object is one whose presence is unquestionable but vaguely disturbing to many critics, and which is not easy to understand. But it is necessary in advance to agree not to underestimate the capacity of the poem for embodying three large-scale objects. The same words will be used two or three times, it may be, in constructing the several objects, though perhaps there will be some words used for one only. The final objects, to be enjoyed fully, may have to be taken more or less in turn. But there will also be the grateful sense of the poem as a whole, whose marvelous economy is such that you can take it quite systematically in three different ways and find in it three different things. Let it be understood, finally, that the three objects do not constitute a Holy Trinity, nor even an Hegelian triad; it is nothing like that!

I hardly know which of two objects should come first, as having the primacy in the poet's interest. But let it be the most obvious one among the three: the logical construct; the big presentable object which most gives its own shape and extension to the whole poem; the object which best asserts its right in the world of affairs, being the social and ethical one, wholly rational and reputable and useful. Clearly this first object is the plot. Sometimes we think we had better call it the argument, as when it is a lyrical poem and the sequence is not of actions; but with all respect to the Aristotelians who for reasons of piety cannot abandon the idea of action. The words of the poem build up this object easily when used in their simple denotative aspect. And surely an object of this kind is good for the imagination to dwell upon; Aristotle will supply the description, and the encomium; it needs no apology.

The second object is harder to find, and perhaps some persons cannot find it. It is the big formless one which develops irresistibly, though hardly without technical consciousness on the author's part, all the time while the public or logical object is being whipped into shape. It is a community of objects rather than a single object; a little world of objects, with new ones constantly entering it as chance allows. On the technical side, there is an energy in the words that makes them unwilling to stop with mere denotation, and a kind of lead given them by the poet, which call the objects into being. And the objects peopling the little world are natural, given, total, and inviolable. If "imitation" is the method of getting the materials for the poetic construction, the imitation which finds such objects as these is freer than Aristotle was prepared for, and the little world it sets up is a small version of our natural world in its original dignity, not the laborious world of affairs. Indeed, the little world is the imitation of our Earthly Paradise, when we inhabited it in innocence.

And now, within the same poem, we can pass from one world to another. The first world is the one we have to live in, and we want it to be handsome as possible. The second world is the one we think we remember to have come from, and we will not let it go.

There is but one big construct left in the poem, and it is entirely visible and audible: the metered one, within which all the words of the poem dutifully assume their places though they may be very busy at other things. The rhythm of the meters envelopes the two other objects, like an atmosphere, a constraint and a blessing too. For it is sounding all the time; it is a low-grade music making an elemental, cosmic, and eternal object. Very diffidently I venture to construe it. I think the meters are an apt imitation of the Platonic Ideas, and in permeating our two other worlds permit us to have them *sub specie eternatatis*. For the worst thing about those two worlds is that the objects and arrangements we sense so exquisitely and cherish so deeply are doomed; they are mortal. That awareness is never withheld from us in the poem, but quite the contrary. Nor is there any possible human equivalent for them, really, in a world of Platonic Ideas. But still that world has the distinction of being the world of the immortals, and we like to sense it presiding over us.

So in the poem we have here or there, and in some confused sense all together, nearly every thing we can possibly desire. It is the best of all possible worlds. Of course it is not really possible. But when we settle down into that grim realization, we are beyond the help of any poems at all.

THE CONCRETE UNIVERSAL

OBSERVATIONS ON THE UNDERSTANDING

OF POETRY, I

 HAVE BEEN READING the new book by Professor W. K. Wimsatt, Jr., entitled *The Verbal Icon* (University of Kentucky Press, $4.00). It is a collection of essays about critical procedures, their hazards and "fallacies," and how to make them secure. Mr. Wimsatt is of reasonable temper, and he has read everything. Being at Yale, he must have associated with both members of the famous partnership of Brooks and Warren, and with one member of the other famous partnership of Wellek and Warren (the two Warrens being not identical of course); and on the whole I believe he is regarded as a kind of "new" critic, a late and technically accomplished one. But we come to the essay where he advises that the understanding of a poem can be fitted pretty well into a kind of Hegelian disposition: for him a poem is a structure which may be viewed as a Concrete Universal. And suddenly we are in the deep waters of one of the great philosophical systems.

The Concrete Universal. Is this the language for a critic? He has his own reduction of the poem to make, but is there not a line to be drawn somewhere? For his usual language, perhaps. We might say that ordinarily the critic's language, though less immediate than the poet's, should be less reductive than the philosopher's; in order that he may remember, and permit his gentle readers to remember, that the language of poetry is the language of feeling, not the language of epistemology. This can be said without prejudice to the rights of epistemology, and of philosophy at large. Perhaps the wisdom which chaste Philosophia loves is always epistemology, i.e. the universal grammar or logic of knowledge, describing serially its various and interlacing forms, itself devoid of any feeling except a rare and strange passion for widest

This essay first appeared in the *Kenyon Review*, XVI (Autumn, 1954), 554–64. From *Poems and Essays* by John Crowe Ransom, copyright © 1955 by Alfred A. Knopf, Inc. Reprinted by permission of the publisher.

perspective; the epistemological passion. Philosophy would then be different even from the pursuit of knowledge by the scientists, which is devoid of feeling for its materials, and supported only by a feeling for its urgent specific objectives; philosophy would suspend even these feelings in order to bring all the knowledges indifferently under the epistemological perspective. The satisfaction destined for the philosopher will be a philosophical satisfaction; the cake which he would bake will be the cake which he will cut. If at that stage he finds it painful to reflect that the love of wisdom has caused him to abandon certain more elementary emotions, he is like some Existentialist who wonders if there is any stage of the poor human panorama to which he might decently go back in order to reclaim his humanity. But at any rate we will locate (perhaps I mean that I should locate) the experience of the poet, and for the most part of his expositor, in the earlier stages.

I might have said that the notion of the poem as a concrete universal must involve us in metaphysics; this way, it would generate more excitement than as epistemology. That would be its consequence with a Hegelian. According to Hegel, the author of the poem is Spirit residing though partially and intermittently in the poet, and identical with that Spirit of the Universe which is God, or that Spirit of History which continually creates in order to objectify itself. This Spirit is of an amplitude which only the plenitude of concreteness can express. It cannot have its being within the servile restrictions of the technical sciences. The scientific universals are hopelessly abstract, they are mere concepts; and though these mean too to go out into the world, it is only to take what each of them characteristically wants of the world, and to reject more than they take. Quite different are the occasions when the world somewhere seems possessed and sustained through and through by the universals of the Spirit; for example, when a natural landscape is utterly beautiful, with every feature toned to the common tone; still better in the more responsive world of human affairs, when there is realized beside some hearth a scene of perfect familial accord, or when a whole people is exalted in a moment of crisis by the consciousness of serving a just State. Coming to the fine arts, and to poetry which he regarded as the best of them all, Hegel found that poems are recapitulations of the Spirit in the act of occupying its world, and are inclined to extend its triumphs even beyond the present limits of actuality. They mean to make us conscious of our own spiritual nature and destiny. We will perhaps try to think of Hegel's passion as an elevated humanism, if

we cling to a secular scruple, but its emotional tone is religious. The
epistemological passion, by comparison, would be fixed upon the techniques of knowledge, and for motivation perhaps it would have to rest,
as the phrase goes, upon "intellectual curiosity."

The trouble for the literary critic is that the poet appears ordinarily
not to have had much of the formidable Hegelian intention; and Mr.
Wimsatt has very little of it. A poem is a concrete universal in some
sense or other, but the emotions it registers are common and elemental
rather than Hegelian. But any view of the poem of course will seem a
little vulgar after Hegel's.

Mr. Wimsatt makes epistemological play with the language of poetry
at many places. It is easy to do this if one is interested in linguistics. I
am thinking of the kind of comment which critics of my general persuasion, and I not least, have liked to pass upon the poem. It is common
to show that some part of the poem is epistemologically interesting.
Here is a paradox, for instance, identifying A with not-A; or a metaphor
identifying the given object with a handsomer or more exotic object
that is not given at all. More generally, here is a passage that belongs
evidently to the logical order, but with various differences that look extraneous to the logical order and demand reference to some other category not easy to name. This is perhaps the primary fact which analysis
discloses in the poetic language. I have to confess that Mr. Wimsatt
does not agree with an old argument of mine that the concrete detail is
partly extraneous to the abstract universal or concept. And it will never
appear so if we won't let it; that is, if we keep qualifying the concept as
he does by every bit of the poem's concreteness, for then it becomes
tautological to say that all the detail qualifies the concept, or that no
reduction of the qualified concept can be equivalent to it. The concept I
had in mind would be one of that efficient sort with which we can do
work, in ethics for example, and which is taken with the minimum of
qualifiers when we define it or use it. But at any rate his view has no
Hegelian consequences. He does not argue that the poetic language is
the perfect Synthesis of the Thesis (or Universal) and the Antithesis (or
Concrete), and does not need to make any further reference to its components. The union is such a loose one (in my view) or such a nominal
or theoretical one (in his view) that it is easily broken up again. Indeed,
it is likely that we prefer one of the components by itself, or that we like
both of them, but independently and for different reasons. It would be
my conclusion that the language which accommodates both at once is

remarkably capacious in a comfortable and ingenious but not mysterious way; and I think this is according to the classical understanding
of poetry.

The complexity of the dialectic about concrete and universal, in the
poem which offers both, is something to drown in if we are not careful,
but I shall go a little farther. Mr. Wimsatt does concede a little to my
view that the two are radically incommensurable. This is how he concludes his essay:

> Croce tells us, as we should expect him to, of the "impossibility of ever
> rendering in logical terms the full effect of any poetry." . . . The situation
> is something like this: In each poem there is something (an individual
> intuition—or a concept) which can never be expressed in other terms. It
> is like the square root of two or like pi, which cannot be expressed by
> rational numbers, but only as their *limit*. Criticism of poetry is like 1.414
> . . . or 3.1416 . . . , not all it would be, yet all that can be had and very
> useful.[1]

I take it that he refers in his parenthesis to the Concrete Universal of
Hegel, where the concrete is supposed to be wholly assimilated to the
universal, and the universal to extend over the whole concretion; and
that the "other terms" which are not adequate to expressing it are those
of successive "logical paraphrases," each being fuller than the last, but
the last still requiring us to say, as everybody says, "The logical paraphrase is not equivalent to the poem." But the slightest irrationality cor-
rupts the integrity of the universal. We are bound to say that the universal does not quite, and therefore not in strict principle, grasp the
concrete.

We might observe that the Idea or Concrete Universal which is already formed subjectively by the Spirit—this is Hegelian language—is
in somewhat the position which Mr. Eliot attributes to Shakespeare in
creating his *Hamlet*. Shakespeare had in hand already his "emotion"—
perhaps an affective version of the concrete universal—but made the
mistake of thinking that the plot he adopted from another play would
make a good "objective correlative" for it. The materials proved too various for the purity of the emotion to assimilate.[2]

Mr. Wimsatt steps on my toes, along with many other toes of course,
with the greatest politeness though firmly. He is referring to a text of

---

1. *The Verbal Icon*, 83.
2. T. S. Eliot, "Hamlet and His Problems," in *Selected Essays of T. S. Eliot* (New York,
1960), 49.

mine which for a long time I have been unable to read (except to look
up his page-references). I do not now like the terms into which my argument fell at that time. The difference between Mr. Wimsatt and me
is that I abandoned much sooner than he does the attempt to make the
concrete-universal formulation work. If the poem is to represent the
moral sensibilities in an action that is adequate to the intention, it may
bring out a multitude of the nicest moral determinations of the speech
and behavior of the agents. But we have other sensibilities too, and
these will find their interest in other aspects of the concrete situation.
Under the jealous rigor of a scientific universal the other sensibilities
are repressed, and we can say we are "wholly" engaged with our scientific business. This cannot mean that all of our sensibilities are engaged, but only that our whole strength at the moment is lent to the
proper sensibilities and the others must wait. (I do not have the psychological language to describe this properly.) But if there is any meaning
for a universal which is described as concrete, and distinguished by
this mark from a scientific universal, I can only suppose that it will pursue its business with a fair degree of effectiveness no doubt, but not
without allowing the unrelated and suggestible sensibilities to keep up
their own play too. Tolerance is the technical distinction of this universal. It is precisely the distinction which most analysts seem to find in a
poetic language. Mr. Eliot speaks not only of the "emotion" which attends the main business of the poem, but also of the "feelings" which
"are not in emotions at all"; they come with the writing of poems. I am
afraid it must be added that if the analysts are idealists too, they are apt
to try presently to bring the random sensibilities into line, and to discover that "somehow" they are serving the universal nevertheless.

I have my own selfish purpose in these observations, aside from
noticing Mr. Wimsatt's able book, and now I must say for the benefit of
the present readers that about fifteen years ago I was thinking of the
poem as having a logical structure or framework, and a texture whose
character was partly irrelevant to the logical form and purpose.[3] My
"texture" in particular has given offense, and the fact is that I had no
sooner uttered it than it struck me as a flat and inadequate figure for
that vivid and easily felt part of the poem which we associate peculiarly
with poetic language. I wish now to recast my definition entirely, though
I shall only employ another figure whose disabilities I am aware of in
advance. It will be an absurd figure, but that has made it more memora-

3. "Criticism As Pure Speculation," present volume, pp. 128–45.

ble for me, so that I have been using it as a mnemonic device, to remind me of the several interests which have got themselves into the compound structure of a poem.

It is the figure towards which many critics in the 18th Century as well as today have gravitated. Suppose we say that the poem is an organism. Then it has a physiology. We will figure its organs, and to me it seems satisfactory if we say they are three: the head, the heart, the feet. In this organism the organs work all at the same time, but the peculiarity of the joint production is that it still consists of the several products of the organs working individually. Of course a good deal of cooperation among the organs was necessary, on the understanding that each would have to push its product at the expense of the others, requiring some compromises all round; but that having been agreed to, it is not too bad if none of the products has been realized in the degree of perfection that may have been coveted.

This figure too will collapse presently, but I take it a little farther. The organs are all intelligent, and can speak. Their joint product is a poem, and it is in a language within which three persistent speakers are speaking in their individual languages; the head in an intellectual language, the heart in an affective language, the feet in a rhythmical language; and it is to be supposed that in the composite language we attend to each of them, though usually with different degrees of consciousness. If we do not identify ourselves with any of the speakers at all, we shall probably think we are not getting sufficient motivation for our trouble, but only a dubious and improvised one: "the emotion of the poem as an organic whole"; and that will be only a kind of epistemological motivation. Each critic has the right to like one of the languages best, but he should be invited to see if the others are not there too, for the other critics, and motivated as well as his own.

As for the language of the head. The poem contains an action of the affections, and an action of the feet, but there is also an intellectual action, and its language probably will not be too badly distorted. Thus we say that the poem will have a beginning, a middle, and an end; these are intellectual distinctions, and with a given poem we may have expected them and received them without any conscious effort; being used to poems which are logical wholes, with whatever additions or qualifications. But here is a poem in which it is not so easy, and how can we be sure of them? Perhaps it is a modern poem, therefore especially cryptic. We cannot be sure, perhaps even after a second reading. Therefore we perform an *explication de texte*, and then a translation of the composite language into the exclusive language of the intellect, which we call the logical paraphrase. The head is quite ready to assist in this labor, in order to recover that absolute perspicuity of language from which it was hindered during the original composition. And suppose it comes off very well, and nobody takes exception. What is it good for? In the event that we have forgotten, the head has its own reasons, and will not lose the chance of disclosing them. A noble cause is involved, since the logical paraphrase exhibits one working of a principle that is moral, or religious, or political, or momentous in some other generalized way. The logical paraphrases of poems are always being crowned by the captains of the noblest causes, for fear that the critics may not have remembered to elucidate their significance.

I think perhaps I used to make it a point of honor to intimate that the intellectuals with their paraphrases were abusing and spoiling our poems. But now I think that may be arrogant and wrong, and surely it is unseasonable and vain. There is nowhere in the world for the logical paraphrase to have come from except the poem, where it is implicit; and it is the intellectuals (in their capacity of formal logicians) who are masters of the science of explicating what is implicit. Nor do they harm the poem by taking their use of it. When we look again, the poem is still there, timeless and inviolable, for the other uses.

Nor do I mean to damn the head's part in the poem by calling it harmless; and I must go farther and say—what anybody could substantiate by a hundred poems of all shapes and sizes, meters, tones—that the universal may be perfectly startling in its own right, or very fine and subtle. If humanists are to prevail in these bad times (when the movement of our culture seems stalled, as if we might have to get a new engine for it, so to speak) there will need to be a moiety of powerful intellectuals among them, and even among the poets. And we should be the wildest ineffectual fanatics if we should say we loved poetry passionately because it agreed with us that intellect is hateful.

We must sometimes be quite justified in not attending too carefully to the language of the head for fear we will miss its import. Often we can see quickly that it is harping on a principle to which we consented ages ago. The poem becomes then an instance of the principle in concrete action. (Mr. Wimsatt's titular idea of the Verbal Icon could have no larger application than when we say the poem is an icon of the play of the affections, and an icon of symbolic rhythm.) Now the weary old universal is wonderfully freshened up by being made to appear in the composite language with bright companions, and that is something that is always happening. Sir Philip Sidney said:

So it is in men, most of which are childish in the best things, till they be cradled in their graves—glad they will be to hear the tales of Hercules, Achilles, Cyrus, Aeneas; and hearing them must needs hear the right description of wisdom, valor, and justice; which, if they had been barely, that is to say philosophically, set out, they would swear they be brought to school again.[4]

But Shelley was a far more strenuous intellectual than Sidney, and he lived in a period of revolutionary ideas. His apology for poetry is very different:

Poets are the hierophants of an unapprehended inspiration; the mirrors of the gigantic shadows which futurity casts upon the present; the words which express what they understand not; the trumpets which sing to battle, and feel not what they inspire; the influence which is moved not, but moves. Poets are the unacknowledged legislators of the world.[5]

Sidney is good enough to regard the poet as a mature personality who is glad to put his gift at the service of the common moralist. Shelley thinks him incapable of intellectual ideas yet the unconscious mind of his age, and in a time of uncertainty actually initiating the new ideas which are required. We could find some good occasional evidences for this view.

But I will cite an easier case. There is one poet whose universals seem to be lost on our critics, though directed specifically to our age and important to it. They are expressed almost as directly as a composite language is likely to allow. Wallace Stevens is not Shelley's poet but a poet of intellectual maturity. Good critics have written at length about his verse, but so far as I have read them none has said anything even remotely to this effect: that the poems of Stevens from the first volume onward may be construed as a set of Notes Toward the Definition of a Secular Culture, and would therefore stand in some opposition to T. S. Eliot's Notes Toward the Definition of Culture as Based on Religion, with which we have been made acquainted both in verse and in prose. But so far as that goes, several years ago Mr. Stevens reinforced the poetic version with a prose version in his essay, "The Noble Rider."[6] The character of our future culture is of considerable concern at the

4. "A Defence of Poetry," in *Miscellaneous Prose of Sir Philip Sidney*, ed. Katherine Duncan-Jones and Jan Van Dorsten (London, 1973), 92.
5. "A Defence of Poetry," in *The Complete Works of Percy Bysshe Shelley*, Vol. VII (New York, 1930), 140.
6. T. S. Eliot, *Notes Towards the Definition of Culture* (New York, 1949); Wallace Stevens, "The Noble Rider and the Sound of Words," in *The Necessary Angel: Essays on Reality and the Imagination* (New York, 1951), 1–36.

moment to intellectuals, and among these are certainly the critics of fiction. I should be sorry to think that the critics of poetry do not share this concern, or, what is more likely, that they do not expect to find any useful pronouncement upon it in poems. The utterances of this poet upon the issue address themselves admirably to the naturalistic thinkers, and I do not mean to anticipate the outcome if I remark that many of us must for a long time have thought it desirable for men of letters generally, including the critics, to solicit the naturalists on behalf of a humanistic culture, and on such terms as they could bring themselves to offer without begging the whole question. Mr. Stevens in his essay thinks the irreducible condition to such a culture is the sense of Nobility. I should have thought it was a little simpler than that: the steady cultivation of the unselfish affections. But nobility would be derivative from them; and he has many poems about them, though it is his habit to take the soldier, dying with perfect acquiescence for the sake of his cause, as the supreme image. On one base or the other the poets can erect their handsome fictions, and I seem to find an always diminishing distance between these and the transcendental structures of religion.

I am wondering if Mr. Stevens may not think it a little odd that his admirers have not identified him intellectually, by his ideas. Would this be bad form?

THE CONCRETE UNIVERSAL

OBSERVATIONS ON THE UNDERSTANDING

OF POETRY, II

Y TITLE employs a famous working-phrase of Hegel's, and in the first of these papers I made some lay observations about that philosopher's understanding of poetry. But Hegel's thought is a special development of Kant's, and the fact is that I am obliged to think of Kant as my own mentor. Kant is closer to modern criticism than Hegel is! So I shall talk of Kant's understanding of poetry, and at even greater length. But perhaps a small apologia is in order, perhaps it is already overdue,—for bringing philosophy into the literary discussion.

I don't know how it is possible to deny to the literary critic the advantages of philosophy; I suppose we have fears that he, or his audience, will be unequal to them. But doesn't he try for a radical and decisive understanding of poetry? I could believe that he should be denied if I thought it must follow that, having once got into philosophy, he would never get out again. This would mean that resiliency had gone for some reason from his working consciousness, that the fateful time had come when the usual succession of its moods and interests must break down; which would be distressing if it did not seem arbitrary.

Probably the critic's ordinary job is to interpret the poem in common language that is not philosophical, and does not stray far from the literary text. We think of him as trying to induce the right public reception of the poem when he has come straight from his own experience of it. And we think his performance will be a little barbarous if some of the warmth of the object does not carry over his presentation, and even some of the graces of its language.

The reading of technical philosophy is the critic's home work. It should be fruitful of radical and decisive ideas—if his mind is strong

This essay first appeared in the *Kenyon Review*, XVII (Summer, 1955), 383–407. Reprinted by permission of Helen Ransom Forman.

enough to take them. But can he afford to immerse his mind in the stiff and graceless language? He will be safe if his passion for his art is incorruptible. Indeed, the whole intention is to save him from unconscious errors, like some cheapening of the poem's effect, or some wretched exclusions that he might feel inclined to make within its meaning,—which would be like having the lie within his soul, more killing than jargon, if we must compare one evil with another. The philosophical understanding of poetry as we have it now is almost entirely a thing that has been achieved by the moderns; Concrete Universal is one of its key phrases. But even here the philosophers do not speak with one voice; as doubtless they never will. It is the critic's privilege to have a mind of his own when caught in the disagreements among the doctors. And he has at least one enormous advantage over the philosophers: he is intimate, and it must be very rare if they are intimate, with the immediate pulsing fact which is his poem. He doesn't promise to accept a philosophical disposition of his poem which seems not to have very much to do with the felt reality of the thing. Must he then assume the burden of being a critic of philosophy as well as literature? But the added labor does not mean the doubling of his burden. His single role is still the understanding of poetry, and while this is made surer and firmer it is really being made easier.

I suppose we can scarcely say that philosophy as a part of the critical discipline is according to Arnold, or according to Eliot. It is according to Richards, and it is according to Coleridge. I find it pleasant to believe that the special revival of Coleridge in our time, in our language, signifies that critics direct their thought again to the heroic time when Augustan poetry, with its intricate surfaces and its abhorrence of passion, had played itself out finally, and was being succeeded by the fresh concert of the Romantics; when the poets themselves were amateurs of philosophy, and aware of the late or even the living philosophers of their art. The new philosophy was German. Schiller was its best spokesman in Germany among the poets and critics, and Coleridge, though scarcely Schiller's equal in speculative force, was his counterpart in English. The great philosophical name, of course, was that of Kant. We are still under the domination of an aesthetic humanism which we must call either Kantian or post-Kantian. And when we plunge into the first-rate sequence of poets which includes Wordsworth, Coleridge, Byron, Shelley, Keats, we at once take the impression that they are purposeful, dedicated, even programmatic, to a degree hardly equaled by another set of individual poets living in a single age. They had a common preoccupation with a certain understanding of poetry, and they had got it partly from the literary critics, but more and more it tended to go back to Kant, or to those critics who had assimilated their own views to Kant's. Now it will be said that they had also a preoccupation with political freedom, and the politics of revolution. But this one was not so leading. Perhaps it is more intense than the other preoccupation in Byron, but the case is just reversed in Keats; and both preoccupations are strong in Shelley. At any rate, as we proceed we come much too soon, for our mood, to Tennyson, and feel a cooling-off of our spirits; the epoch must have gone already, for here the succession passes once more to the nondescript, the poet who has received many gifts from the Muses but must take a long time deciding what had best be done with them,—and there won't be anything particularly philosophical in his decision when he makes it.

A little later we come to Browning, and Browning has a great deal of the Romantic philosophy in his equipment. Whether he borrows or originates it I do not know, though the former seems the more likely; but at any rate there has been the break already, and we do not associate him with the movement.

Then there is the third Victorian poet, Matthew Arnold, about whom we shall always have very mixed feelings. His beginnings may inspire us to fancy that Keats has come to life again. But there is quickly a breakdown, the Keatsian strain is stifled, as Arnold proceeds to argue himself out of the Romantic movement. The effect is to convert the author of "The Strayed Reveller," and of the Callicles part of "Empedocles," into an intellectual poet, or an academic poet; though he may still indulge himself occasionally in some nostalgic echo of his early self. Arnold criticized the Romantics because they "did not know enough"; in England they had then no proper "current of ideas" to nourish them. Let us say simply, Nobody knows enough; or hardly anybody. Let that be the ample blanket which will cover the Romantics; but it must cover Arnold too; he did not fail to acquaint himself with the German literary critics, but he did not take them in their Kantian phase. When he talks about poetry we know that Kant's firm understanding of it has never reached him, or at least that it has never touched him. The physical death of Keats at an early age is painful to us, but worse, perhaps, is the death of the poet in the living Arnold, and I for one, on the present occasion, will not be consoled by thinking of the value of the public man who emerged from the ruin. I am ready to agree that Arnold was the happiest of all the rhetoricians in our language who have dedicated

themselves to the public cause; that is to say, the most engaging schoolmaster who ever teased and scolded his bad pupils into bothering about
"the best that had been thought and uttered in the world." But Arnold
was not congenitally interested in the radical and decisive thought of
the philosophers.

Concrete universal is a useful term for systematic philosophy. Hegel hit
upon it, but Kant might easily have used it, and I think he would have
explained scrupulously the difference if he should have used it for two
different kinds of occasion. Let us return to the vernacular to clear up
this term, if we think that the critic may feel a little bewildered by the
jargon, but that it allows of being translated into something more commonplace with which he is bound to be familiar. A Universal in Hegel's
favorite sense is any idea in the mind which proposes a little universe,
or organized working combination of parts, where there is a whole and
single effect to be produced, and the heterogeneous parts must perform
their several duties faithfully in order to bring it about. Thus the formula of a chemical reaction; the recipe for a dish; the blue-print of a
machine; or even, to the extent in which it is practicable, Newman's
"idea of a university." It becomes a Concrete Universal when it has
been materialized and is actually working. The Universal by itself is the
design as it exists in the understanding, and if we ask what is the Concrete by itself we must say, I imagine, that it is the objective element in
which the Universal in all parts is to be materialized.

Nevertheless, when we read Kant and Hegel, it must occur to us
that there appear to be two kinds of Concrete Universal which are radically distinct. First, as the easier one by far for us to follow, there is the
Concrete Universal as we find it exemplified a thousand times in the
operations of applied science. We do not there raise a question which
has agitated many recent literary critics when they think of a poem as a
Concrete Universal: whether the Concrete or working Universal real-
izes in precise measure the blue-print, the Universal in the mind, or
whether there is more Concreteness than is actually needed. Science
means to have its Concrete Universal just right, and has it so; and the
crucial factor in getting it right would perhaps be the determination of
the scientist, if he does not find the right parts already existing in the
state of nature, to alter the materials he does find, prepare them, till
they become right; compound them or purify them, grow them or man-
ufacture them, fit them to size and shape, and so on; in the universal as
designed there are specifications which they must meet. So the parts of

the finished Concrete Universal do have their blue-print perfection, perhaps as follows: Not one necessary part missing; nor one unnecessary part showing; nor a part showing which is either excessive or deficient in its action even though some one might be (by the carelessness of the designer, or the stubbornness of the material), and still not fail to do its work after a fashion.

If we insist that engines and scientific processes are never perfect, and as a matter of fact are continually being improved upon, the answer is that at any rate they are perfectible; and in particular that the scientists are free to make any possible use of nature to obtain the specified parts, and are not to be deterred by any sentimental regard for nature.

But it is odd that literary critics should claim, so many of them (they would be banking heavily on Aristotle the ancient critic), that this same rigorous organization obtains within a poem; that the Universal or logical plan of the poem is borne out perfectly in the sensuous detail which puts it into action; and that this Concrete is used up so completely in the service of the Universal that there is no remainder. I believe this notion could not have occurred to either Kant or Hegel, because of one radical consideration which must have seemed to them too obvious to dwell upon.

A poem has a rather wide and indefinite purpose, as compared with a scientific or practical operation. Kant offered a new version of the essential human history behind a poem, and Hegel accepted it without any particular question. Speaking broadly, we are given to saying that applied science attends busily to our explicit appetitive or organic needs, and a scientific Universal is a workable concept seen in that perspective. Now the Universal of the poem is a moral Universal. There is difficulty enough, as we are well aware, when we try to locate the common moral impulse in the animal perspective of human nature, and many humanists follow Kant in saying that it is a "higher" impulse and requires us ultimately to posit a Supreme Being and an eternal Moral Order, if we mean to find a steady perspective in which to regard it objectively. That is, the understanding of common morality takes some metaphysical speculation to accomplish; or, if that is not everywhere accepted, at the least it requires of whatever thinker a far more radical and imaginative psychology and anthropology than existed in Kant's time. All the same, the moral Universal often enough is perfectly explicit; that is, when we are in a situation where we see our duty clearly, and do it without question. That is morality in action, and Kant has treated it firmly in his *Critique of Practical Reason*, second of the big books in his trilogy. In a moral action we treat other persons as ends, not means; and if we propose to confer material benefits upon them we shall have to treat nature as a means and not an end, precisely as the scientists or other practical people do in working their Universals.

And there might conceivably be a poetry aiming simply at our moral improvement, representing the most exemplary behaviors in order to move us to like behaviors. Doubtless there actually is such a poetry; but Kant despises it if he notices it, and Hegel after him. A little less disreputable (less absurdly simple) would be a kind of poetry given to representing moral situations where it is difficult not so much to do one's duty, as to know just which among the several possibilities is the duty one must do; exemplary in its practical judgments, in the nicety of its distinction among the moral ideas. Here we come close to Hegel's weakness and, by the same token, to Hegel's strength. But still this is not poetry as Kant conceives it consistently, or as Hegel conceives it ideally.

The moral Universal whose Concrete embodiment is a poem is different in its technique from that moral Universal, or from any other practical Universal, which exacts from nature its prescribed parts and goes to work with them. Its object in a poem is surely "reflective," but since that is a weak word let us say it is metaphysical, as we must construe it; it is of an elemental importance which we feel profoundly even if we do not easily identify it. But we may start with the technical distinction, which is this: the moral Universal of the poem does not use nature as a means but as an end; it goes out into nature not as a predatory conquerer and despoiler but as an inquirer, to look at nature as nature naturally is, and see what its own reception there may be. The moral Universal takes a journey into nature, so to speak, and the Concrete element is an area of nature existing in its natural conformations as these are given, and discovered, not a Concrete element which it means to ransack for materials which are to be exacted of nature. It is for this reason that it seems idle for literary critics to raise the question whether, within the traversed region of nature, the unpredictable and highly particular detail of the local "manifold of sense" is going to enter precisely and without remainder into the formal Universal. That is too much to expect. We shall be glad to settle for much less than that. The sort of hospitality offered to our moral Universal by the Concrete of the natural world will need to be convincing, if it is to do us any good, but on the other hand the Universal is a mannerly and modest sort of tourist. I shall have to go into that topic by stages; it is not an easy topic; it is

Kant's topic, and he makes it very clear in principle, but does not offer many case-histories for the benefit of the weak laity's understanding of poetry.

Let me clear up my feeling with regard to Hegel, in order to continue the better with Kant. There is a temperamental difference between Kant and Hegel. I think of Hegel as a benign yet extremely aggressive spirit to whom we have to attribute at last an intention as ambitious and simple as the following: to push the moral Universal like any other common Universal out into the objective world, where it is to enforce its presence, and in doing so to make that world over, even if only a little at a time; it will amount finally (in a "power age" like ours) to a reformation of nature, as when it takes the form of substituting modern urban life for the old agrarian life. Up to a certain point the new world will be the natural one, so long as its forms may seem suited to our primitive moral feeling. And poetry will record its happiest moments. But under the speed-up of the Universals, the moral pressure grows so brisk and demanding that the natural world simply becomes humanized, so-cialized, and made over, a pure convenience which in its own right is quite disregarded. There will be an endless evolution in the complexity of human society, in its manners and ideals, its institutions and states, and this is one way to make the best of our curious existence; it is a very muscular way. There will be no poetry at this stage, because no honor can be wasted on nature. Poetry has already had its day, says Hegel. He speaks with a proud candor of the beauty which vanished with the classical arts (when even deities were anthropomorphic and could be sculptured from living models), and of that modern phase which he calls Romantic art, and in which nature appears only as atomized and re-combined into forms which the moral Universal contrives for it. I offer some samplings of his temper:[1]

> In the Romantic, therefore, we have two worlds. The one is the spiritual realm, which is complete in itself—the soul, which finds its reconciliation within itself, and which now for the first time bends around the otherwise rectilinear repetition of genesis, destruction and renewal, to the true circle, to return-into-self, to the genuine Phoenix-life of the spirit. The other is the realm of the external, as such, which, shut out from a firmly cohering unity with the spirit, now becomes a wholly empirical actuality, respecting whose form the soul is unconcerned. . . .
>
> Here . . . has vanished that ideal beauty which [has sought to] replace

1. Translated by W. M. Bryant from *Lectures in Aesthetics* in the recent *Philosophy of Hegel*, edited by Carl J. Friedrich. Mouton Library. (Ransom's note)

its imperfect development by the blooming beauty of existence. Romantic Art no longer has for its aim this free vitality of actual existence, in its infinite calmness and submergence of the soul in the corporeal, nor even this *life*, as such, in its most precise significance, but turns its back upon this highest phase of beauty. Indeed, it interweaves its inner being with the accidentality of external organization, and allows unrestricted play room to the marked characteristics of the ugly. . . .

Thus though the soul is still destined to pass through the world, it no longer pursues merely worldly aims and undertakings. Rather, it has for its essential purpose and endeavor the inner struggle of man within himself, and his reconciliation with God, and brings into representation only personality and its conservation, together with appliances for the accomplishment of this end. . . .[2]

Hegel is already at the point of abandoning nature, for the sake of realizing the modern society. But it is clear to him—he is in that degree still a Kantian—that this means the abandonment of poetry and art. He is the prototype of all "moderns" who work at the organization of society. His position is little different from that of the "social" school of literary critics who hold on to prose fiction as an art while virtually abandoning poetry. My own feeling would be that in spite of the pressures of modern urban society, Hegel's example is not obligatory upon critics and artists; and that it is a very real question whether there is an art or a fiction which has no poetry in it.

If I read Kant correctly, his is the more poetic soul, and the greater piety. I have come to think of him as the most radical and ultimate spokesman for poetry that we have had. We must approve his philosophical background. It was a British philosopher who woke him from his "dogmatic slumber," and conditioned him to the sort of intellectual scruple with which an empirical thinker faces the facts of life and of nature. The immediate consequence was one which lasted a painful while; the grim conviction that we must divide our effort between two sundered worlds, the free moral world which is wholly inner, and the natural world which is external but determinate and mechanical. (We know about the mechanical universe which Newton and his successors had furnished by Kant's time.) But finally he made the epoch-making discovery which seemed to bridge the abyss between them. To put this as simply as I can. There is no specific, singled-out event in nature which the understanding cannot regard as altogether externally caused. But nature when we look hard refuses to be specific and single; it is

2. *The Philosophy of Hegel* (New York, 1953), 364, 361.

everywhere itself, a dense "manifold of sense," a tissue of events whose effects are massive and intricate beyond the grasp of the understanding. It is Kant's monumental achievement to have discerned how it is that nature nevertheless sometimes appears beautiful. These are the times when, preoccupied with our own freedom and purpose, we find that nature likewise seems free and purposive. To be sure, Kant will not allow us to say that nature's purpose is the same as ours, or that we quite understand it; we cannot claim, for example, that it is a moral purpose; but at least it seems sympathetic with our moral purpose. And the happiest consequences follow. The human kingdom and the natural kingdom appear like free and harmonious powers, collaborating with each other in dignity and peace; and in the sequel the poetic imagination is able to set up memorials of art which bear witness to their concord. Or if we require a bourgeois figure: we do not have to feel still that the natural world is our alien habitation, for now it is our home. Or it is "our element." So it is not as if we have been deposited in a world in which we could not live with dignity unless we should build us a city and immure ourselves in a society.

Kant cites readily an instance or so of natural beauty. In a garden the foliage or the blossoms of the plants will answer insofar as the general profile is concerned to the gardener's geometrical Universal, yet their configuration in its profuse detail is much too intricate, and spontaneous-looking to account for, and implies energies not used up by the Universal. It is as if the plants obeyed the law of their placement only to exhibit their own freedom beneath it the more luxuriantly. We have learned to think that this is just the right condition in which they will manifest their grace, or their beauty. And Kant has supplied the paradigm of natural beauty. (Was there anticipation of this paradigm? Not quite, I think, on philosophical grounds.) Nature seems to have no inclination to reject or even to resent the human Universal, for now obtains the condition of "freedom under the law," and its consequence of beauty. In these or similar terms the paradigm is recited nearly everywhere.

If this is natural beauty, what is poetry? Kant's view is simple, and for all except the new "symbolist" critics who desire for poetry a "creativity" upon which there are to be no limits, it will be adequate: Poetry is the representation of natural beauty. The spectacular faculty of Imagination is its agent. Kant calls it the faculty of presentation, and says it is equivalent in the poet to Genius. The play between the understanding with its moral Universal on the one hand, and on the other hand

Imagination presenting the purposive Concrete of nature, is unpredictable and inexhaustible. Coleridge, at least by the time of the *Biographia Literaria*, made a sort of official English version of Kant's view,
and critics are familiar with it. No statement is more studied than the
sudden and enormous sentence at the bottom of Chapter XIV (in lieu of
a great deal of promised text) in which the understanding and the
imagination are paired ten times or so; the one which begins: "This
power [Imagination], first put in action by the will and understanding
and retained under their irremissive, though gentle and unnoticed,
control (*laxis effertur habenis*) reveals itself in the balance or reconciliation of opposite or discordant qualities. . . ." But I do not think it
can be said that Coleridge explains the purpose of the pairings. The understanding is possessed by its own universal and lacks language to
utter it; the imagination supplies it, in fact over-supplies it, with a natural or metaphorical expression.

Kant hammered many times on the right way to construe the complex
experience of beauty. He did not develop all the implications, nor provide systematic illustration. I will have to quote a small English poem
which makes nature purposive with an almost excessive clarity, and indeed carries a tag of identification so pointed as to be embarrassing:

> The year's at the spring
> And day's at the morn;
> Morning's at seven;
> The hill-side's dew-pearled;
> The lark's on the wing;
> The snail's on the thorn:
> God's in his heaven—
> All's right with the world.

Little Pippa sings this song in passing, and a pair of guilty lovers recall
their lost innocence and take to quarreling, like Adam and Eve after
their Fall. Pippa's Universal is a feeling of joy, intense but diffused over
every act and thought. (She is innocent, and this is her holiday from
the silk mills.) She spends three lines dating the occasion very precisely, as Wordsworth might have identified his moment of illumination
by way of his note-book, or even in the poem itself. Then come three
details which constitute the Concrete: the hillside, the lark, the snail. A
poem cannot and need not list all the details of the "manifold," only
enough, and in variety startling enough, to make a fair sampling. We
are given to understand that everything is joyful like Pippa, that all na-

ture is animated in the morning light. And that would be the poem;
except that she must conclude by putting in her theological Universal,
in which she has been well instructed: the world rejoices because
Pippa's God is now its God too, and he is in his heaven ordering all.

Kant would not have approved her tag. He was solicitous that the
flowering of nature should not be subjected to the moral and theological Universals; for it could easily be that these are peculiar to the human understanding. It might be self-deception if we had wanted to discover that nature was moral and then proceeded to discover it. The
nature-lover who studies actual nature, and the poet who imagines nature, must be on their guard against this possibility. The veteran critics
of poetry today need no prompting to be on their guard.

Here is a passage in which the poet does not impose human responsibility upon nature quite so complacently. Shakespeare lived before the
Romantics built up their great volume of business with nature, and in
Cymbeline we observe his royal boys (who have been reared in the lap
of nature, housed in a cave) as they stand by the grave of Fidele and
improvise a funeral service. One of them says:

> With fairest flowers
> While summer lasts and I live here, Fidele,
> I'll sweeten thy sad grave; thou shalt not lack
> The flower that's like thy face, pale primrose, nor
> The azured harebell, like thy veins, no, nor
> The leaf of eglantine, whom not to slander,
> Outsweetened not thy breath: the ruddock would,
> With charitable bill,—O bill! sore-shaming
> Those rich-left heirs, that let their fathers lie
> Without a monument,—bring thee all this;
> Yea, and furred moss besides, when flowers are none,
> To winter-ground thy corse.[3]

This is so handsome that we think, and perhaps we are not wrong, that
Shakespeare has lent his own feeling to it. The flowers are gathered by
human hands, and they resemble Fidele only in exterior features, not
spiritually. But the speaker adds that if he were not bringing them, the
red-breast (or ruddock) would; which might be crucial except that this
sort of thing may be according to the folklore of red-breasts. (I find a
small evidence in the new *Standard Dictionary of Folklore*.) It is an
enticing idea all the same, for the poet goes on into an aside over the

3. *Cymbeline*, Act IV, Sc. ii, 219–28.

bird's "charitable bill" and offers the apostrophe beginning "O bill!" It is a mawkish moment of danger. But the other prince, the practical younger one, saves the situation when he scolds his brother for the speech:

> Prithee, have done,
> And do not play in wench-like words with that
> Which is so serious.[4]

And Shakespeare has put up his guard, his decent Kantian reservation.

It would be wrong to give the impression that in a poem, necessarily, the intellectual Universal has always disappeared from sight and now exists only in the Concrete. It is my impression that as often as not a poem will recite its two versions, side by side. Thus Portia, commending mercy, explains that mercy does not come by compulsion but spontaneously or by grace: its quality is "not strained," or, as we would say, "unconstrained." That is the moral Universal. Then comes the poetic consummation. As if this abstract talk of the Universal might not be quite intelligible, she adds, "It droppeth as the gentle rain from heaven / Upon the place beneath." And in the following passage the poet Yeats, who likes to show the strain of his intellectual ideas, looks hard at his metaphor or Concrete before he accepts it for his Universal:

> Some moralist or mythological poet
> Compares the solitary soul to a swan,
> I am satisfied with that,
> Satisfied if a troubled mirror show it,
> Before that brief gleam of its life be gone,
> An image of its state:
> The wings half spread for flight,
> The breast thrust out in pride,
> Whether to play or to ride
> Those winds that clamor of approaching night.[5]

But it may be quite otherwise. By a *tour de force* which for more reasons than one we are apt to call "metaphysical," the Universal of a poem may be wholly translated into a natural image, or a series of them, and never expressed in the abstract language of the understanding at all; as in that Shakespearian sonnet which begins the first of three images with "That time of year thou mayst in me behold."

Probably it is normal, when the Universal receives a metaphorical or

4. *Cymbeline*, Act IV, Sc. ii, 229–31.
5. "Nineteen Hundred and Nineteen."

natural image, for the Universal to come first; tenor precedes vehicle, as we say it today. But we must observe that this order may be reversed. A natural object or conformation strikes our attention because it seems significant of more than mechanical effect, and we proceed to equate it metaphorically with the appropriate human Universal. In this case we start with nature and humanize it; in the other case we started with the human Universal and naturalized it. How, for example, shall the modern poet explain his depression over the late evening that has not even the dignity of a sunset sky? It is "spread out against the sky / Like a patient etherized upon a table"; as if it might not survive the operation. Kant himself observes that the poem may begin at either end of the process. He quotes "a certain poet" observing the sunrise and then moralizing it:

> The sun arose
> As calm from virtue springs.

Here the observer was not satisfied with noting for the calendar, or the meteorological record, the fact that the sun rose clear, but elected to find, in Kant's words, that it "diffuses in the mind a multitude of sublime and restful feelings and a boundless prospect of a joyful future, to which no expression measured by a definite concept [i.e., keeping to the tenor] completely attains."

Marvell combines with his sophistication or worldliness an extravagant love of gardens and nature. He often begins a metaphor with a natural object, and sometimes humanizes it almost absurdly. But his guard is up, too, and his tone is therefore apt to be waggish. Thus his Mower addresses the Glowworms in one poem:

> Ye living lamps, by whose dear light
> The nightingale does sit so late,
> And studying all the summer night
> Her matchless songs does meditate;
>
> Ye country comets, that portend
> No war nor prince's funeral,
> Shining unto no higher end
> Than to presage the grass's fall. . . .

His famous "Garden" poem has burlesque moments along with its proper beauties; he pretends to picture the Garden as his preferred and adequate element, supplying him with natural satisfactions which are of the same kind as those he could have had in the human society:

No white nor red was ever seen
So amorous as this lovely green.
Fond lovers, cruel as their flame,
Cut in these trees their mistress' name:
Little, alas, they know, or heed,
How far these beauties hers exceed!
Fair trees, wheresoe'er your barks I wound
No name shall but your own be found.

And he is quite direct and not metaphorical in "Bermudas" where the colonists sing of the kindness of the natural element with which God has provided them:

He gave us this eternal spring,
Which here enamels everything;
And sends the fowls to us in care,
On daily visits through the air.
He hangs in shades the orange bright,
Like golden lamps in a green night.
And does in the pomgranates close
Jewels more rich than Ormus shows.
He makes the figs our mouths to meet;
And throws the melons at our feet.
But apples plants of such a price,
No tree could ever bear them twice.
With cedars, chosen by his hand,
From Lebanon, he stores the land,
And makes the hollow seas that roar,
Proclaim the ambergris on shore.
He cast (of which we rather boast)
The gospel's pearl upon our coast.
And in these rocks for us did frame
A temple, where to sound his name.

The category for the Universal here would be that of literal religious faith. The purpose of nature is identified completely with the purposes of Providence; and this naïveté is justified dramatically, since the pious colonists are made to row their boat to the beat of the hymn, but it does not square with the canon.

Wallace Stevens has written a poem expressly under the title of "The Motive for Metaphor," and Kant, I think, would have accepted it as a stylized but competent variation upon his own view:

You like it under the trees in autumn,
Because everything is half dead.
The Wind moves like a cripple among the leaves
And repeats words without meaning.

In the same way, you were happy in spring,
With the half colors of quarter-things,
The slightly brighter sky, the melting clouds,
The single bird, the obscure moon—

The obscure moon lighting an obscure world
Of things that would never be quite expressed,
Where you yourself were never quite yourself
And did not want nor have to be.

Desiring the exhilaration of changes:
The motive for metaphor, shrinking from
The weight of primary noon,
The A B C of being,

The ruddy temper, the hammer
Of red and blue, the hard sound—
Steel against intimation—the sharp flash,
The vital, arrogant, fatal, dominant X.

That is to say, I think, something like the following. You like metaphor
in the autumn, because you cannot express yourself, except to say that
the wind cannot express itself, either. You like it in the spring, because
instead of trying to express what you feel then, you can speak of how
the obscure moon lights an obscure world. You like it because it is ex-
hilarating, and alternative to the dreary searching of your own mind for
the meaning of your state. [There must be many a moral Universal
seeking its poetry though it is no better than a moral feeling; so much
of the moral life turns on feeling, and on half-successful reflection, and
can scarcely ever be satisfied except with a poetic expression or its
homely equivalent.] The moral Universal is intolerably harsh and simple, when you phrase it, not equal to what you want it to mean, and in
fact it is the "vital, arrogant, fatal, dominant X"; it is inexpressive, like
the sign of an unknown quantity. So much more visible, more audible,
more tangible, better focussed for observation, are the behaviors of nature which the poet can draw upon because they are expressive. This
poem makes an important remark in a very casual manner, and many
of us will already possess a notion, as I imagine, that no poet has written more verse about the understanding of poetry than Stevens has
done, unless it was Wordsworth. If it had not been Richard Blackmur

who wrote recently about Stevens as a poet not only dandiacal but un-philosophical, I should have boggled at both ascriptions, and thought that Blackmur's own guard was down, most unaccountably.[6] But it *was* Blackmur, and Blackmur as a critic is so far from having an impediment in his speech that he excels other critics in the plenitude of his contexts, so that I dare say there are intimations in the one on Stevens which amount to proper qualifications; or amount partly to them.

The fullest quotation of verse in Kant's own writing seems to be the one from the poem by Frederick the Great written in French: "Sur les vaines terreurs de la mort et les frayeurs d'une autre vie." Although Kant translated the verse into German for his own text, our English editor and translator supplies it in the original language:

> Oui, finissons sans trouble et mourons sans regrets,
> En laissant l'univers comblé de nos bienfaits.
> Ainsi l'astre du jour au bout de sa carrière
> Répand sur l'horizon une douce lumière;
> Et les derniers rayons qu'il darde dans les airs,
> Sont les derniers soupirs qu'il donne à l'univers.[7]

The King at the end of his full life is metaphorically represented by the sun taking a last look around upon the world he has illuminated before he goes down. That is all, but the sun's moment is a rich one. Kant comments that here

> the great King . . . quickens his rational Idea of a cosmopolitan disposition at the end of life by an attribute which the Imagination (in remembering all the pleasures of a beautiful summer day that are recalled at its close by a serene evening) associates with that representation, and which excites a number of sensations and secondary representations for which no expression is found.

No expression is found in the tenor for the sensations and secondary representations, which therefore are assigned to the vehicle to express. Is it that no expression *can* be found in the tenor, that the language of feeling is too dumb, too poor, to allow of that? I take it so. And if it is so, then, Kant in effect is saying precisely what Mr. Cleanth Brooks as a modern critic has been saying to his own public over and over: that "there is no other way" for language to express what it wants to express

6. R. P. Blackmur, "The Substance That Prevails," *Kenyon Review*, XVII (Winter, 1955), 94–110.

7. *Kant's Critique of Pure Reason*, translated and edited by J. H. Bernard. Second edition. (London, 1914), p. 200. (Ransom's note)

without having recourse to metaphor; without going to the concrete of nature for its analogy. I cannot think that Kant would have repudiated his implication, but that he would have stated it with his usual boldness—if he could have foreseen the difficult passages, and the *impasses*, which the subsequent course of literary criticism would encounter, and the need of developing his own principles to cover many possibilities.

The understanding of poetry which I have attributed to Kant in these notes is less than the whole of that philosopher's deliverance; but I think I have indicated the burden of it. I have ventured to furnish him with a word which perhaps will describe in our time, and for our critics, the way of the imagination in giving objective or Concrete existence to the homeless moral Universal. The word is metaphor, and Kant makes no particular use of it. He has not supplied poetic studies detailed enough, or in number enough, to have fixed on it for his regular word. But it would seem a decisive word for his understanding of poetry; it gives us the sense of nature accepting the Universal readily into its infinite system, and lending to it what metaphysical sanction is possible.

Many critics of our time, starting let us say with Richards and coming on now at least to Professor Wimsatt, have uttered bold ideas about metaphor, and I have not gone far beyond some of them. To say "metaphor" tirelessly, with brutal repetition, is one militant way of defending nature as the element to which the Universal is referred, and therefore the element to which poetry has to look. I think the defenders of poetry would not mind saying that they are not prepared to abandon nature, because that would be the abandonment of poetry; which, when they have weighed it, would be a serious abridgment of the range of human experience. The alternative to sticking by nature and poetry is to follow Hegel's view that the moderns are now so far advanced with their perfectly specific and practicable Universals, their faith in these is so sure, and the conduct of them fulfills so completely the range of our demands, that nothing remains for the human spirit but to put all this strength into society and politics. My critics are scarcely going to agree with that.

But critics are notoriously impressionistic, as perhaps it is their business to be; and every day I have a new sense of the wide spread of that Hegelian type of modernity. I can liken myself modestly to Arnold in the respect that, though I am not an inspector of schools, I have done a long turn as a schoolmaster of poetry, and even acquired some professional anecdotes of my own. The latest one is not ten days old. A former pupil, after spending several years in business employment, came to me to say that he wished now to go on to a graduate school for further studies in literature; and to ask if I might tell him at what university he might find teachers whose interest was concentrated upon modern fiction, therefore upon the social sensibility. As for the teachers of poetry, who abound in the universities, he explained that in his business life he had been so impressed with his social responsibility that he could no longer bear to read works in that old-fashioned art. And though I was shocked by his apostasy, I was not so shocked but that I was able with a straight face to tell him what he wanted to know, so far as my information permitted. I assured him with all sincerity that the masters of morality nowadays were indeed the sociologists, who understood the moral pressures of modern society, and that among the ablest sociologists, and even among the most learned sociologists, were many literary critics whose professional occupation was with fiction.

I have also had experiences showing how a certain practical kind of religiosity, like practical morality when it possesses us, is capable of getting in between the soul and its reception of poetry and literature. This is when the soul is a timid soul and prefers the security of dogma to the dreadful facts of life and the pusillanimous dialect by which poetry deals with them. But I do not wish to recite these experiences; they are not pretty stories and even the humor of them is painful. I remark that the poet's theology is metaphorical, and the poet knows it is metaphorical, and insists like Keats in holding by a rule of Negative Capability,—which is not a Kantian phrase, but sounds like one, and might have been one if Kant, once more, had elaborated his views further than he did. By this rule a theological representation is in terms of our understanding of this world, and though it is hopeful it is far from determining about any other world. And if people are young enough and adventurous enough to go to college, they ought not to cheat themselves of those beautiful yet mortal representations offered them in literature.

To go only a little further. What is, characteristically, the religious faith of a poet? Or, if strictly speaking he has nothing quite orthodox to show under that head, what is the sort of faith which he does have? The faith of Kant the philosopher was formed on intellectual grounds, it was other-worldly yet of extreme Protestant severity, quite declining to let the imagination of this world give it a form. I should say that we might call the poet's piety a "natural" piety, his gift being for finding the natural world not merely mechanical but hospitable to the moral Universals. In literature this piety is recorded perhaps in that later mood of Wordsworth's, arrived at during the years between the other-worldly opening of the "Ode on Imitations of Immortality" and its more modest and slightly sad conclusion. But, regardless of what might have been Kant's professional feelings, I would like to borrow here from another philosopher. The poet's faith, I should say, is that this is "the best of all possible worlds"; inasmuch as it is not possible for imagination to acquaint us with any other world. It is a horrid as well as a beautiful world, but without the horror we should never focus the beauty; without death there would be no relish for life; without danger, no courage; without savagery, no gentleness; and without the background of our frequent ignominy, no human dignity and pride. (These are excellent and rather Hegelian commonplaces.) Wordsworth at the beginning of his Ode advanced the ancient doctrine of metempsychosis, without remarking that there is provided traditionally, betwixt the residence of the soul in one world and its residence in another world, a Lethean bath to bring forgetfulness of that nature which the soul has just lived with; in order that it may adapt to whatever nature may be next in order.

Most of Kant's understanding of poetry—if we except the middle section of the work which is concerned with the sublime—is devoted to that high moment in which we suddenly perceive what we may call the Epiphany of Beauty. It uses up the whole of a poetry, with the Universals of the mind deploying against the natural metaphors, and then our recognition of the consequence, to create this show. Kant's understanding therefore chooses to regard poetry as a single and powerful though complicated action; and that is the kind of view which is deeply coveted by the modern critics. It is a complete view—except for one reservation which is anticlimactic, and a little embarrassing, and after all not exactly trifling.

Kant's description is of a poetic phrase, or passage, or of a short poem: it is the description of a lyrical effect—if we can divorce that term from the idea of music, which does not come under Kant's notice as essential—or of a moment of illumination; it is the soul of poetry caught briefly, but completely and characteristically.

And yet—what are we to say about the long poems? about philosophical poems, or epics, or poetic narratives, or poetic dramas? It cannot often be that the action focusses upon a single metaphorical or metaphysical moment. The chances are, overwhelmingly, that the moral Universal in such cases is a considerable and organized sequence of intellectual ideas, or of historical events, embodied for action and working themselves out; or, it is just possible, not clearly embodied, and only talking themselves out; and the best we can hope for, as Kantians, is that there are many happy metaphorical transformations, or little poetries, in the course of the poem, and perhaps a conclusion suited to the faith of a poet. This order of poetry will be much more put together, or synthetic, than the lyric, and more capable, indeed more demanding, of being separated by analysis into its primary parts. A different thing.

And a different story for critics, though not altogether. With poetry of this sort I have sometimes been at pains to defend the right of the intellectuals (the moralists or religionists) to isolate the ideas and discuss them on their intellectual merits; inasmuch as the ideas are surely in the poetry; and ideas demand discussion by intellectuals, the very best intellectuals who will offer. This is a poetry that can be taken apart. And yet if it is really a poetry it cannot be hurt; and Kantians can come back to the whole poetry and see what is poetical about it.

NEW POETS AND OLD MUSES

I HAVE RISKED making a disorderly beginning to this paper, which must be an unpardonable self-indulgence—if it was mistaken on my part to imagine that there is a certain public interest in the strange motions of the mind when it is working in the mode of poetry. There is a particular ghost which had to be laid before I seemed able to begin. No sooner had I adopted my high-flown title with its figure of the Old Muses, and made myself ready to let it work its way with me, than it seemed I had opened the door too wide, to figuration unlimited. Many of this audience will know from experience how the figures of some famous and unusually tuneful poem will begin suddenly to ring in one's head, and to force themselves into one's most oppressive problems as if they belonged there. So suggestible are we as we look for answers to the problems; such free and detachable and obliging busybodies are the poetic figures that form and float in the world of imagination—as if they would come and serve us on whatever occasion if we would let them.

The poem which came to haunt me was E. A. Robinson's "Eros Turannos." I had known it and liked it a long time, but apparently had not fully realized it before. It came all the way from its New England seaboard town, where it had to do with two lovers and their doom, and was so admirably suited to its own occasion that I have been aware of a certain absurdity in trying to adapt it to my very different uses. But did not Mr. Eliot introduce to the modern audience a way of composing a poem by juxtaposing poetic fragments without showing their logical relations; and did he not accustom us to a new use of the epigraph—that placement of a bit of another poet's verse (which might be divergent in style and theme from his verse) just under the title and over the text of his poem, as an item which might throw its light upon what would follow? The Robinson poem is my epigraph, and seems to be a sort of large metaphor or parable to give advance notice of what is coming. The part

This essay is reprinted from Ransom's *American Poetry at Mid-Century* (Washington: Reference Department, Library of Congress, 1958), 1–14. Reprinted by permission of Helen Ransom Forman.

of the poem which kept sounding in my ears was especially the fourth stanza and the sixth or last stanza. The fourth stanza is climactic and goes like this:

> The falling leaf inaugurates
>   The reign of her confusion;
> The pounding wave reverberates
>   The crash of her illusion;
> And home, where passion lived and died,
> Becomes a place where she can hide—
> While all the town and harbor-side
>   Vibrate with her seclusion.

The able students of Eliot have told us to "study the epigraph"; and even more than that, to study the context of the epigraph, the whole passage in which it was embedded; and then, though we may have to repair to the library, the play or book or even the theological system in which it figured. So I will offer a few notes about my epigraph. Earlier in the poem we were given the situation, where the aggressive new man comes to the town, and offers his hand to a lady who is accustomed to the town's old and ceremonious way of life. In spite of herself she has fallen in love with the new man. He imagines he will like the fashion of life as she will have it conducted; she reads his character and knows he is not suitable. Nevertheless she accepts him, and the sequel is ruinous; it is the one told in the stanza I have just read. This is a peculiar poet. He declines to tell the factual detail of his story. He does not employ a narrative style, nor yet a proper dramatic style, either of which would have required him to report the commonplace of the event. One of his unique characteristics is to evade the telling of the story at many crucial points by employing a sort of algebraic x which the reader must solve for himself: "We knew—what we knew." Even the opening stanza of "Eros Turannos" contains some x's, which I will emphasize as I read it:

> She fears him, and will always ask
>   *What fated her* to choose him;
> She meets in his engaging mask
>   *All reasons* to refuse him;
> But *what she meets* and *what she fears*
> Are less than are the downward years
> Drawn slowly from the foamless weirs
>   Of age, were she to lose him.

What he reports in our fourth stanza is the *affect* of the event, as it registers in the woman's feelings, and these we identify sympathetically by the tremendous urgency of the natural metaphors. The language is sharply stylized. It is intended for an accomplished reader, using latinate words to make a mighty rhetorical clang (as latinate words will do if they are sparse, and cunningly placed), and altogether it is in the diction of the universities. Yet it is assimilated successfully to a stanza made of the folk line. I think there may be in our reception of the poem a slightly humorous but still delicious satisfaction over what an extraordinary thing has been attempted in that way, and pretty well carried off. Metrically the stanza is too elaborate for ballad, or even for Mother Goose, but I think we are likely to find it set to full music on certain pages of the hymnbook, if we are churchgoers.

The sixth and final stanza is the poet's epilogue upon the whole unhappy affair and his part in it:

> Meanwhile, we do no harm; for they
>   Who with a god have striven,
> Not hearing much of what we say,
>   Take what the god has given;
> Though like waves breaking it may be,
> Or like a changed familiar tree,
> Or like a stairway to the sea
>   Where down the blind are driven.[1]

Its author, the poet, is an anonymous citizen of the town, one of its "vibrators" whose sensibility is ravaged by the event; he is a good judge of such matters, and records his observations both in wise maxims like a Greek chorus, and in the heroic natural images. He has a right to his judgment, because the event is of public importance. And he does no harm, whether by advising against it in the first place, or by talking about it afterwards, because it was always the god who would determine it.

And now I must try to show why this poem came into my mind as if it had a bearing upon my own argument. I think I can do it. The new man stands for the new poet, and he addresses his suit of course not to the lady of the old town but to the Old Muses of my title. When they do not reject him they, like himself, are destroyed. But this is awkward for

1. The 24 foregoing lines from the *Collected Poems* of Edwin Arlington Robinson (Copyright 1935, 1937, 1946, by the Macmillan Company) are reprinted by courtesy of the publisher. (Ransom's note)

immortal Muses; and what is a Muse anyway? In prose we want to deal with such reality as we can feel sure of, and therefore we must break out of the whole clutter of the Greek mythology, which itself provides us only with figures and parables. The Muses, it will occur to us at once, might translate into the Spirit of Poetry; but this is not much better. Let them stand for whatever public authority there really is who accepts or rejects the new poet; the wise public censor if there could be such an officer; and failing that, the town and harbor-side, the corporate community of poetry-lovers who are anonymous citizens; perhaps including occasional professional critics, and editors. It is they whom the new poet solicits, and against their accepting him too easily comes the warning of my epigraph against a too-aggressive kind of new man. If the poetic community accepts him hastily and then he proves unworthy, both they and he are brought to public shame.

But most of all, surely, I felt the power of the god, the *deus ex machina* of the poem, as necessary to my argument. In the poem he is Eros Turannos, the god who decrees that the man and the woman shall fall in love. For my argument he is a mode of Necessity imposing itself at the right time upon the human experience; he is one of those Universals which bind the intricately constituted mind of man. In the terms offered by Immanuel Kant, which are the best for me though I choose to understand them rather too simply and to recite them too rapidly to suit a strict Kantian, the god is the Subjective Universal of Poetry; or, better as I think, the Poetic Category of the Mind, imposing the poetic mode of experience upon us when we have come into the need of it, and the capacity for it. Poetry is an advanced pattern of public behavior in the series or hierarchy of patterns. I should imagine that this is quite according to the understanding of the anthropologist. The anthropologist is the analyst and historian who identifies the essential cultural forms of a society on the assumption that man is the measure of all things. That is a very modern sort of assumption, we are apt to think; and evidently Kant is a modern philosopher with an anthropological habit of mind, provided we may attribute to anthropology the fullest and most elevated humanism. The essential cultural forms would be those which represent the different powers of the mind engaging in common experience; and a form remains essential or categorical even though, as the anthropologist becomes comparative and goes from race to race and from age to age, its embodiments will not all turn out to be just alike. As an *a priori* mode of the mind, poetry, along with the other fine arts, is one of the categories or grand divisions of ultimate experience. The categories which are its peers would be morality and theology. Perhaps morality and theology precede it in development, in that order. Logically prior to these categories, of course, are the mathematical categories of time and space which order the data of the senses, and then the twelve so-called categories of the understanding which make up the grammar or logic of language; it is these which permit consecutive or rational discourse about the sense data, and achieve finally the great structure of natural science itself. These categories do not fail to enter into the discourse of morality and religion and art, and to keep them rational and economical, as they must be if they would be practicable behaviors and not morbid or crazy behaviors. By these (the fundamental and prior categories) we maintain physical life and material welfare; by those (the later and more metaphysical categories) we advance to the good society and to religion and beauty. Indeed, the latter ones might be said, as indeed in Germany and Italy they are said, to be the categories of the spirit, by comparison with the earlier ones which would be the categories of the animal man. But the comparison of course would not be quite accurate; for though the later ones do not condition the earlier ones (a healthy physical man is not necessarily a lover of poetry), yet the earlier ones do condition the later ones (a lover of poetry is still obligated not to sacrifice his animal necessities nor his discreet provision for them).

The florid recital of the categories which I have just offered may have had a certain air of making fanfare. That was very nearly the intention. I hope you will take my anthropologist seriously, as he would take himself, and as he would take the object of which he treats. Poetry as an art by itself, or at any rate poetry as augmented by the sister arts, makes up a massive and distinct though fluid area of the human culture, and the anthropologist as I conceive him will admit it readily. He will honor it in the matter-of-fact respect which he is prepared to offer to its masterpieces; and perhaps he will respect at least equally the sheer bulk of its production, and the steady essential character it maintains at all levels and grades in a mixed society. It seems to me advisable to record our conviction that the bulk of our working poetry at any time is much larger than that authorized by the scholars of the universities or by the editors of *avant-garde* reviews. The anthropologist will scarcely confine his survey to the culture of an élite class. Yet it is good if he is torn between his respect for the idea of poetry as a functional pattern of the total culture and his own love for the showpieces which it achieves in its highest development. If we are lovers of poetry we are familiar with this conflict in ourselves. It is not more painful than it is comfortable to live with. The anthropologist, if he exists as I have described him, or we ourselves if we are amateur statesmen as well as addicts to poetry, obtains at least as much sense of dignity from its universality as from its choice and almost miraculous exhibits. Poetry is not a narrow accomplishment, nor a private one. We may well venture occasionally to apprise the new poets of the dignity of their calling as public functionaries.

Matthew Arnold was confident about the immensity of the future of poetry. But surely crises arise in its history. At this particular time it is not easy to say what the new poets are worth. But at least it can be said that there is immensity in their numbers; which only makes it harder to assess their quality. They number many thousands; they cannot be counted. There is a sense in which it may be properly said, as we hear it said, that there are more writers of verse than there are readers. In this sense: there are more new poets whose intentions are serious, and have to do with the creation of masterpieces, than there are readers who care to look seriously into their work. And this would be true even with respect to their published work, and aside from their mere manuscripts. The late Christopher Morley, author of many pleasantries, once remarked how, leaning over the brink of the Grand Canyon, he let fall a rose-leaf and listened for the reverberation of its landing; and before this terrific event found time to liken himself to the new poet waiting for the applause to greet his first book of poems.[2]

The editors of *Poetry*, at Chicago, the most official organ of contemporary poetry in this country, have stated in print that they receive annually 50,000 manuscripts of verse. Other editors see less verse than those editors, though they are scarcely greater perfectionists or more exacting in their requirements. If they do not make 50,000 judgments a year, the number is still in the thousands, and I believe they have a harrowing time of it. The new poets are often aggressive in the claims with which they offer their poems, or the objections they make to the editor's judgment when it is given. This is not a consideration to hold against them. They are in their duty, and they mean business. The editor is perhaps as close as anybody to actually arriving at the status of literary anthropologist; he has to idealize this scientist, who seems as yet to have scarcely appeared in the eminent profession of anthropology

2. Christopher Morley (1890–1957), novelist, poet, essayist, and influential columnist for *Saturday Review of Literature*.

as we observe it; the editor has to enact him, though remotely. Editors regard poetry as an official public function, or an estate, or perhaps a cult, which needs its neophytes or apprentices. Many offer for this cult, where few are chosen. But it is honorable to offer, and what is more, it is compulsive to offer, when the imperative of the behavior called poetry calls to the imaginative young man (or woman) who thinks his talent is verbal, and sufficient. Of course the anthropologist is by the way an ecologist, and as ecologist he is used to the consideration that Nature, as if to insure the survival of a species, creates its members with wasteful profusion; as for example the fertile seeds which more likely than not will fall in the wrong places and never take root, or take root but never find nourishment enough to survive; or the young of the animal kingdom who, because the species is already numerous beyond the prospects of subsistence, are exposed to death as soon as they have come to birth. Happily the ecologist takes the long view which immunizes him from being too much harrowed. And after all he remembers that poets who fail do not thereby lose their lives, nor are they therefore put to death. To an editor it does not seem likely that new poets who once have set themselves to be poets on the high sophisticated level— the level at which they approach the editor—will ever be good poets at the popular levels. But they may enter other vocations, even advanced and honored public vocations; as for example the teaching profession, where they may instruct the readers of poetry, perhaps adverting sometimes to the failures as well as the successes of this art.

Between the editor and the new poet correspondence is apt to arise; the editor has returned the manuscript, with some mention of the seeming flaws in the poem, and presently he finds himself reciting certain homely rules or maxims for the insistent poet's attention. He is asking the poet to observe that "this is the way it is done by experienced poets." And, for example, he says that the meters are ragged; or that the argument is not clear. Or there are places where the language is "not figurative enough," or the figures are not striking enough, and he may remind the poet of Doctor Johnson's observation that a simile, or metaphor, to be successful must not only "illustrate" but "ennoble." On the contrary, the figures may be too extravagant and far-fetched. Maxims are rules of procedure, as they have developed and become standard in the history of poetry. The content of the *Ars Poetica* is largely maxims, and the content of the *Essay on Criticism* is largely maxims.[3] Many a

3. Horace, *Ars Poetica*; Alexander Pope, *An Essay on Criticism*.

good critic, like George Saintsbury, has managed very well with maxims for the staple of his critical apparatus.[4] Many of the best poets,
though surely not very many, have composed with them.

Coleridge at his best had piercing philosophical insights, but a good
half of the time he is not at his best, by a defect of temperament, or
perhaps of physical constitution. The revival of Coleridge in our time
has been concerned principally, I think, with what I take to be a rule of
practice, a maxim; but perhaps the largest and most compound maxim
that could be recommended to the attention of new poets. This is the
famous rule that the imagination of the poet must still be under the
control or censorship of right reason. The two powers must work together in harmony, and for reasons so obvious, at the maxim level, as
not to need to be recited; because without rational purpose and order
the unfettered imagination will not be consecutive, and people will not
care to follow it; and because the poem of reason from which imagination is absent becomes a plain morality, or a theological dogma, and is
not art at all. This is not good enough for my anthropologist, but it goes
a long way, and has been useful. (It is the maxim in which the young
poets are particularly instructed at college, but it does not necessarily
persuade the aggressive new poet who thinks it is time for a new poetry
and a new maxim.)

The word for imagination at the universities nowadays is sensibility.
An editor comes upon many new poets of fine sensibility, and verbal
power quite equal to reporting it handsomely, perhaps just as nicely as
the eminent poets of our time do it. We read the new poet with technical admiration, from line to line, and image to image. But presently the
poem seems to be getting nowhere, and we cannot continue. Sensibility is doing beautifully here, we say, but what a dangling or undirected sensibility! If only the well-turned phrases could touch and
move the massive affective economy! Mr. Eliot would have put it this
way: If only the little feelings which respond to the details could be incidental to the registration of some grand emotion or passion! But to
keep within my own frame of reference: If only sensibility had attached
itself somehow to a moral situation; or even to a systematic theology.
We can surely say now that in our time there has been so much experiment with the educated yet aimless sensibility that we have found its
limit by going beyond it to the point of no return. Your speaker is him-

4. George Saintsbury (1845–1933), British literary critic best remembered for his
Short History of English Literature (1898).

self an editor, as you will have suspected, and his impression of talented sensibility working without direction is a frequent one. There are times when he wonders if he might not have waked up the new poet by saying severely: You are lacking in character, for you register no causes, passions, prejudices, nor obsessions; very possibly the failure in your development is past remedy now, because to take the remedy you would have to change your life. But that might not necessarily be quite true, and any exaggeration in the charge would not be decent. If we were editing a popular journal of poetry, I have no doubt the charge would be, as a rule, quite the obverse of this one. We might want to say: Your verse indicates a very sound morality, but what you need is a sensibility; you are a moralist rather than a poet.

Before leaving the topic of the undirected sensibility, I have one quick digression to make, because I think its pertinence will have occurred surely to some members of my audience. There is the famous case of the Symbolists, in France. My remark cannot be that of a master at the reading of the French language. But surely the Symbolists were provided with an astonishing proficiency in what we may call the pure poetic sensibility, of the kind which notes in the physical setting of the action, as for example in the landscape of the physical world, and the fauna and the flora, those configurations and motions which are dramatic in the human sense of the drama. For its implement they cultivated probably the most elevated poetic language in Western history; provided we mean by poetic the language which refuses always to lapse into a rhetorical resonance with a vague meaning, but keeps the edge of its detail very sharp. There are poems by Mallarmé, Rimbaud, and Valéry, where the sensibility works beautifully in every turn of phrase, in every achieved image; yet to our infinite regret seems at the end to have gone nowhere and to have no consequence. These are poets' poets, who show the extreme refinements of sensibility. But it would be rather beyond the reach of dull moralizing poets to ponder them; and their best service would be to just those new poets of considerable sensibility who are bent on perfecting it, but yet are well instructed in the maxim about the presidency of reason.

It might be said that the occasion of a poem is a *moral* situation. But immediately it must be added as a correction that the occasion of a poem is a moral *situation*. The moral is never to be emphasized as if the poem existed just for its sake, but must stay implicit in the situation. And that is rather curious. We may recite our maxim to that effect without having the faintest conscious idea of the advantage of making the moral and the situation go their way together. It sounds like a primitive wisdom, and primitive wisdom does not explain itself; or like Oriental wisdom, and we fancy that Oriental means oblique and occult. Mr. Eliot told us that about the time of the English Restoration there was a dissociation of sensibility from thinking, so that later poets have had to feel and think by turns, when they should have been combining both in one unified experience. But we still ask: Why is it better to have them together, in a single experience; and finally we ask: What is the intention of poetry anyway, that it should not covet a perfect logical clarity as prose does, but clutter its discourse incessantly with figures? So we must leave the area of the maxims, if we would find an answer to those questions. We must return to the idea of the literary anthropologist, who not only regards the distinctive forms of experience as functional, but can tell what their functions are, and how they are carried out. Again, however, we must improvise this literary anthropologist, who may not yet actually exist; but who if he did exist might be the top economist among the senior economists in the public service.

We are not entirely helpless. For there is the philosopher Kant, to whom I have attributed an anthropological cast of mind, and who was capable of probing very deeply into the economy of the spirit. And there is William Wordsworth, who is not nearly so articulate, nor so consistent, but who had a passion for exploring the depths of his poetic consciousness.

If I read Kant correctly, he has suffered a strange neglect so far as concerns that third of the famous *critiques*, the *Critique of Judgment*; I think I have never seen mention of the answer he provides for our question. But of course it is the fact that Kant was so much the pioneer in this field that his account, though repetitive, is not elaborated with much illustration, and his very technical language is exasperating.

Let us make a fresh start, at a place remote from this discussion up to here, but familiar to the anthropologist. Suppose the purpose of the poem is to heal the appalling loneliness that human creatures suffer, especially when they are good creatures who act with scrupulous justice toward their fellow creatures, and even with love and charity. (Ordinarily the moral of the situation is commonplace, and the poet is a man of complete moral sense, addressing himself to his peers.) They are isolated, and not only from men and women who do not share their moral sentiments, but even more irreparably from the physical and non-human world in which all things seem to move relentlessly on their mechanical or vegetative or animal ways. In such a world they do not feel at home. But now, in the poem, this world figures as the setting or stage within which the human characters are placed. The action of the human agents is in intimate association with the stage properties, so to speak; such as a view, or birds and beasts, or inanimate objects like winds, waters, stones, trees, lights and shadows. And what happens is, simply, that the stage properties soon begin to figure in the poem as if they were moral agents too. They are not moral strictly, or at least we cannot know that they are, as Kant was careful to say; but they seem wonderfully understanding; they seem "expressive," and what they express seems to be their sympathy with the moral actions and speeches of the principals. John Ruskin is the observer who has made the fullest report on the expressiveness of natural objects, though he would not allow it to seem immoderate past the bounds of credulity, and had a stern eye for the gross representations of it by poets whom he charges with a "pathetic" (or sympathetic) fallacy. Shakespeare is perhaps still the poet who used it most easily and spontaneously in his verse. The consequence is that the poet and his readers receive suddenly a wonderful epiphany, the vision of a "society" in which nature seems to associate herself with the lonely moralists, and no longer to be hostile or indifferent. It is as if the moral order embraced and governed the whole world; at least for the time being. I should think that is a kind of cosmic or religious experience, though not the dogmatic or theological one in which persons see marvelous prospects opening to them as the result of a sustained and difficult act of faith. Both experiences would suffer from being identified with each other. We do not ordinarily name the experience as either a religious experience, or a moral experience, but as a poetic or artistic experience, and the form of its happiness is the entrancing and massive satisfaction called beauty.

We may well believe that Wordsworth will always rate as having been the most determined Nature-poet in the history of literature. For some five or six years he attached himself to a mystical dogma which accounted miraculously for the claim Nature made upon his affections. He declared that the deity by special providence entered into the particular natural scene, and the impression the poet took of it was that of a Presence, or a Voice, which manifested itself to him for his instruction, or his comfort; it calmed his spirits or aroused them, according to his need. Nature taught him more than books by human hands. But Wordsworth could not maintain his rapturous belief; it made Nature too aggressive to be quite natural; so that finally Nature with its Voices and Presences became simply—common nature, to which after a period of disillusionment he resorted as habitually as ever, not as to a God but as to a kind foster-mother or nurse. The animation of nature in these homely terms is as absolute as in the others, but these are not so grim and authoritarian. In the earlier period the poetry about Nature was better, as if by an overflow of the poet's high spirits. But the nature which figures in the later period is the one which is common, or orthodox, among the poets. This would be according to the sophistication which we attribute professionally to the poets. As children we came into the power of make-believe early, and learned presently to distinguish what we pretended to be from what we really were. Not without saying to ourselves, even in our cooler moments, that we *meant* somehow and some time to be what we had played at being; the playing idealized our total economy. Then we were given fairy tales, where miracles occurred when the beasts, or it might be the trees, came to the aid of the good child in his horrid straits. Our parents and teachers were very sure that these would not seriously impair our sense of reality. The fairy tales were just right to serve for our literature at that stage. Then we grew up, and fictions for grown-ups replaced the fairy tales, with characters which were stronger than ourselves, and better, and endings which were righter than we could easily find in life. But best of all came the poems, if we managed to find our initiation into that kind of make-believe. If Nature did not necessarily figure in the fictions, it was a primary consideration in the poems. But the wonders in the poems, when we entered into the society of Nature, were far more discreet than they had been in the fairy tales, as they must be to be reputable for our intelligence, and effective. We have found ourselves moved as deeply by the poems as we once were moved by the fairy tales. Indeed, since we are bigger than we were then, and more complex, there is *more* commotion in us made by the poems, more displacement. Wordsworth employed for his special ode the title, "Intimations of Immortality." The first word there is a very discreet one. What the poets give us is an incessant stream of miraculous intimations about nature, and "Intimations of Goodness in the Body of This World" might have been the title which Wordsworth would have employed if he had been following Kant's conception of the office of poetry. The intimations are tonic for us. They lend us morale; it is an excellent effect in an Age of Anxiety; and so far as we know every age is an age of anxiety. The poets are responsible public functionaries for doing this service; or so I think our anthropologist would say.

There is a special device to which poets have always been habituated, contributing to the dominant intention. It is the linguistic invention which we know as metaphor; the figure which towers over all the others in the poetic handbook. As if for fear the natural properties of the setting cannot be animated by direct methods in poems as in the fairy tales, as if they cannot be suddenly and heroically transformed for adult readers out of their prose or common functions, metaphor breaks into the poetic argument at any moment to endow the natural object with a human sentience. Metaphor is the equation of the human action to that of some natural object; the object really is extraneous to the human action, but it is made to involve itself in that action anyway, which in effect is to be humanized. In the Robinson poem, for example, there are such metaphors, where nature answers to human passion with like passion; at the climax of the action when all is lost, "the falling leaf inaugurates," and "the pounding wave reverberates"; at the dismal conclusion there is the "changed familiar tree" and the "stairway to the sea / Where down the blind are driven." Metaphors are metamorphoses, though they are never so grossly miraculous as the effects described in the cruder medium of the poet Ovid.

The difference between fiction and poetry perhaps becomes clearer at this point. Many fictions are inextricably mixed with poetry; the natural setting of the great scenes being chosen to "suit the action," so to speak; the narrator speaking a language that is stylized and imaginative, perhaps luminous sometimes with modest metaphors. But there are plain fictions where the art seems most specialized and distinct. They deal with moral situations—as all arts in some sense have to do—but their emphasis is on the moral. They may work at great length and with much subtlety. Mr. [Lionel] Trilling has said that the proper subject for fiction is manners, which always profess moral attitudes, but sometimes hypocritically.[5] So there may be opposition between the good manners of a set of people and the evil which they actually do; and always there will be open opposition between our own good people and those other people who are obviously bad. But now and then, and it is especially happy if this comes at the end, there is the fine scene where the good people triumph conclusively, and the evil people are removed or converted to goodness; and so massive has been the progress and the preparation toward the event that it seems to us like a vision of goodness prevailing everywhere. It is as if the whole family of mankind had turned to goodness, or might someday turn to goodness. The "intima-

5. "Manners, Morals, and the Novel," *Kenyon Review*, X (Winter, 1948), 11–27.

tion" is of the good society established and regnant on earth. But the earth is not involved. We have a great happiness, but it is a social or family happiness, and that is not the same as the lyrical happiness we received in poetry from the participation of nature. I think the two happinesses do not feel the same. But I hope the lovers of fiction will not mind the haste and simplicity with which I have put this distinction.

The new poet today looks back upon a half-century which may have been more eventful for new poetry than any other in the history of our language, with the exception of the second half of the 16th century, and possibly its successor the first half of the 17th century. The exhibition must be rather bewildering to review. Mr. Ezra Pound advised the poets early to "Make It New," and there was never a better time for this advice than the impoverished period from which they had to start. They founded many innovations, and engineered many revolutions. Before long an *avant-garde* was galloping off in almost every direction, and it was difficult in the confusion to tell which one the main troops were going to follow. That was a magnificent confusion. All possible poetries were being tried, and nothing could have been better for the times.

A great deal was gained in the understanding of what the capability of a poem is, and what its limits are. That is coming to light steadily, if my own impression is correct, in the utterances of critics. But the farther we stand from the peak of all that confusion, the more possible it seems that there is still going to be a continuity between the old poetry and the poetry of the future. And perhaps the reason would be that the genius of the art will refuse to go very far from the genius of the language, which is its medium; and that the possibilities of the medium were rather thoroughly explored by the able pioneers of 1550 to 1650, and other companies of pioneers who came after them and found new discoveries always harder to make. The chances are not so bright now for poetries which are radically new. But in saying this I do not mean anything which might be taken as disputing our conviction that every age must present to the anthology a poetry of its own, which must be at least new enough to distinguish it. We cannot use a tradition which is not adaptable to our own society. But at least it has appeared in recent years that the newest poets are not particularly revolutionary.

I have even noticed that the newest poets appear much more often than not to be picking up again the meters, which many poets in the century had thought they must dispense with; and by way of conclusion it seems imperative to say something about the meters, in order not to neglect altogether the half of the poetic effects made possible by the medium, which is the spoken language. This language has its meaning, as we know very well; and necessarily it makes oral sounds, which have no value at all in themselves when we are attending strictly to the meaning, but do have value in themselves if the poet makes them fit into a kind of music having fixed units like bars and measures, line-lengths and stanzas. The metered language is a double medium, with two systems of effects, which at first sight seem to have very little to do with one another. The effects which I have been remarking up to this point are almost entirely on the meaningful side of the medium, and might very well have been realized in free verse, which has no fixed system of sounds at all. Indeed, such effects have been realized in the free verse of our own century, and by admirable poets. And my feeling would be, like yours, that the meaningful effects represent the better half of poetry when it doubles its medium and has two halves. But now the question of the anthropologist must be: What is the good of the meters as the old poets regularly, and the new poets increasingly, have elected to employ them? What do they mean?

I hope everybody in the audience knows how the meters go, so that I need only to offer my guess as to what they are for.

Though we might prefer to attend only to the meaning of the poetic language, the meters would have us attending also to their music. It is not an advanced kind of music, but it is a steady music, and its simple rhythmic unit is infinitely repetitive. At long last, and against our will perhaps, we are compelled to hear it; always after that we have to be listening for it in advance. If we were provided as the ancients were with the actual oral delivery of poetry by a public rhapsode with a musical sense, we would be extremely sensitive to the meters, and never miss hearing them. But even if we are our own readers and have some slight musical sense, we will still find ourselves attending more or less to the meters, though we read in armchairs, and silently. What do they signify to us?

I think meters confer upon the delivery of poetry the sense of a ritualistic occasion. When a ritual develops it consists in the enactment, or the recital over and over again, of some experience which is obsessive for us, yet intangible and hard to express. The nearest analogue to the reading of poetry according to the meters, as I think, is the reading of an ecclesiastical service by the congregation. Both the genius of poetry and the genius of the religious establishment work against the same difficulty, which is the registration of what is inexpressible, or metaphysical. The religious occasion is a very formal one, with its appointed place in the visible temple, and the community of worshippers congregated visibly; it defines itself sharply and publicly for the anthropologist. The reading of poetry is not, since the invention of printing, so communal, so formal, so formidable. But the anthropologist will have to pay his respects to it anyhow, and give it what dignities he can. (All this is being said much too briefly.)

Mr. Eliot has referred to his verse as being "free verse." But that is not quite accurate, as he would know very well. He never has sustained his free verse, because, as I am obliged to think, free verse is not good enough for his purpose. Mr. Blackmur, writing about Eliot as a leading poet (and he was the master whom the new poets most followed), did not fail to remark upon the beauty of his music, and one might have thought the reference was to some sort of prose music in the free verse; for prose may have itself an irregular beauty, a free beauty which is different from the formal beauty of a measured language.[6] But Mr. Blackmur protected himself by making two quotations from the poems, each of which was a perfect or metered unit of oral language. One was from *The Waste Land*:

> A woman drew her long black hair out tight
> And fiddled whisper music on those strings;

and the other was from one of the *Four Quartets*:

> The salt is on the briar rose.
> The fog is on the fir-tree.

We cannot doubt that Mr. Blackmur was aware that the first is from the great metrical family of blank verse, an intellectual and university-bred family; and the second is from the other great family, the folk line. He could not have displayed more briefly or more sharply Mr. Eliot's exceeding command of the meters. These metered bits, and the others in his verse, are telling, and final, when we come to take our sense of him as a poet. Incidentally, as I understand it, they go along precisely with Mr. Eliot's concern with religion and ritual, as we know it from his public deliveries other than the poems. If he turned largely to free verse, we may suppose he had decided that his age wanted and needed new and informal kinds of verse, and that this was the quickest road to loosening their language and bringing vitality back into it. As for the next age, I can imagine that he might not have in mind for it the same strategy now.

6. "Lord Tennyson's Scissors: 1912–1950," *Kenyon Review*, XIV (Winter, 1952), 1–20.

THE IDEA OF A LITERARY
ANTHROPOLOGIST

AND WHAT HE MIGHT SAY OF THE

PARADISE LOST OF MILTON

A Speech with a Prologue

(THE PROLOGUE)

N MAY of last year there was dedicated a new Phi Beta Kappa Hall at the College of William and Mary, where the Society was founded, in Williamsburg. A literary speech was made, and has been printed and distributed by the College as part of the Proceedings. I had the honor to make that speech. Until now I have not thought it suitable for periodical publication. It is so very likely that the intellectual ideas of a speech will be too blunt and unqualified to address to learned readers, or that the warmth of the oratorical style will seem too factitious to address to dainty readers. But now after all I think perhaps it may do as an item in this *Review*, following upon the beautifully perfected essay by Mr. Roy Harvey Pearce on "Historicism Once More," which appeared in the previous issue.[1] If Mr. Pearce recommended to critics a kind of historicism, the speech will be recommending a kind of anthropologism, as if by way of reply.

We may imagine many occasions for a telling use of Mr. Pearce's historicism, but the speech will propose that there is a common and elemental sort of occasion where it does not suit at all. I found myself unexpectedly caught in that sort of occasion, and had to abandon my historicism. So I make a small prologue in order to talk briefly about the perspective of the literary anthropologist as an alternative to that of the historicist. Then the speech will appear, with slight revisions meant to

This essay first appeared in the *Kenyon Review*, XI (Winter, 1959), 121–40. Reprinted by permission of Helen Ransom Forman.

1. *Kenyon Review*, XX (Autumn, 1958), 554–91.

sharpen it for the printed occasion; and a new over-all title has been supplied. But it is still the fact that my anthropologist appeared in the original text. I was already thinking about his peculiar virtues.

And what is a literary anthropologist? I suppose that no such gifted person as yet perfectly exists—a professional anthropologist who is at the same time deeply accomplished in the understanding of literature. He is my notion of an anthropologist working in a special and difficult field. But it has occurred to me that if the critics would imagine him, and keep his image firmly beside them, he might admonish them much to their advantage sometimes when they were at their own professional labors.

The most inclusive principle which Mr. Pearce professes is "humanitas," and the literary anthropologist must needs be a great humanist. But as an anthropologist in the first place he will have conceived himself as more radically a scientist than our historians are expected to be. He will be a good naturalist, or economist, and his understanding of literature (with its literary theology), as of the culture of a society generally, must have to do with its adaptation to the natural economy.

Early in his essay Mr. Pearce mentioned many pairs of opposed considerations which, though opposites, must still be accommodated to each other somehow in our understanding of literature; and the final pairing was, art vs. life. Perhaps the anthropologist might choose to put this a little more sharply, in justice to one member of the pair: art vs. the facts of life. That is to say, he would be thinking of art not as its own end, nor as ever escaping from some vital motivation which is responsible for art but which is not art, however he might construe that. And presently Mr. Pearce offered his Condition in the Pluperfect Subjunctive, in order to show exactly how we receive comfort and reinforcement from studying and finally accepting a literary work from a bygone age. We say to ourselves (says Mr. Pearce), "If there had been such a person as X, living in a specified situation, etc., he would have acted in this way." That is, we the readers would have acted in this way; it was altogether a vital and a human kind of action. In this consent of ours we feel that we have discovered an evidence of the continuity of our culture, and indeed of our human nature.

I should not care to rush into an impiety by withholding consent on my part too wilfully. But surely many a masterpiece from the past tries us painfully when we try to consent to it. Sometimes there is a special reason for this. The great work, for example an epic, may owe its very fulness and perfection to the fact that it waited till that final stage of a

historic period when the intellectual culture was dead ripe, and ready
to fade; so that actually we find ourselves trying to overcome a natural
resentment against so accomplished an author who nevertheless committed himself to it so grandly and precariously. Mr. Pearce's Contrary
to Fact Condition often would have us surrendering to a sense of the
facts of life other than our own. Perhaps that is only for the time being;
but it goes against the grain. In the speech which follows we shall be
thinking of poor Milton's predicament. The *Paradise Lost* is a product
of Milton's own historicism. However bold a revolutionary we may have
reckoned this poet, he is elaborating with unexceptional piety upon the
grandest of narratives, majestic in its tone of authority and finality, yet
one of the most ancient: the Book of Genesis. If my feelings are just,
Milton's poem must have for us something of the effect of an anachro-
nism doubled. We have to try our own historicism upon a work which is
itself historistic.

A narrative note for the reader. I was getting on with my drafting of
the speech, using Milton for my text, and steeped in the serenest historicism, when the shock came which changed everything. A kind Vir-
ginian informed me that the year was 1957, the 350th anniversary of
the settlement at Jamestown, and that not a speech would be delivered
all year in Virginia which did not make proper reference to the settlers.
This bit of prompting threw the plan of my speech into an impossible
confusion. It smashed my historicism, which I believe has withdrawn
completely from the text finally arrived at. I think it would have smashed
Mr. Pearce's historicism; for the time being. For he is a moderate man
having very wide resources, and I am sure he suspects that there are
limits to a historicism, or to any other doctrine which has the quality, as
it has the terminology, of an *ism*; just as already I am apprehensive
about the risks of my anthropologism, and determined to give it only a
short run.

(THE SPEECH)
OUR AGE AMONG THE AGES

Your speaker does not feel equal to the platform on an occasion so re-
splendent as this one. But I can ask credit for choosing for my speech a
title sufficiently elevated. I am not sure what the general public thinks
about our Phi Beta Kappa Society; it is just possible that the very general public does not think about our Society, period. But at this time and
place, and among highly literate persons such as those in this audi-

ence, there may be a rather fixed impression of the Phi Beta Kappa personality; and I should hope that the image you have received is of something large in the style and something idealistic in the intellectual tone. My title means that I shall be asking dutifully the question which seems in order on this very official occasion: What is our age coming to? In every age, of course, there are persons who ask that, but surely the members of our Society do it pre-eminently; we seem exactly the sort of people of whom it is expected. I have heard the members asking, and you have heard them.

In approaching this question, I have kept in mind the letter of instruction, which said that I was to deliver a literary address. I am grateful for that. A speaker uses language as his medium (which appears to be more capacious and harder to manage than the medium of any other art), and therefore has at his disposal about all the range of reference in the world; but so do the literary artists even more completely, and he is happy if he can borrow from their fine phrases something to confirm his own prosy remarks. And there is no trouble finding what he will require. Literature is more many-sided than other arts, and more articulate. It exhibits not only our behaviors, but our thoughts, and even our feelings. The point of departure which I have elected is the *Paradise Lost* of the poet Milton; which means that I shall be employing the theological approach, though my qualifications are most irregular. I have even found in this work the text which will suit my argument perfectly. It is in the Fourth Book where Satan spies upon Adam and Eve in order to find where lies their weakness, and tempt them to his own designs; and overhears them talking about a peculiar Tree called the Tree of Knowledge of Good and Evil, whose fruit they must not taste on pain of death. This is the news Satan has been waiting for. But it surprises him, and though Milton by this time has made him hateful, he responds to it with a generous burst of real indignation:

> One fatal Tree there stands of Knowledge call'd,
> Forbidden them to taste. Knowledge forbidden?
> Suspicious, reasonless. Why should their Lord
> Envie them that? Can it be sin to know,
> Can it be death?[2]

At this point in the story I believe that some complacent readers, including perhaps even some members of our Society, who would never

2. *Paradise Lost*, Bk. IV, 514–18.

be the ones to forget that what they are reading is a great classic in our literary tradition—at this point some easy readers nevertheless may have felt their flesh constricting suddenly in a little shiver of horror. The matter seems so personal to their own careers! But Milton's theology is unfolding deliberately, according to the book. It is according to the Book of Genesis. There are passages where you can see, if you are versed in theological history, that Milton was an independent theologian. But this is not one of them, here in the crucial disposition of his story. In Milton's time and place theology had been breaking up into theologies, each having its own adherents and binding them explicitly to its particular revelation of the human destiny; and all meaning to derive faithfully from the single ancient authority. The intellectual community, including the scientists and philosophers, and everybody except the mutinous freethinkers, seems not to have wanted to exempt itself from the common theological perspective to which decent people were supposed to have committed themselves indifferently.

In recent years there has been a great splash of new essays and books which have revived the study of Milton, and greatly advanced it. I am familiar with some of them, and these lead me to the conviction that the Milton scholars have not altered their old style of operation; they like to display their author and his work with complete fulness, and everywhere with the utmost scruple in the detail, yet still they seem to be shackled by one remarkable reservation.[3] We know the type of the old-fashioned scholar who has devoted himself to his Chaucer, or it may be his Spenser, or Shakespeare, or Milton, or Wordsworth. We may think of him perhaps as a dedicated hero-worshipper, and that would indicate a piety which is conspicuously endearing in the human records of our society; the disciple putting on the precise heroism of his hero. We have to be for him much more than against him. A scholar of this sort means to enter into the mind of his author, acquiring of course the language and the style, and assimilating just as faithfully the moral and theological ideas too, till he is accomplished in his author's whole "sense of life." This intimate possession he then presents to the public domain with his compliments. But the self-effacing scholar is so identified with his author that he is deterred, though he may not know it, from risking the fateful incidence of a common humanistic criticism. Doubtless this is

3. Three books which were on my desk as I wrote, all coming in the year 1957, were: *Milton's Ontology, Cosmology, and Physics*, by Walter Clyde Curry; *Heroic Knowledge* by Arnold Stein; and *Images and Themes in Five Poems by Milton*, by Rosamund Tuve. They are first-rate, but the old-style historian is operating in them all. (Ransom's note)

one of the chief occupational hazards of the literary scholar. Now literature perhaps, like free capitalism, though much more idealistic in its
temper, is an expanding economy, and arrives now and again at blazing
new affirmations of the human dignity which do not consist with the
dogmatic faith of many an old author. (If this were not so, there would
hardly have been in our time that worried debate among critics over the
question of how we can make use of a poet whose beliefs we cannot
now subscribe to.) Your speaker was himself for some years an uncritical Milton scholar, though a small one, acquainting himself with his
hero through the work of the established scholars. Today, being out of
school, he thought he might confront the pious scholars, to see
whether Milton's ideas about the Tree of Knowledge should inspire our
affection, or our disaffection.

We need not suppose that the conscience of the tender modern
reader is necessarily blunted because he reads Milton. We may rule out
"tender" from this sort of human context. With a certain "willing suspension of disbelief" at various crises of the argument, according to a
procedure which has been highly recommended, he will have his reward at other places. I will mention some of them. Among the long
poems of our language the *Paradise Lost* is the grandest, and it sustains its narrative and philosophical tension the best. Musically, I imagine it may be supreme among the long poems of Western literature; the
music is stately, and keeps to its laws without becoming tired and mechanical. Like Shakespeare's plays, this poem mounts incessantly into
lyrical moments; I could recite fifty of the passages, and many of you
would easily identify them all. But there is a barrier of language which
the modern reader has to overcome. Mr. T. S. Eliot early pointed out a
flaw of Milton's language, and some twenty-five years later withdrew
his objections as being not too important in view of the excellence of
the language for its purpose.[4] It was not *colloquial*; i.e., not according to
the spoken idiom of language for our age, or for that matter not for
Milton's own age, as we have it for example in Dryden. Eliot's concern
was on behalf of young poets struggling in a dull period to find a proper
language; he advised them that Milton's language was artificial. And
indeed there is a quaintness in Milton's diction, by common speech-
standards; the inkhorn has got into it, or as we say now it has a quality
which we must call "academic." The young poets of 1920 needed to
have this point made. Milton is not widely read by the moderns now,

4. See T. S. Eliot, "Milton II," in *On Poetry and Poets* (New York, 1957), 181.

and Eliot's reproach had a good deal to do with this. But then we must suppose that what Eliot was doing, partly at least, was to size up prophetically a turn of poetic language which the modern taste was already developing, and must have achieved anyhow. What Eliot did was partly to cause and partly to accelerate this development.

I am obligated by my instructions, I think, to go a little further in this line; for this is a "literary" moment. So I will read a sentence from Milton's poem and make a few comments. Since Milton has become for most persons, and even for many highly educated persons, a poet of the academy, I think it will occur to some of you that the sentence I shall quote is not so graceless and cold as you may have expected; and perhaps those of you who know it already will not mind hearing it again. It is not one of the longer sentences; it contains only fifteen lines, and scarcely more than a hundred words. My first comment will be in advance. I should like to ask you to listen to the developing sentence as having a most unusual structure. It will take some of the sting from Mr. Eliot's reproach if you will observe how far this sentence is, though uncolloquial in many ways, from being a periodic sentence. The periodic sentence has a beginning and a middle and finally an ending; by the faculty of reason you know exactly when it is ended, and before that point you could not possibly have stopped it. But Milton liked to keep a sentence going anyway, by just adding one thing after another, with the most casual connections, so that you will not be able to tell when it is ended without watching for the visible period on the page, or waiting to hear the speaker's voice fall and pause decisively. In such a sentence a man of proud self-conscious learning is thinking aloud in his privacy, holding on pretty firmly to the situation in hand, but letting his mind play with it freely. His mind in its progress is not very much like a steamship plowing straight ahead on its course, but rather like a sailing ship making headway yet veering and tacking luxuriously in the wind. Perhaps we would think of this informal kind of sentence as being found more in the prose poetry of the time than in the verse.

My sentence occurs where the fallen angels are exploring their Hell, while their chieftain is gone on his grand new adventure against the Almighty. They do not like what they find:

> Thus roving on
> In confus'd march forlorn, th' adventrous Bands
> With shuddring horror pale, and eyes aghast
> View'd first their lamentable lot, and found
> No rest; through many a dark and drearie Vaile

> They pass'd, and many a Region dolorous,
> O'er many a Frozen, many a Fierie Alpe,
> Rocks, Caves, Lakes, Fens, Bogs, Dens, and shades of death,
> A Universe of death, which God by curse
> Created evil, for evil only good,
> Where all life dies, death lives, and nature breeds,
> Perverse, all monstrous, all prodigious things,
> Abominable, unutterable, and worse
> Than Fables yet have feign'd, or fear conceiv'd,
> *Gorgons* and *Hydras*, and *Chimeras* dire.[5]

I have two after-remarks. Midway in this sentence occurs the line so famous in prosodical dispute:

> Rocks, Caves, Lakes, Fens, Bogs, Dens, and shades of death,

where Milton, like any other poet who has the resources for it, makes startling use of the figure of Not Quite Co-ordinate Series; and where many prosodists have declared that the six initial monosyllabic nouns are so perfectly co-ordinate as to be equal in weight, so that the iambic rule of pairing a lightly stressed syllable always with a heavily stressed one no longer obtains, but every syllable obtains full stress; where, therefore, the meter breaks down. I cannot think so. It does not seem too difficult for the ear to make out the usual bars, or feet, each made of a light stress and a heavy. *Rocks* is indifferent as a feature of landscape, but its partner *Caves* is a Gothic and dangerous item, which outstresses it; *Lakes* is neutral, but its partner *Fens* is ominous; and *Bogs* may make us a little apprehensive, but it is outdone by *Dens*, which brings to mind the savage creatures who inhabit there, and may be the stimulus which drives Milton's imagination on to those climactic monsters, the *Gorgons*, etc., of the final line. It would seem to me that it is either an obtuseness of sensibility, or else an acquired habit of oracular monotony, which would prevent the reader from rendering the iambic pattern here as elsewhere.

My other comment is prosodical too, but it is a sort of occasional remark, when I remember that I am speaking here in old Virginia. There is a trace of Virginia speech in Milton's language. His musical system obliges us to pronounce his *lamentable, abominable, unutterable,* in the way I have said them, with heavy stress on the *able.* So it is with many other similar words of his, and so with *comfortáble,* a word which I have heard pronounced a good many times by Virginians with this

5. *Paradise Lost,* Bk. 2, 615–28.

very emphasis. It is pretty certain that word would have been said this way at Jamestown in 1607, the year before Milton was born—if the settlers at Jamestown had any use for the word—and at Williamsburg in 1693 when the College of William and Mary was founded, and in 1776 at the College when our Society was founded. I hope the old word still prevails; and that there are many occasions for employing it.

And now to go ahead with our argument. There are times when the doctrine of Genesis and of Milton suits us very well, and seems perfectly exemplary; it consists with the theology of the Greek playwrights, for instance, as when a great man sins by arrogating to himself a more than human ambition. There are many uses for a theology which enforces humility. It might be called our Sunday theology, which we put off on Monday and Tuesday when we resume the hard program of the secular life. But I have to venture now upon a little theologism of my own at Milton's expense. I do so without worrying much over the question of its orthodoxy. There is much in Milton's career to suggest that he himself, in a later and more liberal century, and under happier private circumstances, might as the independent theologian have uttered something of the sort. I have heard sermons of the sort from Christian pulpits, from blameless divines who apparently were unconscious of their trespass against the letter of their theology. But they were not unconscious of it. The wise priest or parson is aware of the manifold of conflicting dogmas that subsist more or less comfortably together in the mind by attending each to its proper occasions. How could it be otherwise? The general principle might be that our orthodox theology, if we profess one, is curiously complemented by private theologisms which suit some occasions better than it does.

The job which Milton laid upon himself was to make a narrative image first of life in Heaven, a place into which even his own imagination was powerless to enter effectively; and then of life in Hell, where he does well enough with the depiction of extreme horrors both physical and psychical; and finally, his ultimate objective, of life on earth, where he has created a total image that is even harsher than he knew, as an aged and embattered Puritan nursing the extremity of his enthusiasm.

Adam and Eve in their primeval or pre-historic existence had no house, nor household implements, nor clothing, nor other food than the fruits which dropped or were ready for dropping from the trees and shrubs, nor fire to concoct the raw foods and establish a cuisine. They were not authorized to cut down the trees, even if they could, for the timber that would have gone into building; or to assault the animals to get their coats for clothing and their flesh for eating. (The animals did not even prey upon each other.) But they were furnished for our own better understanding with one thing extremely advanced in the scale of culture, as the anthropologist uses the term: a wonderfully flexible and poetic language in which they could express their mutual affection and praise their Creator. The climate was perfect, the fruits were delicious, and the regimen so wholesome that it did not admit of sickness. Existence in the Garden was one long state of bliss, provided the happy creatures did not worry about their condition and have recourse to the "sciential sap" which was within the forbidden fruit. But if Adam was contented, Eve was not; it would seem that Eve became bored a little by the elevated discourse of her husband, and the rude state of housekeeping. I was once a member of a group of young men in Tennessee who made a public diversion in favor of an agrarian way of life which was fast becoming outmoded, even in that happy region. And I recall how it was a commonplace in our observation that it was always the woman of the house who made her husband sell the farm and move to the city, where her own drudgery would be lightened, and her children could go to proper school; we never found the right words to address to the woman.

According to my rough calculations, following the action of the story in Milton's account, Adam and Eve inhabited in the Garden for a period somewhere between fourteen and twenty-one days, the period, so to speak, of a honeymoon. Then Eve fell victim to Satan's wiles and ate of the fruit of the tree, and Adam joined her in sin, and immediately they were cast out of the Garden into the harsh outer world where some science is necessary to establish any sort of stable economy. Yet I believe it is now the impression of all Milton scholars that Adam and Eve, as they pass under the flaming sword of Michael and leave the gates of Paradise, do not seem to find the occasion quite so dreadful as one has been led to expect. Milton could not quite accomplish what his severe piety intended. His humanity had never quite dismissed that sense of life which produces societies, civilizations, and histories and gives occupation to anthropologists who review the rich organization of the collective human experience. And I think I must repeat, for emphasis, that the knowledge which was forbidden on theological grounds is the knowledge which means to improve, and in any event is going to alter profoundly, the given human economy. That knowledge is science; we may even turn this proposition around, and say perhaps that science is knowledge which bears directly or indirectly upon the economy.

In Scripture and in *Paradise Lost* the eating of the apple had consequences not immediately related to the economic changes. But there are implications that both the Scriptural authors and Milton are fully conscious of impending economic events. With the abandonment of the Garden begins at once the series of economic stages out of which will come eventually the human society as we know it and as the anthropologists have taught us to figure it.

It is finally for shame that Adam and Eve try to improvize clothing to hide their nakedness, but there must have been immediately another shame for the poor job they made of it. As they are about to leave the Garden to serve their punishment, Messiah himself kindly furnishes them with raiment made of animal skins, whether sloughed off by the animals or even, as Milton seems to intimate, taken in predatory style from the slain animals. That does not seem to matter now; the animals are already preying upon each other. And we find Adam speculating about some method of catching and preserving fire to keep the cold away; he is looking for his Prometheus, so to speak. But there are many stories in the oldest Scriptures which have economic significance, and Milton manages to assimilate some of them into his narrative.

Adam and Eve have a son Abel who keeps sheep. Here we have the pastoral economy, and it is as if a whole later society, with a priesthood, had been projected backward into one small family, to simplify and memorize a crucial event. There is another son named Cain, who is a tiller of the ground, which signifies that he has discovered a revolutionary economy. Upon the altar Abel sacrifices a lamb, which pleases God, but Cain offers the first fruits of his field, and God is displeased. Dispute arises, and Cain slays Abel, and is cast out of that society into a deadly wilderness. But we know that his economy will prevail.

One story that Milton does not find room for has a certain pathos in its implications. The last son of Adam is Seth, replacing Abel, and from him the line descends to David, and from David to the Messiah who is to come on earth. But first we are given the descent of Cain through a number of generations, bearing names very nearly the same as those which will appear in the line of Seth, until suddenly Cain's line breaks off, like an item that is not wanted after all in the official history of the race. We come to Lamech, sixth in the line which begins with Cain. One of his wives bears him a son named Jabal, and another son whom I will mention presently, while a second wife bears him a son named Tubal-Cain. Jabal is characterized as the father of such as dwell in tents and of such as have cattle; he is a second Abel. But Tubal-Cain is characterized as "an instructor of every artificer in brass and iron"; which signifies that one of Cain's line has invented metallurgy and is about to lead his people out of the Stone Age. But that would seem a revolution against the old order which is sinful, and inevitably there is strife. At any rate Lamech comes rushing to his wives to cry, "I have slain a man to my wounding, and a young man to my hurt," and to exclaim that his curse will be heavier than Cain's had been. We are not told whom he has killed, but as we think of the killer his ancestor we cannot but conclude that he has sided with his son Tubal-Cain and slain his son Jabal. Violence marks these economic revolutions, though they cannot be undone. Yet there had been something new and appealing in the role of the second or middle son, by the first wife, whose name is Jubal; he is characterized as the father of all such as handle the harp and the organ. I do not know anything about those instruments as the Scriptural author knew them, but I like to imagine that they had to be constructed by Tubal-Cain and his workmen, the sinful crew of metallurgists; who with the versatility of modern manufacturers would have wished to furnish to Jabal and all the faithful the instruments on which they might make better music in God's honor. There is a great irony here, and a moral which has something to do with tolerance, with coexistence.

Much in the ancient Scriptures has to do with the wickedness of cities, which represent a stage in the economy far removed from dwelling in tents. When Abraham and his nephew Lot journeyed westward toward the Jordan to find a new habitation, Lot parted company with his uncle in order to live in the cities of the plain, while the good Abraham kept to the hills and tended his flocks. But the sin of Sodom and Gomorrah was very great, and Abraham's pleas could not save them from the vengeance of the Lord, who destroyed them. It is not necessary to remind you that Sodom and Gomorrah were not the last of cities,

A theological compulsion was upon Milton in these ancient stories to side with the Old Order when there is division within an economic society. And perhaps there has been an inclination on your part to do so, as there has often been on the part of your speaker. His performance has been insignificant, but he may have written a little, and made a few speeches, to justify that side. But as he has grown older it seems less and less important, and less and less possible, to be consistent, so that he is here today to talk for the other side. It is a little disturbing to observe that the order of his opinions is just opposite to the sequence of positions as Milton held them. From his earlier position Milton had written the *Areopagitica*, in defense of the freedom of individual opinion. When the Civil Wars came he had not supported the party of the anointed King and the old landowners and farm-folk; and by his public arguments for the regicides he had made himself into a virtual accessory after the fact to what the voice of England was shortly to pronounce a heinous crime. There must often be an economic and social appendage to a dogmatic theology. But the one that is indicated in the *Paradise Lost* is not the one which Milton would have cared to represent when it was a question of the massive economic and social revolution which had been going on ceaselessly in the England of his own youth.

I am not intimately acquainted with the mentality of the anthropologist, but I believe he is a historian of the facts of life, observing in their widest range the patterns of behavior which become organized in the collective cultures; and after that a close psychologist who understands the motivation behind the behaviors. I assume, and I cannot believe this is mistaken, that he is philanthropic or humanistic in his sentiments; a lover of life as he finds its historic manifestations. The culture as he sees it includes not only the technical ways of livelihood, but the morals and manners, the arts, and the rites and ceremonies attending upon the religious institution. I should not like to imagine the anthropologist who would not care to take into consideration the religion, and the theology which undertook to justify it; the act of faith by which the community had asserted its peculiar destiny. He would seem needlessly brutal and misanthropic. But I think the anthropologist hardly singles out some one theology to set up as the absolute; his studies seem to be of comparative theology. If there is a great change in the economic life, its leaders will probably feel the same compulsion which Milton felt, to "assert eternal Providence / And justify the ways of God to men." But the new theologies will probably not have the same authoritarian tone as the old ones; and as things go increasingly, they need not.

The new theological notions are probably tacit; it may make unnecessary trouble if they are not. Nevertheless, after this discreet apologia, I do not mind offering a simple version of the theology which I wish Milton might have uttered, following upon the Story of Creation. (I must remark that the race does not arrive at its public professions of faith in quite this informal way.) He might have declared with suitable gravity that God had endowed his new creatures deliberately and knowingly with a prodigious adventurousness, but with mental powers to match; and set them down in the midst of an infinitely tangled wilderness of a world which would be far more seductive presently to them than their idyllic bower. He had them start their existence in the Garden, and waited to see that would happen, in the perfect confidence which goes with good planning. There is no dispute between Milton and the authors of Genesis as to what happened next. They did leave the Garden. But if there was grief in Heaven to see them go, Milton might have parted company with Genesis here and said that the Creator smiled as if to say: "That is what I wanted, what I intended; for I made them free. You would not understand the world which I created for them, because it is subject to much contingency; indeed it has pain in store for them, and sickness and death, but there is also possible a strength, and a happiness, which are not to be obtained in any other way. These are my pioneers." At this point I believe I am arguing that not the dull sheltered Garden, but the unknown forbidding world at large, is what we must identify in all piety, using the famous phrase of the philosopher, as "the best of all possible worlds." Milton could not have known Leibnitz'[6] phrase when he wrote. But we can neither wish nor imagine this world much different. If it did not call forth fear in its inhabitants, it would never generate their courage; if not their savagery in the pursuit of survival and wealth, then not their gentleness; and if they had not to live in the constant prospect of death, then there could have been little relish in the living. But it was indispensable that the small creatures so piteously exposed in this world should have keen wits, to seek the knowledge of the world's secrets and put them to work. They must have science.

So we cannot but feel that it was odious of Milton to have them damned for their seeking of knowledge as great sinners, especially at his particular period of history, which we regard in this year 1957 with a very special perspective. Milton's life almost spanned the great wave of settlements which his countrymen were establishing on the American seaboard, where they were writing what we have been well instructed, in our secular schools if not in Sunday School, to think of as a noble chapter of human history. He was indifferent to it. Let us in all charity concede that he had other matters to occupy him.

And now to return to my title and speak briefly about our own age. Again we have a new economy, and it is painfully arriving at a new total culture, and doubtless at a new theology, tacit and private perhaps

6. Gottfried Wilhelm Leibnitz (1646–1716), German philosopher and mathematician.

mostly, to justify it. Milton in the 17th Century could not have foreseen our economy, nor could anybody in the 18th Century, and very few public men even at the end of the 19th. Our own country was chiefly its native seat. Of course I am talking in general about the Industrial Revolution, which has long been understood in principle, but in particular about the accelerated form it took at last, which was not foreseen at all. The Western world was used to the power-driven machines of human invention, and the division of labor. But the new forms of power came so fast that before we had any theoretical understanding of it we were in the Age of Mass-production. Even economists were scarcely ready to accept the condition upon which mass-production depends; and that is, mass-consumption. Technically, mass-consumption means purchasers with income proportionate to the volume of production. It may be said that for at least two decades now this consideration, forced upon us by hideous experience, is overwhelmingly in our consciousness; it is of such a magnitude that it dwarfs any differences supposed to lie between the policies of the Republican and the Democratic parties. Possibly, it might even be argued that mass-production was the result of the encouragement which the Republicans extended to business, but that when it was here the Democrats had to be called in to channel mass-production off by a program of distributing income; whereupon it might be argued next that the Democrats entered with such zeal into their program that the Republicans had to be recalled to administer it with moderation. As for myself, I believe in a two-party system, and count myself an independent voter.

At any rate, the old ways of life have been disappearing much too rapidly for comfort, and we are in a great cultural confusion. Many millions of underprivileged persons now have income and leisure which they did not have before. They have the means to achieve the best properties of a culture, if they know how to spend their money wisely. And it is the fact that they spend handsomely on education. Now, I am in the education business, and I can report my observations on that. It is as if a sudden invasion of barbarians had overrun the educational institution; except that the barbarians in this case are our neighbors and friends, and sometimes they are our own children, or they are ourselves, they are some of us gathered here on this very fine occasion. We should not fear them; they are not foreigners, nor our enemies. But in the last resort education is a democratic process, in which the courses are subject to the election of the applicants, and a course even when it has been elected can never rise above the intellectual passion of its pupils, or their comparative indifference. So, with the new generation of students, Milton declines in the curriculum; even Shakespeare has lost heavily; Homer and Virgil are practically gone. The literary interest of the students today is ninety percent in the literature of their own age; more often than not it is found in books which do not find entry into the curriculum, and are beneath the standard which your humble servants, the teachers of literature, are trying to maintain. Chaucer and Spenser and Milton, with their respective contemporaries, will have their secure existence henceforth in the library, and of course in the love and intimate acquaintance of a certain academic community, and there they will stay except for possible periods when there is a revival of the literature of our own antiquity. Our literary culture for a long time is going to exist in a sprawling fashion, with minority pockets of old-style culture, and some sort of majority culture of a new and indeterminate style. It is a free society, and I should expect that the rights of minorities will be as secure as the rights of individuals.

But in conclusion I would make one more observation about something which has been very much on my mind. It may be that we in the elite tradition of Phi Beta Kappa have held too hard and too long by our traditional literature, and have become culturally a little effete and devitalized. Milton implored his Muse to find "fit audience, though few" for his verse. That is the cry of the avant-garde in any generation, and of most of the artists we count best. But the poet Whitman said, "To have great poets, there must be great audiences, too." It has been feared, and I think with much justification, that he had in mind the audience which was great not so much in the superfine quality of its responses, but principally in its numerosity, in being constituted by "the people" itself. I have been wondering if this was an unreasonable aspiration in Whitman. The barbarians who are our friends, the new people who write books, and prepare the programs for radio and television, these may now and then, I imagine, have more vitality and power than we like to allow. It is possible that what the arts need now is some tough but low-rated new strain in the stock which enters into the making of our artists. That is the suggestion with which I conclude.

Appendix A

From a Letter to Allen Tate, September 5, 1926

The three moments in the historical order of experience are as follows:

I FIRST MOMENT.

Bear in mind that the moments as I shall describe them are immensely simplified and ideal. The first moment is the original experience—pure of all intellectual content, unreflective, concrete, and singular; there are no distinctions, and the subject is identical with the Whole.

II SECOND MOMENT.

The moment after. This moment is specific for human experience as distinguished from the ideally animal experience. Biologically man is peculiar in that he must record and use his successive experiences; the beasts are not under this necessity; with them the experience is an end in itself, and takes care of itself. In the second moment cognition takes place; never mind the fact that cognition is always recognition, and presupposes *two* moments.—for we can say that the first moment must be *repeated* before the time arrives for the (qualitatively) second moment. The feature of the second moment is it is now that the record must be taken of the first moment that has just transpired. This record proceeds inevitably by way of *concepts* discovered in cognition. It is the beginning of science. Its ends are practical: but its means are *abstractions*; and these, it must be insisted, are subtractions from the whole. Now what becomes of the whole in this operation? A feature, or several features, are taken up and spread upon the record; let us say, they are written down on lasting tablets; at the least, they go into the Ready Memory where items of knowledge are constantly in use, and constantly available. The rest goes somewhere and is preserved, else we could never miss it; it goes, according to Bergson, into Pure Memory; according to the modern school of psychologists, into the Unconscious, where it is far from idle, and whence it somewhere, sometime, will come up again. So experience becomes History, conceptualized knowledge, in respect to a part, and Unconscious Knowledge, lost knowledge, in respect to the vast residue of the unconceptual. So also is generated the cognitive or scientific habit; which is that which disposes us to shorten the subsequent First Moments of our experience to the minimum, to dwell upon our subsequent fresh experiences only long enough to reduce them as here; and which is so powerful when formed that many of us unquestionably spend most of our waking lives in entertaining or arriving at concepts.

III THIRD MOMENT.

We become aware of the deficiency of the record. Most of experience is quite missing from it. All our concepts and all our histories put together cannot add up into the wholeness with which we started out. Philosophical syntheses do no good—the Absolutists are quaint when they try to put Humpty-Dumpty together again by logic—they only give us a Whole which, as Kant would say, is obtained by *comprehensio logica* and not by *comprehensio aesthetica*—a Whole which it is only necessary to say fails to give us satisfaction. The world of science and knowledge which we have laboriously constructed is a world of illusion: not one of its items can be intuited. We suddenly appear to ourselves as monsters, as unnatural members of humanity; and we move to right ourselves again. (The scientific world, as seen on these terms, quite clearly appears as an artificial or *phenomenal* world, and so our objection is quite regular and eclectic.) How can we get back to that first moment? There is only one answer: By images. The Imagination is the faculty of Pure Memory, or unconscious mind; it brings out the original experiences from the dark storeroom, where we dwell upon them with a joy proportionate to our previous despair. And therefore, when we make images, we are regressive; we are trying to reconstitute an experience which we once had, only to handle and mutilate. Only, we cannot quite reconstitute them. Association is too strong for us; the habit of cognition is too strong. The images come out mixed and adulterated with concepts. Experience without concepts is advocated by some systems, and has some healing power, but it is not an adult mode; it cannot really produce images without concepts but only an imageless and conceptless state; as in the Dionysian state of Nietzsche or the Orientalism of Schopenhauer. What we really get, therefore, by this deliberate recourse to images is a mixed world composed of both images and concepts; or a sort of practicable reconciliation of the two worlds. Therefore we are not really opposed to science, except as it monopolizes and warps us; we are perfectly content to dwell in the phenomenal world for much of our time; this is to be specifically human; we would not be babes or beasts; we require merely the fullness of life, which is existence in the midst of all our faculties. And our Aesthetic can never deny science wholly, which would be wildly romantic, and not reasonable, if not suicidal. This leads us to a distinction between *Romantic* or *Pure* tendencies, *Gothic* or *Mixed*, which is like the distinction between the *East* and the *West*. Science is a kind of blindness, but necessary and useful; exactly as the typical successful mercenary appears blind to the poet. . . . An important detail is to show why, with our formal cognitive habit or apparatus, we cannot have fresh experience of first moments; because they disintegrate as fast as they come. And this corollary: In Nature as compared with Art, our sense of Wholeness is extremely vague and unsatisfying; the artistic contemplation of nature is better, a very advanced state, in which we are conscious of the scene as we might have conceptualized it, and at the same time of the scene as we actually do persist in intuiting it. But this is quite like art: a mixture.

Appendix B

Chronology

1888   John Crowe Ransom born April 30, in Pulaski, Tennessee

1909   B.A., Vanderbilt University

1910–13   Rhodes Scholar

1913   Teacher of Latin at the Hotchkiss School, Lakeville, Conn.

1914   Joined faculty of Vanderbilt University

1915   "The Question of Justice"

1919   *Poems About God*

1920   Married Robb Reavill, December 22

1922–25   Helped edit the *Fugitive*; most of best poetry written

1923   "Waste Lands"

1924   *Chills and Fever*; *Grace After Meat*; "The Future of Poetry"

1925   "A Man Without a Country"; "Mixed Modes"; "Prose: A Doctrine of Relativity"

1927   *Two Gentlemen in Bonds*; wrote *The Third Moment* (not published); "The ABC of Aesthetics"

1928   "The South—Old or New"

1929   "Classical and Romantic"; "The South Defends Its Heritage"; "Flux and Blur in Contemporary Art"

1930   *God Without Thunder*; "Reconstructed but Unregenerate"; "Statement of Principles"

1931–32   Spent year in England on Guggenheim grant; wrote *Land!*

1932   "Land! An Answer to the Unemployment Problem"; "The State and the Land"

1933   "A Capital for the New Deal"; "Happy Farmers"; "A Poem Nearly Anonymous"; "A Poem Nearly Anonymous: The Poet and His Formal Tradition" (published in *The World's Body* as "Forms and Citizens"); "Shall We Complete the Trade?"

1934   "The Aesthetics of Regionalism"; "Hearts and Heads"; "Poetry: A Note in Ontology"; "Regionalism in the South"

1935   "The Cathartic Principle"; "The Mimetic Principle"; "Modern with the Southern Accent"; "Poets Without Laurels"; "A Psychologist Looks at Poetry"; "The Tense of Poetry"

1936   "A Cathedralist Looks at Murder"; "Characters and Character"; "The Contents of the Novel: Notes Toward a Critique of Fiction"; "Fiction Harvest"; "The Making of a Modern: The Poetry of George Marion O'Donnell"; "Sentimental Exercise"; "The South Is a Bulwark"; "What Does the South Want?"

1937   Became professor of English at Kenyon (later Carnegie Professor of Poetry)
        "Art and Mr. Santayana"; "Criticism, Inc."; "The Poet As Woman"

1938   *The World's Body*; "Shakespeare at Sonnets"

1939   Became editor of the *Kenyon Review*. (Retired in 1959)
        "The Aesthetics of Finnegan's Wake"; "The Arts and the Philosophers"; "The Teaching of Poetry"; "Was Shakespeare a Philosopher?"; "Yeats and His Symbols"

1940   "Apologia for Modernism"; "Honey and Gall"; "The Mimetic Principle"; "Old Age of a Poet"; "The Pragmatics of Art"; "Strategy for English Studies"; "The Thing About Poetry"

1941   *The New Criticism*: "The Aesthetics of Music"; "All Verse is Not Poetry"; "Criticism as Pure Speculation"; "Eliot and the Metaphysicals"; "The Irish, the Gaelic, the Byzantine"; "Moholy-Nagy's New Arts"; "Muses and Amazons"; "Ubiquitous Moralists"; "Wanted: An Ontological Critic"; "The Younger Poets"; "Yvor Winters: The Logical Critic"

1942   "An Address to Kenneth Burke"; "Mr. Russell and Mr. Schorer"; "On the Brooks-MacLeish Thesis"; "Poetry As a Primitive Language"

1943   "The Forster Revival"; "The Inorganic Muses"; "Positive and Near Positive Aesthetics"

1944   "Artists, Soldiers, Positivists"; "Art Needs a Little Separating"; "The Bases of Criticism"

1945   *Selected Poems*; "Art and the Human Economy"; "Art Worries the Naturalists"; "The Severity of Mr. Savage"

1946   "These Little Magazines"

1947   "On Shakespeare's Language"; "Poetry: The Formal Analysis"; "Poetry: The Final Cause"

1948   "The Literary Criticism of Aristotle"; "On Being Modern with Distinction"

1950   "*All the King's Men*: A Symposium"; "The Understanding of Fiction"; "William Wordsworth: Notes Toward an Understanding of Poetry"

1951   Bollingen Award in Poetry; Russell Liones Award in Literature; edited
       The Kenyon Critics
       "The Poetry of 1900–1950"; "William Faulkner: An Impression"

1952   "An Age of Criticism"; "The Communities of Letters"; "Hardy—Old
       Poet"; "Why Critics Don't Go Mad"

1953   "Alienation of a Century Ago"; "Empirics in Politics"; "More Than Ges-
       ture"; "A Reply to Wayne Booth"; "Symbolism: American Style"

1954   "The Concrete Universal: Observations on the Understanding of
       Poetry, I"

1955   *Poems and Essays*; "The Concrete Universal: Observations on the Un-
       derstanding of Poetry, II"; "Old Age of an Eagle"

1956   "Emily Dickinson: A Poet Restored"; "The Strange Music of English
       Verse"

1958   "New Poets and Old Muses"

1959   "The Idea of a Literary Anthropologist and What He Might Say of the
       Paradise Lost of Milton"; "In Amicitia"

1961   Edited *Selected Poems of Thomas Hardy*

1962   Academy of American Poets Fellowship

1963   *Selected Poems*

1964   Book of the Year in Poetry Award
       "On 'Master's in the Garden Again'"; "The Planetary Poet"

1966   "Gerontion"; "Theory of Poetic Form"

1967   "The Rugged Way of a Genius: A Tribute to Randall Jarrell"

1968   "T. S. Eliot: A Postscript"

1969   *Selected Poems*

1972   *Beating the Bushes*; "Beating the Naturalists with the Stick of Drama"

1974   Died in Gambier, Ohio, on July 3

Appendix C

A Checklist of Ransom's Critical Essays

"The ABC of Aesthetics," *New Republic*, LIII (December 14, 1927), 104 (Letter).

"The Aesthetic of Regionalism," *American Review*, II (January, 1934), 290–310.

"The Aesthetics of *Finnegan's Wake*," *Kenyon Review*, I (Autumn, 1939), 425–28.

"The Aesthetics of Music," *Kenyon Review*, III (Autumn, 1941), 494–97.

"An Address to Kenneth Burke," *Kenyon Review*, IV (Spring, 1942), 218–37.

"An Age of Criticism," *New Republic*, CXXVI (March 31, 1952), 18–19.

"Alienation of a Century Ago," *Kenyon Review*, XV (Spring, 1953), 335–36.

"*All the King's Men*: A Symposium," *Folio*, XV (May, 1950), 2–22.

"All Verse Is Not Poetry," *Hika*, IX (December, 1941), 22–25.

"Apologia for Modernism," *Kenyon Review*, II (Spring, 1940), 274–81.

"Art and the Human Economy," *Kenyon Review*, VII (Autumn, 1945), 683–88.

"Art and Mr. Santayana," *Virginia Quarterly Review*, XIII (Summer, 1937), 420–36.

"Artists, Soldiers, Positivists," *Kenyon Review*, VI (Spring, 1944), 276–81.

"Art Needs a Little Separating," *Kenyon Review*, VI (Winter, 1944), 114–22.

"The Arts and the Philosophers," *Kenyon Review*, I (Spring, 1939), 194–99.

"Art Worries the Naturalists," *Kenyon Review*, VII (Spring, 1945), 282–99.

"The Bases of Criticism," *Sewanee Review*, LII (Autumn, 1944), 556–71.

"Beating the Naturalists with the Stick of Drama," *Beating the Bushes*, 119–27.

"A Capital for the New Deal," *American Review*, II (December, 1933), 129–42.

"The Cathartic Principle," *American Review*, V (Summer, 1935), 287–300.

"A Cathedralist Looks at Murder," *Southern Review*, I (Winter, 1936), 609–23.

"Characters and Character," *American Review*, VI (January, 1936), 271–88.

"Classical and Romantic," *Saturday Review of Literature*, VI (September 14, 1929), 125–27.

"The Communities of Letters," *Confluence*, I (December, 1952), 86–92.

"The Concrete Universal: Observations on the Understanding of Poetry, I," *Kenyon Review*, XVI (Autumn, 1954), 554–64.

"The Concrete Universal: Observations on the Understanding of Poetry, II," *Kenyon Review*, XVII (Summer, 1955), 383–407.

"The Contents of the Novel: Notes Toward a Critique of Fiction," *American Review*, VI (Summer, 1936), 301–18.

"Criticism As Pure Speculation," *The Intent of the Critic*. Edited by Donald A. Stauffer. Princeton: Princeton University Press, 1941, pp. 91–124.

"Criticism, Inc.," *Virginia Quarterly Review*, XIII (Autumn, 1937), 586–602.

"Eliot and the Metaphysicals," *Accent*, I (Spring, 1941), 148–56.

"Emily Dickinson: A Poet Restored," *Perspectives USA*, XV (Spring, 1956), 5–20.

"Empirics in Politics," *Kenyon Review*, LI (Autumn, 1953), 648–58.

"Fiction Harvest," *Southern Review*, I (Autumn, 1936), 399–418.

"Flux and Blur in Contemporary Art," *Sewanee Review*, XXXVII (July, 1929), 353–66.

"The Forster Revival," *Kenyon Review*, LI (Autumn, 1953), 618–23.

"The Future of Poetry," *Fugitive*, III (February, 1924), 2–4.

"Gerontion," *Sewanee Review*, LXXXIV (Spring, 1966), 389–414.

"Happy Farmers," *American Review*, I (October, 1933), 513–35.

"Hearts and Heads," *American Review*, II (March, 1934), 554–71.

"Hardy—Old Poet," *New Republic*, CXXVI (May 12, 1952), 16, 30–31.

"Honey and Gall," *Southern Review*, VI (Summer, 1940), 2–19.

"Humanism at Chicago," *Kenyon Review*, XVI (Autumn, 1952), 647–59.

"The Idea of a Literary Anthropologist and What He Might Say of the *Paradise Lost* of Milton," *Kenyon Review*, XI (Winter, 1959), 121–40.

"In Amicitia," *Sewanee Review*, XCVII (Fall, 1959), 528–39.

"The Inorganic Muses," *Kenyon Review*, V (Spring, 1943), 278–300.

"The Irish, the Gaelic, the Byzantine," *Southern Review*, VII (1941–42), 517–46.

"Land! An Answer to the Unemployment Problem," *Harper's Magazine*, CLXV (July, 1932), 216–24.

"The Literary Criticism of Aristotle," *Kenyon Review*, X (Summer, 1948), 382–402.

"The Making of a Modern: The Poetry of George Marion O'Donnell," *Southern Review*, I (Spring, 1936), 864–74.

"A Man Without a Country," *Sewanee Review*, XXXVI (July, 1925), 301–307.

"The Mimetic Principle," *American Review*, V (October, 1935), 536–51.

"Mr. Russell and Mr. Schorer," *Kenyon Review*, IV (Autumn, 1942), 406–407.

"Mr. Tate and the Professors," *Kenyon Review*, II (Summer, 1940), 348–50.

"Mixed Modes," *The Fugitive*, IV (March, 1925), 28–29.

"Modern with the Southern Accent," *Virginia Quarterly Review*, II (April, 1935), 184–200.

"Moholy-Nagy's New Arts," *Kenyon Review*, III (Summer, 1941), 374–84.

"More Than Gesture," *Partisan Review*, XX (January–February, 1953), 108–111.

"Muses and Amazons," *Kenyon Review*, III (Spring, 1941), 240–42.

"New Poets and Old Muses," *American Poetry at Mid-Century*. Washington: Reference Department, Library of Congress, 1958, pp. 1–14.

"Old Age of a Poet," *Kenyon Review*, II (Summer, 1940), 345–47.

"Old Age of an Eagle," *Poems and Essays*. New York: Vintage Books, 1955, pp. 79–87.

"On Being Modern with Distinction," *Quarterly Review of Literature*, IV (1948), 136–42.

"On 'Master's in the Garden Again,'" *The Contemporary Poet As Artist and Critic*, edited by Anthony Ostroff, Boston: Little, Brown, 1964, pp. 134–40.

"On Shakespeare's Language," *Sewanee Review*, LV (Spring, 1947), 181–98.

"On the Brooks-MacLeish Thesis," *Partisan Review*, IX (January, 1942), 40–41.

"The Planetary Poet," *Kenyon Review*, XXVI (Winter, 1964), 233–64.

"A Poem Nearly Anonymous," *American Review*, I (May, 1933), 179–202.

"A Poem Nearly Anonymous: The Poet and His Formal Tradition," *American Review*, I (September, 1933), 444–67; reprinted as "Forms and Citizens," in *The World's Body*.

"The Poet As a Woman," *Southern Review*, II (Spring, 1937), 783–806.

"Poetry: A Note in Ontology," *American Review*, III (May, 1934), 172–200.

"Poetry As Primitive Language," *Michigan Alumnus Quarterly Review* (Summer, 1942), 278–84; reprinted in *The Writer and His Craft*.

"The Poetry of 1900–1950," *Kenyon Review*, XIII (Summer, 1951), 445–54.

"Poetry: The Final Cause," *Kenyon Review*, IX (Autumn, 1947), 640–58.

"Poetry: The Formal Analysis," *Kenyon Review*, IX (Summer, 1947), 436–56.

"Poets Without Laurels," *Yale Review*, XXIV (March, 1935), 503–18.

"Positivists and Near Positive Aesthetics," *Kenyon Review*, V (Summer, 1943), 443–47.

"The Pragmatics of Art," *Kenyon Review*, II (Winter, 1940), 76–87.

"Prose: A Doctrine of Relativity," *The Fugitive*, IV (September, 1925), 93–94.

"A Psychologist Looks at Poetry," *Virginia Quarterly Review*, XI (October, 1935), 575–92.

"The Question of Justice," *Yale Review*, IV (July, 1915), 684–98.

"Reconstructed But Unregenerate," *I'll Take My Stand: The South and the Agrarian Tradition*, by Twelve Southerners (New York: Harper, 1930).

"Regionalism in the South," *New Mexico Quarterly*, IV (May, 1934), 108–18.

"A Reply to Wayne Booth," *Kenyon Review*, XV (Spring, 1953), 301–304.

"The Rugged Way of Genius: A Tribute to Randall Jarrell," *Southern Review*, III (Spring, 1967), 363–87.

"Sentimental Exercise," *Yale Review*, XXVI (December, 1936), 353–68.

"The Severity of Mr. Savage," *Kenyon Review*, VII (Winter, 1945), 114–17.

"Shakespeare at Sonnets," *Southern Review*, III (Winter, 1938), 531–53.

"Shall We Complete the Trade," *Sewanee Review*, LXI (April, 1933), 182–90.

"The South Defends Its Heritage," *Harper's Magazine*, CXIX (June, 1929), 108–18.

"The South Is a Bulwark," *Scribner's Magazine*, XIX (May, 1936), 229–33.

"The South—Old or New," *Sewanee Review*, XXVI (April, 1928), 139–47.

"The State and the Land," *New Republic*, LXX (February 17, 1932), 8–10.

"Statement of Principles," *I'll Take My Stand: The South and the Agrarian Tradition*, by Twelve Southerners (New York: Harper, 1930), ix–xxl.

"The Strange Music of English Verse," *Kenyon Review*, XVIII (Summer, 1956), 460–77.

"Strategy for English Studies," *Southern Review*, VI (Autumn, 1940), 226–35.

"Symbolism: American Style," *New Republic*, CXIX (November 2, 1953), 18–20.

"The Teaching of Poetry," *Kenyon Review*, I (Winter, 1939), 81–83.

"The Tense of Poetry," *Southern Review*, I (Autumn, 1935), 221–38.

"Theory of Poetic Form," *Texas Quarterly*, IX (Spring, 1966), 190–201.

"These Little Magazines," *American Scholar*, XV (October, 1946), 550–51.

"The Thing About Poetry," *Hika*, VI (May, 1940), 9–11.

"Thoughts on the Poetic Discontent," *The Fugitive*, IV (June, 1925), 63–64.

"T. S. Eliot: A Postscript," *Southern Review*, n.s. III (Summer, 1968), 579–97.

"Ubiquitous Moralists," *Kenyon Review*, III (Winter, 1941), 95–100.

"The Understanding of Fiction," *Kenyon Review*, XII (Spring, 1950), 189–208.

"Wanted: An Ontological Critic," *The New Criticism* (Norfolk, Conn.: New Directions, 1941), pp. 279–336.

"Was Shakespeare a Philosopher?" *Kenyon Review*, I (Winter, 1939), pp. 75–80.

"Waste Lands," *Literary Review*, III (July 14, 1923), 825–26.

"What Does the South Want?" *Virginia Quarterly Review*, XII (April, 1936), 180–94.

"Why Critics Don't Go Mad," *Kenyon Review*, XIV (Spring, 1952), 331–39.

"William Faulkner: An Impression," *Harvard Advocate*, CXXXV (November, 1951), 17.

"William Wordsworth: Notes Toward an Understanding of Poetry," *Kenyon Review*, XII (Summer, 1950), 498, 519.

"Yeats and His Symbols," *Kenyon Review*, I (Summer, 1939), 309–22.

"The Younger Poets," *Kenyon Review*, III (Autumn, 1941), 491–94.

"Yvor Winters: The Logical Critic," *Southern Review*, VI (Winter, 1941), 558–83.

Index

349